iPad® and iPhone® Tips and Tricks

Jason R. Rich

Que®
800 East 96th Street
Indianapolis, Indiana 46240 USA

iPAD® AND iPHONE® TIPS AND TRICKS
THIRD EDITION

ISBN-13: 978-0-7897-5237-6

ISBN-10: 0-7897-5237-9

Library of Congress Control Number: 2013950964

Printed in the United States of America

First Printing: November 2013

TRADEMARKS

WARNING AND DISCLAIMER

BULK SALES

Que Publishing offers excellent discounts on this book when ordered in quantity for bulk purchases or special sales. For more information, please contact

U.S. Corporate and Government Sales
1-800-382-3419
corpsales@pearsontechgroup.com

For sales outside of the U.S., please contact

International Sales
international@pearsoned.com

EDITOR-IN-CHIEF
Greg Wiegand

ACQUISITIONS EDITOR
Laura Norman

DEVELOPMENT EDITOR
Jennifer Ackerman-Kettell

MANAGING EDITOR
Sandra Schroeder

SENIOR PROJECT EDITOR
Tonya Simpson

INDEXER
Lisa Stumpf

PROOFREADER
Sarah Kearns

TECHNICAL EDITOR
Greg Kettell

PUBLISHING COORDINATOR
Cindy Teeters

INTERIOR DESIGNER
Anne Jones

COVER DESIGNER
Alan Clements

COMPOSITOR
Bumpy Design

CONTENTS AT A GLANCE

TABLE OF CONTENTS

ABOUT THE AUTHOR

Jason R. Rich (www.JasonRich.com) is the bestselling author of more than 55 books, as well as a frequent contributor to a handful of major daily newspapers, national magazines, and popular websites. He also is an accomplished photographer and an avid Apple iPhone, iPad, Apple TV, and Mac user.

Jason R. Rich is the author of the books *Your iPad at Work*, Fourth Edition, as well as *OS X Mountain Lion Tips and Tricks*, both published by Que Publishing. He has also written *How To Do Everything MacBook Air*, *How To Do Everything iCloud*, Second Edition, and *How To Do Everything iPhone 5* for McGraw-Hill, and *Ultimate Guide to YouTube For Business* for Entrepreneur Press.

More than 150 feature-length how-to articles by Jason R. Rich, covering the Apple iPhone and iPad, can be read free online at the Que Publishing website. Visit www.iOSArticles.com and click on the Articles tab. You can also follow Jason on Twitter (@JasonRich7) or read his blog, called *Jason Rich's Featured App Of The Week*, to learn about new and useful iPhone and iPad apps (www.FeaturedAppOfTheWeek.com).

DEDICATION

I am honored to dedicate this book to Steve Jobs (1955–2011), a true visionary, entrepreneur, and pioneer who forever changed the world. This book is also dedicated to Nick and the rest of my family.

ACKNOWLEDGMENTS

Thanks once again to Laura Norman at Que Publishing for inviting me to work on all three editions of this book, and for all of her guidance as I've worked on this project. My gratitude also goes out to Greg Wiegand, Tonya Simpson, Cindy Teeters, Jennifer Ackerman-Kettell, Greg Kettell, and Paul Boger, as well as everyone else at Que Publishing/Pearson who contributed their expertise, hard work, and creativity to the creation of this all-new edition of *iPad and iPhone Tips and Tricks*.

Finally, thanks to you, the reader. I hope this book helps you fully utilize your iOS device in every aspect of your life and take full advantage of the power and functionality your iPhone and/or iPad offers.

WE WANT TO HEAR FROM YOU!

As the reader of this book, *you* are our most important critic and commentator. We value your opinion and want to know what we're doing right, what we could do better, what areas you'd like to see us publish in, and any other words of wisdom you're willing to pass our way.

We welcome your comments. You can email or write to let us know what you did or didn't like about this book—as well as what we can do to make our books better.

Please note that we cannot help you with technical problems related to the topic of this book.

When you write, please be sure to include this book's title and author as well as your name and email address. We will carefully review your comments and share them with the author and editors who worked on the book.

Email: feedback@quepublishing.com

Mail: Que Publishing
ATTN: Reader Feedback
800 East 96th Street
Indianapolis, IN 46240 USA

READER SERVICES

Visit our website and register this book at quepublishing.com/register for convenient access to any updates, downloads, or errata that might be available for this book.

Introduction

Apple's iPhone smartphones and iPad tablets have revolutionized the way people communicate and handle their everyday computing needs while on the go. These devices have also altered our perceptions of the capabilities of smartphones and tablets.

In just over five years, hundreds of millions of people from around the world have incorporated an Apple iOS mobile device into their lives. With each new iPhone or iPad model and each revision of the iOS operating system, these mobile devices become more powerful and introduce us to new features and functionality that seem as if they have been lifted directly from the pages of science fiction novels.

Released on September 17, 2013, iOS 7 has been redesigned from the ground up. It offers an entirely new user interface, hundreds of new features, plus better integration with online social networking services such as Facebook and Twitter, as well as Apple's own iCloud service.

NOTE Throughout this book, an "iOS mobile device" refers to any Apple iPhone, iPad, or iPod touch that's running the iOS 7 operating system. If you plan to continue using iOS 6 with your iOS mobile device, pick up a copy of the earlier edition of *iPad and iPhone Tips and Tricks*, which focuses on the older version of Apple's mobile device operating system.

If you're a veteran iPhone or iPad user, when you upgrade from iOS 6 to iOS 7, you're in for a pretty major surprise. Just about everything displayed on the device's touchscreen will now look and operate somewhat differently. In some cases, the finger taps and gestures you use to interact with your iOS mobile device are also now different.

By adopting the philosophy that "change is good," and investing some time getting reacquainted with your iPhone and/or iPad, you'll quickly discover that iOS 7 offers a remarkable and powerful platform through which you can truly harness the capabilities of your device as a communications, productivity, and organizational tool, as well as a mobile entertainment center, in both your personal and professional life.

For those who are first-time iPhone or iPad users, congratulations! Now is the perfect time to introduce yourself to these mobile devices or switch from another smartphone or tablet to what Apple has to offer. Not only can you expect an exciting experience as you begin using your new iPhone or iPad hardware, but you have the opportunity to access the App Store to access any of the hundreds of thousands of third-party apps that can greatly expand the capabilities of these mobile devices.

Whether you're a veteran iPhone or iPad user or you're first learning how to use an iOS mobile device, this book will teach you what you need to know to quickly become proficient using the device itself and the majority of the apps that come bundled with it. The focus of this all-new third edition of *iPad and iPhone Tips and Tricks* is to quickly get you acquainted with iOS 7 and help you adapt to this new operating system while learning how to best utilize the features and functions it offers.

NOTE The iOS operating system is compatible with the iPhone 5S, iPhone 5C, iPhone 5/4/4S, as well as the iPad Air, iPad 2, iPad with Retina Display, iPad mini, and iPad mini with Retina Display.

HOW TO UPGRADE FROM iOS 6 TO iOS 7

While the new iPhone 5S and iPhone 5C, along with the iPad Air, for example, automatically come with iOS 7 installed, anyone who purchased their iPhone, iPad, or iPod touch before September 17, 2013 will need to upgrade to iOS 7. The easiest way to do this is to connect your mobile device to a Wi-Fi hotspot or wireless home network to establish a high-speed Internet connection. Then, from the Home screen, launch Settings.

TIP Before upgrading your iOS mobile device from iOS 5 or iOS 6 to iOS 7, be sure to create a backup of your iPhone or iPad using the iTunes Sync Backup feature or the iCloud Backup feature. After you install the iOS 7 operating system, all of your apps and related data will automatically be restored.

Next, tap on the General option from the main Settings menu, and then tap on the Software Update option (shown in Figure I.1). If your device is running iOS 5 or iOS 6, a message appears indicating that an operating system upgrade is available. Follow the onscreen prompts to download and install iOS 7 for free. The upgrade process will take between 20 and 45 minutes, depending on which iPhone or iPad model you're using, its internal storage capacity, and how much information is currently stored on your device.

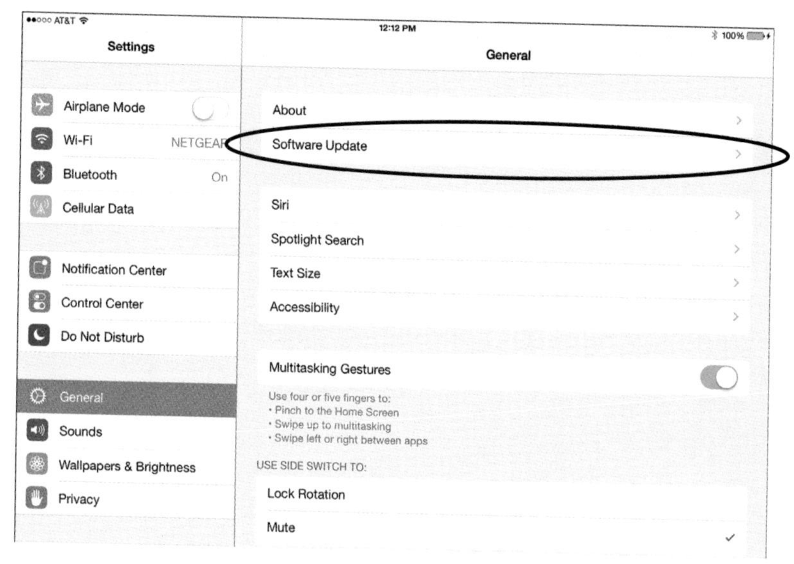

FIGURE I.1

The easiest way to upgrade your iPhone or iPad from iOS 6 to iOS 7 is to access the Software Update option from within the General Settings options.

INTERACTING WITH YOUR iPHONE OR iPAD

If you're a veteran iPhone or iPad user, you already know that Apple's iOS enables you to interact with your mobile device using its touchscreen. Data entry is typically done using the virtual keyboard displayed on the screen when it's needed. Based on the type of information you're entering and the app you're using, the keyboard's layout will adapt automatically.

When not using the virtual keyboard, much of your interaction with the iPhone or iPad will be done using a series of taps, swipes, and other finger gestures on the touchscreen display.

You can also communicate with your iPhone or iPad using your voice, thanks to Apple's Siri (which now has a new look) and the Dictation features, or utilize an optional external keyboard and/or pen-shaped stylus.

TOUCHSCREEN TECHNIQUES YOU'LL NEED TO MASTER

To navigate your way around iOS 7 on your iPhone or iPad, you'll need to master a series of basic taps and finger gestures. Keep in mind that with the new look and user interface offered by iOS 7, some of the gestures and the direction you swipe to accomplish specific tasks have changed.

Just as when using previous editions of the iOS with an iPhone or iPad, from the moment you turn on your device (or take it out of Sleep mode), aside from pressing the Home button, virtually all of your interaction with the smartphone or tablet is done through the following finger movements and taps on the device's highly sensitive multitouch display:

- **Tap**—Tapping an icon, button, or link that's displayed on your device's screen serves the same purpose as clicking the mouse when you use your main computer. And, just as when you use a computer, you can single-tap or double-tap, which is equivalent to a single or double click of the mouse.
- **Hold**—Instead of a quick tap, in some cases, it is necessary to press and hold your finger on an icon or onscreen command option. When a hold action is required, place your finger on the appropriate icon or command option, and hold it there with a slight pressure. There's never a need to press down hard on the smartphone or tablet's screen.
- **Swipe**—A swipe refers to quickly moving your finger along the screen from right to left, left to right, top to bottom, or bottom to top, in order to scroll left, right, up, or down, depending on which app you're using.
- **Pinch**—Using your thumb and index finger (the finger next to your thumb), perform a pinch motion on the touchscreen to zoom out when using certain apps. Or "unpinch" (by moving your fingers apart quickly) to zoom in on what you're looking at on the screen when using many apps.

TIP Another way to zoom in or out when looking at the device's screen is to double-tap the area of the screen on which you want to zoom in. This works when you're surfing the Web in Safari or looking at photos using the Photos app, as well as within most other apps that support the zoom in/out feature. To zoom out again, double-tap the screen a second time.

- **Pull down**—Using your index finger, swipe it from the very top of the iPhone or iPad's screen quickly in a downward direction. This will cause the Notification Center window to appear, alerting you of incoming email messages, text messages, alarms, and other time-sensitive actions that need to be dealt with. You can hold the device in either portrait or landscape mode for this to work. As you'll discover in Chapter 1, "Tips and Tricks for Customizing Settings," the functionality of Notification Center has been enhanced in iOS 7.

TIP Use a pull-down gesture that starts in the middle of the iPhone or iPad's Home screen to access iOS 7's Spotlight Search feature. Use this to quickly find any information that's stored on your mobile device, such as a Contacts entry, Calendar event, or content within an email message. Enter a keyword or search phrase into the Search field that appears, tap on the Search key on the virtual keyword, and then tap on one of the search result listings to access the data or content by automatically launching the related app. It can also be used to quickly find an app, such as one stored in an app folder.

- **Swipe up**—At any time, swipe your finger in an upward direction from the bottom of the screen to make the new Control Center appear. From here, you can access a handful of iOS 7 functions depending on your device. On the iPhone, you can turn on/off Airplane Mode, Wi-Fi, Bluetooth, the Do Not Disturb feature, and the Screen Rotation Lock, plus access screen brightness controls, Music app controls, and AirDrop and AirPlay functions. The Control Center also provides access to the Flashlight, Clock, Calculator, and Camera apps. You can use the swipe up gesture to access Control Center from the Lock screen. The Control Center is covered in more detail in Chapter 1.
- **Five-finger pinch (iPad only)**—To exit out of any app and return to the Home screen, place all five fingers of one hand on the screen so that they're spread out, and then draw your fingers together, as if you're grabbing something. Be sure, however, that the Multitasking Gestures are turned on in the Settings app (found under the General heading).

TIP Return to the Home screen at any time by pressing the Home button once, regardless of which app is being used. Or, as you're scrolling through supplemental Home screens, press the Home button once to return immediately to the primary Home screen.

- **Multi-finger horizontal swipe (iPad only)**—When multiple apps are running simultaneously, swipe several fingers from left to right, or from right to left on the screen to switch between the active app and the other apps that are running in the background. In some situations, a two-finger rotation gesture can also be used, such as when adjusting the map view orientation within the Maps app.

HOME BUTTON QUICK TIPS

Positioned on the front of your iPhone or iPad below the main touchscreen is the Home button. Here's how to use some of the Home button's main functions when using iOS 7:

- **Activate Siri**—Press and hold down the Home button for two to three seconds from the Home screen or when using any app.
- **Access the multitasking bar**—From any app (or from the Home screen), quickly press the Home button twice. Press the Home button again to exit out of the multitasking bar.
- **Exit an app and return to the Home screen**—When using any app, press the Home button once to exit it and return to the Home screen.
- **Reboot the device**—Press and hold the Home button and the Power button simultaneously for about five seconds, until the Apple logo appears on the screen. Doing this will not delete any data, apps, or content from your iOS mobile device.
- **Return to the main Home screen**—When viewing any of the other Home screens on your mobile device, press the Home button once to return to the main Home screen.
- **Wake up the device from Sleep mode**—Press the Power button or the Home button once when the device is in Sleep mode. If the device is powered down, press and hold the Power button for several seconds to restart it.

TIP If you're an iPhone 5S user, the Home button has the Touch ID sensor built in, so it can be used to unlock your smartphone and confirm iTunes Store, App Store, iBookstore, and Newsstand purchases using your fingerprint.

HOW TO MAKE THE BEST USE OF THE VIRTUAL KEYBOARD

To enter data into your iPhone or iPad, use the virtual keyboard that pops up on the bottom portion of the screen when it's needed. The virtual keyboard typically resembles a typewriter or computer keyboard; however, certain onscreen keys have different purposes, depending on which app you're using. When you access the Spotlight Search screen, you will notice the large Search key on the right side of the keyboard. However, when you use the Pages word processor app, the Search key becomes the Return key. When you're using an app that involves numeric data entry, such as Numbers, the layout and design of the virtual keyboard can change dramatically.

> **TIP** As you're using the virtual keyboard, some keys have hidden characters that you can access and use by holding your finger down on the key and then tapping on your alternate character selection. Hidden characters include letters with accent marks.
>
> Some keys have different characters available depending on which app you're using. When using Safari, for example, press and hold the question mark ("?") key to access .us, .edu, .com, .net, and .org website extensions. When sending a message or using Pages, however, press and hold the question mark key to access quotation marks.

VIRTUAL KEYBOARD QUICK TIPS

Use these tips to help you more easily work with the virtual keyboard on your iPhone or iPad:

- **Divide the virtual keyboard in half (iPad and iPad mini only)**—Make it easier to type on the virtual keyboard with your two thumbs while holding the device. To split the keyboard, use the index fingers on your right and left hand simultaneously, place them in the center of the virtual keyboard when it's visible, and then move them apart.
- **Undock and move the virtual keyboard upward (iPad and iPad mini only)**—Hold down the Hide Keyboard key (displayed in the lower-right corner of the keyboard) and select Undock from the pop-up menu. You can also choose to split or merge the keyboard.

- **Turn on/off the keyboard's key click sound**—Launch Settings, tap on the Sounds option, and then from the Sounds menu, scroll down and tap the virtual switch associated with Keyboard Clicks (shown in Figure I.2) to toggle it on or off.

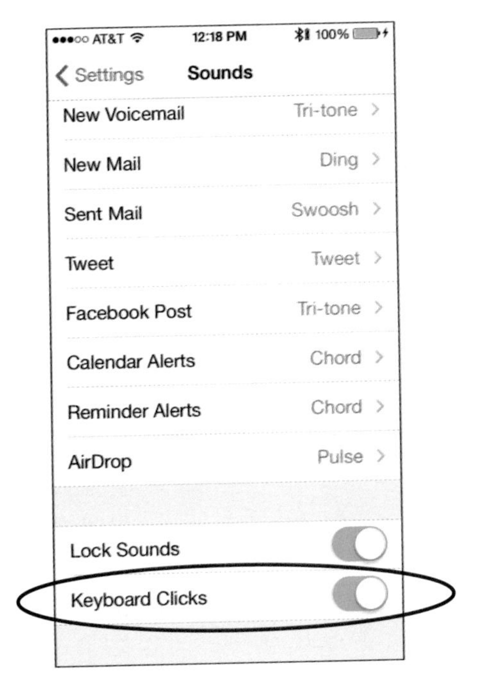

FIGURE I.2

In Settings, it's possible to customize a handful of virtual keyboard-related features, such as whether you hear the key click sound every time you tap a key.

- **Adjust auto-capitalization, autocorrection, check spelling, enable caps lock and the keyboard shortcuts options**—Launch Settings, tap on the General option, and then tap on the Keyboard option to access the Keyboard menu. Tap the virtual switch associated with each option to toggle it on or off.

> **TIP** To turn on Caps Lock when using the virtual keyboard, quickly double-tap the Shift key (it displays an upward-pointing arrow). Tap the key again to turn off Caps Lock.

- **Hide the virtual keyboard**—You can often tap anywhere on the screen except on the virtual keyboard itself, or you can tap on the Hide Keyboard key (iPad and iPad mini only) located in the lower-right corner of the keyboard.

- **Make the virtual keyboard appear**—If you need to enter data into your iPhone or iPad after you have dismissed the virtual keyboard, simply tap on an empty data field to reopen it. An appropriately formatted virtual keyboard appears.
- **Make the keys on the virtual keyboard larger**—For some people, this makes typing easier. Simply rotate the iPhone or iPad from portrait to landscape mode.
- **Create keyboard shortcuts**—If there's a sentence, paragraph, or phrase you need to enter repeatedly when using an app, it's possible to enter that text just once and save it as a keyboard shortcut. Then, instead of typing a whole sentence, you can simply type a three-letter code that you assign to that shortcut and the virtual keyboard will insert the complete sentence. How to create your own keyboard shortcuts is covered in Chapter 1.
- **Change keyboard layouts**—A handful of alternative keyboard layouts are built in to iOS, some offering emoticons, such as Emoji, and some that offer characters from various foreign languages. This is also covered in Chapter 1.

SOMETIMES, AN OPTIONAL EXTERNAL KEYBOARD OR STYLUS WORKS BETTER

If you expect to do a lot of data entry or word processing on your iOS mobile device, instead of using the virtual keyboard, you can purchase an optional external keyboard that connects to the phone or tablet using either the device's 30-pin dock connector port or lightning port. You'll also find a vast selection of wireless Bluetooth keyboards that work with the iPhone and iPad.

MORE INFO Apple (store.apple.com), Brookstone (www.brookstone.com), Logitech (www.logitech.com), and Zagg (www.zagg.com) are just a sampling of companies that offer optional, external iPhone or iPad keyboards. Some of these keyboards are built in to phone or tablet cases that also double as stands.

Some apps for the iPhone or iPad enable users to handwrite or draw on the phone or tablet's screen using an optional stylus (a pencil-shaped device with a special tip that's designed to work with the touchscreen display). The Hex3 JaJa stylus ($89.99, www.hex3.co/products/jaja) is an example of a pressure-sensitive stylus that works with a growing number of drawing and art-related, photo editing, and PDF file annotation apps. Much less expensive, nonpressure-sensitive styluses are also available.

TIP The Siri and Dictation features in iOS 7 have also been enhanced. You'll discover tips and strategies that focus on how to communicate with your iPhone or iPad using your voice from Chapter 2, "Using Siri, Dictation, and iOS in Your Car to Interact with Your Mobile Device."

HOW TO TURN THE iPHONE OR iPAD ON OR OFF VERSUS PLACING IT INTO SLEEP MODE

Your iOS mobile device can be turned on, turned off, placed into Sleep mode, or placed in Airplane mode.

- **Turned on**—When your phone or tablet is turned on, it can run apps and perform all the tasks it was designed to do. To turn on the iPhone or iPad when it's powered off, press and hold the Power button located near the top-right corner of the device for about five seconds, until the Apple logo appears on the screen. Release the Power button, and then wait a few additional seconds while the device boots up. When the Lock screen appears, you're ready to begin using the iPhone or iPad.
- **Turned off**—When your iPhone or iPad is turned off and powered down, it is not capable of any form of communication, and all apps that were running are shut down. The device is dormant. To turn off your phone or tablet, press and hold down the Power button for about five seconds, until the Slide To Power Off banner appears on the screen. Using your finger, swipe your finger along this red-and-white banner from left to right. The device will shut down.
- **Sleep mode**—To place your iPhone or iPad into Sleep mode, press and release the Power button once. To wake up the device, you can press the Power button or the Home button. In sleep mode, your device's screen is turned off but the phone or tablet can still connect to the Internet, receive incoming calls (iPhone) or text messages, retrieve emails, and run apps in the background. Notification Center also remains fully operational, so you can be alerted of preset alarms, for example. Sleep mode offers a way to conserve battery life when you're not actively using your phone or tablet.

NOTE By default, when left unattended for two minutes, your iOS mobile device automatically enters into Sleep mode. To change this, launch Settings, tap on the General option, and then select the Auto-Lock option.

TIP On the iPad, you can place the tablet into Sleep mode by placing an Apple Smart Cover (or compatible cover) over the screen, assuming the iPad Cover Lock/Unlock option is turned on from the General menu within Settings.

You can also place the device into Do Not Disturb mode. This automatically routes incoming calls directly to voice mail. As you'll discover, you can customize the Do Not Disturb feature to allow preselected people to reach you when you otherwise want to be left alone. See Chapter 9, "Make and Receive Calls with an iPhone," for more information on this useful feature. On the iPad, the Do Not Disturb feature works with FaceTime calls.

DISCOVER SOME OF WHAT'S NEW IN iOS 7

iOS 7 is chock full of brand-new features, as well as hundreds of enhancements to existing features that were found in previous versions of Apple's mobile operating system. Among the major enhancements to iOS 7 are the ways it enables your iPhone or iPad to communicate and easily share data and information wirelessly with others. You'll also discover better integration with online social networking services, as well as with Apple's own iCloud service.

Let's take a quick look at some of the major new features and enhancements made to iOS 7. You'll learn strategies for best utilizing the majority of these features later in the book, but here's a rundown of what's new and noteworthy about iOS 7:

- **New customization options within Settings**—The Settings app, which you'll learn more about in Chapter 1, has been redesigned for iOS 7. However, it continues to offer more than 100 customizable options that you can adjust to personalize how your iPhone or iPad will perform and function.
- **Control Center**—This new, easy-access menu offers a fast way to adjust certain popular iPhone or iPad settings and access commonly used apps. See Chapter 1 to learn more about how to customize Control Center.
- **Enhanced Notification Center**—Notification Center offers a centralized place where your iPhone or iPad keeps track of alerts, alarms, and notifications related to the apps you're running and the phone or tablet's functions you're using. Notification Center runs continuously in the background and then displays alerts, alarms, and notifications both on the Lock screen and within the Notification Center window. In Chapter 1, you discover strategies for managing Notification Center and learn how to customize the information it tracks and displays.

- **Enhanced multitasking**—Your iPhone or iPad can run multiple apps simultaneously, although you can work with only one app at a time on the screen; the rest continue running in the background. To quickly switch between apps that are running, or shut down one or more apps, access the multitasking bar on your device. To do this, press the Home button twice quickly.

  The new multitasking bar (shown in Figure I.3) displays icons and thumbnail images for all the apps currently running on your device.

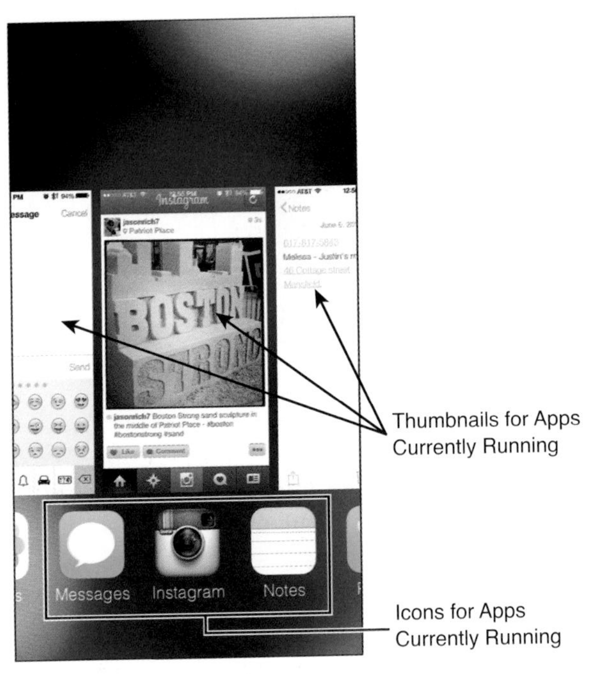

FIGURE I.3

The new multitasking bar of iOS 7 is shown here on an iPhone 5.

  Scroll from right to left or from left to right (using a swipe motion with your finger) to see all the apps that are running. To switch to a different app and make it active, tap on its thumbnail or app icon.

  To shut down an app while in the multitasking bar, swipe your finger in an upward direction along the thumbnail image for the app you want to close.

- **Improved camera and photo editing/organization**—The digital photography capabilities using the cameras built in to the iPhone and iPad, along with the redesigned Camera app, continue to improve. iOS 7 offers a handful of new features when it comes to shooting still images and video. The redesigned Photos app provides many few features for viewing, organizing, sharing, printing, editing, and enhancing your photos. Learn more about these features in Chapter 8, "Shoot, Edit, and Share Photos and Videos."

- **AirDrop for iOS**—In the past, to share information between your iPhone or iPad and another computer or mobile device user, you needed to use email or text message. Now, when you're in close proximity to another iOS mobile device user, you also can use AirDrop to share app-specific data, such as contact entries from the Contacts app, documents, files, and photos. This is a wireless form of data communication.
- **New Web surfing features in Safari**—The Safari web browser that comes bundled with iOS 7 has been redesigned, giving users more features that make surfing the Web, as well as organizing and sharing bookmarks and related information, much easier and more efficient. Be sure to read Chapter 12, "Surf the Web More Efficiently Using Safari," to discover strategies for using all of Safari's newest features.

iOS 7 WHAT'S NEW With the iOS 7 version of Safari, Apple has introduced iCloud Keychain. Now, when you visit a new website that requires you to create a username and password, Safari automatically remembers this information and logs you in to that website anytime you revisit it in the future. Because this feature is tied directly into iCloud, all website-related usernames and passwords are synced with your iCloud account and made accessible on all your Macs and iOS mobile devices that are linked to the same iCloud account.

- **iTunes Radio**—Built in to the Music app that comes bundled with iOS 7 is Apple's new streaming music service. In the past, if you wanted to listen to music on your iPhone or iPad, you needed to download and store the music files on your device. Now, in an effort to compete with online-based services like Pandora, iTunes Radio offers a free streaming music service that enables you to listen to custom-created "stations" whenever your phone or tablet has Internet access. This service is free and, as you'll discover in Chapter 14, "Get Acquainted with the Music, Videos, and iTunes Store Apps," is highly customizable.
- **Improved Siri functionality**—With iOS 7, Siri has been given a new look, a new sound, and additional functionality. For example, when you ask Siri a question, the feature can now access more online sources to find the answer. You can also use Siri to control more iPhone or iPad functions, such as playing music, accessing voicemails, or controlling iTunes Radio. The focus of Chapter 2, "Use Siri, Dictation, and iOS in Your Car to Interact with Your Mobile Device," explains how to effectively "talk" to Siri.

iOS 7 WHAT'S NEW If you own a 2013 or 2014 (or later) model year vehicle from one of more than a dozen car manufacturers, including General Motors, your vehicle can probably wirelessly link to your iPhone or iPad. Using Siri Eyes Free and other iOS In The Car functionality, it's possible to control certain features and functions of your iPhone through your car's in-dash infotainment system and issue commands using your voice, but never have to take your eyes off of the road to look at the iPhone's screen.

- **New features in all of iOS 7's core apps**—Your iPhone or iPad comes with a handful of preinstalled apps, including Contacts, Calendar, Reminders, Notes, Mail, Safari, Maps, Photos, Camera, App Store, iTunes Store, Music, and Messages. The iOS 7 versions of these and other preinstalled apps have all been redesigned and enhanced with new features and functions that will be explained throughout this book.

NOTE Several other apps developed by Apple, including the iWork for iOS and iLife for iOS apps, which include Pages, Numbers, Keynote, iPhoto, GarageBand, and iMovie, are now offered free from the App Store.

- **Better integration with iCloud**—In addition to serving as an online-based file sharing and data backup service, iCloud works seamlessly with many core iOS 7 functions and bundled apps. Thus, what's possible using iCloud directly from your iOS mobile device to sync, back up, and share app-specific data is more impressive and useful than ever.

NOTE Some iCloud-related functions can be utilized from your iPhone or iPad using a 3G or 4G (LTE) cellular data connection; however, to utilize some other features, such as iCloud Backup, a Wi-Fi connection is required.

- **Improved communication tools through iOS 7's app-related sharing buttons**—Certain apps that come preinstalled with iOS 7, such as Contacts and Photos, enable you to share app-specific data with others. The latest versions of these and other apps offer enhancements in terms of how you can share app-specific data via the Mail or Messages app, Facebook or Twitter, or the new AirDrop for iOS feature. You'll discover these improvements in most apps that feature a Share button, including the optional iWork for iOS apps (Pages, Numbers, and Keynote).

Figure I.4 shows the Share menu screen that's displayed on the iPhone 5S after tapping on the Share icon in the Photos app. As you can see, digital images stored on an iOS mobile device can now be shared via AirDrop, Messages, Mail, iCloud, Twitter, Facebook, or Flickr. From this menu screen, the Copy, Slideshow, Airplay, Save to Camera Roll, Assign to Contact, Use as Wallpaper, and Print commands are also available, and thumbnails of selected images are displayed.

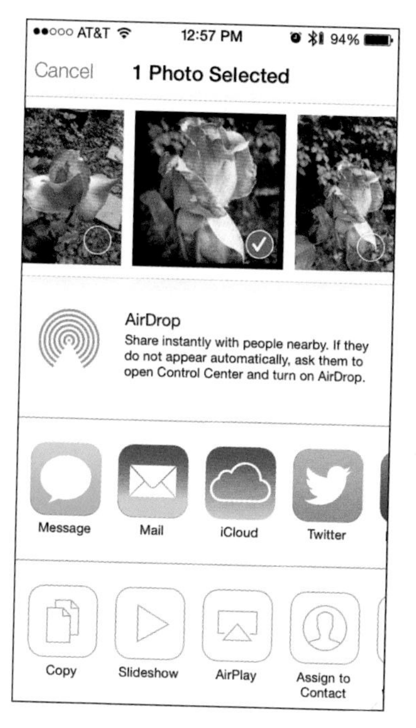

FIGURE I.4

The newly expanded Share menu screen in the iOS 7 version of the Photos app.

- **New security features**—The Find My iPhone/iPad feature, which you can access using the optional and free Find My iPhone app or by visiting www.icloud.com/#find from any computer's web browser, enables you to pinpoint the exact location of your iOS mobile device on a detailed map if it gets lost or stolen. Find My iPhone/iPad then offers features to help you retrieve your device and/or protect your data from being accessed by authorized people. Now, thanks to iOS 7, if your iPhone is stolen, someone will need to know your Apple ID and related password to delete its contents and reactivate it.

NOTE The iPhone 5S also offers enhanced technology built in to its cameras. To fully utilize this technology and be able to shoot better photos and videos, additional options are offered when using the Camera app, for example. These are covered in Chapter 8.

USING THE NEW TOUCH ID FINGERPRINT SENSOR

The iPhone 5S includes the Touch ID sensor built in to the Home button. This fingerprint scanner is a cutting-edge security tool that enables the user to unlock his iPhone using his fingerprint, as opposed to manually entering a passcode. The same sensor can also be used to approve an iTunes Store, App Store, iBookstore, or Newsstand purchase, without having to manually enter an Apple ID password.

NOTE The Touch ID sensor is available only in the iPhone 5S. This information does not apply to any of Apple's older smartphone or tablet models.

As with most iPhone-related features, use of the Touch ID sensor is optional. Upon activating and setting up the device for the first time, users are prompted to set up the Touch ID on a compatible device by scanning their fingerprint and turning on the features associated with this sensor. However, this feature can be activated, modified, or deactivated at any time in Settings.

CUSTOMIZE THE TOUCH ID SETTINGS

To customize settings related to the Touch ID sensor, launch Settings, tap on the General option, and then tap on the Passcode & Fingerprint option (shown in Figure I.5). If the feature is already active, you'll be prompted to enter your four-digit passcode to confirm your identity.

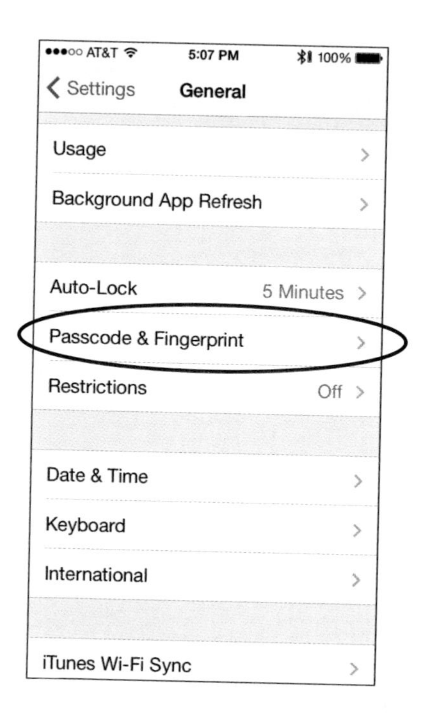

FIGURE I.5

After launching Settings, tap on the General option, and then tap on the Passcode & Fingerprint option to customize Touch ID-related options.

Then, from the Passcode & Fingerprint menu in Settings (shown in Figure I.6), it's possible to turn on or off the Passcode feature, determine when the Passcode will be required, turn on or off the Simple Passcode option and manage the fingerprints stored in the iPhone 5S.

From this menu, it's also possible to turn on or off the Erase Data option, which causes the iPhone to automatically erase its contents if an unauthorized person attempts to gain access to the device more than 10 times in a row with an incorrect passcode.

After tapping on the Fingerprints option that's displayed about halfway down on the Passcode & Fingerprint menu, the Fingerprints menu (shown in Figure I.7) is displayed.

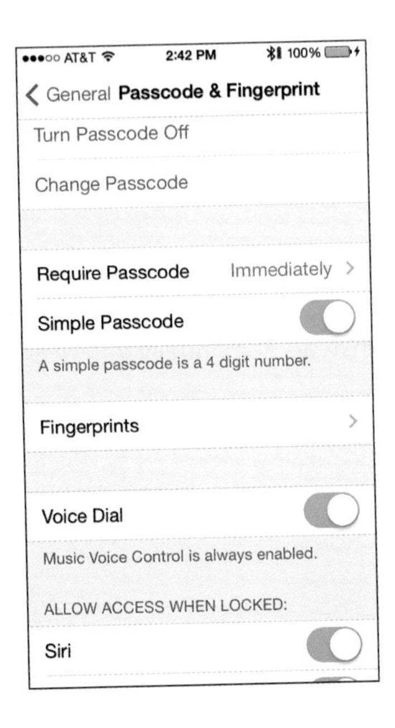

FIGURE I.6

Turn on or off iOS 7's Passcode option from the Passcode & Fingerprint menu shown here.

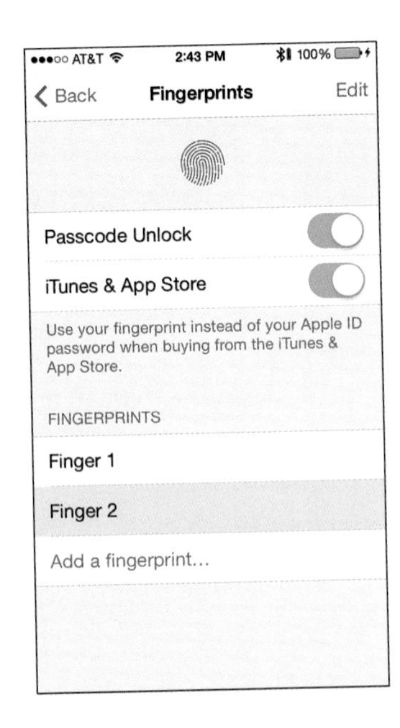

FIGURE I.7

From the Fingerprints menu, you can turn on or off the ability to use the Touch ID sensor to unlock your iOS mobile device, as well as approve iTunes Store and App Store purchase decisions.

From here, you have three options:

- You can turn on or off the Passcode Unlock feature. When turned on, this feature enables you to unlock your iOS mobile device using your fingerprint scan.
- You can turn on or off the virtual switch that's associated with the iTunes & App Store option. When turned on, your iPhone 5S enables you to use a fingerprint scan to confirm your iTunes Store, App Store, iBookstore, and Newsstand purchases, instead of manually entering your Apple ID password.
- Under the Fingerprints heading, you can tap on the Add a Fingerprint option to enable the iPhone 5S to scan and store additional fingerprints that it will accept. Use this option to allow additional users access to your iOS mobile device by scanning their fingerprint(s), or you can add an additional fingerprint of your own.

NOTE After a fingerprint scan is stored in your iPhone 5S, the data is encrypted and is never shared with Apple, app developers, or other third parties. Fingerprint scan data does not sync with iCloud.

iOS 7 WHAT'S NEW Depending on how you hold your iPhone 5S, sometimes you might find it convenient to use your thumbprint with the Touch ID sensor. However, at other times, you might opt to use your index finger. For the Touch ID sensor to accept both your thumb and index finger fingerprints, each must be scanned into the device separately.

To do this, tap on the Add a Fingerprint option, and then as instructed, lift and rest your finger on the Home button repeatedly so that your iOS mobile device can accurately scan and store each fingerprint. The Success screen (shown in Figure I.8) displays when your iOS mobile device has captured and stored each new fingerprint.

FIGURE I.8

When prompted, place your finger on the Home button and then remove it. Do this repeatedly until your iPhone fully scans your fingerprint and this Success screen is displayed.

The process of scanning a fingerprint needs to be done only once (per finger or user). If you opt to scan the fingerprint of other authorized users into your iPhone 5S, but later want to revoke access to your smartphone, return to the Fingerprints menu in Settings and swipe from right to left across the listing for a fingerprint scan that you want to delete. They're listed as Finger 1, Finger 2, and so on. Next, tap on the red-and-white Delete button to confirm your decision.

NOTE When a fingerprint is deleted from your iPhone 5S, the Touch ID sensor built in to the smartphone will no longer recognize that fingerprint. If you have revoked someone else's access to your device, however, it might be necessary to also change the Passcode programmed into your iPhone if the other person knows this four-digit code or password.

UNLOCKING THE iPHONE 5S AND MAKING iTUNES STORE PURCHASES

After you've activated the Touch ID sensor, anytime you turn on or wake up your iPhone, place and hold your finger on the Home button for a second or two to unlock the device and proceed from the Lock screen to the Home screen to begin using your iPhone 5S.

If you've also turned on the ability to confirm iTunes Store purchases in Settings, after tapping on the Price icon for the app or content you want to purchase, tap on the Buy button. When the Scan Fingerprint pop-up screen appears, place and hold your finger on the Home button to confirm your purchase. The app or content will begin downloading to your tablet almost immediately. This works when purchasing apps from the App Store, as well as content from the iTunes Store, iBookstore, or Newsstand.

> **NOTE** The Touch ID sensor built in to the iPhone 5S is an extremely powerful security feature that can be used to protect your data, documents, and files. iOS 7's Passcode feature is used as a backup for accessing your smartphone if, for some reason, a fingerprint can't be scanned properly or recognized, or if you want to grant someone else access to your device without first scanning in and storing their fingerprints.

WHAT THIS BOOK OFFERS

This all-new third edition of *iPad and iPhone Tips and Tricks* helps you quickly discover all the important new features and functions of iOS 7 and shows you how to begin fully utilizing this operating system and its bundled apps so that you can transform your iPhone, iPad, iPad mini, or iPod touch into the most versatile, useful and fun-to-use tool possible.

You'll discover strategies for finding and installing optional third-party apps from the App Store, plus learn all about how to experience various other types of content—from music, TV shows and movies, to eBooks and digital editions of magazine, plus learn how to best organize, view, and share your own digital photos.

In terms of using your iPhone or iPad as a powerful communications tool, you'll also discover strategies for efficiently making and receiving calls (iPhone only), sending and receiving text messages, participating in FaceTime calls (videoconferencing), and participating on social networking services such as Facebook and Twitter, while simultaneously making full use of iOS 7's latest features. The book also explores how to take full control of and customize your phone or tablet using the tools and features available from Settings, Control Center, and Notification Center.

ATTENTION, PLEASE...

Throughout the book, look for Tip, Note, Caution, What's New, and More Info boxes that convey useful tidbits of information relevant to the chapter you're reading. In each chapter, you'll also discover Quick Tips sections, which quickly outline how to perform a series of common tasks related to the iOS 7 features, functions, or apps that are being discussed.

The What's New boxes highlight new features or functionality introduced in iOS 7, while the More Info boxes provide website URLs or list additional resources that you can use to obtain more information about a particular topic.

IN THIS CHAPTER

- How to personalize your iPhone or iPad by adjusting the options available from within Settings
- How to customize the Lock screen and Home screen
- How to use Control Center
- Discover what's possible from the Lock screen

1

TIPS AND TRICKS FOR CUSTOMIZING SETTINGS

Thanks to iOS 7, the functionality of your iPhone or iPad is highly customizable. You can adjust many device and app-related options from within Settings, plus use Notification Center to help you manage alerts, alarms, notifications, and certain content in one centralized location. Meanwhile, the new Control Center gives you quick access to a handful of commonly used features and functions.

This chapter focuses on personalizing and customizing your iOS mobile device and getting you acquainted with using Settings, Control Center, and Notification Center.

> **TIP** To access Settings, simply tap on the Settings app icon from the Home screen (shown in Figure 1.1). Like so many of the apps that come bundled with iOS 7, the Settings app icon has a new look.

FIGURE 1.1

Many of the Home screen icons for apps that come preinstalled with iOS 7, including Settings, now have a new look. (Shown here on the iPad.)

To make your iPhone or iPad handle so many tasks and integrate functionality between apps, a lot automatically happens behind the scenes that's controlled by iOS 7. From within Settings, however, you can personalize and customize many different options that give you more control than ever over how your iPhone or iPad responds to you, while managing your apps, files, content, and data.

After iOS 7 is installed and fully operational on your iPhone or iPad, you'll definitely want to manually adjust some of the options in Settings, as opposed to relying entirely on their default settings.

> **TIP** As you install additional apps onto your iPhone or iPad, if those apps enable you to customize specific features within the app, those customization options will often be available to you from within Settings, as well.

USING THE SETTINGS APP

After you launch Settings, the menus and submenus are displayed in a hierarchical structure. Under the main Settings heading, you'll see a handful of main menu options relating to various apps and functions offered by your iPhone or iPad (shown in Figure 1.2). When you tap on many of these options, a submenu often displays. From that submenu, additional but related options, some of which have submenus themselves, become accessible.

iOS 7 WHAT'S NEW When you access Settings (shown in Figure 1.3), you'll immediately discover some new menu options that were not available in iOS 6. Plus, the virtual on/off switches associated with many menu options now have a new look. When a virtual switch is positioned to the right and you see green, that option is turned on. When the switch is positioned to the left, it's turned off.

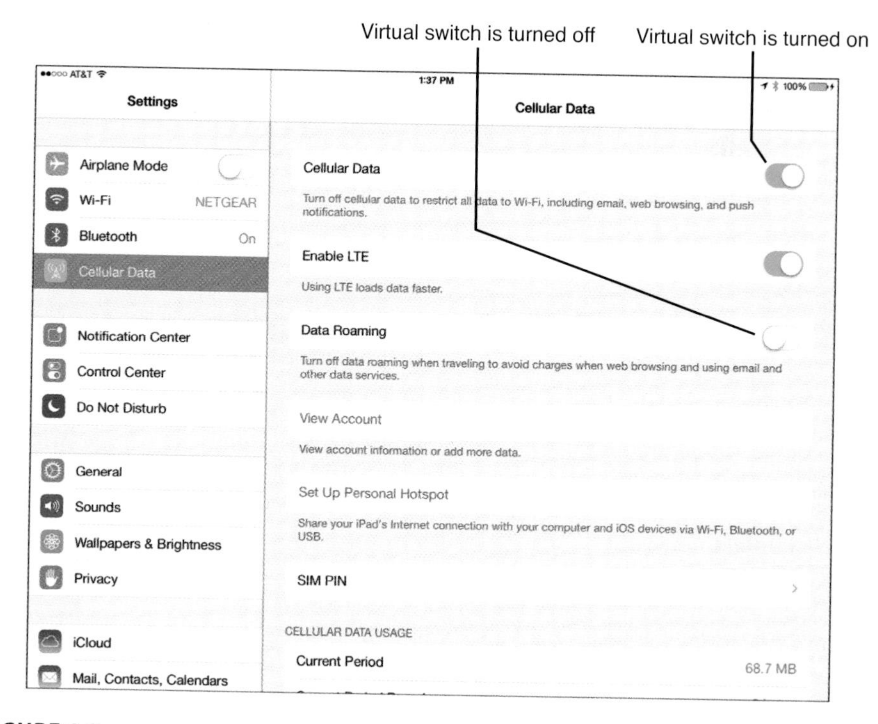

FIGURE 1.2

On the iPad, the left side of the screen shows the main Settings menu. To the right are available submenu options.

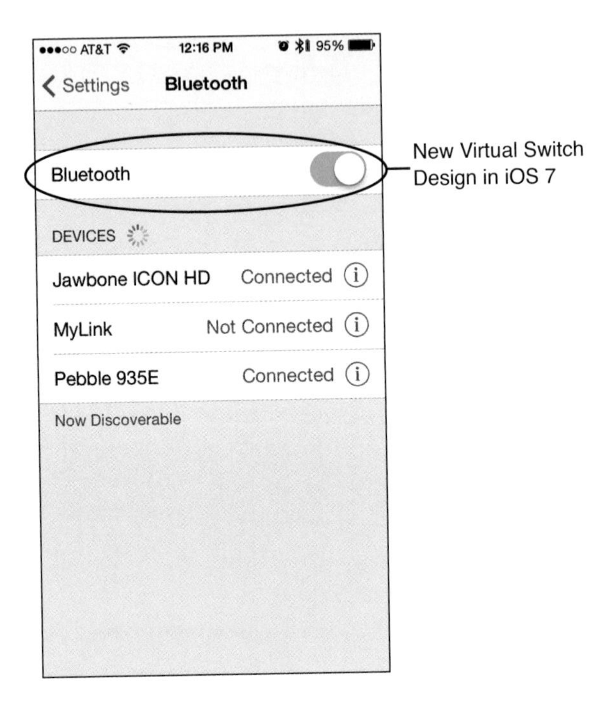

FIGURE 1.3

The virtual on/off switches in Settings have a new look. To turn on a feature (shown here), the switch should be positioned to the right.

> **NOTE** The user-customizable options available from within Settings will also vary based on what model iOS device you're using and whether it offers 3G/4G (LTE) cellular Internet connectivity.

For example, if you tap on the Brightness and Wallpaper option, the submenus associated with controlling the screen brightness and personalizing the Lock screen and Home screen wallpaper are shown.

By tapping on the wallpaper thumbnails displayed under the Wallpaper submenu, additional submenu options are displayed.

As you work your way deeper into each submenu, a left-pointing icon appears near the upper-left corner of each submenu screen that enables you to exit out of each Settings submenu and move a step back toward the main Settings menu.

At any time, tap on this left-pointing arrow icon to exit out of the submenu you're in (before or after you've made adjustments to the various option settings). If you opt to make adjustments, those changes will automatically be saved when you exit out of the menu or submenu within Settings. Or if you exit out of a menu or submenu without making any changes, nothing will be altered.

MAIN OPTIONS AVAILABLE FROM THE SETTINGS APP

The following is a summary of the main options available from the Settings app, which will vary slightly based on whether you're using an iPhone, an iPad, or another iOS device.

NOTE If you're using an iPhone 5S or an iPad model released after September 2013, additional options pertaining to the Touch ID sensor (Home button), as well as the built-in cameras are offered within Settings.

AIRPLANE MODE (iPHONE/iPAD CELLULAR + WI-FI MODELS)

This Settings option has no submenu but offers a virtual on/off switch. It's used to switch your device into Airplane Mode. Ideal for when you're on an airplane or traveling overseas, putting your device in Airplane Mode shuts down its capability to access a 3G/4G (LTE) cellular Internet connection and keeps the unit from sending or receiving cellular transmissions. However, all its other features and functions remain fully operational.

In Airplane Mode, a small airplane icon appears in the upper-left corner of the iPhone or iPad's screen, as shown in Figure 1.4.

FIGURE 1.4

In Airplane Mode, a small airplane icon appears in the upper-left corner of your iPhone or iPad's screen. (Shown here on the iPad.)

Even while your device is in Airplane Mode, you can still turn on Wi-Fi and/or Bluetooth, allowing the iOS device to access the Web via a Wi-Fi hotspot (to utilize the wireless web access available on some commercial aircrafts, for example), and also communicate with a Bluetooth-enabled wireless keyboard or headset.

TIP When you turn on Airplane mode, the Wi-Fi and Bluetooth features of your iPhone or iPad get turned off automatically. You can, however, turn them back on manually while still in Airplane mode. This is done in Settings or the Control Center.

If you refer to Figure 1.4, you'll see that the iPad is in Airplane Mode (the airplane icon is displayed in the upper-left corner of the screen). However, the tablet is also connected to a Wi-Fi network. You can see the Wi-Fi signal strength icon displayed in the upper-left corner of the screen, near the Airplane Mode icon. In addition, this tablet has Bluetooth turned on and a Bluetooth-compatible external speaker connected. You can tell this from the Bluetooth icons displayed in the upper-right corner of the screen, next to the battery indicator icon and percentage meter.

WI-FI (iPHONE/iPAD)

Located directly below the Airplane Mode option is the Wi-Fi option. When you tap this option, a submenu containing a virtual on/off switch is displayed. When it's turned on, a listing of available Wi-Fi networks is displayed directly below the Choose a Network heading.

TIP When you're reviewing a list of available Wi-Fi networks, look to the right side of each listing to determine whether a lock icon also appears. This indicates that the Wi-Fi hotspot is password protected. Tap on a hotspot that does not display a lock icon unless you possess the password for that network.

Also on the right side of each listing is the signal strength of each Wi-Fi hotspot in your immediate area.

To choose any Wi-Fi hotspot listed, simply tap on it. In a few seconds, a check mark appears to the left of your selected Wi-Fi hotspot, and a Wi-Fi signal indicator appears in the upper-left corner of your device's screen, indicating that a Wi-Fi connection has been established.

If you select a Wi-Fi network that is password protected, when you tap on it, an Enter Password window appears on your screen. Using the device's virtual keyboard, enter the correct password to connect to the Wi-Fi network you selected. You will often have to do this when connecting to a Wi-Fi hotspot offered in a hotel, for example.

> **NOTE** If you attempt to access a public Wi-Fi hotspot—in an airport, library, or school, for example—you might not need a password but you might be required to accept terms of a user agreement before Internet access is granted. In this case, your iOS device will say it's connected to a Wi-Fi hotspot, but until you launch Safari and accept the user agreement terms, your various apps will not be able to access the Internet.

BENEFITS OF CONNECTING TO A WI-FI HOTSPOT TO ACCESS THE WEB

There are several benefits to connecting to the Internet using a Wi-Fi connection, as opposed to a cellular-based 3G/4G (LTE) connection (if you're using an iPhone or iPad Cellular + Wi-Fi model), including the following:

- A Wi-Fi connection is typically faster than a 3G/4G (LTE) connection. (Although if you're within a 4G LTE coverage area, you might experience faster connectivity using it as opposed to Wi-Fi.)
- When connected to the Internet via Wi-Fi, you can send and receive as much data as you'd like without worrying about using up the monthly wireless data allocation that's associated with your cellular data plan.
- Using a Wi-Fi connection, you can download large files, such as movies and TV show episodes, from the iTunes Store directly onto your device. You also can create wireless backups of your iPhone or iPad that are stored on iCloud.

> **NOTE** The main drawback to using a Wi-Fi connection is that a Wi-Fi hotspot must be present, and you must stay within the radius of that hotspot to remain connected to the Internet. The signal of most Wi-Fi hotspots extends for only several hundred feet from the wireless Internet router. When you go beyond this signal radius, your Internet connection will be lost.

If you leave the Wi-Fi option turned on, your iPhone or iPad can automatically find and connect to an available Wi-Fi hotspot, with or without your approval, based on whether you have the Ask to Join Networks option turned on or off. When the Ask To Join Networks feature is turned off, your iPhone or iPad will re-connect automatically to wireless networks and Wi-Fi hotspots that you have connected to previously, such as each time you return to your home or office.

TIP By turning off the Ask To Join Networks option found in the Wi-Fi submenu of Settings, your iOS mobile device automatically joins known Wi-Fi networks without first asking you for permission.

BLUETOOTH (iPHONE/iPAD)

Turn on Bluetooth functionality to use compatible Bluetooth devices such as a wireless headset, external keyboard, or wireless speakers with your iOS mobile device. In Settings, tap Bluetooth and then turn on the virtual switch in the submenu. The first time you use a particular Bluetooth device with your iOS mobile device, you will probably need to pair it. Follow the directions that came with the device or accessory for performing this initial setup task. Some Bluetooth 4.0 devices automatically pair with your iOS device. The pairing process should take only about a minute or two. Multiple Bluetooth devices can be used simultaneously with your iPhone or iPad.

NOTE After an optional device has been paired once, as long as it's turned on and in close proximity to your iOS device and the iOS device has the Bluetooth feature turned on, the two devices will automatically establish a wireless connection and work together.

TIP If you're using your iPhone or iPad without having a Bluetooth device connected, turn off the Bluetooth feature altogether. This helps extend the battery life of your iOS device. When you turn on this feature, your iPhone or iPad automatically seeks out any Bluetooth-compatible devices in the vicinity.

CELLULAR (iPHONE) OR CELLULAR DATA (iPAD WITH CELLULAR + WI-FI)

When the Cellular or Cellular Data option is turned on, your iOS mobile device can access the wireless data network from the wireless service provider to which you're subscribed. When this option is turned off, your device can access the Internet only via a Wi-Fi connection, assuming that a Wi-Fi hotspot is present.

The Data Roaming option appears on the Cellular submenu. When turned on, Data Roaming enables your iPhone or iPad to connect to a cellular network outside the one you subscribe to through your wireless service provider. The capability to tap in to another wireless data network might be useful if you must connect to the Internet, there's no Wi-Fi hotspot present, and you're outside your own service provider's coverage area (such as when traveling abroad).

> **! CAUTION** When your iPhone or iPad is permitted to roam and tap in to another cellular data network, you will incur hefty roaming charges, often as high as $20 per megabyte (MB). Refrain from using this feature unless you've prepurchased a cellular data roaming plan through your service provider, or be prepared to pay a fortune to access the Web. In late October 2013, T-Mobile introduced free global data roaming to its customers with specific plans. This enables users to access a 3G/4G LTE cellular data network when visiting any of more than 200 countries, with no additional roaming charges.
>
> When your device can't find a compatible 3G or 4G (LTE) network, it will seek out an older 2G network, which is much slower.

From the Cellular menu within Settings, you can determine which apps and iPhone or iPad features can use your phone or tablet's cellular data network to connect to the Internet. Scroll down and set the virtual switch that's associated with each app or device feature to turn it on or off. When turned on, Internet access via a cellular data network and/or Wi-Fi will be granted. When turned off, only Wi-Fi Internet access will be granted.

Depending on your service provider, you might be able to transform your iOS device into a personal hotspot so other devices can connect wirelessly to the Internet via Wi-Fi using your iPhone or iPad's cellular data connection. If your provider allows, this option is available from main Settings menu or within the Cellular submenu.

The Cellular menu also enables you to track call time (on the iPhone) and cellular data usage.

NOTIFICATION CENTER (iPHONE/iPAD)

This Settings option (shown in Figure 1.5) enables you to determine which apps function with Notification Center, plus it enables you to determine the other ways in which apps that generate alerts, alarms, or notifications notify you.

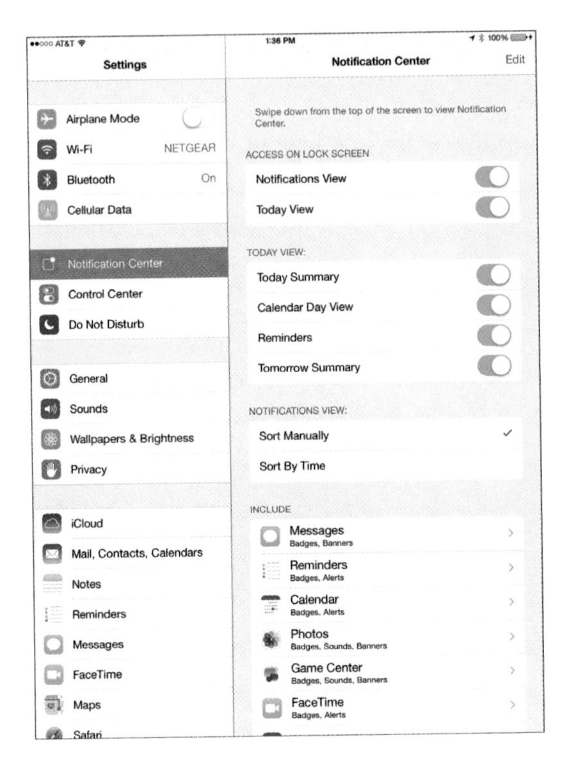

FIGURE 1.5

Apps that are set to exchange data with Notification Center are listed under the heading Include when you select the Notifications option from within the Settings app (shown here on the iPad).

iOS 7 **WHAT'S NEW** Thanks to iOS 7, you can now customize additional content that's displayed in the Notification Center window, beyond just how alerts, alarms, and notifications are presented. It's now possible to toggle the appearance of the Today Summary, Tomorrow Summary, Calendar Day View, Reminders, Stocks (iPhone), and Next Destination (iPhone) options.

Displayed near the top of the Notification Center window are three tabs: Today, All, and Missed. The Today tab displays a summary of the day's weather forecast, along with an overview of your appointments and tasks for the day that are stored in the Calendar and Reminders apps. The All tab reveals a listing of alerts and notifications generated by all the apps that Notification Center is monitoring. When you tap on the Missed tab, it displays a summary of alerts or notifications you missed while the iPhone or iPad was in Sleep mode. On the iPhone, this would include missed incoming calls.

When you tap on the Notifications Center option and scroll down, a section of the submenu under the Include heading lists apps currently installed on your iPhone or iPad that are compatible with Notification Center, and that are set to automatically share data with Notification Center.

These apps include Phone (iPhone only), Messages, Passbook (iPhone only), Calendar, Reminders, Game Center, Photos, FaceTime, Mail, and App Store, which all come preinstalled with iOS 7. However, additional apps that you install later might also be compatible with Notification Center, and will ultimately be listed here as well.

Below the Include heading is another heading, Do Not Include. Here, other apps that are capable of generating alerts, alarms, badges, or notifications are listed. However, the apps listed here are not currently set to exchange data with the Notification Center app.

TIP To move an app between the Include and Do Not Include section, tap on its listing under the heading it currently appears and toggle the virtual switch associated with Show In Notification Center to the on or off position. When turned on, the app is monitored by Notification Center and listed under the Include heading. When turned off, the app is ignored by Notification Center and included under the Do Not Include heading.

As you review each app listed under the Include or the Do Not Include heading, you can tap on it to reveal a secondary submenu pertaining specifically to that app.

The submenu associated with each app related to Notification Center enables you fully customize how alerts, sounds, and badges generated by that specific app are presented to you. Notifications can be viewed in the Notification Center window, as a banner or alert when using your phone or tablet, on the Lock screen, and/or as a badge on the app icon.

From the Notification Center submenu, one at a time, tap on an app that's listed under the Include menu, such as Calendar. Then, adjust the settings listed in its respective submenu screen.

By selecting an Alert Style, you can choose whether a banner or alert should be displayed on the screen, even when you are using another app.

If you choose Banners, a pop-up window appears at the top of the screen with the alert-related information. It appears for a few seconds and then automatically disappears. The alert style for the Messages app, for example, defaults to a banner.

If you choose the Alerts option, a pop-up window displays on the iPhone or iPad's screen until you tap on it to dismiss or address the alarm. The Calendar app generates alerts by default if you set an alarm for an upcoming event.

If you select the None option, no app-specific banner or alert will be displayed while you're using the iPhone or iPad. A notification can still be displayed in the Notification Center screen, however, if the app appears in the Include list in the Notification Center Settings submenu.

By turning on the virtual switch associated with the Badge App Icon option, the app you're customizing can display a badge on the Home screen along with its app icon. Some, but not all, apps can utilize Home screen badges.

NOTE A badge (as shown in Figure 1.6) is a small red-and-white circular graphic that can appear in the upper-right corner of an app icon on your device's Home screen. The badge contains a number used to graphically show you that something relating to a specific app has changed. For example, a number will appear as a badge on your Mail app icon when you've received new incoming email messages. The number indicates how many new messages were received.

FIGURE 1.6

On this iPhone 5 Home screen, the Phone, Mail, and Facebook app icons are all displaying badges.

Also from the submenu associated with customizing app-specific Notification Center options, you can adjust the alert sound that's generated if that app is capable of playing sounds with alerts, alarms, or notifications. From the Calendar submenu in the Notification Center settings, for example, tap on the Calendar Alerts option to access another submenu that enables you to choose a sound to be associated with event alarms.

Under the Alerts heading, turn on the virtual switch associated with Show In Notification Center if you want alerts related to that app to be displayed in the Notification Center window. Then, tap on the Include option to determine how many related alerts generated by the selected app will be listed at any given time in the Notification Center window. Your options include 1, 5, or 10 recent items. As you're first starting to use this iOS 7 feature, keep the number of alerts manageable by selecting just five per app. You can always add more for specific apps that are more important to you.

Finally, you can determine whether notifications generated by a particular app will be displayed on the Lock screen when your device is otherwise in Sleep mode. When enabled, the phone or tablet will be woken up automatically to display new notifications on the Lock screen for anyone to see, without the device first needing to be unlocked.

NOTIFICATION CENTER QUICK TIPS

- To avoid getting bombarded by excessive notifications from apps that aren't too important to you, manually set the capability of Notification Center to work with specific apps.
- At the bottom of the Notification Center settings are two new features—AMBER alerts and Emergency Alerts. When turned on, if the government issues an AMBER alert in your area or a message is broadcast over the emergency broadcast system, an alert appears on your device. These features work only with iPhones.
- To protect your privacy, you can set up Notification Center to refrain from having alerts displayed on your Lock screen. To do this, tap on each app under the Include heading and turn off the Show On Lock Screen option.
- As you customize how Notification Center displays notifications, the options available to you vary by app. For example, for the Messages app, you can assign Notification Center to repeat alerts between one and ten times, at two-minute intervals, to get your attention. You also can opt to preview an incoming message in alerts and banners and in the Notification Center window, plus decide whether you want to be alerted of all incoming messages or just messages from people who have entries in your Contacts database.

CONTROL CENTER (iPHONE/iPAD)

The Control Center is an entirely new feature added to iOS 7 on both the iPhone and iPad. It grants you quick access to a handful of phone- or tablet-related functions and apps. In the Settings app, tap the Control Center option to choose whether the Control Center will be accessible from the Lock screen or while using an app.

When the Access on Lock Screen option is turned on, you can swipe your finger from the bottom of the screen up to display Control Center from the Lock screen. When the option is turned off, Control Center will be accessible only after the device is unlocked. If Access Within Apps is turned off, you can access Control Center from the Home screen but not while you're using an app.

GENERAL (iPHONE/iPAD)

When you tap the General option in the Settings app, various other options become available. Unless otherwise noted, each option is available using an iPhone or iPad. Because many of these options remain consistent from iOS 6, only the most important or new settings are discussed here. Thus, some of the General options include the following:

- **Software Update**—Use this option to update the iOS operating system wirelessly, without having to connect your iPhone or iPad to your primary computer and use the iTunes sync procedure.
- **Siri**—Enable or disable Siri functionality on compatible devices, and adjust specific settings related to this feature. See Chapter 2 for more information about using Siri.

> **TIP** The iPhone offers a Raise To Speak option. When this is turned on, Siri engages anytime you physically pick up the iPhone and hold it up to your ear. Otherwise, you must press and hold down the Home button for about two seconds to activate Siri.

> **iOS 7 WHAT'S NEW** From the Siri menu in Settings, you can now give Siri a male or female voice. To do this, launch the Settings app, access the General menu, and then tap on the Siri option, followed by the Voice Gender option.

- **Spotlight Search**—Upon tapping this option, you can determine which portions of your iPhone or iPad are searched when you use the Spotlight Search feature built in to the device.

> **TIP** To access Spotlight Search from the Home screen, perform a swipe downward that originates from the center of the screen to make the Spotlight Search screen appear. If you swipe from the top of the screen, you open the Notification Center, so be sure your swipe originates from the center.
>
> Separate Search fields also appear in some other apps.

- **Text Size**—Control the text size within all apps (such as Mail and Safari) that support Dynamic Type. This enables you to automatically display text using a larger font size to make it easier to read on the screen.
- **Multitasking Gestures (iPad)**—There are several iPad-exclusive finger gestures for interacting with the multitouch display. You can opt to turn on or off recognition of these gestures by adjusting the virtual on/off switch that's associated with the Multitasking Gestures option. The gestures are listed on the General submenu beneath this option.
- **Use Side Switch To (iPad)**—Located on the right side of your iPad just above the volume button is a tiny switch. From the General Settings screen, you can set this switch to be used as either a Lock Rotation switch or a Mute switch.

  If you choose Lock Rotation, when the switch is turned on, you can physically rotate your iPad but the screen will not automatically switch between landscape and portrait mode.

  When it's used as a Mute switch, this turns off the iPad's built-in speaker so that no sounds are heard, such as alarms. This is useful when using your iPad in a meeting or in a quiet area, such as a library.

> **TIP** On the iPhone, the Ring/Silent switch silences call-related ringers and many alert sounds that your iPhone is capable of generating. It is located on the left side of the handset, above the Volume Up and Volume Down buttons.

- **Usage**—Tap on this option to see how the storage capacity of your device and your iCloud account are being utilized. From the Battery Usage option displayed on this screen, you can decide whether to display your device's battery life as a numeric percentage (for example, 73%) or as a battery icon graphic.

- **Background App Refresh**—This new iOS 7 feature enables you to control the capability of apps to automatically access the Internet to refresh app-specific content and/or Location Services data when the device has Internet access. A listing of compatible apps, such as Stocks and Weather, is displayed in the submenu.
- **Auto-Lock**—Anytime your iPhone or iPad is turned on, if you don't do anything for a predetermined amount of time, it can be set to automatically switch into Sleep mode to conserve battery life.
- **Restrictions**—This feature provides a way to "childproof" your iPhone or iPad by enabling a user to gain access to only specific apps or content. To activate it, tap the Restrictions option and then tap Enable Restrictions from the submenu. Set a passcode for the restrictions. You can then customize which apps are allowed, block the installation or deletion of apps, prevent in-app purchases, or set ratings limits for content.

! CAUTION If you choose to utilize this feature, make sure you remember the passcode you associate with it. If you forget the passcode, it might be necessary to erase your entire iOS device and reload everything from scratch.

- **Keyboard**—You can make certain customizations from the Setting screen that impact how your virtual keyboard responds as you're typing. Tap on the Keyboard option when using the Settings app, and you'll discover several customizable settings, such as whether Auto-Capitalization, Auto-Correction, and Check Spelling are turned on.
- **International**—If you purchased your iPhone or iPad in the United States, the default language and keyboard options are for English; however, you can adjust these settings by tapping on the International option. Even without changing the primary language, it's possible to add additional language keyboards so you can access them anytime as you're using your device.
- **Reset (iPhone/iPad)**—Every so often, you might run in to a problem with your iPhone or iPad such that the system crashes or you need to reset specific settings. For example, to restore your iPhone or iPad to its factory default settings and erase everything stored on it, tap on the Reset option, and then tap on the Erase All Content and Settings option. In general, you should refrain from using any of these settings unless you're instructed to do so by an Apple Genius or a technical support person.

! CAUTION Before using any of the options found under the Settings Reset option, which could potentially erase important data from your iPhone or iPad, be sure to perform an iTunes sync or back up your device wirelessly to iCloud and create a reliable backup of your device's contents. See Chapter 4, "Sync, Share, and Print Files and Data Using iCloud, AirDrop, Airplay, and AirPrint," for step-by-step directions for how to do this.

You'll probably never need to tinker with or adjust several options found under the General heading. Leave them at their default settings. Others you'll need to utilize often as you use your iPhone or iPad for different tasks.

SOUNDS (iPHONE/iPAD)

Tap on this option to adjust the overall volume of the iPhone or iPad's built-in speaker (or the volume of the audio you hear through headsets), as well as to turn on or off various audible tones and alarms your phone or tablet generates.

From this menu, you can also assign specific audio tones, sounds, or ringtones to specific types of app-specific alerts and alarms, plus turn on or off the click noise associated with pressing keys on the iPhone or iPad's virtual keyboard.

It's also possible to turn on the Vibrate mode so that the iPhone handset shakes, instead of or in addition to playing a ringtone. You can control the ringer volume using an onscreen slider, and adjust the custom ringtones and audio alerts associated with various features and functions of your iPhone. Your iPhone has an all-new library of different audio alarms and alerts, as well as ringtones built in, plus you can download additional ringtones from iTunes.

TIP On your iPhone, you can manually adjust the ringer and speaker volume using the Volume Up and Volume Down buttons located on the left side of your handset. You also can control the vibration of the phone and choose different vibration patterns to alert you of different things. This can be customized from the Sounds menu within Settings. Volume controls are also now accessible from the Control Center.

BRIGHTNESS & WALLPAPER (iPHONE/iPAD)

The Brightness & Wallpaper options (shown in Figure 1.7 on the iPad) enable you to control the brightness of your iPhone or iPad's screen and customize the wallpaper of your device's Lock screen and Home screen.

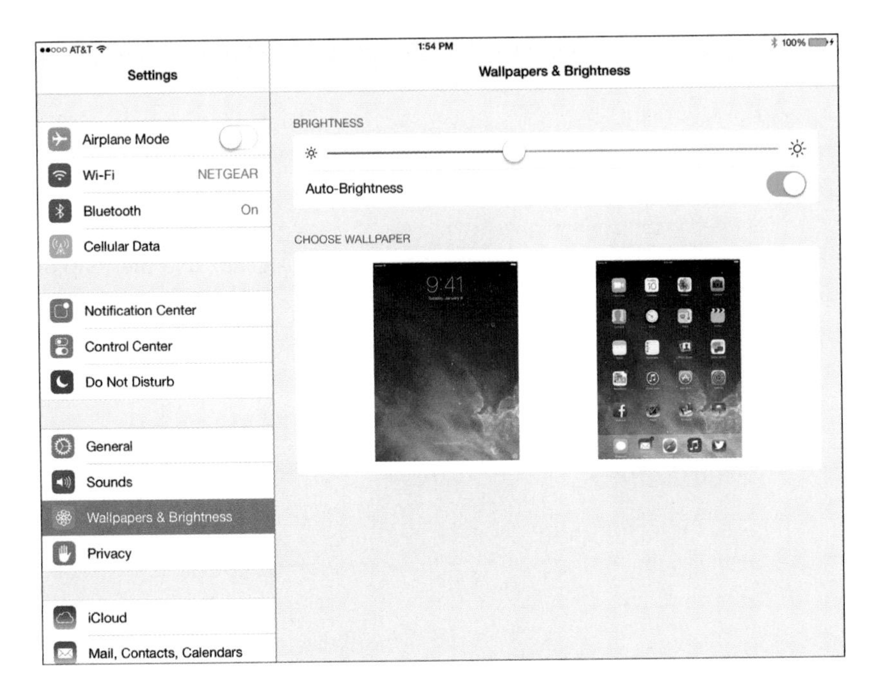

FIGURE 1.7

Use the brightness slider to control how light or dark your iPhone or iPad's screen appears.

When you tap on this option, the Brightness & Wallpaper submenu appears. At the top of this submenu is a brightness slider. Drag the white dot to the right to make the screen brighter or to the left to make the screen darker. This sets the screen brightness for the current lighting conditions.

The Auto-Brightness option displayed under the brightness slider has a virtual on/off switch associated with it. When it's turned on, your device takes into account the surrounding lighting where you're using your Phone or iPad, and then adjusts the screen's brightness accordingly.

The default setting for the Auto-Brightness feature is the on position. Leave it there unless you consistently have difficulty seeing what's displayed on your iPhone or iPad's screen based on its brightness setting.

Customize Your Lock Screen and Home Screen Wallpaper

Below the brightness slider is the Wallpaper option. Your iPhone or iPad has more than two dozen preinstalled wallpaper designs built in, plus you can use any digital images stored on your device (in the Photos app) as your Lock screen or Home screen wallpaper. Here, you see a thumbnail graphic of your iPhone or iPad's Lock screen (left) and its Home screen (right).

Tap on either of these thumbnail images to change its appearance. When you do this, the Settings screen changes, and two options are listed. On top is the Wallpaper option. Below it is the Camera Roll and Photos app Albums options (where photos shot with your iPhone or iPad or that are being stored on your device are stored).

Tap on the Wallpaper option to display thumbnails for the preinstalled wallpaper graphics you can choose from (as shown in Figure 1.8), and then tap on your selection.

FIGURE 1.8

When looking at the collection of Stills wallpaper graphics, tap on the one you'd like to use. (Shown here on the iPhone 5.)

iOS 7 **WHAT'S NEW** If you select an Apple wallpaper for your Lock screen or Home screen, it's then necessary to choose between a dynamic or still wallpaper. The dynamic wallpaper is animated and appears multidimensional, while the still images are static.

Next, on the iPad's screen, the graphic you select is displayed in full-screen mode. In the bottom-right corner of the screen are three command icons labeled Set Lock Screen, Set Home Screen, and Set Both.

On the iPhone, after tapping on your wallpaper selection, tap the Set button and then select whether to set the Lock screen, Home screen, or both to display that graphic (shown in Figure 1.9).

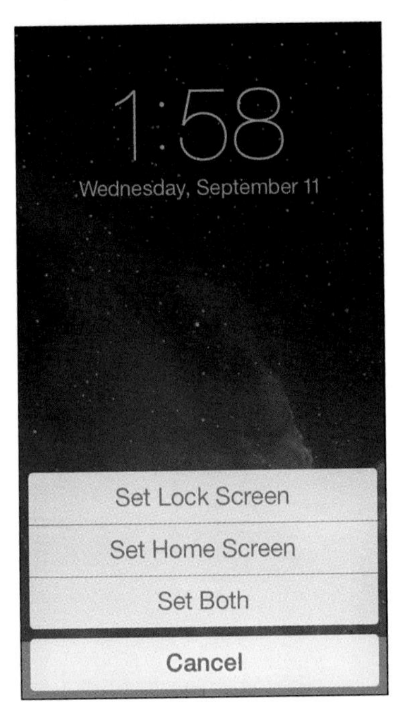

FIGURE 1.9

After selecting a wallpaper graphic to use, and then tapping on the Set button, tap on one of the four buttons to determine where the graphic is displayed—on your Lock screen, Home screen, or both.

After making your selection, when you return to the iPhone or iPad's Lock screen or Home screen, you see your newly selected wallpaper graphic displayed.

Instead of choosing one of the preinstalled wallpaper graphics, you also have the option of using photos you've transferred to your iOS device and have stored in the Photos app or photos you've shot using the Camera app.

TIP Using any search engine, enter the keyword "iPhone wallpaper" or "iPad wallpaper" to find free wallpaper graphics you can download.

To select one of your own photos to use as your Lock screen or Home screen wallpaper, tap on the Brightness & Wallpaper option within Settings, and then tap on the thumbnails that appear showcasing your iPhone or iPad's Lock screen and Home screen.

This time, in the Photos heading located below the Wallpaper option, tap on the folder that contains the image you want to use as your wallpaper. Then tap on the image you want to use as your wallpaper for your Lock screen and/or Home screen. When the photo you selected appears in full-screen mode, you might need to crop or reposition the image within the onscreen frame, and then tap the Set button.

After you've made your selection, your newly selected wallpaper graphic appears on your Lock screen and/or Home screen, as you can see in Figure 1.10 and Figure 1.11.

FIGURE 1.10

A newly selected Lock screen graphic, chosen from a photo stored on the iPhone 5 in the Photos app.

FIGURE 1.11

The still wallpaper selected from within Settings is now displayed as your Home screen wallpaper, behind your app icons (shown here on the iPad).

PRIVACY (iPHONE/iPAD)

This newly enhanced menu option in Settings gives you much greater privacy control in terms of how information is shared between apps and shared with other people.

From this Settings submenu screen, you can control specifically which apps have access to the iOS device's Location Services feature, for example, plus which other apps can share data with certain pre-installed apps (including Contacts, Calendar, Reminders, and Photos).

Certain apps and services, such as Maps or Find My iPhone (or Find My iPad), utilize the capability to pinpoint your exact location. It's important to customize the Location Services options if you're concerned that certain apps will be able to potentially share this information.

TIP If you utilize the Find My Friends app, which enables authorized people to track your whereabouts in real time, customize the Location Services options related to Find My Friends, and from within the app, to determine who can "follow" you and when. You can enable or disable this functionally quickly whenever you like, but you must remember to turn it off when you want your privacy.

When the master virtual switch for Location Services option is turned on, your iPhone or iPad can fully utilize its GPS capabilities, in addition to crowd-sourced Wi-Fi hotspots and cell towers, to determine your exact location. When it's turned off, your device cannot determine (or broadcast) your location. However, some of your apps will not function properly.

TIP When the Location Services option is turned on and you snap a photo or shoot video using the Camera app, the exact location where that photo or video was shot will be recorded and saved. This feature is deactivated if you turn off the Location Services option. You can also leave the master Location Services feature for your device turned on, but turn off this feature with specific apps, such as the Camera app.

iOS 7 WHAT'S NEW From the Privacy menu within Settings, you determine which apps can share information with each other and with the public when you use Facebook, Twitter, or other online social networking apps. Click on the Advertising option from the Privacy menu to limit ad tracking for in-app ads and ads you see in Safari when surfing the Web.

iCLOUD (iPHONE/iPAD)

You learn all about using iCloud with your iPhone or iPad in Chapter 4.

MAIL, CONTACTS, CALENDARS (iPHONE/iPAD)

If you use your iPhone or iPad on the job, three apps you probably rely on heavily are Mail, Contacts, and Calendars. From the Settings app, you can customize a handful of options pertaining to each of these apps, and you can set up your existing email accounts to work with your phone or tablet.

For information about how to use the Settings app to customize the Mail app-related settings, see Chapter 11, "Send and Receive Emails, Text, and Instant Messages with the Mail and Messages Apps." You can find details about customizing the settings of the Contacts and Calendar apps in Chapter 13, "Calendar and Contact Management Strategies."

TIP Under the Calendars heading of the Mail, Contacts, Calendars option, one useful setting is Default Alert Time. Tapping on this option reveals the Default Alert Times menu screen, from which you can automatically set advance alarms for birthdays, events, and all-day events stored in your Calendar app. Each of these options can be individually set to alert you at 9:00 on the morning of the event, one or two days prior, or one week before the event, based on your preference.

If you fill in the Birthday field as you create contact entries in the Contacts app, these dates can automatically be displayed in the Calendar app to remind you of birthdays. The advance warning of a birthday gives you ample time to send a card or a gift.

MORE APP-SPECIFIC OPTIONS WITHIN SETTINGS

As you scroll down on the main Settings menu on your iPhone or iPad, you'll see specific apps listed, including some of the core preinstalled apps (such as Notes, Reminders, Messages, FaceTime, Maps, Safari, Music, Newsstand, and Videos), as well as optional Apple-created apps if they're installed on your device (such as iBooks).

As you continue scrolling down, you'll see listings for Twitter, Facebook, Flickr, and Vimeo, which lead to submenus that offer the capability to fully customize integration with these online social networking services with many of the apps you'll soon be using, including Photos.

TIP To customize your ability to make and manage app and content purchases from the iTunes Store and the App Store, tap on the iTunes and App Store option found under the main Settings menu. From this submenu, you can manage your Apple ID, turn on/off the optional iTunes Match service, plus activate automatic downloads for music, apps, books, and updates using a cellular and/or Wi-Fi Internet connection.

USER-INSTALLED APPS

By scrolling toward the bottom of the Settings menu, you'll discover a listing of other individual apps that you have installed on your iPhone or iPad and that have user-adjustable options or settings available. Tap on one app listing at a time to modify these settings. Remember, as you install new apps in the future, additional app listings will be added to this section of the Settings menu and can be modified accordingly.

CONTROL CENTER GIVES YOU QUICK ACCESS TO POPULAR FEATURES AND FUNCTIONS

At any time, regardless of what you're doing on your iPhone or iPad, it's possible to access the new Control Center. To do this, simply place your finger near the bottom of the screen and swipe upward. This causes the Control Center window to appear (shown in Figure 1.12).

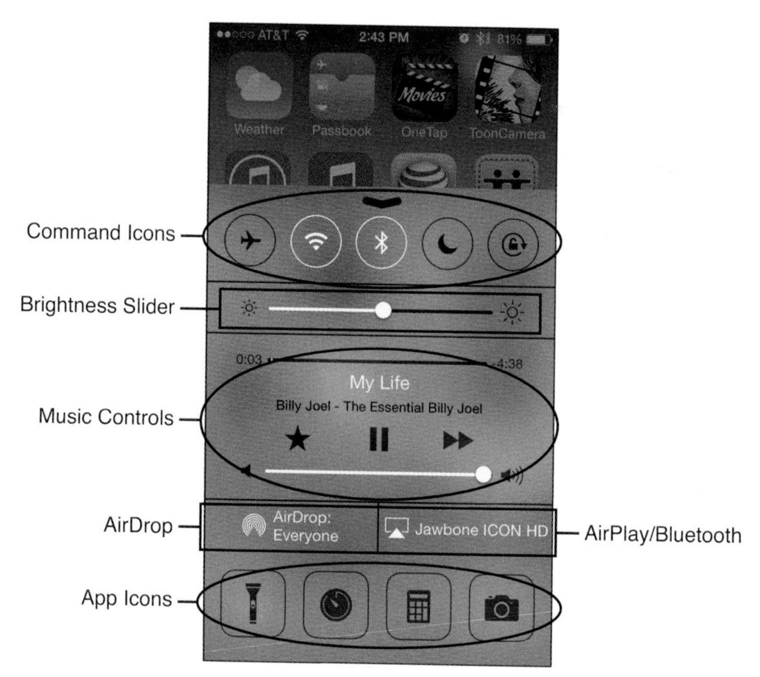

FIGURE 1.12

The new Control Center window on the iPhone.

On the iPhone, you'll see five circular icons near the top of the Control Center window, each of which enables you to control a frequently used iPhone feature. From left to right, the icons include

- **Airplane Mode**—Quickly place your iPhone or iPad into Airplane mode.
- **Wi-Fi**—Turn Wi-Fi on or off with a single tap, without having to access Settings.
- **Bluetooth**—Turn Bluetooth on or off so that your iPhone or iPad can link to Bluetooth devices it has already been paired with.
- **Do Not Disturb**—Manually turn on the Do Not Disturb feature after you've customized this option from within Settings.
- **Rotation Lock**—Normally, when you rotate your iPhone sideways, the screen automatically switches from portrait to landscape mode. To prevent this from happening when the phone is rotated, turn on the Rotation Lock feature by tapping on its icon.

Displayed below these icons is the screen brightness slider, and below that are the Music app controls, which enable you to play currently selected music (or Playlists) without launching the Music app.

Moving down within Control Center, you'll see two additional command buttons, labeled AirDrop (left) and AirPlay (right). Tap on AirDrop to quickly activate this feature and determine what content or data you want to wirelessly share with nearby iPhone or iPad users. Tap the AirPlay button to select where AirPlay-compatible apps will direct content.

TIP When AirDrop is turned on, your iPhone or iPad is discoverable by any iPhone or iPad user that's in your immediate vicinity that also has the AirDrop feature turned on. You can then wirelessly transfer data from certain apps, like Contacts and Photos. To protect your privacy when out in public, consider keeping this feature turned off unless you specifically want to use it. Keep in mind that only the latest model iPhones and iPads are compatible with this feature.

Displayed along the bottom of the Control Center window on the iPhone are four app-related icons. Tap on the flashlight icon to turn on the iPhone's flash so that it serves as a bright flashlight. Tap on the alarm icon to set and manage alarms. This serves as a shortcut to the Clock app.

Tap on the Calculator icon to launch the Calculator app quickly. Finally, tapping on the Camera icon offers yet another way to quickly launch the Camera app and begin snapping photos. This can also be done quickly from the Lock screen placing your finger on the Camera icon and flicking upward.

The Control Center on the iPad is similar to that of the iPhone; however, as you can see from Figure 1.13, the layout of the options is different. The Control Center on the tablet is displayed as a bar across the bottom of the screen. The Music controls and volume slider are displayed on the left, the five command icons (Airplane Mode, Wi-Fi, Bluetooth, Do Not Disturb, and Rotation Lock) are displayed near the center, while the Clock/Alarm and Camera app icons and screen brightness slider can be found on the right.

FIGURE 1.13

The new Control Center feature on the iPad.

To close the Control Center window, tap anywhere near the top of the iPhone's screen, or tap on the down-pointing arrow icon that's displayed near the top of the window.

ORGANIZE APPS ON YOUR HOME SCREEN WITH FOLDERS

If you're like most iPhone and iPad users, you'll probably be loading a handful of third-party apps onto your device. After all, there are several hundred thousand third-party apps to choose from. To make finding and organizing your apps easier from the iPhone or iPad's Home screen, and to reduce onscreen clutter, you can place app icons in folders.

Utilizing the Folders feature is easy. From the Home screen, press and hold down any app icon until all the app icons begin shaking on the Home screen. Using your finger, drag one app icon on top of another, to automatically place both of those apps into a new folder.

You can organize your apps in folders based on categories, like Games, Travel, or Productivity (shown in Figure 1.14), or you can enter your own folder names, and then drag and drop the appropriate app icons into the folders you create. After your app icons are organized, simply press the Home button again on the iPhone or iPad to save your folders and display them on your Home screen.

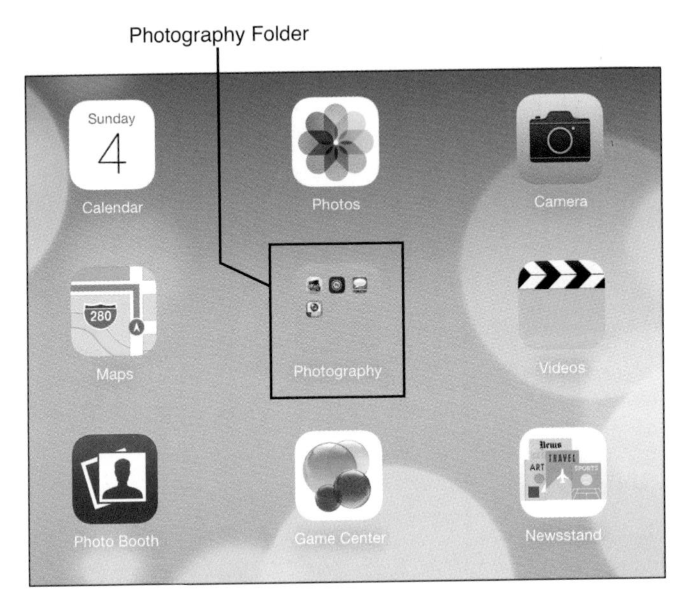

FIGURE 1.14

On this iPad, a Photography folder has been created. It contains four different photography-related apps.

WHAT'S NEW As you're creating app folders, thanks to iOS 7, you are no longer limited in terms of how many apps you can place into each folder.

If you later want to remove an app icon from a folder so that it appears as a stand-alone app icon on your Home screen, simply press and hold any of the folder icons until all the onscreen icons start to shake. The folder's contents are displayed.

When the app icons are shaking, simply drag the app icons, one at a time, back onto the Home screen. Each will then be removed from the folder. Press the Home button to finalize this action.

MOVING APP ICONS AROUND ON THE HOME SCREEN

To move app icons around and reorganize them on the Home screen, press and hold down any app icon with your finger. When the app icons start to shake, you can use your finger to drag one app icon at a time around on the Home screen.

Your iPhone or iPad can extend the Home screen across multiple pages. (Switch pages by swiping your finger from left to right, or right to left when viewing the Home screen.)

To move an app icon to another Home screen page, while it's shaking, hold it down with your finger and slowly drag it to the extreme right or left, off of the screen, so that it bounces onto another of the Home screen's pages.

When you switch pages, the row of up to four app icons displayed at the very bottom of the iPhone's screen (or up to six app icons on the iPad's screen) remains constant. Place your most frequently used apps in these positions so that they're always visible from the Home screen.

As the app icons are shaking on the Home screen, you can delete the icons that display a black-and-white "X" in the upper-left corner from your iPhone or iPad by pressing that "X" icon. You'll discover that the preinstalled (core) apps related to iOS 7, such as Contacts, Calendar, Reminders, Notes, App Store, and Settings, cannot be deleted. They can only be moved.

ADD FREQUENTLY USED WEB PAGE ICONS TO YOUR HOME SCREEN

Many people constantly return to their favorite websites for updates throughout the day or week. Instead of first accessing the Safari browser on your iPhone or iPad, and then choosing your favorite sites from your Bookmarks list, you can create individual icons for your favorite web pages and display them on your Home screen. This enables you to access that web page with a single tap of the finger from the Home screen.

Depending on the website, when you create a web page icon, it either uses a thumbnail image from the website itself or a predesigned logo or graphic. In Figure 1.15, the Jason R. Rich icon shows a thumbnail for the JasonRich.com website, while the CNN icon is for CNN.com.

FIGURE 1.15

A web page icon (such as the one for JasonRich.com or CNN.com) on your Home screen looks similar to an app icon; however, when you tap it, Safari is launched and the web page that the icon is associated with is loaded automatically.

To create a web page icon on your Home screen, access Safari and visit your favorite web page. Next, tap the Share icon that's located next to the Address Bar (shown in Figure 1.16), and tap the Add to Home Screen option that appears.

The menu that appears when you tap on the Share icon contains several features, which you'll learn more about in Chapter 12, "Surf the Web More Efficiently Using Safari."

When you return to your Home screen, the icon for that web page is now displayed and looks very much like an app icon. To access that web page in the future, simply tap the appropriate icon on the Home screen.

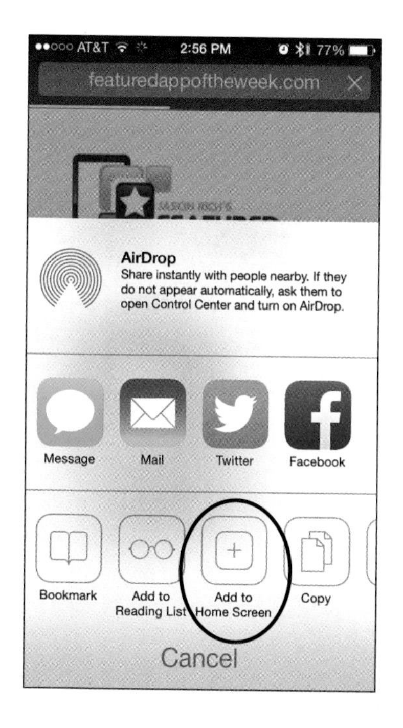

FIGURE 1.16

To create a web page icon that appears on your Home screen, use the Add to Home Screen command displayed when you tap the Share icon within Safari (shown here on the iPhone 5).

DISCOVER WHAT'S NOW POSSIBLE FROM THE LOCK SCREEN

iOS 7 now offers additional functionality that you can access directly from the Lock screen. From within Settings, however, you can opt to turn off most of this functionality to protect your privacy. Thus, if you turn on Passcode Lock, strangers will not be able to pick up and use your phone or tablet or access any content from it.

The Lock screen automatically displays the current time and date, the Slide To Unlock feature, as well as the Camera icon. You can also set it up so app-specific alerts or banners are displayed on the Lock screen when applicable, plus you can decide whether you want the ability to access the Control Center directly from the Lock screen. These features can be customized from within Settings.

MANAGE YOUR CUSTOMIZED NOTIFICATION CENTER SCREEN

Accessing the Notification Center window/screen from the iPhone or iPad at any-time continues to be possible simply by placing your finger near the top of the screen and swiping downward. From the newly designed Notification Center, you can see all alerts, alarms, and notifications generated by your device in one place.

Thanks to iOS 7, however, the Notification Center screen (shown in Figure 1.17) now displays additional content beyond just app-specific notifications.

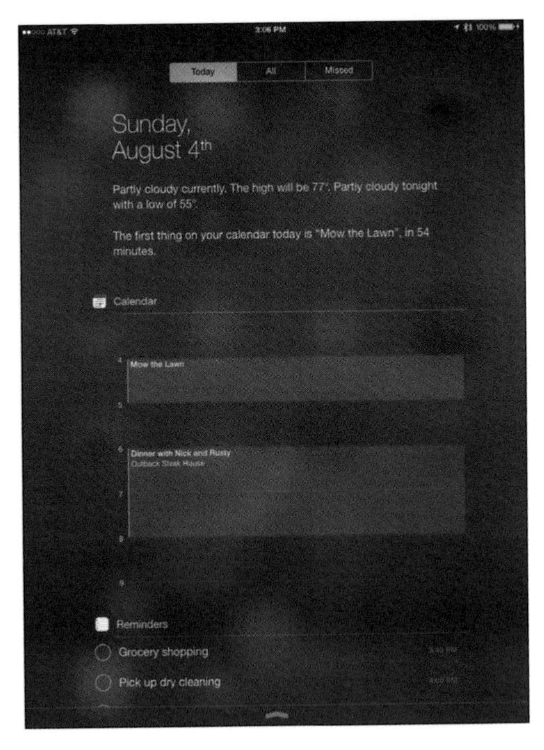

FIGURE 1.17

The newly designed Notification Center screen shown here on the iPad. From within Settings, what's displayed here is customizable.

Along the top of the Notification Center are three command tabs: Today, All, and Missed. Tap on Today to see the current day and date, along with the weather forecast, plus a preview of upcoming appointments from the Calendar app. Scroll down on this screen to see a preview of tomorrow's schedule.

Tap on the All tab to see notifications recently generated by all compatible apps running on your phone or tablet. The name and app icon for each compatible app is displayed, followed by the preselected number of alerts, alarms, or notifications related to that app. (Keep in mind which apps are displayed and how many alerts, alarms, or notifications from each app can be customized from within Settings.)

To clear all notifications related to an app that's displayed in Notification Center, tap on the small "X" icon that's displayed to the right of the app's name and icon.

> **TIP** To control the order in which app-related alerts, alarms, and notifications are displayed in the Notification Center window/screen, launch Settings, select the Notification Center option, and then under the Notifications View, tap on the Sort Manually option.
>
> Then, tap on the Edit option (near the top-right corner of the screen) and use your finger to move apps listed under the Include heading either up or down on the list. To do this, hold your finger on the Move icon that's displayed to the right of each app listing, and then drag it.
>
> To view this information by the date and time each alert, alarm, or notification was generated, select the Sort By Time option instead.

To quickly launch a specific app that's related to a notification you're viewing, tap on that listing.

Tap on the Missed button displayed along the top of the Notification Center to display a listing of missed calls, messages, and other alerts or alarms that occurred while the phone was turned off or in Sleep mode.

IN THIS CHAPTER

- Introduce yourself to Siri
- How to use Siri with your iPhone or iPad
- Use the Dictation feature as an alternative to the virtual keyboard
- Use your iPhone "Siri Eyes Free" with iOS In The Car

2

USING SIRI, DICTATION, AND iOS IN YOUR CAR TO INTERACT WITH YOUR MOBILE DEVICE

While Siri was first introduced on the iPhone 4S with iOS 5, it has now been enhanced in iOS 7 to work with all the latest iPhone and iPad models and to offer a variety of new features, plus improved accuracy.

Thanks to Siri, instead of having to utilize the touchscreen to interact with your phone or tablet, simply use your voice and speak using normal sentences. There are no commands to memorize.

Right from the start, understand that Siri doesn't know or understand everything, and it does have limitations in terms of what it can do and which apps it works with. Once you get accustomed to working with Siri, however, you'll discover this feature can make you much more efficient using your iPhone or iPad.

In addition to using cutting-edge voice recognition, Siri uses advanced artificial intelligence, so it doesn't just understand what you say, it interprets and comprehends what you mean, and then translates your speech to text. And if you don't initially provide the information Siri needs to complete your request or command, you'll be prompted for more information.

iOS 7 **WHAT'S NEW** One aspect of Siri's evolution with iOS 7 is that it can now speak using a male or female voice.

TIP To get the most out of the Siri feature, turn on your iOS device's master Location Services functionality, and then make sure Location Services is set up to work with Siri.

To do this, launch Settings, tap on the Privacy option, and then tap on the Location Services option. Turn on the virtual switch that's associated with Location Services, as well as the virtual switch that's associated with the Siri option.

WHAT YOU SHOULD KNOW BEFORE USING SIRI

For Siri to operate, your phone or tablet must have access to the Internet via a cellular or Wi-Fi connection. Every time you make a request or issue a command to Siri, your iOS mobile device connects to Apple's data center. Thus, if you're using a cellular data connection, some of your monthly wireless data allocation is used up (if data allocation is imposed by your wireless service provider).

TIP Because a Wi-Fi connection is typically significantly faster than a 3G/4G (LTE) cellular connection, you'll discover that Siri responds faster to your requests and commands when you use a Wi-Fi connection.

You should also understand that heavy use of the Internet, especially when connected via a cellular data connection, depletes the battery life of the iPhone or iPad faster. So, if you constantly rely on Siri throughout the day, the battery life of your device will be shorter.

! CAUTION If your iPhone or iPad is placed in Airplane mode (and Wi-Fi connectivity is turned off), Siri will not function. You'll receive a verbal message stating that Siri is unavailable.

WAYS TO ACTIVATE SIRI

As you go about using your iPhone or iPad, if you want to use the Siri feature, you first must activate it. There are four ways to do this:

- Press and hold the Home button on your iPhone or iPad for two to three seconds.
- Pick up your iPhone and hold it up to your ear. Siri will activate automatically. However, this iPhone-specific feature first must be turned on from within Settings, as explained later.
- Press and hold the Call button on your wireless Bluetooth headset that is paired with your iPhone or iPad. This enables you to speak to Siri on your device from up to 30 feet away.
- If you're using Apple EarPods or an original Apple headset (headphones), press the middle button on the controls found on the cable.

TIP If you're using your iOS device with a Bluetooth headset, when you activate Siri, to the right of the microphone icon will be a Bluetooth icon. Tap on it to choose between using the iPhone's built-in microphone or your headset's microphone when talking to Siri.

When Siri is activated, the message, "What can I help you with?" displays on the screen, along with a circular microphone icon (shown in Figure 2.1). You'll simultaneously hear Siri's activation tone. As you're speaking, the microphone icon transforms into an animated sound wave graphic.

Do not start speaking to Siri until this tone is heard. Then, you have about 5 seconds to begin speaking before the microphone deactivates. To reactivate it, simply tap on the microphone icon or repeat one of the previously mentioned steps.

As soon as you hear Siri's activation tone, speak your question, command, or request. For the most accurate results when using Siri, speak directly into the iPhone, iPad, or headset. Try to avoid being in areas with excessive background noise. Also, speak as clearly as possible so Siri can understand each word in your sentences.

FIGURE 2.1
When Siri is activated, the "What can I help you with?" message appears, and you hear Siri's activation tone. (Shown here on the iPhone 5.)

SETTING UP SIRI TO WORK ON YOUR iPHONE OR iPAD

Before you start using Siri, you must turn it on from within Settings. Follow these steps to do so:

1. Launch Settings from the Home screen.
2. From the main Settings menu, tap on the General option.
3. From the General menu screen, tap on the Siri option.
4. From the Siri submenu (shown in Figure 2.2), turn on the virtual switch associated with the Siri option by tapping on it.
5. Select your language. The default setting is English (United States); however, many other languages are now supported by Siri with iOS 7.

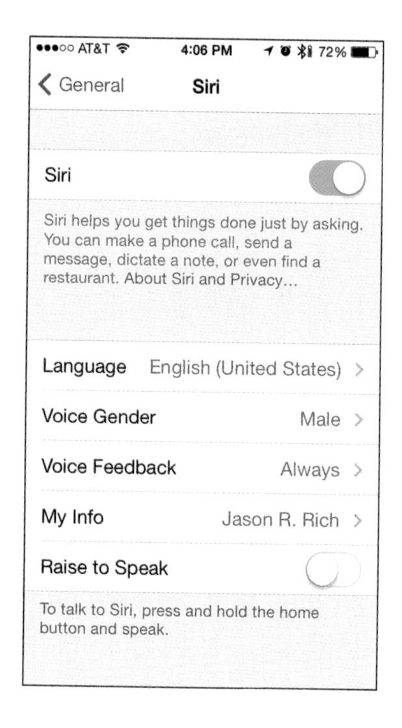

FIGURE 2.2

The Siri menu in Settings.

6. Tap on the new Voice Gender option to choose between giving Siri a male or female voice.
7. Tap on the Voice Feedback option to determine whether Siri will respond to you verbally for every request you make, or just when using the feature's hands-free mode. If Voice Feedback is turned off, text-based Siri prompts will appear on the iPhone or iPad's screen but you will not hear Siri's voice.
8. Tap on the My Info icon to link your own Contacts entry with Siri. It's important that you create an entry for yourself in the Contacts app and fill in all the data fields related to your phone numbers, addresses, email addresses, Twitter username, Facebook account, and so on, and that you properly label each data field. For example, if your Contacts entry has three phone numbers (Home, Work, and iPhone), be sure each has the appropriate label associated with it.

   Likewise, your home and work addresses, and the various email addresses you use, should be properly labeled with the Home and Work (or other appropriate) labels. The more information about yourself you include in your Contacts entry, the better Siri will be able to serve you.

TIP Siri also utilizes information stored in the Related People fields available to you from the Add Field option as you create or edit a contact. By tapping on this field, you can add a relationship title, such as mother, father, brother, or sister to a Contacts entry. Then, when using Siri, if you say, "Call Mom at home," Siri knows exactly to whom you're referring.

If you activate Siri and say, "Call my mom at home," the first time you use Siri for this task, you're asked who your mother is. As long as you have a Contact entry for your mother stored in the Contacts app, when you say your mother's real name, Siri links the appropriate contact and remembers this information. This applies to any nickname or title you have for other people, such as "wife," "husband," "son," "daughter, "mother," "father," "dad," or even "Uncle Jack."

9. At the bottom of the Siri menu on the iPhone, the Raise To Speak option is listed. When the switch is turned on, Siri automatically activates when you pick up the phone and hold it up to your ear.

In addition to customizing the options offered from the Siri menu screen in Settings, it's important that you enable Siri to pinpoint your location. After you complete this procedure, Siri will have the basic information needed, as well as access to content stored on your iPhone or iPad, that it needs to function. As you use Siri, it periodically asks you for additional information, which it then saves for future use.

CHECK OUT HOW SIRI CAN HELP YOU

The great thing about Siri is that you don't have to think too much about how you phrase a command, question, or request. Siri automatically interprets what you say.

NOTE When you're finished issuing your command or request or asking a question, simply stop speaking. If additional information is required, Siri prompts you for it as needed.

To get the most out of using Siri—with the least amount of frustration as a result of Siri not being able to comply with your requests—you must develop a basic understanding of which apps this feature works with and how Siri can be used with those apps.

In general, Siri can be used with most of the apps that come preinstalled with iOS 7, plus Siri can find information on the Internet by performing web searches. You can use Dictation mode, however, in any app where the microphone key appears on the iPhone or iPad's virtual keyboard.

NOTE Dictation mode offers an easy way to speak into your iPhone or iPad and have what you say translated into text and inserted into the app you're using, instead of typing using the virtual keyboard.

The following sections provide a sampling of what Siri can be used for and tips for how to use Siri effectively. Apple and third-party app developers are continuously working to upgrade Siri's capabilities, so you might discover additional functionality as you begin using Siri with various apps.

SIRI QUICK TIPS

- Siri is one of the few features that work from the Lock screen. Thus, even if you have the Passcode Lock feature turned on, someone can potentially pick up your device and access your data using Siri without your permission. To keep this from happening, set up the Passcode feature on your device. Then, from within the Passcode Lock submenu in the General options of the Settings app, turn off the Siri option.
- Siri can be used to verbally launch any app. To do this, activate Siri and say, "Launch [app name]." If it's a game you want to play, simply say, "Play [game name]." Another option is to say, "Open [app name]."
- For more information about how Siri can be used, activate Siri and say, "What can you do?" or tap on the information ("i") icon that's displayed on the screen when Siri is activated.

FIND, DISPLAY, OR USE INFORMATION RELATED TO YOUR CONTACTS

Your Contacts database can store a vast amount of information about people or companies. Every field within a Contact's entry is searchable and can be accessed by Siri. Or you can ask Siri to look up a specific contact for you and display that contact's Info screen.

Again, the more information you include in each entry stored in your Contacts database, the more helpful Siri can be. To have Siri look up and display information stored in Contacts, say something like the following:

- "Look up John Doe in Contacts."
- "What is John Doe's phone number?"
- "What is John Doe's home phone number?" (See Figure 2.3.)

FIGURE 2.3

When you ask, "What is John Doe's home phone number?" the appropriate number from your Contacts database displays.

- "What is John Doe's work address?"
- "Where does John Doe live?"
- "Where does John Doe work?"

> **TIP** When Siri displays the Info screen for a Contact, it is interactive; therefore, you can tap on a displayed phone number to initiate a call (iPhone only), or tap on an email address to launch the Mail app to send email to that address. If you tap on a regular address, the Maps app launches, and if you tap on a website URL, Safari launches and opens that web page.

Siri can also use information stored in your Contacts database to comply with various other requests, such as:

- **"Send John Doe a text message"**—This works if you have an iPhone-labeled phone number or iMessage username or email address saved in John Doe's Contacts entry. On the iPhone, it also works with the phone's SMS text messaging feature if you have a phone number in someone's Contacts entry that's associated with the "mobile" label.

- **"Send John Doe an email"**—This works if you have an email address saved in John Doe's Contacts entry.
- **"Give me directions to John Doe's home"**—This works if you have a home address saved in John Doe's Contacts entry. The newly revamped Maps app launches, and directions from your current location are displayed.
- **"When is John Doe's birthday?"**—This works if you have a date saved in the Birthday field in John Doe's Contacts entry.
- **"What is John Doe's wife's name?"**—This works if you have a spouse's name saved in John Doe's Contacts entry.

INITIATE A CALL

On the iPhone, you can initiate a call by activating Siri and then saying, "Call [name] at home," or "Call [name] at work." This works if that person has a Contacts entry associated with their name, as well as a phone number labeled Home or Work, respectively. You could also say, "Call [name]'s mobile phone," or "Call [name]'s iPhone." If you just use the command call, and that person has several phone numbers in their Contacts entry, Siri gives you the option to select which number you want to call.

If you request someone's work phone number and Siri finds a contact's name but not a corresponding phone number, Siri responds with, "There is no work number for John Doe in your contacts." This is followed by a listing of whichever phone numbers are available for that contact.

NOTE When issuing a command to Siri, you have flexibility in terms of what you say. For example, say, "Call John Doe at work," "Call John Doe work," or "Call the work number for John Doe," and in all these cases, Siri initiates a call to John Doe's work number.

Alternatively, if someone's contact information or phone number is not stored in your iPhone, you can say, "Call" or "Dial" followed by each digit of a phone number. Thus, you'd say, "Call 212 555 1212."

TIP You can also ask Siri to look up a business phone number or address by saying, "Look up [business name] in [city, state]." Or, you could say, "Look up [business type, such as a dry cleaner] in [city, state]."

On the iPhone, when Siri finds the phone number you're looking for, Siri says, "Calling [name] at [location]," and then automatically initiates a call to that number by launching the Phone app. Siri also has the capability to initiate FaceTime video calls. Use a command, such as, "FaceTime with [name]."

FIND YOUR FRIENDS

The optional Find My Friends app is available free from the App Store. If you install it and begin following friends, coworkers, or family members (with their permission), at any time, you can ask Siri, "Where is [name]?" or say, "Find [name]," and Siri finds that person and displays a map showing that person's exact whereabouts. This feature is great for keeping tabs on your kids or teenagers, especially if they miss a curfew or claim to be studying at the library on a Friday evening.

For this feature to work, however, you need to be logged in to your free Find My Friends account via the app.

TIP If you're using the Find My Friends app to track your kid's whereabouts, be sure to activate the Restrictions feature on their iOS device so they can not deactivate the Find My Friends app. To do this, launch Settings, tap on the General option, and then select the Restrictions option. Adjust the Location Services feature and the Find My Friends feature so your child can't change those settings.

SET UP REMINDERS AND TO-DO ITEMS

If you constantly jot down reminders to yourself on scrap pieces of paper or sticky notes, or manually enter to-do items into the Reminders app, this is one Siri-related feature you'll truly appreciate. To create a reminder (to be utilized by the Reminders app), complete with an alarm, simply activate Siri and say something like, "Remind me to pick up my dry cleaning tomorrow at 3 PM."

Upon doing this, Siri creates the to-do item, displays it on the screen for your approval, and then saves it in the Reminders app. On the appropriate time and day, an alarm sounds and the reminder message is displayed.

NOTE A handful of optional list management apps available from the App Store, such as Things, are also Siri compatible. Some of these apps offer more robust features than the Reminders app.

TIP When creating a Reminder using Siri, you can provide a specific date and time, such as "tomorrow at 3 pm" or "Friday at 1 pm" or "July 7th at noon." You can also include a location that Siri knows, such as "Home" or "Work." For example, you could say, "Remind me to feed the dog when I get home," or "Remind me to call Emily when I get to work."

Because the Reminders app on the iPhone can handle location-based alerts, you can create them using Siri. Learn more about using location-based alerts in Chapter 5, "Organize Your Life with Reminders and Notes."

READ OR SEND TEXT MESSAGES

When you receive a new text message but can't look at the screen, activate Siri and say, "Read new text message." After Siri reads the incoming message, you're given the opportunity to reply to that message and dictate your response.

Using Siri with the Messages app, you can also compose and send a text/instant message to anyone in your Contacts database by saying something like, "Compose a text message to John Doe."

You are asked to select an email address or mobile phone number to use. To bypass this step, say, "Send a text message to John Doe's mobile phone," or "Send a text message to John Doe's iPhone." Then, Siri says, "What do you want to say to John Doe?" Dictate your text message.

When you're finished speaking, Siri says, "I updated your message. Ready to send it?" The transcribed message is displayed on the screen, along with Cancel and Send icons. You can tap an icon or speak your reply.

CHECK THE WEATHER OR YOUR INVESTMENTS

The Weather app can display a current or extended weather forecast for your immediate area or any city in the world, and the Stocks app (on the iPhone) can be used to track your investments.

However, Siri has the capability to automatically access the Web and obtain weather information for any city, as well as stock-related information about any stock or mutual fund, for example.

After activating Siri, ask a weather-related question, such as

- **"What is today's weather forecast?"**—Siri pinpoints your location and provides a current forecast.

- **"What is the weather forecast for New York City?"**—Of course, you can insert any city and state in your request.
- **"Is it going to rain tomorrow?"**—Siri accesses and interprets the weather forecast, and then vocalizes, as well as displays a response.
- **"Should I bring an umbrella to work?"**—Siri knows the location of your work and can access and then interpret the weather forecast to offer a vocalized and displayed response.

If you have stock-related questions (using the iPhone or iPad), you can ask about specific stocks by saying something like

- "What is [company name]'s stock at?"
- "What is [company]'s stock price?"
- "How is [company name]'s stock performing?"
- "Show me [company name] stock."

When you request stock information, you get a verbal response from Siri along with information about that stock displayed on the iPhone or iPad's screen, as you can see in Figure 2.4.

FIGURE 2.4

Just by asking, Siri can tell you how a specific stock is performing.

FIND INFORMATION ON THE WEB OR GET ANSWERS TO QUESTIONS

If you want to perform a web search, you can manually launch the Safari browser, and then use a keyboard to find what you're looking for in the Search field. Or, you can ask Siri to perform the search for you by saying something like

- "Look up the [company] website."
- "Access the website cnn.com."
- "Find [topic] on the web."
- "Search the web for [topic]."
- "Google information about [topic]."
- "Search Wikipedia for [topic]."
- "Bing [topic]." (Bing is a popular search engine operated by Microsoft.)

You also can ask a question, and Siri will seek out the appropriate information on the Web.

> **NOTE** When you ask Siri a question that requires your iPhone or iPad to seek out the answer on the Internet, this is done through Apple using Wolfram Alpha. To learn more about the vast topics you can ask Siri about, from unit conversions to historical data, visit www.wolframalpha.com/examples.

SCHEDULE AND MANAGE MEETINGS AND EVENTS

Like many of the apps that come preinstalled with iOS 7, the Calendar app is fully compatible with Siri, which means you can use Siri to create or modify appointments, meetings, or events by using your voice. To do this, some of the things you can say include

- "Set up a meeting at 10:30am."
- "Set up a meeting with Ryan at noon tomorrow."
- "Meet with Emily for lunch at 1pm."
- "Set up a meeting with Rusty about third-quarter sales projections at 4pm on December 12th."

SEND EMAIL AND ACCESS NEW (INCOMING) EMAIL

If you want to compose an email to someone, activate Siri and say, "Send an email to [name]." If that person's email address is listed in your Contacts database, Siri will address a new message to that person. Siri will then say, "What is the subject of your email?" Speak the subject line for your email. When you stop speaking, Siri will say, "Okay, what would you like the email to say?" You can now dictate the body of your email message.

When you're finished speaking, Siri composes the message, displays it on the screen, and then says, "Here is your email to [name]. Ready to send it?" You can now respond "yes" to send the email message, or say "cancel" to abort the message. If the message isn't what you want to say, you can edit it using the virtual keyboard, or ask Siri to "Change the text to...".

SET AN ALARM OR TIMER

Siri can control the Clock app that comes preinstalled on your iOS device so that it serves as an alarm clock or timer. You can say something like, "Set an alarm for 7:30am tomorrow" or "Set a recurring wakeup call for 7:30am" to create a new alarm. Or, to set a 30-minute timer, say, "Set a timer for 30 minutes." A countdown timer will be displayed on the iPhone or iPad's screen, and an alarm sounds when the timer reaches zero.

You can also simply ask Siri, "What's today's date?" or "What time is it?" if you're too busy to look at the iPhone or iPad's screen, such as when you're driving.

GET DIRECTIONS USING THE MAPS APP

Pretty much any feature you can use the Maps app for—whether it's to find the location or phone number for a business, obtain turn-by-turn directions between two addresses, or map out a specific address location—you can access using Siri.

To use Maps-related functions, say things like the following:

- "How do I get to [location]?"
- "Show [address]."
- "Directions to [contact name or location]."
- "Find a [business type, such as gas station] near [location]."
- "Find a [business or service name, such as Starbucks Coffee] near where I am."
- "Where is the closest [business type, such as post office]?"
- "Find a [cuisine type, such as Chinese] restaurant near me."

If multiple businesses or locations are found that are directly related to your request, Siri asks you to select one, or all related matches are displayed on a detailed map.

CONTROL THE MUSIC APP

In the mood to hear a specific song that's stored on your iPhone or iPad? Maybe you want to begin playing a specific playlist, you want to hear all the music stored on your iOS device by a particular artist, or you want to play a specific album? Well, just ask Siri. You can control the Music app using your voice by saying things like the following:

- "Play [song title]."
- "Play [album title]."
- "Play [playlist title]."
- "Play [artist's name]."
- "Play [music genre, such as pop, rock, or blues]."

You can also issue specific commands, such as "Shuffle my [title] playlist," or speak commands, such as "Pause" or "Skip" as music is playing. However, Siri is unable to search for and display song or album listings. For example, if you say, "Show music," or "Show song playlists," you will receive a response saying, "Sorry, [your name], I can't search that content." Thus, to use Siri to control your music, you must know what music is stored on your iPhone or iPad.

FORGET STICKY NOTES—DICTATE NOTES TO YOURSELF

The Notes app that comes preinstalled with iOS 7 is used to compose notes using a text editor (as opposed to a full-featured word processor, such as Pages). Siri is compatible with the Notes app and enables you to create and dictate notes.

To create a new note, activate Siri and begin a sentence by saying, "Note that I... " You can also say, "Note: [sentence]." What you dictate will be saved as a new note in the Notes app.

SIRI KNOWS ALL ABOUT SPORTS AND MOVIES TOO

If you're looking for the latest scores related to your favorite professional team or sporting event, you can ask Siri. It's also possible to ask sports-related questions and then have Siri quickly research the answers via the Internet. When it comes to sports, here are some sample questions or requests you can use with Siri:

- "Did the Yankee's win their last game?"
- "What was the score of last night's Patriots game?"

- "What was the score the last time the Yankees and Red Sox played?"
- "Show me the baseball scores from last night."
- "When do the Dallas Cowboys play next?"
- "Who has the most home runs on the New York Mets?"
- "Show me the roster for the Patriots."
- "Are any of the Bruins players currently injured?"

When it comes to movies, Siri can also help you decide what to go see, determine where movies are playing, look up movie times, and provide details about almost any movie ever made. Here are some sample questions or requests you can use with Siri that relate to movies:

- "Where is [movie title] playing?"
- "What's playing at [movie theater]."
- "Who directed the movie [movie title]."
- "Show me the cast from [movie title]."
- "What's playing at the movies tonight?"
- "Find the closest movie theater."
- "Show me the reviews for [movie title]."
- "What movie won Best Picture in [year]."
- "Buy two tickets to see The Smurfs 2 tonight at the Showcase Cinema de Lux in Foxboro, MA."

MORE SIRI QUICK TIPS

- Siri is a mathematical genius. Simply say the mathematical calculation you need solved, and Siri presents the answer in seconds. For example, say, "What is 10 plus 10?", "What's the square root of 24?", or "What is 20 percent of 500?" This feature is particularly useful for helping you calculate the server's tip when you receive the check at a restaurant.
- When asking Siri to look up businesses, landmarks, popular destinations, or restaurants, in addition to just displaying a location on a map, Siri integrates with the Yelp! online service to provide much more detailed information about many businesses and restaurants. Plus, with the online-based Open Table service, Siri can be used to book a restaurant reservation for you, without you having to call that restaurant.

  For example, you can activate Siri and say, "Find Morton's Steak House in Boston." Once found, Siri will display detailed information about that restaurant from Yelp!. As you're looking at this listing on your screen, activate Siri again and say something like, "Book a table for two tonight at 8pm." You will then receive a confirmation for your reservation.

- Send a Tweet or update your Facebook page using your voice. Activate Siri and say something like, "Send a Tweet that says, 'I am at Starbucks, come join me.'" To update your Facebook wall, say something like "Write on my wall, 'I just landed in New York City and I am leaving the airport now.'"

  When dictating a Tweet, you can add the phrase, "Tweet with my location," to have Siri publish your current location with the outgoing Tweet you're dictating.
- If you need to turn on or off certain iPhone or iPad features, activate Siri and say, "Turn on Wi-Fi" or "Turn off Bluetooth."
- In addition to controlling the Music app, Siri can be used to verbally control iTunes Radio. Start with a command like, "Launch iTunes Radio," once you've activated this service from the Music app.

PRACTICE (WITH SIRI) MAKES PERFECT

Right from the start, Siri will probably understand most of what you say. However, as you begin using this feature often, you will become acquainted with the best and most efficient ways to communicate questions, commands, and requests to generate the desired response.

Keep in mind that Siri translates what you say phonetically, so periodically, you might encounter names or commands that Siri can't understand or match up with correctly spelled information stored on your iPhone or iPad. This occurs most frequently with unusual names that sound vastly different from how they're spelled or used.

> **! CAUTION** Before allowing Siri to send any message or text, be sure to proofread it carefully on your device's screen. Keep in mind that some words sound the same when spoken, and Siri might choose the wrong word when translating your speech to text. This could lead to embarrassing situations or dramatically change the meaning of what you intended to say.

Siri can streamline how you interact with your device and make certain tasks much easier to accomplish. Based on the questions you ask, you might also discover that Siri has a sense of humor. For example, try asking, "Siri, what do you look like?", "Siri, are you attractive?", or "What is the best smartphone on the market?"

USE DICTATION MODE INSTEAD OF THE VIRTUAL KEYBOARD

Even if you're using an app that Siri is not yet compatible with, chances are you can still use your iPhone or iPad's Dictation mode. In many situations when the iPhone or iPad's virtual keyboard appears, a microphone key is located to the left of the spacebar. When you tap on this microphone key, Dictation mode is activated (shown in Figure 2.5). You'll see an animated sound wave graphic displayed on the screen as you speak.

FIGURE 2.5

Use Dictation mode to enter text using your voice, instead of typing on the virtual keyboard. (Shown here on an iPhone 5 running the Notes app.)

You can now say whatever text you were going to manually type using the virtual keyboard. You can speak for up to 30 seconds at a time. When you're finished speaking, it's necessary to tap the Done key so that your device can translate your speech into text and insert it into the appropriate onscreen field.

For the fastest and most accurate results, speak one to three sentences at a time, and have your device connected to a Wi-Fi Internet connection.

TIP While using Dictation mode, you can easily add punctuation just by saying it. For example, you can say, "This is a sample dictation period," and Siri will add the period (".") at the end of the sentence. You can also use words like "open parenthesis" or "close parenthesis," "open quotes" or "close quotes," or "comma," "semicolon," or "colon" as you dictate.

CONNECT OR LINK YOUR iPHONE TO YOUR CAR TO USE THE iOS IN THE CAR FEATURE

Thanks to the Siri Eyes Free and iOS In The Car functionality that's built in to iOS 7, it's possible to connect or wirelessly pair your iPhone with some of the 2013 and 2014 model year cars offered by about a dozen car manufacturers.

Typically, when you use Siri, information that's requested is displayed on the iOS device's screen. Siri Eyes Free, however, offers much of the same functionality as Siri but turns off the iPhone's screen altogether. Thus, it offers only verbal responses to a user's requests, commands, and questions.

Siri Eyes Free offers the perfect solution to drivers who must pay attention to the road yet want to access content from their Internet-connected iOS mobile device to initiate calls, look up information, access email or text messages, or obtain turn-by-turn driving directions to a specific location.

When an iPhone is paired with a compatible car via Bluetooth, you can press the Siri or voice recognition button that's built in to your steering wheel or your car's in-dash infotainment system. This activates Siri Eyes Free on the iPhone while the phone remains in your pocket, purse, or glove compartment. There is never a need for you to even momentarily divert your eyes to the phone's screen.

Thanks to Siri Eyes Free, all compatible cars now have access to GPS navigation; can utilize Internet connectivity; and be used for a growing selection of voice-activated tasks, such as accessing weather forecasts, finding nearby gas stations, looking up or adding appointments, obtaining sports scores, locating nearby restaurants, and playing music that's stored on the iOS device.

Siri Eyes Free does not handle features that would ordinarily require Siri to display content on the screen. For example, if you ask for a weather forecast, Siri Eyes Free says the current temperature but does not display a graphic-intensive extended forecast on the screen.

Likewise, Siri Eyes Free can read aloud an incoming email or text message and allow a response to be verbally created, but the message does not appear on your screen as you're driving.

All conversations between you and Siri are conducted through the speaker(s) and microphone built in to the vehicle itself—not through the iPhone or a Bluetooth headset that can otherwise be linked to the phone. Thus, privacy between you and Siri isn't possible, as all in-vehicle passengers will hear your interactions.

Each car manufacturer is implementing this technology different into its vehicles. Chevrolet, for example, allows drivers to control the Music app on their iPhone but play that music wirelessly through the vehicle's speaker system for all to enjoy. Chevrolet's Sonic and Spark cars can also play Pandora or TuneIn Internet radio that's streaming via an iPhone, plus use the optional BringGo app to provide a full-featured navigation system to the vehicle. Maps generated by the iPhone are displayed on the in-dash infotainment system's screen.

In the near future, vehicles from Audi, BMW, Ferrari, Honda, Jaguar, Land Rover, Mercedes-Benz, and Toyota, among others, will also be compatible with the iPhone and Siri, in conjunction with the in-dash infotainment systems built in to their respective 2013 or 2014 model year vehicles.

> **NOTE** The ultimate goal of iOS In The Car and Siri Eyes Free is to enable a driver to press a single button located on his steering wheel, activate his iPhone remotely, and then take advantage of the phone's cellular Internet connection to transform his iPhone and the car he's driving into a hands-free and eyes-free virtual assistant.
>
> To accomplish this task, even experienced iPhone users who have mastered how to utilize Siri experience a slight learning curve because communicating with an iPhone using only one's voice while driving and not having access to the phone's screen is an entirely new skill and experience.

When using Siri Eyes Free and iOS In The Car functionality, handling certain tasks, such as initiating a call, are straightforward.

Other tasks that you can utilize via Siri, such as finding a restaurant and then making a reservation or accessing movie listings and finding the closet theater that's playing a certain movie, are handled slightly differently using Siri Eyes Free. For example, if you ask a question such as, "What is the state flag of Massachusetts?", Siri displays the flag on the iPhone's screen, but Siri Eyes Free informs you that the requested task is not possible while you're driving.

Any time you leave your vehicle or manually activate a Bluetooth headset to use with your iPhone, Siri Eyes Free automatically deactivates and gives you full access to all of Siri's regular features, including the full use of the iPhone's touchscreen.

IN THIS CHAPTER

- Install optional apps to your iOS mobile device using the App Store
- How to determine what's different about iPhone-specific, iPad-specific, and Hybrid apps
- How to determine the difference between iPhone, iPad, and hybrid apps

3

STRATEGIES FOR FINDING, BUYING, AND USING THIRD-PARTY APPS

The collection of preinstalled apps that comes with iOS 7 enables you to begin utilizing your iPhone or iPad for a wide range of popular tasks without first having to find and install additional apps.

However, one of the things that has set the iPhone and iPad apart from its competition, and has made these devices among the most sought-after and popular throughout much of the world, is the vast library of optional apps available for them.

Whereas other smartphones or tablets might offer a collection of a few hundred or even a few thousand optional apps, third-party developers have created an ever-growing collection of iPhone and iPad apps that's now in the hundreds of thousands of choices.

All the apps currently available for your iOS device can be found in Apple's online-based App Store. Then, as needed, iOS 7 can automatically update your apps to ensure you're always working with the most recently released version.

TIP From the App Store, several Apple-created (or endorsed) iPhone and iPad apps are available. Some of these free apps include iBooks (for downloading and reading books), Find My Friends (for tracking the whereabouts of your friends and family and allowing them to track your location in real time), iTunes U (for accessing the incredible collection of personal enrichment and educational content compiled by Apple), the official Twitter app (for managing one or more Twitter accounts from your iPhone or iPad), the official Facebook app (for managing all aspects of your Facebook account), and Find My iPhone.

APP STORE BASICS

There are two ways to access the App Store: directly from your iPhone or iPad (using the App Store app that comes preinstalled on your device) or using the iTunes software on your primary computer.

The App Store app is used exclusively for finding, purchasing (if applicable), downloading, and installing apps directly on your device from the App Store. Other apps are used to access additional types of content. iTunes on your primary computer is used to access the App Store as well as many other types of content.

HOW NEW APPS INSTALL THEMSELVES

If you're shopping for apps directly from your iPhone or iPad, tap on the Price icon, followed by the Buy icon, to make a purchase. You might be asked to supply your Apple ID password to confirm the transaction. The app automatically downloads and installs itself on your device. After it is installed, its app icon appears on your iPhone or iPad's Home screen and is ready to use.

You can also shop for apps from your primary computer and transfer them to your iPhone or iPad, or sync apps between your various mobile devices using the iTunes Sync process or iCloud.

FREE OR PURCHASED?

Some apps available from the App Store are free. To download them, you go through the same process as you do for purchasing an app; however, instead of tapping on the Price icon, followed by the Buy icon, you must tap on the Free icon associated with the app, followed by the Install App icon.

You are not charged for downloading a free app. You do, however, still need to supply your Apple ID password to confirm the transaction. Your newly acquired app is also stored in your online-based iCloud account, so it can be reinstalled later or installed onto your other compatible iOS mobile devices.

In addition to apps, you can add a wide range of content to your iPhone or iPad, such as music, movies, TV shows, podcasts, audiobooks, and eBooks. How to acquire and enjoy this content is mentioned later in this chapter.

RESTORING OR REINSTALLING APPS YOU'VE ALREADY DOWNLOADED

To download an app onto your iPad that has already been purchased or downloaded onto another computer or device, tap on the Purchased icon that's displayed at the bottom of the screen in the App Store app. On the iPhone, tap on the Updates icon, and then tap on the Purchased option that's displayed near the top of the Updates screen. All your app purchases to date are displayed.

TIP As an app is downloading from the App Store to your mobile device, to pause the process, tap on the Download icon that's displayed in the app description or app preview box in the App Store, or tap on the app icon as it's installing on the Home screen. To resume the download and installation process, tap the icon again.

NOTE At the top of the Purchased screen on the iPhone or iPad, tap on the All tab to view all of the apps you've purchase to date for that device. You also have the option to tap on the Not On This iPhone/Not On This iPad tab to view apps you've acquired in the past but that are not currently installed on the device you're using.

Instead of a Free or Price icon being associated with each app description, you will see an iCloud icon indicating the app is available through your iCloud account. Tap on the iCloud icon to download the app (without having to pay for it again) to the iOS device you're currently using. You can only install already purchased apps that are compatible with that iOS device. For example, you can't install an iPad-specific app onto an iPhone or iPod touch. You can, however, install iPhone-specific or hybrid apps onto an iPad or iPad mini.

TIP From the Settings app, you have the option of having your iOS device automatically download and install any new (and compatible) apps, music, or eBooks purchased using your Apple ID on any other computer or device. To set this up, launch Settings, select the iTunes & App Store option from the main Settings menu, and then adjust the Automatic Downloads options, which include Music, Apps, and Books. You also can decide whether this feature will work with a cellular data Internet connection or just when a Wi-Fi connection is available.

WHERE TO FIND APPS, MUSIC, AND MORE

If you're shopping for apps, music, movies, TV shows, podcasts, audiobooks, eBooks, ringtones, or other content from your primary computer, with the goal of transferring what you acquire to your iPhone or iPad later via the iTunes sync process or via iCloud, use the latest version of the iTunes software on your Mac or PC computer.

However, from your iPhone or iPad, acquiring and then enjoying different types of content is done using a handful of different apps. Table 3.1 explains which app you should use to acquire and then enjoy various types of content on your iOS device.

Table 3.1 How to Acquire and Enjoy Various Types of Content on Your iPhone or iPad

Content Type	Buy with App	Run with App
Apps	App Store	The app itself that you download and install
Digital editions of publications (including newspapers and magazines)	Newsstand	The digital publication's proprietary app
Music	iTunes Store	Music
Movies	iTunes Store	Videos
TV Shows	iTunes Store	Videos
Podcasts	Podcasts**	Podcasts
Audiobooks	iTunes (or the optional Audible app)	Music (or the optional Audible app)
eBooks*	iBooks (to access iBookstore)	iBooks
PDF files	Mail, iCloud, iTunes Sync	iBooks or another PDF reader app

Content Type	Buy with App	Run with App
iTunes U Personal Enrichment and Educational Content	iTunes U***	iTunes U
Ringtones (and Alert Tones)	iTunes Store	Phone, FaceTime, Messages (or other apps that generate audible alarms or ringtones)

** eBooks can also be purchased from Amazon.com and read using the free Kindle app, or purchased from BN.com and read using the free Nook app.*

*** The Podcasts app is available for free from the App Store. It was developed by Apple and is designed to help you find and experience free podcasts on your iOS mobile device.*

**** The iTunes U app serves as a gateway to a vast selection of personal enrichment and educational courses, lectures, workshops, and information sessions that have been produced by leading educators, universities, and other philanthropic organizations. All iTunes U content is provided for free.*

EVERYTHING YOU NEED TO KNOW ABOUT APPS

Apps are individual programs that you install on your iPhone or iPad to give it additional functionality, just as you utilize different programs on your primary computer. For the iPhone or iPad, all apps are available from one central (online-based) location: the App Store.

When you begin exploring the App Store, you'll discover right away that there are literally hundreds of thousands of apps to choose from, which are divided into different categories.

The App Store's app categories include Books, Business, Catalogs, Education, Entertainment, Finance, Food & Drink, Games, Health & Fitness, Lifestyle, Medical, Music, Newsstand, Photo & Video, Productivity, Reference, Social Networking, Sports, Travel, Utilities, and Weather.

COMPATIBILITY: DOES THE APP RUN ON MULTIPLE DEVICES?

In terms of compatibility, all iOS apps fall into one of three categories:

1. **iPhone-specific**—These are apps designed exclusively for the various iPhone models that might not function properly on the iPad. Most iPhone-specific apps will run on an iPad but will not take advantage of the tablet's larger screen. Most iPhone-specific apps have been optimized to work with the larger screen of the iPhone 5 and later models.

Figure 3.1 shows what an iPhone-specific app (in this case, Instagram for iPhone) that's running on an iPad looks like. The app functions fine but does not take full advantage of the tablet's larger screen. A useful trick is to tap on the 2x icon in the lower-right corner of the iPad's screen to double the size of what the iPhone app is displaying on the screen (as shown in Figure 3.2). However, in some cases, this causes text and graphics to become slightly distorted.

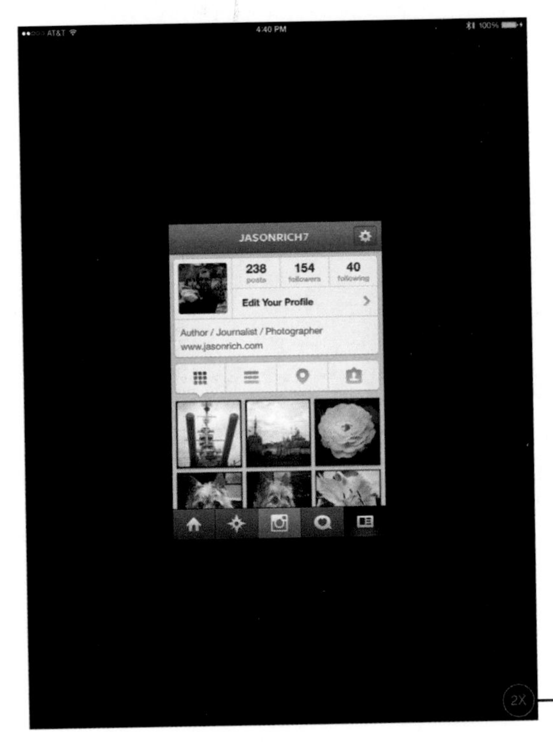

FIGURE 3.1

Instagram is an iPhone-specific app, shown here running on an iPad. It utilizes only a small portion of the tablet's screen that's equivalent to the screen size of an iPhone.

FIGURE 3.2

Tapping the 2x icon doubles the size of the app on the tablet's screen.

2. **iPad-specific**—These are apps designed exclusively for the iPad. They fully utilize the tablet's larger display. They will not function on the iPhone or on other iOS devices. All iPad-specific apps do, however, function flawlessly on the iPad mini.
3. **Hybrid**—Although you might encounter a few exceptions, these are apps designed to work on all iOS devices, including the iPhone and iPad. These apps detect which device they're running on and adapt.

> **TIP** When reading the App Store description of any app, tap on the Details tab and scroll down to the Information heading. Here, you can see a listing of which iOS devices the app is compatible with.

TIP If you own two or more iOS devices, such as an iPhone and an iPad (or an iPod touch), and all the devices are liked to the same Apple ID account, you can purchase a hybrid (or iPhone-specific) app once but install it on all of your iOS devices. This can be done through iTunes Sync or via iCloud after an app is initially purchased or downloaded.

When you're browsing the App Store from your iPhone, by default it displays all iPhone-specific apps followed by hybrid apps, but the App Store will not display iPad apps. When you're browsing the App Store from your iPad, iPad-specific, hybrid and iPhone-specific apps are listed. Tap on the Phone or iPad tab that's displayed near the top-center of the screen when viewing many areas of the App Store.

If you're shopping for apps using the iTunes software on your primary computer, click the iPhone or iPad tab that's displayed near the top center of the iTunes screen (shown in Figure 3.3) to select which format apps you're looking for.

FIGURE 3.3

When shopping for apps using iTunes on your primary computer, click the appropriate tab to indicate which format apps you're looking for, keeping in mind that iPhone-specific apps will run on an iPad (but not take advantage of the tablet's larger screen), but iPad-specific apps do not run on an iPhone.

TIP Because some app developers release the same app in both an iPhone-specific and an iPad-specific format, many iPad-specific apps have "HD" for High-Definition in their title, to help differentiate them from iPhone or hybrid apps. For example, the popular game Angry Birds is for the iPhone, whereas Angry Birds HD is for the iPad.

Some iPad-specific apps include the words "for iPad" in their titles, such as GoodReader for iPad.

QUICK GUIDE TO APP PRICING

Regardless of whether you use the App Store app from your device or visit the App Store using the iTunes software on your primary computer, you must set up an Apple ID account and have a major credit card or debit card linked to the account to make purchases.

TIP If you don't have a major credit card or debit card that you want to link with your Apple ID account, you can purchase prepaid iTunes Gift Cards from Apple or most places that sell prepaid gift cards.

iTunes Gift Cards are available in a variety of denominations and can be used to make app and other content purchases. They are distinct from Apple Gift Cards, which are only redeemable at Apple Stores or Apple.com.

The first time you access the App Store and attempt to make a purchase, you are prompted to enter your Apple ID account username and password or set up a new Apple ID account, which requires you to supply your name, address, email, and credit card information. For all subsequent online app purchases, you simply need to enter your Apple ID password, and the purchase is automatically billed to your credit or debit card or deducted from your iTunes Gift Card balance.

TIP An Apple ID account can also be referred to as an iTunes Store account. To learn more about how an Apple ID account works or to manage your account, visit www.apple.com/support/appleid. The same Apple ID you use to make purchases can also be used as your username when you're using FaceTime for videoconferencing, Messages to access the iMessage service, or to access your iCloud account.

Some families opt to share an Apple ID account, so that their purchases can be shared between their computers and devices. If you share an Apple ID account for content purchases, create a separate Apple ID account for yourself that you can use with iMessage, iCloud, and FaceTime.

Originally, when the App Store opened, there were two types of apps: free apps and paid apps. The free apps were often demo versions of paid apps (with limited functionality) or fully functional apps that displayed ads in the app. Paid apps were typically priced between $.99 and $9.99.

As the App Store has evolved, additional payment options and fee structures for apps have been introduced, giving app developers new ways to generate revenue and iPhone and iPad users different methods of paying for apps and content.

The following sections summarize the different types of apps from a pricing standpoint.

FREE APPS

Free apps cost nothing to download and install on your phone or tablet. Some programmers and developers release apps for free out of pure kindness to share their creations with the iPhone- and/or iPad-using public. These are fully functional apps.

There are also free apps that serve as demo versions of paid apps. In some cases, certain features or functions of the app are locked in the free version, but are later made available if you upgrade to the paid or premium version of the app.

A third category of free apps comprises fully functional apps that display ads as part of their content. In exchange for using the app, you must view ads, which offer the option to click on offers from within the app to learn more about the product or service being advertised.

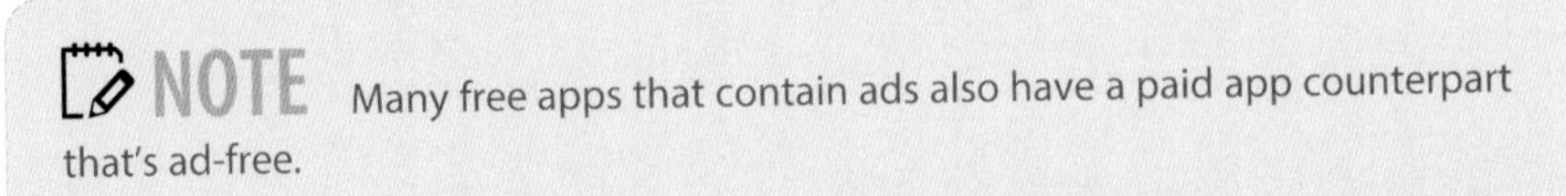

NOTE Many free apps that contain ads also have a paid app counterpart that's ad-free.

A fourth category of free apps serves as a shell for premium (paid) content that must be loaded into the app to make it fully functional. For example, many newspaper and magazine publishers offer free apps related to their specific publications, but require users to pay for the actual content of the newspaper or magazine, which later gets downloaded into the app.

The final type of free app enables the user to make in-app purchases to add features or functionality to the app or unlock premium content. The core app, without the extra content, is free, however.

> **TIP** Some fully functional apps are free because they're designed to promote a specific company or work with a specific service. For example, to use the free HBO Go app, you must be a paid subscriber of the HBO premium cable channel through your cable TV or satellite provider.
>
> Likewise, to use the free Netflix app, you must be a paid subscriber to this streaming movie service. The AmEx for iPad app is useful only to people with an American Express Card, but the free Target app is useful to anyone who shops at Target stores.

When you're looking at an app listing or description in the App Store, if the app is free, it will have a Free icon instead of a Price icon, associated with it (as shown in Figure 3.4). Read a free app's description carefully. Look for the heading In-App Purchases. This indicates that optional in-app purchases are available, and in some cases, these purchases are required to fully use the app.

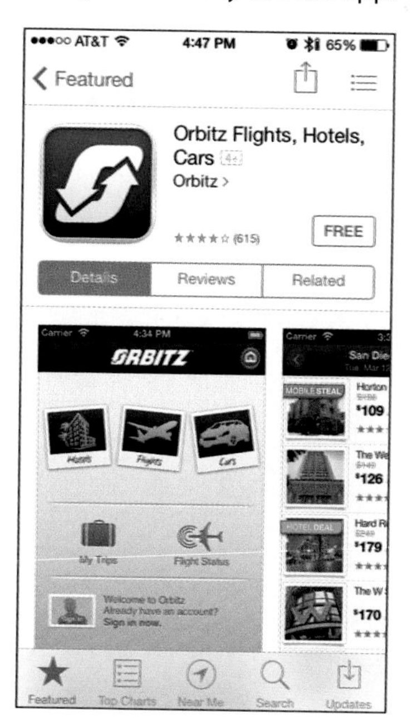

FIGURE 3.4

A free app has a Free icon displayed in its App Store listing or description (shown here on the iPhone 5).

PAID APPS

After you purchase an app, you own it and can use it as often as you'd like, usually without incurring additional fees (although in-app purchases may be possible). You simply pay a fee for the app upfront, which is typically between $.99 and $9.99. Typically, future upgrades of the app are free of charge.

SUBSCRIPTION-BASED APPS

Digital editions of magazines and newspapers can be purchased from the Newsstand app that comes preinstalled on your device. These publications each require their own proprietary app (also available from the App Store) to access and read the publication's content. Digital editions of many popular publications are available from the Newsstand app.

These apps are typically free, and then you pay a recurring subscription fee for content, which automatically gets downloaded into the app. Many digital editions of newspapers, such as the *New York Times* and the *Wall Street Journal*, utilize a subscription app model, as do hundreds of different magazines.

Typically, the main content of the digital and printed version of a publication are identical. However, you can view the digital edition on your iPhone or iPad and take advantage of added interactive elements built in to the app. If you're already a subscriber to the print version of a newspaper or magazine, some publishers offer the digital edition free, while others charge an extra fee to subscribe to the digital edition as well. Or you can subscribe to just the digital edition of a publication.

With some magazines, you can download the free app for a specific publication and then, in the app, purchase one issue at a time, including past issues. There is no long-term subscription commitment, but individual issues of the publication still need to be purchased and downloaded. Or you can purchase an ongoing (recurring) subscription and new issues of that publication will automatically be downloaded to your iPhone or iPad as they become available.

IN-APP PURCHASES

This type of app might be free or might be a paid app. As you're actually using the app, you can purchase additional content or add new features and functionality by making in-app purchases. The capability to make in-app purchases has become very popular and is being used by app developers in a variety of ways.

As you read an app's description in the App Store, if an app requires in-app purchases, it is revealed in the text included in the app description screen. Look for the heading within an app's description that says In-App Purchases and tap on it.

! CAUTION The price you pay for an app does not translate directly to the quality or usefulness of that app. Some free or very inexpensive apps are extremely useful and packed with features and can really enhance your experience using your iPhone or iPad. There are also costly apps (priced at $4.99 or more) that are poorly designed, filled with bugs, or don't live up to expectations or to the description of the app offered by the app's developer or publisher.

The price of each app is set by the developer or programmer that created or is selling the app. Instead of using the price as the only determining factor if you're evaluating several apps that appear to offer similar functionality, be sure to read the app's customer reviews carefully, and pay attention to the star-based rating the app has received. These user reviews and ratings are a much better indicator of the app's quality and usefulness than the price.

HOW TO SHOP WITH THE APP STORE APP

From your iPhone or iPad's Home screen, to access the App Store, tap on the blue-and-white App Store app icon. Your device must have access to the Internet via a cellular or Wi-Fi connection.

When you access the App Store app (shown in Figure 3.5 on the iPad), a handful of command icons at the top and bottom of the screen are used to navigate your way around the online-based store.

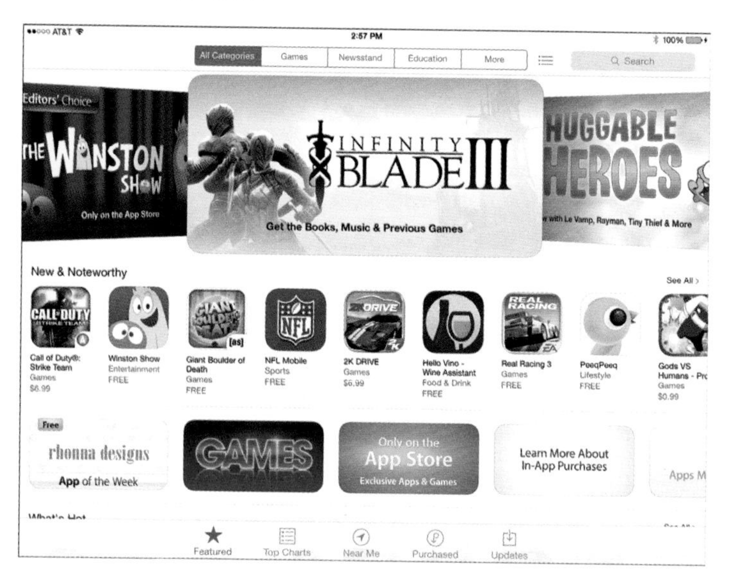

FIGURE 3.5

The main App Store app screen on the iPad. Find, purchase, download, and install apps directly from your tablet.

If you already know the name of the app you want to find, purchase, download, and install, tap on the Search field, which is located near the upper-right corner of the screen in the iPad version. On the iPhone, tap on the Search option displayed at the bottom of the App Store app's screen (as shown in Figure 3.6).

FIGURE 3.6

From your iPhone, tap on the Search icon to search for any app in the App Store by name or keyword. Here, the keyword "Sonic" was used to locate the various Sonic The Hedgehog games from Sega that have been adapted for the iPhone and iPad.

Using the virtual keyboard, enter the name of the app. Tap the Search key on the virtual keyboard to begin the search. You can also perform a search based on a keyword or phrase, such as "word processing," "to-do lists," "time management," or "photo editing."

In a few seconds, matching results are displayed on the App Store screen in the form of app previews.

If you're shopping for apps from your iPad, as you browse the App Store, iPad-specific apps are displayed if you tap on the iPad tab near the top-center of most areas within the App Store.

TIP At the bottom center of the main App Store screen on the iPad are several command icons, labeled Featured, Top Charts, Near Me, Purchased, and Updates. On the iPhone, the icons along the bottom of the screen are labeled Featured, Top Charts, Near Me, Search, and Updates. If you don't know the exact name of an app you're looking for, these command icons will help you browse the App Store and discover apps that might be of interest to you.

THE FEATURED COMMAND ICON

Tap on the Featured command icon near the bottom of the App Store screen to see a listing of what Apple considers "Featured" apps. These are divided into a handful of categories. Either flick your finger from right to left to scroll horizontally through the apps listed, or tap on the See All option that's displayed to the right of the category heading.

Near the top of the screen are large graphic banners that constantly change. In Figure 3.7, the banner simply says "Kickstart Your School Year"; however, it constantly scrolls and often showcases specific apps. These banner graphics promote what Apple considers the "App of the Week," as well as other noteworthy apps the company wants to promote.

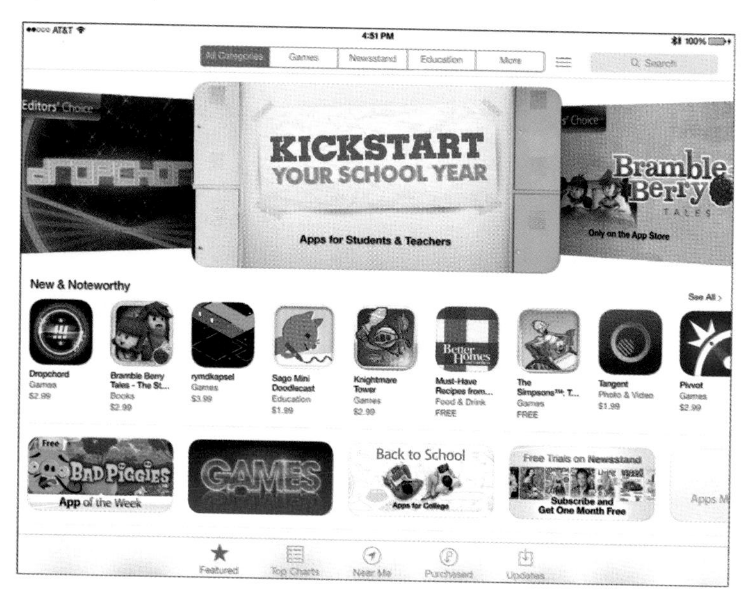

FIGURE 3.7

View apps that Apple is featuring within specialized categories in the App Store. The banner for "Kickstart Your School Year" is shown here.

THE TOP CHARTS ICON

When you tap on the Top Charts command icon, located near the bottom center of the App Store app's screen, a listing of Paid, Free, and Top Grossing apps are displayed (shown in Figure 3.8). These charts are based on all app categories. To view charts related to a specific app category, such as Business or Games, first tap on the Charts button, then tap on the Categories button and choose a category.

FIGURE 3.8

From the App Store app on the iPad, tap on the Top Charts icon at the bottom of the screen to view a list of popular free, paid, and top-grossing apps.

Three new category-specific charts—Free, Paid, and Top Grossing—display. Tap on the See All option to the right of each heading to view up to 300 related apps.

MANAGE YOUR ACCOUNT AND REDEEM ITUNES GIFT CARDS

When you scroll down to the very bottom of the Featured screen in the App Store, you'll see several command buttons displayed.

Tap on the Redeem button to redeem a prepaid iTunes Gift Card. Tap on the Apple ID [Your Apple ID Username] button to manage your Apple ID account and update your credit card information, for example. When the Apple ID window appears, tap on the View Apple ID option. When prompted, enter your password.

Tap on the Apple ID account button to manage your recurring paid subscriptions, as well. When the Account Settings screen is displayed (shown in Figure 3.9), scroll down to the Subscriptions heading and tap on the Manage button. You'll then be able to modify or cancel your paid recurring subscriptions to digital newspapers or magazines, for example. If you don't yet have any active subscriptions, this option does not appear.

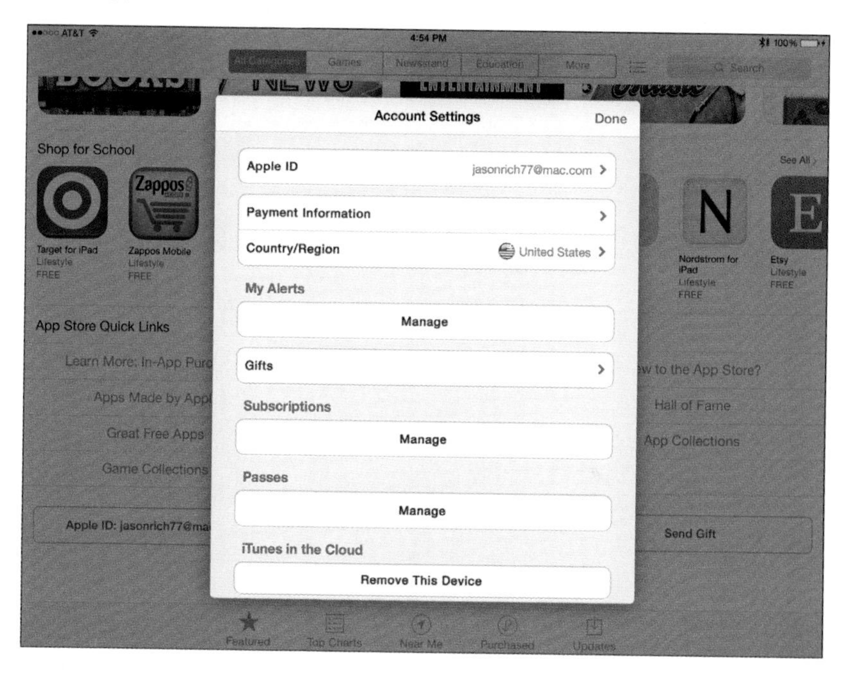

FIGURE 3.9

From the View Account option, you can change or cancel your recurring paid subscriptions for digital editions of newspapers and magazines.

Tap on the Send Gift option to send an iTunes Gift Card to someone else. Their gift will arrive via email and they can redeem it almost instantly from the App Store, iTunes Store, iBookstore, or Newsstand.

FEATURES OF AN APP LISTING

As you browse the App Store, each screen is composed of many app listings (or more information-packed app previews). Each listing promotes a specific app and displays the app's title, graphic icon or logo, what category the app falls into, and its price.

Within an app preview (shown in Figure 3.10), the app's title, its logo/graphic, the app's developer, its average star-based rating, how many ratings the app has received (the number in parenthesis), the price icon, and a sample screen shot from the app itself are displayed.

FIGURE 3.10

A sample app preview contains important, at-a-glance details about that app, including its title and price. Here, a search was performed on the iPad using the phrase "Angry Birds," and app preview boxes for several of the Angry Birds iPad-specific search results are displayed.

LEARN BEFORE YOU BUY: ACCESSING THE APP'S DESCRIPTION PAGE

Before committing to a purchase, as you're looking at an app's listing or preview in the App Store, you can tap on its title or graphic icon to view a detailed description. When you do this on the iPhone, the App Store screen is replaced with a detailed description of the app. On the iPad, a new app description window is displayed over the App Store screen.

An app description screen (like the one shown in Figure 3.11) displays the app's title and logo near the top of the screen, along with its price icon, average star-based rating, and the number of ratings it's received.

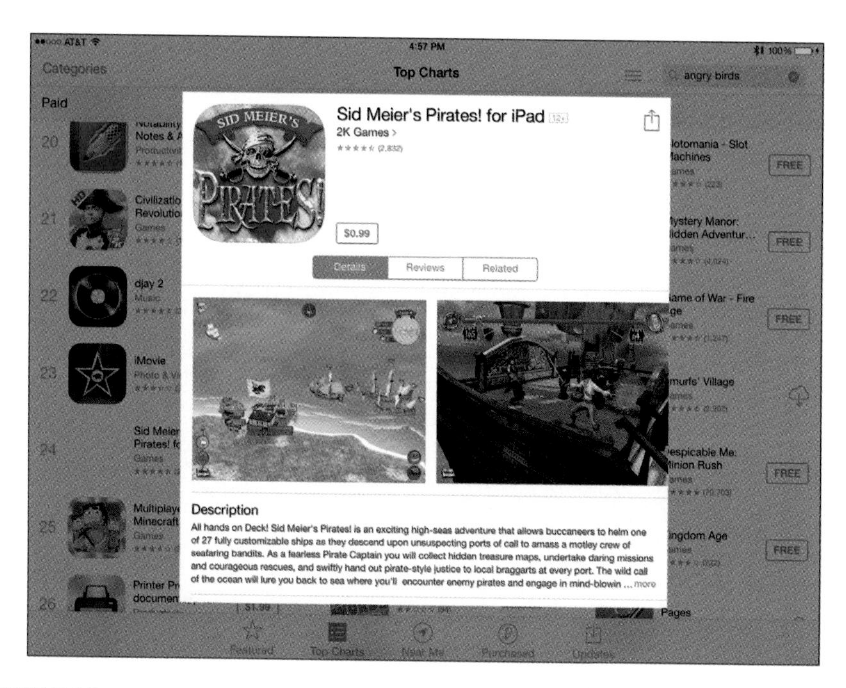

FIGURE 3.11

From an app's description screen (shown here for the Sid Meier's Pirates! for iPad), you can learn all about a specific app. This information can help you decide whether it's of interest to you, or relevant to your needs.

You then see three command tabs, labeled Details, Reviews, and Related. Tap on the Details tab to view a detailed description of the app. Tap on the Reviews tab to view a star-based ratings chart for that app, as well as detailed text-based reviews written by your fellow iPhone and iPad users. Tap on the Related tab to view similar apps that are available from the App Store.

Displayed immediately below the Details, Reviews, and Related tab are sample screen shots from the app itself. Swipe your finger horizontally to scroll through the sample screen shots, or scroll down to view the Details, Reviews, or Related information, based on which command tab you've tapped.

What's Offered When You Tap the Details Tab

Immediately below the sample screen shots from the app is a text-based description of the app that has been written and supplied by the app's developer. This description is a sales tool that's designed to sell apps.

Below the description is information about what new features have been added to the app in the most recent version. Look for the What's New heading.

Displayed beneath the What's New heading, if applicable, is the Supports heading. Here, you can quickly determine whether the app is compatible with Apple's Game Center online service. As you scroll down on this screen, the Information section offers more useful facts about the app.

Below the Information section, tap on the In-App Purchases option, if this option is available, to discover what in-app purchases are available and their cost.

Tap on the Version History option to see information about all revisions to the app that have been released since it was first introduced.

Tap on the Developer Info link to discover other apps available from the same developer or publisher. Tap on the Developer Website option to access the website operated by the app developer or the app-specific website. When you do this, Safari automatically launches and then loads the applicable website.

What's Offered When You Tap the Reviews Tab

When you tap on the Reviews tab, the App Store Ratings chart is displayed (shown in Figure 3.12). This graphically shows how many ratings the app has received, its overall average rating, and the total number of ratings. A top rating is five stars.

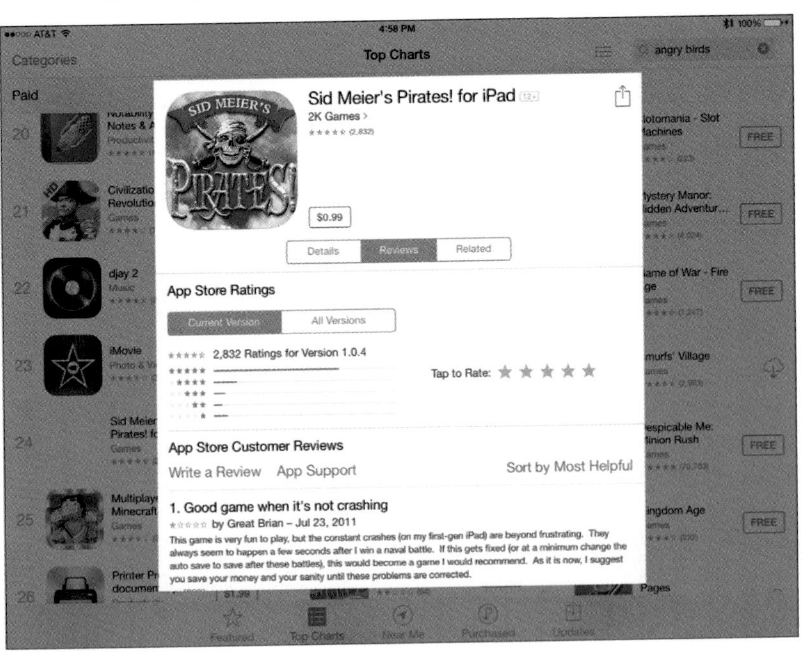

FIGURE 3.12

Every app description contains an average rating and a rating summary chart. Use it to quickly see what other users think about the app you're currently looking at.

Below the App Store Ratings chart are text-based reviews that have been written by other App Store customers.

TIP Obviously, an app with a large number of five-star ratings is probably excellent, whereas an app that consistently earns three stars or less is probably not that great or is loaded with bugs.

TIP As you're looking at an app's Description screen, when you tap on the Reviews tap, above the App Store Ratings chart is a Facebook "Like" button, which enables you to "Like" the app and share details about it on your Facebook page with your online friends. You must have Facebook integration set up on your iOS mobile device to do this. To "unlike" an app you've previously "liked," click the "Like" button again.

Additional options for sharing details about an app with others are offered when you tap on the Share icon that's displayed near the top-right corner of the Description screen. For example, the Gift option enables you to purchase and send a paid app to someone else.

What's Offered When You Tap the Related Tab

These are listings for other apps, usually similar in functionality to the app you're looking at.

On the iPhone, to exit an app's description page and continue browsing the App Store, tap on the left-pointing arrow icon that's displayed near the top-left corner of the screen. On the iPad, tap anywhere outside the app's description window.

KEEP YOUR APPS CURRENT WITH THE UPDATES COMMAND ICON

One of the command icons that's constantly displayed at the bottom of the App Store app's screen is the Updates icon. This is used to keep your currently installed apps up to date. More information about this feature is included in the section, "Keep Your Apps Up to Date with the Latest Versions."

MORE INFO If you opt to shop for apps using the iTunes software on your Mac or PC, you can transfer those apps to your iOS mobile device using the iTunes Sync process or download your purchases from iCloud by tapping on the Purchased option in the App Store app on your mobile device.

To learn more about using the iTunes software on your computer and the iTunes Sync process, visit www.apple.com/support/itunes.

QUICK TIPS FOR FINDING APPS RELEVANT TO YOU

As you explore the App Store, it's easy to get overwhelmed by the sheer number of apps that are available for your iOS device. If you're a new iPhone or iPad user, spending time browsing the App Store introduces you to the many types of apps that are available, and provides you with ideas about how your phone or tablet can be utilized in your personal or professional life.

However, you can save a lot of time searching for apps if you already know the app's exact title or if you know what type of app you're looking for. In this case, you can enter either the app's exact title or a keyword description of the app in the App Store's Search field to see a list of relevant matches. If you're looking for a word-processing app, you can either enter the search phrase "Pages" into the App Store's Search field, or enter the search phrase "word processor" to see a selection of word-processing apps.

If you're looking for vertical market apps with specialized functionality that caters to your industry or profession, enter that industry or profession (or keywords associated with it) in the Search field. For example, enter keywords like "medical imaging," "radiology," "plumbing," "telemarketing," or "sales."

As you're evaluating an app before downloading it, use these tips to help you determine whether it's worth installing on your phone or tablet:

- Figure out what type of features or functionality you want to add to your iPhone or iPad.
- Using the Search field, find apps designed to handle the tasks you have in mind. Chances are, you'll easily be able to find a handful of apps created by different developers that are designed to perform the same basic functionality. You can then pick which is the best based on the description, screenshots, and list of features each app offers.
- Check the customer reviews and ratings for the app. This useful tool quickly determines whether the app actually works as described in its description.

Keep in mind, an app's description in the App Store is written by the app's developer and is designed to sell apps. The customer reviews and star-based ratings are created by fellow iPhone or iPad users who have tried out the app firsthand. If an app has only a few ratings or reviews, and they're mixed, you might need to try out the app for yourself to determine whether it will be useful to you.

- If an app offers a free version, download and test that first before purchasing the premium version. You can always delete any app that you try out but don't wind up liking or needing.
- Ideally, you want to install apps on your iPhone or iPad that were designed specifically for that device if you have a choice. So if you're using an iPhone 5S, choose the iPhone-specific version of an app that's been enhanced for use with the iPhone 5S, or if you're using an iPad, download the iPad-specific version of an app.

KEEP YOUR APPS UP TO DATE WITH THE LATEST VERSIONS

Periodically, app developers release new versions of their apps. One new feature of iOS 7 is that it will automatically update your installed apps as long as your iPhone or iPad has access to the Internet.

To customize this auto-update option, launch Settings and then tap on the iTunes & App Store option. From the iTunes & App Store menu, you can set up automatic downloads for Music, Apps, Books, and Updates. Make sure the virtual switch associated with the Updates option is turned on.

Next, scroll down to the Use Cellular Data option. Choose whether you want apps to update using a cellular data connection to the Internet. Keep in mind that some apps which have a large file size associated with them will require a Wi-Fi Internet connection to update.

At any time, you can see which apps have been updated and read a summary of what functionality or features have been added to the app update (as well as which bugs have been fixed) by launching the App Store app and tapping on the Updates option.

If an app listed on the Updates screen has an Open button associated with it, the app has been recently updated. The date of the update is listed. Tap on the app icon or its title to read about the update. Tap on the Open button to launch the app and use it on your iPhone or iPad.

From the Updates screen, if an Open button is not displayed, you might see a progress meter indicating the app is currently being updated and downloaded to your device. If an update is available but has not yet been downloaded and installed, an Update button, instead of an Open button, is displayed with that app.

As you're viewing the Updates screen, apps are listed in chronological order, based on when they were updated. Pending updates are displayed near the top of the screen (shown in Figure 3.13).

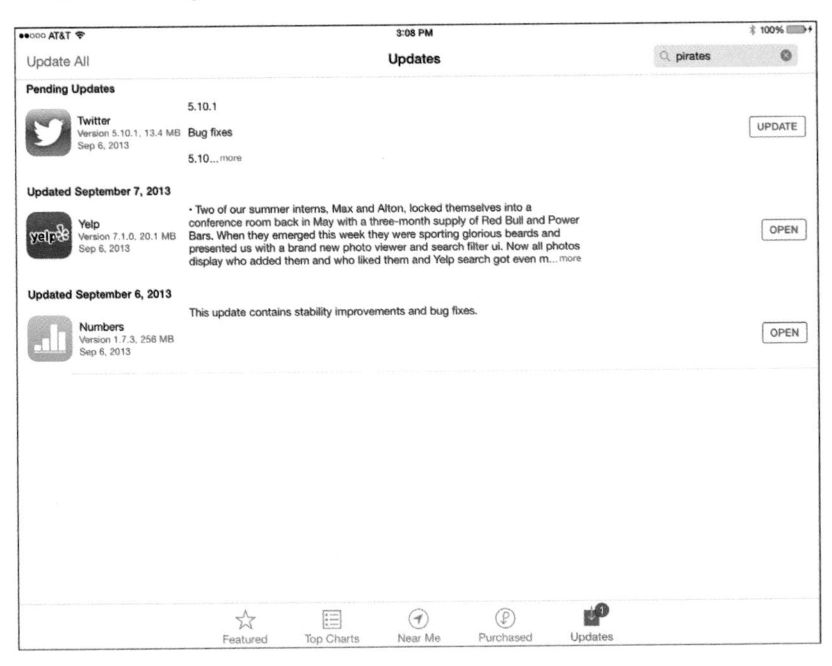

FIGURE 3.13

iOS 7 can now automatically download and install updates to apps. The Updates screen shows which apps have been recently updated and what's new in those updates.

IN THIS CHAPTER

- How to get started using Apple's iCloud service
- How to synch files, documents, and data via iCloud
- Use AirDrop to share data with other nearby Mac, iPhone, and iPad users
- Print files wirelessly to a compatible AirPrint printer

4

SYNC, SHARE, AND PRINT FILES USING iCLOUD, AIRDROP, AIRPLAY, AND AIRPRINT

Initially, you might think that iCloud is just another cloud-based file-sharing service. However, for iOS 7 users, iCloud does much more than simply enable you to store content on a remote server located somewhere in cyberspace.

In fact, iCloud introduces a handful of useful features and functions to your iPhone or iPad that you'll soon be wondering how you ever lived without. There are several compelling reasons to begin using iCloud with your iOS device (and primary computer).

First, an iCloud account is free. When created, your iCloud account includes 5GB of online storage space for your personal data and files, plus an unlimited amount of additional online storage space for all your iTunes Store, App Store, iBookstore, and Newsstand purchases.

The additional storage space needed to store your My Photo Stream and Shared Photo Stream images is also provided, for free, from Apple. Thus, the 5GB of online storage space is used only for your iCloud Backup and iCloud Keychain files, iCloud-related email, and iWork files, as well as to sync and store app-specific files and data "in the cloud."

An iCloud account also includes a free @icloud.com email account, which you can use to send and receive email from all your devices that are linked to your iCloud account. Once it's set up, iCloud automatically keeps your email account synchronized on all devices.

NOTE If you have an older Apple ID account that has an associated @mac.com or @me.com email address, its @icloud.com equivalent can automatically be used as the email address that's associated with your iCloud account.

If you need to upgrade your iCloud account to utilize additional online storage space, it can be purchased directly from your iOS device for an annual fee (as shown in Figure 4.1).

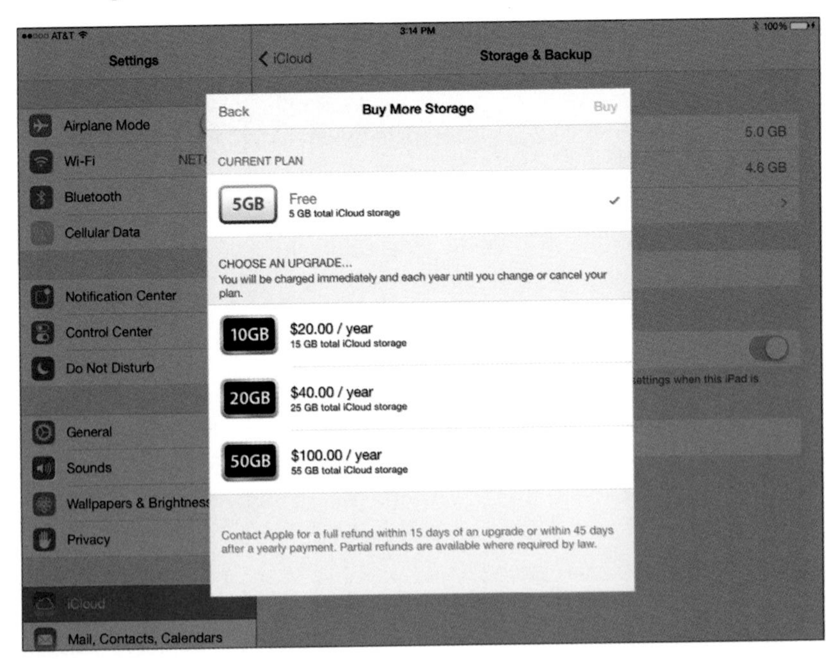

FIGURE 4.1

Launch Settings, select the iCloud option followed by the Storage & Backup option, and then tap on the Change Storage Plan option to acquire additional iCloud online storage space.

CONTENT SAVED TO iCLOUD IS AVAILABLE ANYWHERE

By default, as soon as you establish your free iCloud account, anytime you acquire and download content from the iTunes Store, App Store, iBookstore, or Newsstand, a copy of that content automatically gets saved in your iCloud account and immediately becomes available on all of your compatible computers and iOS devices (including Apple TV) that are linked to that iCloud account. This includes all past purchases and downloads, as well.

So, if you hear an awesome new song on the radio while you're out and about, you can immediately purchase and download it from the iTunes Store using your iPhone. As always, that song becomes available on your iPhone within a minute.

Then, thanks to iCloud, you can access that same newly purchased song from your primary computer, iPad, iPod touch, and/or Apple TV device, without having to repurchase it. This feature also works with TV shows and movies purchased from the iTunes Store.

Another benefit to using iCloud is that syncing can be done from anywhere via the Internet, without using iTunes Sync or requiring a connection between your iOS mobile device and your primary computer.

NOTE The iTunes Sync process is also still possible by installing the iTunes software onto your primary computer, and then connecting your iOS mobile device using the supplied USB cable, but this process for backing up and syncing data is less convenient than using iCloud.

Because using the iTunes Sync process is now considered an antiquated way to sync and backup data, this book focuses on using iCloud. If you're still interested in using iTunes Sync, however, visit Apple's website (http://support.apple.com/kb/PH12117) for more information on how to use this feature.

It's still possible to use the Wireless iTunes Sync process between your iOS mobile device and primary computer that's running the iTunes software, as long as the iPhone or iPad and the computer are connected to the same wireless network.

If you ever opt to delete a purchase from your iOS device, for whatever reason, you always have the option of downloading and installing it again, free, from iCloud.

TIP Depending on how you set up the iTunes Store, the App Store, iBookstore, and Newsstand to work with iCloud, you can automatically have all of your computers and iOS devices download all new music, app, and eBook content you purchase, or this can be done manually. To adjust these Automatic Downloads settings, launch Settings, select the iTunes & App Stores option, and then turn on or off the virtual switches associated with Music, Apps, and Books that are listed under the Automatic Downloads heading.

In iOS 7, you can also set up your iPhone or iPad to automatically update all of your apps as new versions of previously installed apps get released. To do this, turn on the virtual switch associated with the Updates option that's listed below the Music, Apps, and Books options.

Due to their large files sizes, automatic downloads are not possible for TV show episodes, movies, or audiobooks acquired from the iTunes Store. However, you can download these purchases manually onto each of your computers and/or iOS mobile devices that are linked to the same iCloud account.

NOTE Although your iTunes Store music purchases might represent a portion of your overall personal digital music library, chances are that library also includes CDs (which you have ripped into digital format), as well as online music purchases and downloads from other sources (such as Amazon.com).

For an additional fee of $24.99 per year, you can upgrade your iCloud account by adding the iTunes Match services. This grants you full access to your entire personal digital music library (including non-iTunes purchases) from all of your computers and devices that are linked to your iCloud account. To learn more about iTunes Match, visit www.apple.com/itunes/itunes-match.

ACCESS YOUR PURCHASED iTUNES STORE CONTENT FROM ANY DEVICE

If you do not have the Automatic Downloads option enabled, you can still manually load iTunes Store purchases onto your device following these steps:

1. Make sure that your iOS device is connected to the Web via a cellular data or Wi-Fi connection.
2. Launch the iTunes Store app on your device. If prompted, when the Apple ID Password window pops up on your screen, use the virtual keyboard to enter your Apple ID password.
3. Tap on the Purchased icon near the lower-right corner of the iTunes app's screen. Then, near the top-center of the screen, tap on the Music, Movies, or TV Shows tab.

NOTE On an iPhone, to access already purchased content, launch the iTunes Store app, tap on the More icon near the bottom-right corner of the screen, and then tap on the Purchased option. Select Music, Movies, or TV Shows; then choose the content you want to download onto the phone.

4. On the iPad, in a column on the left side of the screen is an alphabetic listing of artists, music groups, or TV shows, depending on which category of content you selected. Tap the one you want to select to see what is available in that listing. If you chose Movies in step 3, you can directly select a movie.
5. On the right side of the screen, songs or episodes of TV shows that you have previously purchased and that are stored in your iCloud account are listed (if you selected Music or TV Shows in step 3). Each listing is accompanied by an iCloud icon (shown in Figure 4.2).

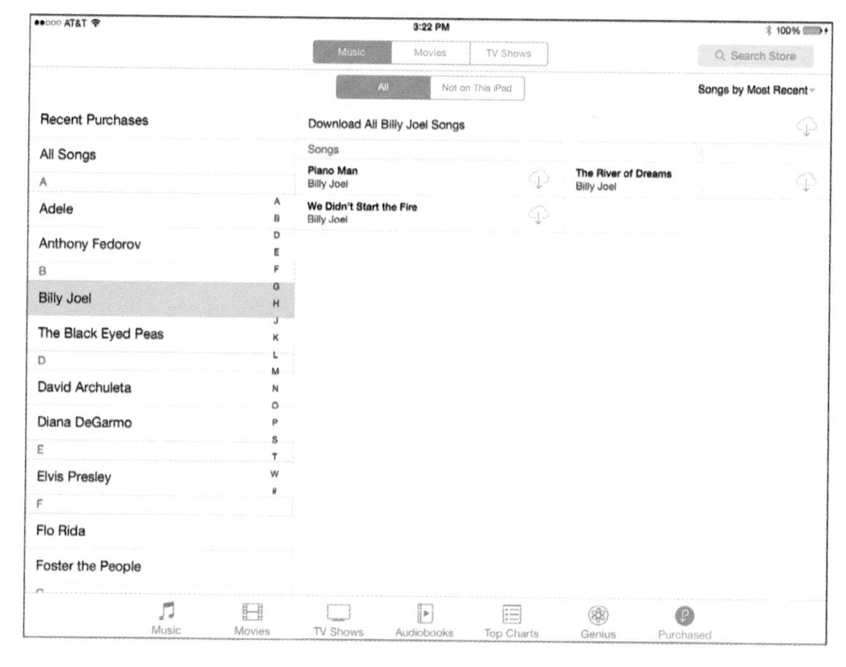

FIGURE 4.2

From any device that runs the iTunes software or the iTunes Store app, you can access and download your previous purchases by tapping on the Purchased icon.

6. Tap on the iCloud icons, one at a time, to select content you want to download onto your iPad. Or to download all of the listed content, tap on the iCloud icon to the right of the Download All option at the top of the list.

> **TIP** If you've acquired audiobooks, an additional tab is displayed alongside the Music, Movies, and TV Shows options.
>
> Below these tabs are two additional tabs, labeled All and Not On This iPad [iPhone]. Tapping on the All tab lists all content of that type you own, while tapping on the Not On This iPad [iPhone] tab displays only related content you own but that's not already stored on the device you're using.

7. Within one to two minutes or so, the content you selected to download is available to listen to on the iOS mobile device you're currently using.
8. Exit the iTunes Store app by pressing the Home button.
9. Launch the Music or Videos app on your iOS device to view your content, as shown in Figure 4.3.

FIGURE 4.3

Billy Joel's music was initially purchased from the iTunes Store on a Mac, but was also downloaded to an iPad connected to the same iCloud account. The music is now stored in the Music app (shown here) on the tablet.

USE iCLOUD TO SYNC YOUR APPS, DATA, DOCUMENTS, AND FILES

Most cloud-based file-sharing services serve mainly as a place in cyberspace to remotely store files. However, you manually must transfer those files to and from the "cloud." Thanks to iCloud's integration with iOS 7, many of the core apps that come with the latest version of the mobile operating system, as well as a growing number of third-party apps, automatically keep data and files created or managed using those apps synchronized with other devices and/or your primary computer that are also linked to the same iCloud account.

From within Settings on your iPhone or iPad, turn on or off iCloud support for all compatible apps on your device. Compatible apps include Contacts, Calendars, Reminders, Safari, Notes, Photos, and Mail (relating only to your free iCloud-related email account).

iOS 7 WHAT'S NEW Related to Safari, iOS 7 has a new feature, called iCloud Keychain, which can automatically store the username, password, and credit card information (for online purchases) related to all the websites you visit. Thus, you no longer need to manually sign in to websites when you revisit them, nor do you need to remember each username and password you associated with a website-related account.

MORE INFO iCloud is also fully compatible with Apple's optional iWork apps for the iPhone and iPad, which include Pages (word processing), Numbers (spreadsheet management), and Keynote (for digital slide presentations). See the section, "Automatically Transfer Documents Using iCloud" to learn more about this functionality.

When you turn on the iCloud functionality related to the Contacts app, for example, your iOS device automatically syncs your contacts database with iCloud. Thus, if you add or update a contact entry on your iPhone, that addition or change automatically synchronizes and becomes available within the Contacts app running on your other iOS devices, as well as within the compatible contact management software that's running on your primary computer (such as the Contacts app or Microsoft Outlook on your Mac). This is also true if you delete a Contacts entry from one device. It is almost instantly deleted from all of your other computers and iOS mobile devices linked to the same iCloud account.

As you surf the Web using Safari, when you turn on iCloud syncing functionality related to this app, all of your Bookmarks and Bookmark Bar data, along with your Reading List information and open browser window/tabs data, are synced via iCloud.

To share your photos between iOS devices, your primary computer, and/or an Apple TV device, you must set up a My Photo Stream or Shared Photo Stream using iCloud. How to do this is explained later in this chapter.

CUSTOMIZING iCLOUD TO WORK WITH YOUR APPS

It's important to understand that the app-related synchronization feature offered by iCloud is different from iCloud Backup, which creates a complete backup of your entire iOS device that gets stored online as part of your iCloud account.

When you set up iCloud to work with a specific compatible app, that app automatically accesses the Web, connects to iCloud, and then uploads or downloads app-related files, documents, or data as needed. iCloud then shares (syncs) that app-specific data with your other computers and devices that are linked to the same iCloud account.

To customize which of your compatible iCloud apps utilize iCloud functionality, follow these steps:

1. Launch Settings from your iPhone or iPad's Home screen.
2. Tap on the iCloud option.
3. When the iCloud Control Panel screen appears (shown in Figure 4.4), at the top of the screen, make sure the Apple ID–linked email address that's associated with your iCloud account is displayed next to the Account option. If it's not, use your existing Apple ID to create or access an iCloud account by tapping on the Account option.
4. Below the Account option is a list of all preinstalled iCloud-compatible apps on your iOS device. To the right of each listing is a virtual on/off switch. To turn on the iCloud functionality associated with a specific app, set its related virtual switch to the on position.

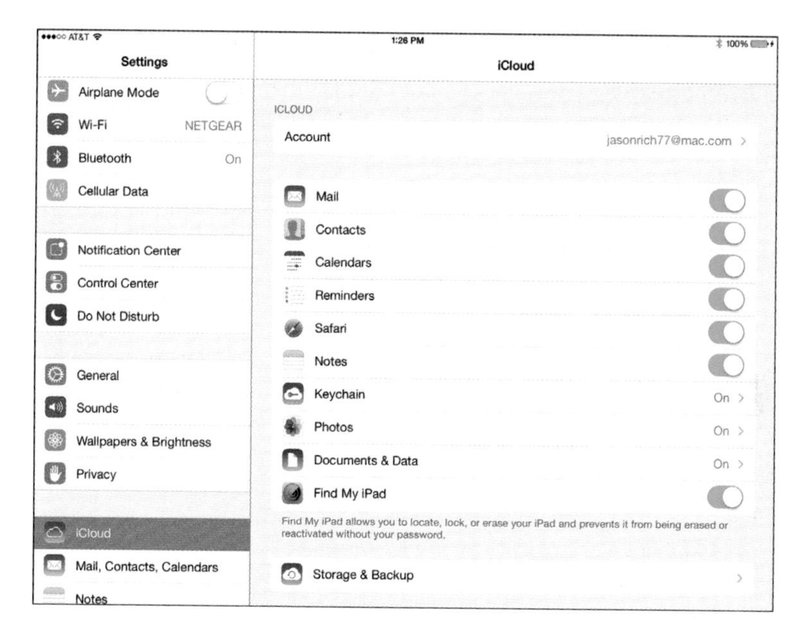

FIGURE 4.4

Turn iCloud functionality on or off for specific apps from the iCloud menu within Settings.

5. When you have turned on the iCloud functionality for all the apps that you want to be able to synchronize via iCloud, press the Home button to exit Settings and save your changes.
6. Repeat this process on each of your iOS devices. So, if you have an iPhone and an iPad, you must turn on the iCloud functionality for Contacts, for example, on both devices to keep Contacts data synchronized via iCloud on both devices.

NOTE After you've turned on the iCloud functionality for specific apps, for the various apps on your iOS devices (and your primary computer) to stay synchronized, each computer or device must have access to the Internet. For this use of iCloud on your iPhone or iPad, a cellular or a Wi-Fi Internet connection works fine. For certain other iCloud features, such as Photo Stream and iCloud Backup, your iOS device will require a Wi-Fi Internet connection.

ACCESS YOUR APP-SPECIFIC DATA ONLINE AT iCLOUD.COM

Another benefit of using iCloud to sync your app-specific data is that using any computer or Internet-enabled devices, you can visit www.iCloud.com, log in using your iCloud username and password (which is typically your Apple ID username and password), and then access Web versions of the Contacts, Calendar, Reminders, and Notes apps. This is shown on a Mac using the Safari web browser in Figure 4.5. Your most up-to-date data appears in the online versions of the apps.

> iOS 7 **WHAT'S NEW** With the release of iOS 7, online versions of the iWork apps, including Pages, Numbers, and Keynote, were also incorporated into the iCloud.com website. This gives you remote access to all of your files, documents, and data related to these popular apps, as long as they have been saved in iCloud rather than on your local hard drive.
>
> The online editions of Pages, Numbers, and Keynote are compatible with Microsoft Office documents and files. It's possible to drag-and-drop a Microsoft Word document into the online-based Pages app, for example, work with that document while online, and then have iCloud sync a Pages-compatible version of the file to your iPhone or iPad.

FIGURE 4.5

Log in to www.iCloud.com to access your app-specific content using online versions of popular iPhone and iPad apps, including Contacts, Calendar, Reminders, Notes, Pages, Numbers, and Keynote.

If you forget your iPhone at home, for example, you can still access your complete Contacts database, your schedule, your to-do lists, and your notes from any computer.

After you log in to iCloud.com, click on the onscreen app you want to access. The online apps are almost identical to the iPad versions of the Contacts, Calendar, Reminders, and Notes apps.

AUTOMATICALLY TRANSFER DOCUMENTS USING iCLOUD

In addition to the iCloud compatibility built in to many of the core (preinstalled) apps that are included with iOS 7, a growing number of other apps also offer iCloud compatibility and enable you to easily and automatically transfer or synchronize app-related documents and files.

This functionality is built in to Apple's iWork apps for the iPhone and iPad, which include Pages, Numbers, and Keynote. Be sure to upgrade your iWork for iOS apps to the latest versions for this functionality to work.

If you turn on iCloud functionality with Pages, Numbers, Keynote, or other compatible third-party apps, when you create or revise a document, that revision is stored on your iOS device and on iCloud. From iCloud, that same app running on your iOS device (or compatible software running on your primary computer) can access that most recent version of your files or documents within seconds.

So, if you're working with the Pages word processor on your iPhone, your iPad, or the Mac, you always know that when you access a specific Pages document from any compatible device, you're working with the most up-to-date version of that document. The synchronization process happens automatically and behind the scenes, assuming that your iOS devices and primary computer are connected to the Internet.

NOTE To use iCloud's "Documents in the Cloud" feature, your iOS device can either utilize a 3G/4G or a Wi-Fi Internet connection.

The processes for turning on iCloud functionality within compatible apps on your iPhone, iPad, and iPod touch are almost identical. To begin, turn on the Documents & Data option from the iCloud menu in Settings. Then, to turn on the iCloud functionality in Pages on an iPad, for example, follow these steps:

1. From your iOS device, launch Settings from the Home screen.
2. Scroll down on the main Settings menu until you find the listing of apps stored on your device (shown in Figure 4.6).

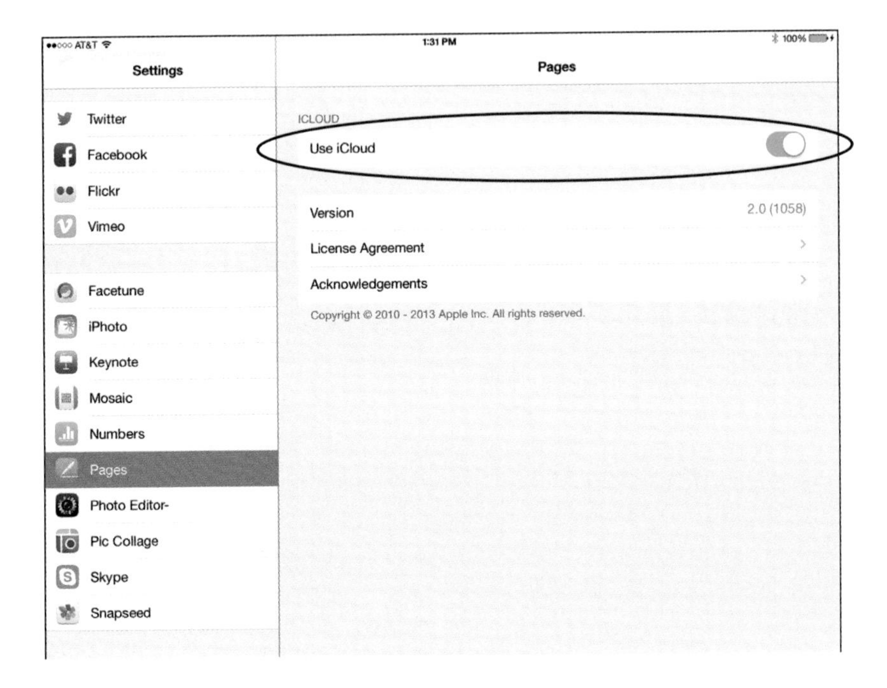

FIGURE 4.6

To control iCloud functionality for apps that don't come preinstalled with iOS 7, scroll down to the specific app listings on the main Settings menu, and tap on the app of your choice, such as Pages (if applicable).

3. Locate the listing for Pages (or the app of your choice) from the Settings menu, and tap on it.
4. When the Pages menu screen appears in Settings, tap on the virtual switch that's associated with the Use iCloud option, and switch it to the on position. If you turn this feature to the off position, your documents are stored only on your device and are not synchronized with other devices via iCloud.
5. Exit Settings. From this point forward, your Pages documents automatically synchronize with iCloud when your device has Internet access.
6. Repeat this process for each iCloud-compatible app, on each of your iOS devices.

NOTE From your iPhone/iPad, to access iWork documents and files created on your Mac, it's necessary to store those documents in your iCloud account. To do this, be sure to turn on iCloud syncing in the Mac version of Pages, as well as in the iCloud option of your Mac's System Preferences. You can also access your iWork documents and files from iWork for iCloud (www.iCloud.com).

CREATE A PHOTO STREAM USING iCLOUD

Apple offers two different types of Photo Streams that work with iCloud. My Photo Stream enables you to automatically share photos between your own computers and iOS mobile devices that are linked to the same iCloud account. Once set up, this sharing process happens automatically and in the background.

The Shared Photo Stream feature also works with the Photos app (and optional iPhoto app). Shared Photo Streams provide an easy way for you to share an unlimited number of designated photos that are stored on your iOS mobile device with specific people who you select. This sharing is done using online galleries that are created using iCloud to showcase your selected images online.

Using this feature, you can create as many separate Shared Photo Stream galleries as you'd like, add and remove photos from them at anytime, plus choose who is granted access to see and download those photos.

To learn more about the My Photo Stream and Shared Photo Stream features and how they work, be sure to read Chapter 8, "Shoot, Edit, and Share Photos and Videos." However, like all iCloud-related features, on each of your iOS mobile devices and computers, the My Photo Stream and Shared Photo Streams features must be turned on separately. This is done by launching Settings, tapping on the iCloud option, and then turning on the virtual switch that's associated with each Photo Stream option.

TIP Photo Stream requires that each of your iOS devices has access to a Wi-Fi Internet connection. It does not work with a cellular data connection. This feature also works with both Macs and PCs, as well as Apple TV.

USING A UNIQUE APPLE ID FOR iCLOUD

When you first create an iCloud account, you're encouraged to use your existing Apple ID and username. This is to encourage Apple computer and device users to use the same Apple ID to make and track all of their iTunes Store, App Store, iBookstore, and Newsstand purchases, plus use that same Apple ID to access Apple's online-based iMessage instant messaging service, the FaceTime videoconferencing service, and utilize all of iCloud's functionality.

If you're the only person who needs access to your iTunes Store, App Store, iBookstore, and Newsstand purchases on your own computer(s) and devices, using the same Apple ID and password for this and to access Apple's other online-based services is practical and efficient.

However, if you want to share your iTunes Store, App Store, iBookstore, and Newsstand purchases with other family members who have their own iPhone, iPad, iPod touch, Mac, or PC, but you do not want those other people to be able to access your iCloud-related files, use your personal iMessage or FaceTime account, or access your iCloud-related email address, create one shared Apple ID account for Apple-related online purchases, and then create a second, personal Apple ID account that you use with some of iCloud's features, as well as iMessage and FaceTime.

NOTE If you do wind up creating multiple Apple IDs, you can decide which ID to use with which app from within Settings. For example, to change the default Apple ID used with the App Store, launch Settings, tap on the iTunes & App Store option, and then tap on the Apple ID option displayed near the top of the iTunes & App Store submenu. Log out of the account you're using and sign in using an alternative Apple ID and password.

To create and manage your Apple ID account(s), visit https://appleid.apple.com from any computer or Internet-enabled device. When you set up iCloud, or use iMessage, FaceTime, or try to access the iTunes Store, iBookstore, or Newsstand for the first time, you also have the option to create a new Apple ID account.

TIP From your iPhone or iPad, to view and manage your Apple ID account, launch Settings, tap on the iTunes & App Stores option, and then tap on the Apple ID option that's displayed near the top of the iTunes & App Store menu screen. Tap on the View Apple ID button to access and manage your account, or tap on the iForgot button to recover a forgotten Apple ID username or password.

If you use multiple Apple IDs, you can view and manage that particular Apple ID from the app to which it's assigned on your iOS mobile device.

BACKING UP WITH iCLOUD

Another useful feature of iOS 7 is the capability to create a backup of your iOS device wirelessly, and have the related backup files stored online ("in the cloud"). Using this iCloud Backup feature, your iOS device can be connected to any Wi-Fi Internet connection. Your primary computer is not needed. Thus, the backup can be created from anywhere, and you can later restore your device from anywhere a Wi-Fi Internet connection is present.

TIP When you activate the iCloud Backup feature, if you connect your iOS device to your primary computer, the iTunes Sync process does not work. If you want to create a backup of your device using iTunes Sync and have the backup files stored on your primary computer's hard drive (instead of on iCloud), you must first turn off the iCloud Backup feature from within the Settings app.

When activated, your iOS device automatically creates a backup to iCloud once per day. For this to happen, your iPhone or iPad also must be connected to an external power source. However, at any time, you can manually create a backup of your device to iCloud from within Settings. This can be done when your device is running on battery.

Follow these steps to activate and use the iCloud Backup feature on an iPhone or iPad:

1. Connect your device to the Internet via a Wi-Fi connection.
2. From the Home screen, launch Settings.
3. Tap on the iCloud option.
4. Tap on the Storage & Backup option that's located near the bottom of the iCloud menu.
5. About halfway down on the Storage & Backup screen, tap on the virtual switch that's associated with the iCloud Backup option.
6. A new Back Up Now option appears near the bottom of the Storage & Backup screen (as shown in Figure 4.7). Tap on it to begin creating a backup of your iOS device. The backup file is stored on iCloud.

TIP The first time you use the iCloud Backup feature to create a wireless backup of your iOS device, the process could take up to an hour (or longer), depending on how much data you have stored on your device.

After the backup process begins, a progress meter is displayed at the bottom of the Storage & Backup screen within Settings. While the backup is being created this first time, refrain from using your iOS device. Just kick back and allow the iPhone or iPad to connect with iCloud and create the initial backup.

In the future, the iCloud Backup process takes place once per day, automatically, when your iOS device is not otherwise in use. These backups save all newly created or revised files and data only, so subsequent iCloud Backup procedures are much quicker.

At the bottom of the Storage & Backup screen within Settings, the time and date of the last backup is displayed. If, for some reason, the backup process could not be completed, such as if the device could not connect to the Internet, an error message displays.

At any time, it's possible to manually create an updated backup via iCloud by tapping on the Back Up Now icon displayed on the Storage & Backup screen.

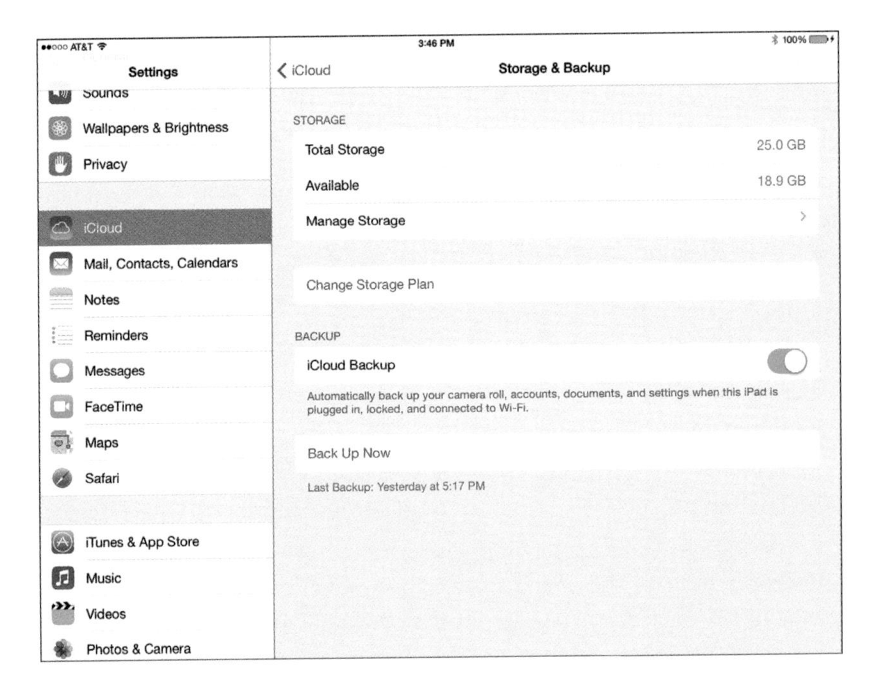

FIGURE 4.7

Manage and launch the iCloud Backup feature from the Storage & Backup screen, accessible from within the Settings app.

The purpose of creating and maintaining a backup of your device is so that you have a copy of all your apps, data, files, content, and personalized settings stored if something goes wrong with your device. If and when you need to access the backup to restore your device using iCloud, when prompted, choose the Restore from iCloud option.

Likewise, if your iPhone or iPad gets lost or stolen and is ultimately replaced, you can restore the content from your old device onto the new one.

iTUNES SYNC IS ALSO A VIABLE BACKUP OPTION

When it comes to syncing data between your primary computer(s) and other iOS mobile device(s), as well as maintaining a backup of your iPhone or iPad, this can be done by connecting your iOS mobile device(s) directly to your primary computer via the supplied USB cable, and then by using the iTunes Sync process.

Because iOS 7 is fully integrated with iCloud, maintaining a backup of your device and syncing app-specific data, as well as transferring data, files, photos, and content between your Mac(s), PC(s), and other iOS mobile device(s) can now be done much more easily using iCloud. When you use iCloud Backup, your iPhone or iPad's backup files are stored online "in the cloud," not on your primary computer's hard drive. Because this is the more popular way to back up and sync data, it's the approach we focus on within this book.

MORE INFO To use the iTunes Sync process between your iPhone or iPad and a Mac or Windows-based PC, you must download and install the latest version of the iTunes software (iTunes 11 of later) onto your computer. To do this, visit www.apple.com/itunes.

To learn more about using the iTunes Sync process to transfer, sync, and back up apps, data, content, and photos, for example, visit www.apple.com/support/itunes.

iCLOUD: MANY USES, ONE STORAGE SPACE

Keep in mind that you are not required to use all of iCloud's various features. You can turn on only those features you believe are beneficial to you, based on how you typically use your iPhone and/or iPad, and what content, data, and information you want to synchronize or back up to your iCloud account.

TIP If you're like most people and wind up storing a lot of content, data, and files on your iPhone and iPad, and you want to use the iCloud Backup feature with each of your iOS devices, you might need to increase your iCloud online storage space allocation (which means incurring an annual fee).

At the top of the main Storage & Backup screen within Settings, the amount of total online storage space you have available on iCloud is displayed next to the Total Storage heading. Below that, the available online storage is listed.

To see how your iCloud online storage is being utilized, tap on the Manage Storage option that's also listed under the Storage heading on the Storage & Backup menu screen. If your online storage allocation is almost filled (or becomes filled), either delete obsolete files and data or tap on the Buy More Storage option to immediately increase the amount of available online storage space you have available.

SHARE DATA WITH OTHER NEARBY iPHONE AND iPAD USERS VIA AIRDROP

If you want to share certain types of app-specific data with other Mac, iPhone, or iPad users, you can send information from the Share menu in many apps via email or text/instant message. To share files between iPhones and iPads, you can also utilize the new AirDrop feature.

AirDrop is a wireless file-sharing tool that enables the device you're using to send and receive certain types of files, photos, documents, and data with other users who are in close physical proximity to you.

Thanks to iOS 7, AirDrop is now available if you have an iPhone 5 or above or a fourth-generation iPad or above. To turn on this feature, access the Control Center by swiping your finger upward, starting near the bottom of the screen. Tap on the AirDrop option. The AirDrop menu includes three options: Off, Contacts Only, and Everyone.

To turn off this feature altogether, tap on the Off option. If you want to be able to share data only with people you know and who have an entry in your Contacts database, select the Contacts Only option. Or, if you want to be able to share data with anyone else who can use the AirDrop feature on their iOS mobile device, select the Everyone option.

Then, from a compatible app, such as Photos, tap on the Share icon and tap on the AirDrop option. Keep in mind, for this feature to work, AirDrop must be active on your mobile device and on the mobile device being used by the other person.

STREAM CONTENT FROM YOUR iPHONE OR iPAD TO OTHER COMPATIBLE DEVICES USING AIRPLAY

AirPlay is another wireless feature that's built in to iOS 7. It enables your mobile device to stream content, such as photos, videos, or audio, to an AirPlay-compatible device, such as Apple TV, Mac, or AirPlay-compatible speakers.

To use AirPlay, your iOS mobile device and the other AirPlay compatible device must be connected to the same wireless home network (via Wi-Fi). Then, when you turn on the AirPlay feature, the two compatible devices will automatically establish a wireless connection.

After the connection is made, an AirPlay icon appears within compatible apps, such as Music, Videos, and Photos, enabling you to transfer (stream) what you would otherwise see on your iPhone or iPad's screen, or what would be heard through the device's speaker, to another compatible device.

In addition to being able to stream photos and video (including iTunes Store TV show and movie purchases and rentals) from your iPhone or iPad to an Apple TV device so that you can watch that content on your HD television set, you can use AirPlay to connect external speakers (without cables) to your iOS mobile device, and then stream music or audio from your device to those compatible speakers.

AirPlay-compatible speakers are available from a handful of different companies, starting around $49.95. To learn about the AirPlay speakers available from the Apple Store and Apple.com, visit http://store.apple.com/us/ipad/ipad-accessories/speakers?m.tsOtherFeatures=airplay.

PRINT FILES WIRELESSLY USING AN AIRPRINT-COMPATIBLE PRINTER

Another wireless feature built in to iOS 7 is AirPrint. It enables compatible apps to wirelessly send documents, data, or photos to be printed on an AirPrint-compatible laser, ink jet, or photo printer. For this feature to work, the iOS mobile device and the AirPrint printer must be connected to the same wireless home network.

Dozens of different AirPrint-compatible printers are now available, from companies such as Brother, HP, Canon, Lexmark, and Epson.

After you've set up an AirPrint-compatible printer, you can use the Print feature built in to many apps, such as Pages, Notes, and Photos, for example, to print out files, documents, data, and photos. To learn more about AirPrint-compatible printers, visit http://support.apple.com/kb/ht4356.

TIP If you're using an AirPrint-compatible printer, it's possible to install specialized software on your Mac, such as handyPrint or Printopia, that will enable your printer to work with the AirPrint feature of your iPhone or iPad as long as your Mac is turned on. These apps are available from the Mac App Store.

IN THIS CHAPTER

- Discover several ways to manage information on your iOS device
- Create and manage to-do lists using the Reminders app
- Use the Notes app to create, manage, share, and sync notes between your iPhone, iPad, and Mac(s)

5

ORGANIZE YOUR LIFE WITH REMINDERS AND NOTES

If you have a busy life, and most of us do, your iPhone or iPad can be used to help you manage your schedule and day-to-day appointments, plus enable you to stay in contact with the people you know and manage those contacts using the Contacts app. Plus, instead of using traditional sticky notes or cocktail napkins to jot notes to yourself, the Notes app is ideal for note taking, keeping track of ideas, and managing text-based information that does not require the full functionality of a word processor.

Using the Reminders app, you can easily manage multiple to-do lists simultaneously, and add alarms and deadlines to individual to-do items, plus you can be reminded of responsibilities, tasks, or objectives exactly when you need this information based on your geographic location or a predetermined time and date. The Reminders app works nicely with Siri, Notification Center, and iCloud (which makes synchronizing your app-related data a straightforward process).

NOTE The Notes app works nicely with the iPhone or iPad's Dictation feature so you don't have to manually type notes into the app.

On the iPad, all information relevant to a specific app or function is typically displayed on a single screen. On the iPhone, however, that same information is often split up and displayed on several separate screens.

USE REMINDERS TO MANAGE YOUR TO-DO LISTS

On the surface, Reminders is a straightforward to-do list manager. However, it offers a plethora of interesting and useful features.

NOTE Reminders is just one option for managing to-do lists on your iPhone or iPad. If you use the Search feature in the App Store (with the keyword "to-do list"), you'll find many more apps created by third parties that can be used for this purpose offering different features.

For starters, you can create as many separate to-do lists as you need to properly manage your personal and professional life or various projects for which you're responsible.

WHAT'S NEW The iOS 7 edition of Reminders enables you to color code to-do lists. Tap on the Edit button displayed to the right of a list's title, and then tap on the Color option. Seven different colors are displayed. Tap on your selection. The list title is displayed in the selected color.

Because your iPhone has Location Services (GPS) capabilities, it always knows exactly where it is. Thus, you can create items within your to-do lists and associate one or more of them with an alarm that alerts you when you arrive at or depart from a particular geographic location, such as your home, office, or a particular store.

For example, you can have your morning to-do list or call list automatically display on your iPhone's screen when you arrive at work if you associate just one item on that list with a location-based alarm. If you use Reminders to maintain a list of office supplies you need to purchase at Staples, you can have it pop up on the screen when you arrive at your local Staples office supply superstore. Again, only one item on the list needs to have a location-based alarm associated with it.

In addition, you can have a reminder alarm set to warn you of an upcoming deadline. This can be displayed on your iPhone or iPad's screen in the Notification Center or as separate alerts or banners, depending on how you have the Reminders app set up to work with your device. To learn how to set up Reminders to work with notifications, see Chapter 1.

As you're setting up an alarm, if you want it to repeat every day, every week, every two weeks, every month, or every year, tap on the Repeat option and make your selection. By default, the Never option is selected, meaning the alarm will not repeat.

TIP Just as you do for other apps, to set up Reminders to work with Notification Center and/or display onscreen alerts or banners, launch Settings, tap on the Notification Center option, and then tap on the listing for the Reminders app. You can then customize the settings on the Reminders menu screen within Settings (shown in Figure 5.1).

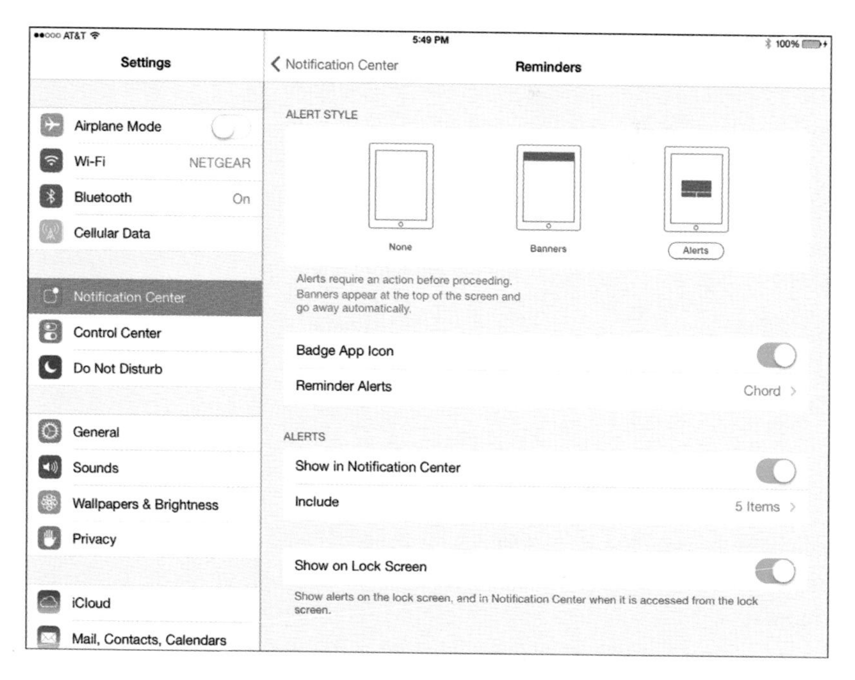

FIGURE 5.1

Customize how you want Reminders to get your attention through Notification Center and/or using Alerts or Banners from this Settings menu screen (shown here on the iPad).

KEEP UP TO DATE WITH REMINDERS

When you launch Reminders for the first time on the iPad, the control center for this app appears on the left side of the screen. On the right side of the screen is a simulated sheet of lined paper. Tap on the Add List button in the bottom-left corner of the screen. The new list on the right side of the screen displays the temporary heading New List. Enter a title for the new list, and then associate a color with it. Tap on the Done option when you're ready to begin populating the list with items (as shown in Figure 5.2), or repeat this process to create another list.

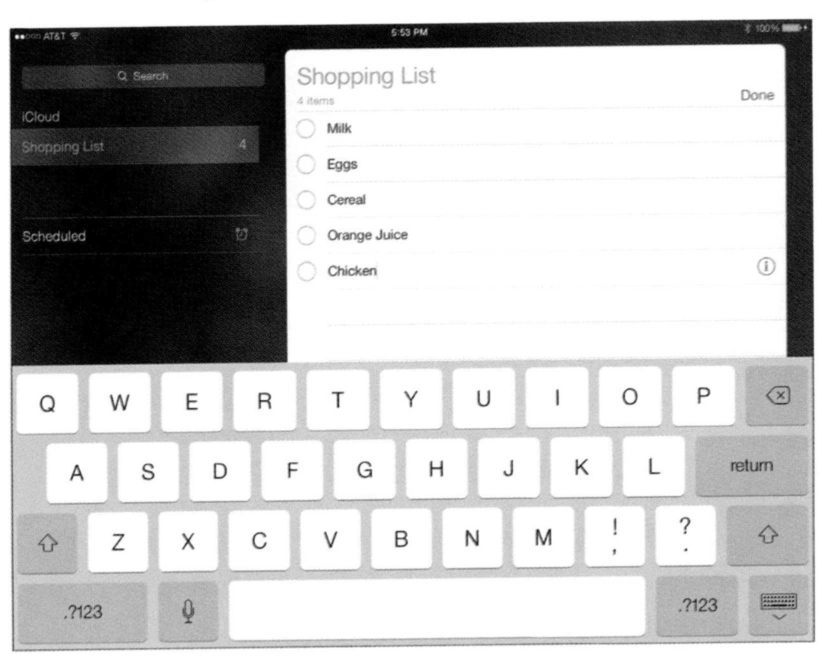

FIGURE 5.2

Using Reminders, you can create and manage one or more to-do lists (shown here on the iPad). Each list can have as many separate items as you wish.

On the iPhone, to create a new list from scratch as you're looking at a list, tap the list name to bring up a master list screen. The New List (+) option is displayed at the top of this screen. Tap on this option, and then type the name of the list and associate a color with it (shown in Figure 5.3). Tap on the Done option. You can then begin populating the list with items or repeat this process to create another list.

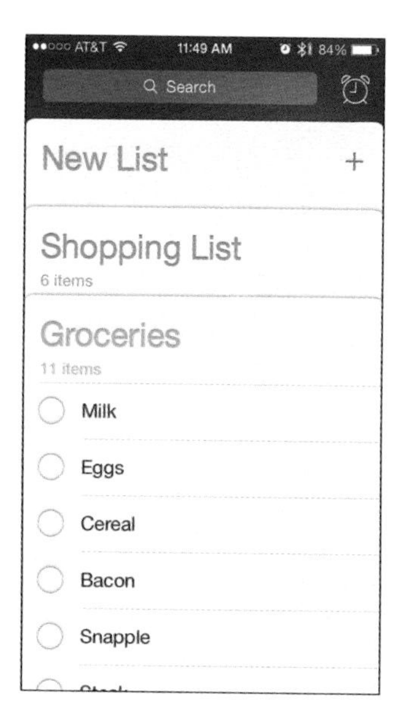

FIGURE 5.3

Swipe your finger in a downward direction to make the New List (+) option appear near the top of the Reminders screen on the iPhone.

When viewing a list, tap on an empty line of the simulated sheet of paper to add an item. The virtual keyboard appears. Enter the item to be added to your to-do list. Next, tap on the Return key on the keyboard to enter another item, or tap on the Details icon (the blue *i* with a circle around it) to the right of the newly added item to associate an alarm, priority, and/or notes with it.

When you're finished adding new list items, tap on the Done option.

To set a date-specific alarm on either the iPhone or iPad, turn the virtual switch associated with Remind Me On a Day to the on position, and then tap on the date and time line that appears below it to set the date and time for the alert.

On the iPhone only, you can set a location-based alarm for that item. To set an alarm based on a location, enter the Details screen, and then turn on the virtual switch associated with the Remind Me At A Location option. Select a location or enter an address, and then decide whether you want to be alerted when you arrive or when you leave that destination by tapping on the When I Arrive… or When I Leave… tab. On the iPad, you can set an alarm only based on a date and time.

TIP On the Mac version of Reminders, you can create location-based alerts and they'll sync with your iPhone via iCloud.

TIP You also have the option to set a priority with each to-do list item. Your priority options include None, Low (!), Medium (!!), and High (!!!).

Although setting a priority for a list item displays that item with one, two, or three exclamations points to signify its importance, adjusting an item's priority does not automatically change its location within the list. You must manually rearrange the order of items on a list.

To do this, while looking at a list, tap on the Edit button. Then place your finger on the Move icon (three horizontal lines) that's associated with the list item you want to move and drag it up or down to the desired location within the list. Tap the Done button to save your changes.

Different alarms can be associated with each item in each of your to-do lists. You also have the option to create a to-do list item but not associate any type of alert or alarm with it.

When an alarm is generated for a to-do list item, a notification automatically appears in your iOS device's Notification Center, assuming that you have this feature turned on.

TIP One additional feature of the Reminders app is that you can display a separate to-do list associated with each day on the calendar. When you use the Remind Me On A Day option, a date becomes associated with that item. Then, to review upcoming items related to a particular day using an iPhone, as you're looking at a list, swipe your finger in a downward direction to reveal the Search field. Displayed to the right is an Alarm Clock icon. Tap on this to display scheduled items for the current day.

On the iPad, tap on the Scheduled option on the left side of the screen.

iOS 7 WHAT'S NEW At the bottom of every to-do list on the iPad is a new Show Completed option. Tap on this to display all items originally added to the list you're viewing but that have since been moved to the Completed list.

To delete an item from a to-do list, swipe your finger from right to left across the item. A More button and a Delete button are displayed. Tap on Delete to confirm your selection, or tap on the More button to reveal the Details window.

As soon as you make changes to a to-do list item, if you have iCloud functionality turned on for the Reminders app and have access to the Internet, your additions, edits, or deletions sync with iCloud. See Chapter 4, "Sync, Share, and Print Files Using iCloud, AirDrop, AirPlay, and AirPrint," to learn more about how the Reminders app integrates with iCloud to sync app-specific data.

HOW TO DELETE AN ENTIRE TO-DO LIST

If you want to delete an entire list, enter the list and click on the Edit button, and then click on Delete List at the bottom of the screen. A warning pops up asking to confirm the deletion.

On the iPad, you can also locate the list you want to delete from the column on the left, and swipe your finger from right to left across it. When the Delete button appears, tap on it.

On the iPad, you also have the option of tapping the Edit button, and then tapping on the negative sign icon that's associated with the list you want to erase. In Edit mode, you can also change the order of your lists by placing your finger on the icon that looks like three horizontal lines that's associated with a list, and dragging it up or down.

To exit Edit mode, tap on the Done option.

NOTE If you also use a Mac that's running OS X Mountain Lion or Mavericks, it comes with the Reminders and Notes apps preinstalled. These are fully compatible with and work just like the iPhone editions of these apps.

TIP If you sync your lists between your Mac and your iOS mobile device(s), it's possible to use the Mac version of the Reminders app to manually rearrange the order of your list items. When the edited lists sync with iCloud, your changes will then be reflected (very quickly) in the Reminders app running on your iPhone and/or iPad as well.

On the iPhone or iPad, to manually reorder a list, tap on the Edit option as you're viewing a list. Then, place your finger on the Move icon to the right of an item listing, and drag that icon up or down. The Move icon looks like three horizontal lines. Tap the Done option to save your changes.

Keep in mind that, when using the iPhone, iPad, or Mac version of Reminders, you can also manually rearrange the order in which your lists are displayed. As you're viewing the directory of lists stored in Reminders, tap on the Edit option. Then, use the Move icon associated with a list to drag it up or down to the desired new location. Tap the Done option to save your changes and view your reordered directory of lists.

PERFORM BASIC TEXT EDITING AND NOTE TAKING WITH THE NOTES APP

While the Reminders app enables you to maintain detailed to-do lists that can be synced between your iOS mobile devices and Mac(s), the Notes app serves as a basic text editor that enables you to create, edit, view, and manage notes.

> **NOTE** The Notes app offers very basic formatting functionality. If you need the features and functions of a full-featured word processor, you should use Pages or another word processing app on your iPhone or iPad. Notes is designed more for basic note taking, not word processing.

Just like Reminders, the Notes app comes preinstalled with iOS 7 on the iPhone, iPad, and iPod touch. In addition, a similar Notes app comes preinstalled on Macs running OS X Mountain Lion or Mavericks, so if you set up this app to work with iCloud, all of your notes remain synced on all of your computers and/or iOS mobile devices that are linked to the same iCloud account.

On the iPhone, the Notes app has two main screens—one that lists each of your note titles and serves as a menu for accessing them (shown in Figure 5.4), and a second for actually creating and viewing each note on a virtual yellow lined notepad (shown in Figure 5.5).

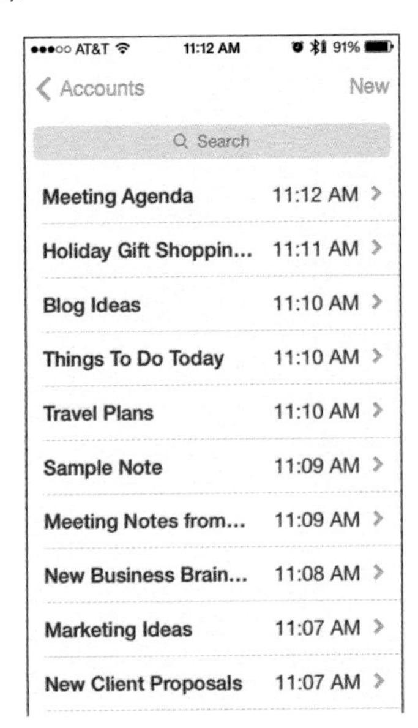

FIGURE 5.4

This Notes list screen displays the heading of each individual note stored on your iPhone. Tap on the listing to view a note.

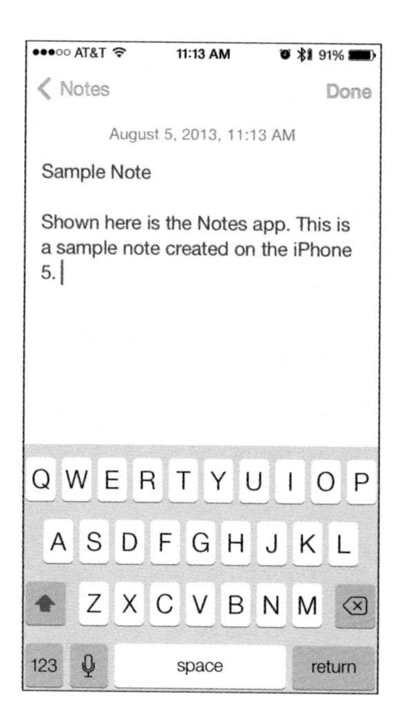

FIGURE 5.5

From the note editing screen on the iPhone, you can create, edit, or view individual notes.

On the iPad, if you hold the device horizontally, the listing of notes is displayed on the left side of the screen, while the right side of the screen displays the individual notes (shown in Figure 5.6).

To create a new note, tap on the New option (iPhone) or the Compose icon (iPad) displayed near the top-right corner of the screen. Begin typing your note using the virtual keyboard, or activate the Dictation function.

NOTE By default, the first line of text you enter into a new note becomes that note's title and is what is displayed on the Notes listing screen/column.

When you're finished typing, dictating, or editing a note on the iPad, you may exit out of the app or select a different note, and your note is saved. On the iPhone, when you're finished typing or viewing a note, tap on the Done key. You can also use the Trash or Share options displayed in the top-right corner of the iPad and bottom of the iPhone screens.

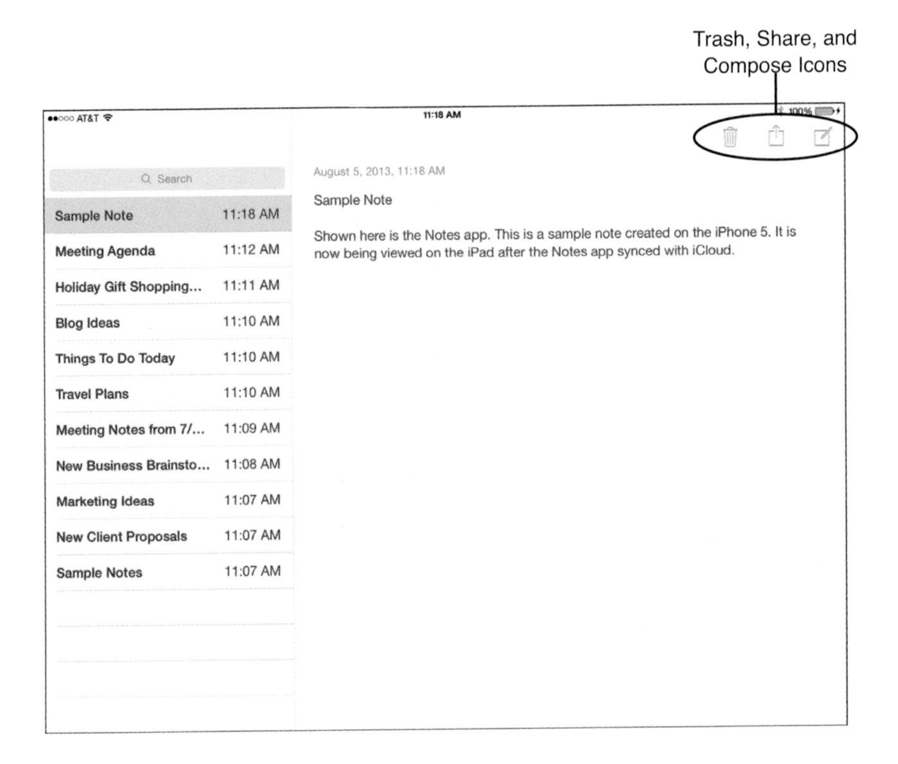

FIGURE 5.6

The iPad displays all aspects of the Notes app on a single screen.

Within a note, tap on the trash can icon to delete the note you're currently viewing.

The main Notes list enables you to see the titles for each note that's stored in the app. To delete a note from this screen, swipe your finger from right to left across the note's title. Confirm your decision by tapping on the Delete button. To open and view a note, tap on its listing.

> **! CAUTION** If you have Notes set up to sync with iCloud and your other iOS mobile devices and/or Mac(s), as soon as you delete or change a note, those changes are reflected almost immediately on iCloud and on your other computers and/or iOS mobile devices that are linked to the same account.

Tap on the Share icon to send the note to one or more recipients via email or the Messages app. You can also print or copy a note by tapping on the appropriate option displayed in the Share menu. When you use the copy command, the note's content gets saved in your iPhone or iPad's virtual clipboard so you can then paste the contents of the note into another app.

TIP The Notes app works with the Select, Select All, Copy, Cut, and Paste features of iOS 7. Thus, you can select and copy text from one note and then paste it into another note or into another app altogether.

As you're creating or viewing a note, press and hold your finger on any word to make the Select All, Copy, Cut, and/or Paste menu options appear. Once you select a word, you'll also see a Define and Replace option displayed (shown in Figure 5.7).

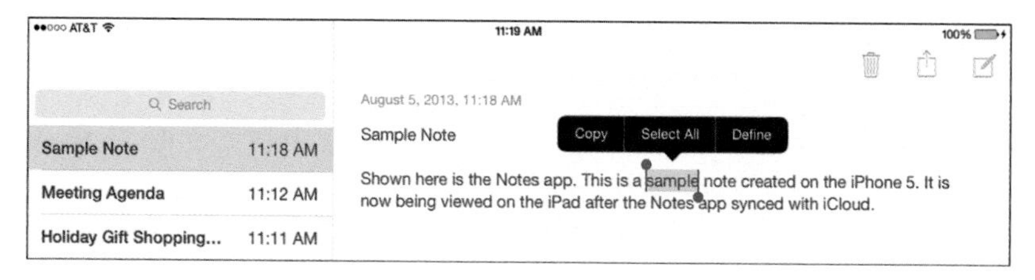

FIGURE 5.7

As you're typing text into the Notes app, hold your finger on a word and tap on the Define option to view a definition (and the correct spelling) of that word.

Tap on Define to look up the definition of the selected work. A pop-up window displaying the definition appears. When you use this feature for the first time, you're promoted to download the Dictionary that can accompany the Notes app. This process takes just 5 to 10 seconds and needs to be done only once.

TIP Syncing notes with iCloud works exactly the same as syncing Contacts, Calendars, or Reminders app-specific data; however, when iCloud is set up on your iOS device, you must turn on the iCloud syncing function that's specific to the Notes app from the iCloud menu screen within Settings.

The Notes app's functionality is relatively basic and straightforward. However, this app comes in particularly handy to jot down ideas or memos without having to worry about formatting text (as you would when using a word processing app). To help keep you organized, the time and date you create each note is automatically saved with the note itself.

QUICK TIPS FOR NOTES

- The Notes app enables you to set up separate accounts, within which you can store multiple notes. On the iPhone, to create or manage accounts, from the main Notes screen, tap on the Accounts option. To view all notes stored in all accounts, tap on the All Notes option. On the iPad, tap on the Accounts option displayed near the top-left corner of the screen to create or manage accounts, which are then listed on the left side of the screen.
- Anytime you include a phone number in a note, it becomes an active link. Tap on it to initiate a call (iPhone) or text message (iPhone or iPad) to that number or to add a contact to the Contacts app. Likewise, when an address is listed, tap on its link to launch the Maps app and view that address on a detailed map. Or when a website URL is included in a note, tap on it to launch Safari and visit that website.
- If there are sentences or phrases that you use often within your notes, set up keyboard shortcuts for them to reduce the amount of typing that's necessary. To do this, launch Settings, tap on General, select the Keyboard option, and then tap on Shortcuts.
- When using the Dictation function with the Notes app, you can speak for up to 30 seconds at a time, allow the iPhone or iPad to translate what you've said into text and insert that text into your note, and then repeat the process as needed. Edit your text using the virtual keyboard.
- To save time entering text into the Notes app, don't forget you can also use Siri. Regardless of what you're doing on the iPhone or iPad, simply activate Siri and begin by saying the word "Note" or "Create Note." For example, say, "Create note: Gather old clothing to donate on Saturday."
- It's possible to sync your Notes with Outlook running on a PC. To do this, be sure to download the iCloud Control Panel software from Apple's website and then turn on the syncing feature associated with the Notes app.

IN THIS CHAPTER

- Use the Maps app to obtain turn-by-turn directions between two locations
- Find and display any address, landmark, point-of-interest, or business on a map
- Discover how the Maps app works in conjunction with other iOS apps and features

6

NAVIGATING WITH THE MAPS APP

In the process of redesigning the Maps app so that it offers extremely detailed maps, accurate driving directions, the capability to quickly look up business and landmark addresses, as well as full integration with other apps and iOS 7 features, Apple has created and implemented a proprietary vector-based mapping system that works nicely on the iPhone or iPad's screen.

The Maps app requires Internet access to function. Although the app works with a Wi-Fi connection, if you plan to use the app's turn-by-turn directions feature, you must use a cellular data connection (which will use up some of your monthly wireless data allocation with each use) because you'll be in motion and will quickly leave the wireless signal radius of any Wi-Fi hotspot. Using the Maps feature with Siri requires even more wireless data usage.

TIP To get the most use out of the Maps app, the main Location Services feature in your iPhone or iPad (as well as Location Services for the Maps app) must be turned on. To do this, launch Settings, tap on the Privacy option, and then tap on Location Services. From the Location Services menu screen, turn on the virtual switch displayed near the top of the screen (associated with Location Services), and then scroll down and make sure the virtual switch associated with the Maps app is also turned on.

GET THE MOST FROM USING THE MAPS APP'S FEATURES

Compared to prior versions of the Maps app, the iOS 7 edition offers a new look and a few new features. Apple has also fine-tuned features introduced with iOS 6, such as the capability to obtain detailed turn-by-turn spoken and displayed directions, interactive 3D map views, and a visually stunning Flyover map view (for many cities and metropolitan areas).

CAUTION Just as when using any GPS device, do not rely 100 percent on the turn-by-turn directions you're given. Pay attention as you're driving and use common sense. If the Maps app tells you to drive down a one-way street or drive along a closed road, for example, ignore those directions and seek out an alternative route. Don't become one of those people who literally drives into a lake or over a cliff because their GPS told them to. Yes, this does happen.

In addition, real-time, color-coded traffic conditions showing traffic jams and construction can be graphically overlaid onto maps, and when you look up a business, restaurant, point-of-interest, or landmark, the Maps app seamlessly integrates with Yelp! to display detailed information about specific locations.

Keep in mind that the Yelp! information screens for each location are interactive, so if you're using an iPhone and tap on a phone number, you can initiate a call to that business or restaurant. Likewise, if you tap on a website URL, Safari launches and the website automatically loads and displays.

TIP To enhance the capabilities of the Yelp! integration, download and install the optional (and free) Yelp! app from the App Store. Without the Yelp! app, when appropriate, the Maps app will transfer you to the Yelp! website.

NOTE Yelp! is a vast online database that contains more than 30 million reviews related to local businesses, stores, restaurants, hotels, tourist attractions, and points of interest. Reviews are created by everyday people, who share their experiences, thoughts, and photos. However, beyond user-provided reviews, Yelp! also offers details about many businesses and restaurants.

Although Maps offers a lot of functionality packed into a standalone app, it's also designed to work with many other apps. For example, as you're viewing an entry in the Contacts app, when you tap on an address, the Maps app launches and displays that address on a map. You can then quickly obtain detailed directions to that location from your current location or from any address you select.

Plus, you can utilize many features built in to the Maps app using voice commands and requests thanks to Siri. For example, regardless of what you're doing on the iPhone or iPad, it's possible to activate Siri and say, "How do I get home from here?" or "Where is the closest gas station?" and then have the Maps app provide you with the directions and map you need.

TIP Anytime you're viewing a map in the Maps app, tap on the My Location icon (which looks like a northeast-pointing arrow) displayed near the bottom-left corner of the screen to pinpoint and display your exact location on the map. Your location is displayed using a pulsating blue dot (shown in Figure 6.1). If for some reason the Maps app loses its Internet signal temporarily, tap on this My Location icon again to reestablish your location.

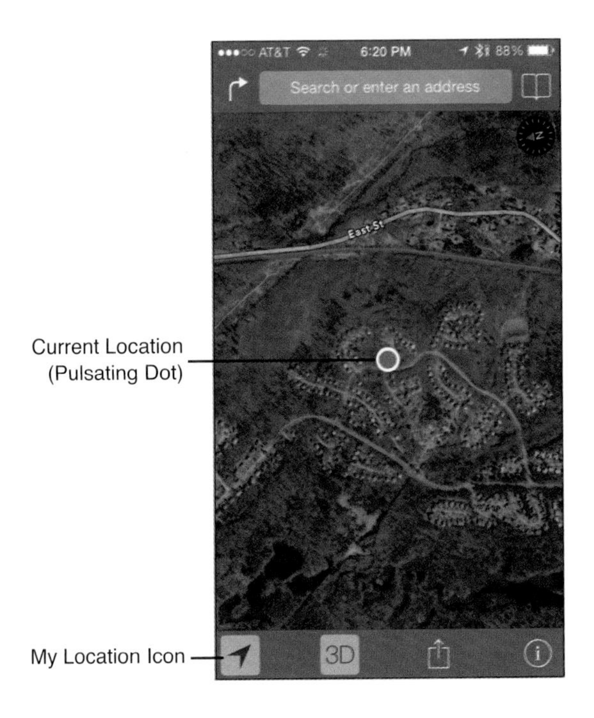

FIGURE 6.1

Tap on the My Location icon (near the lower-left corner of the screen) to pinpoint and display your exact location on a map using a pulsating blue dot.

OVERVIEW OF THE MAPS APP'S SCREEN

On the iPhone, the main screen of the iOS 7 edition of the Maps app now displays a tiny compass near the upper-right corner (below the Bookmarks icon). On both the iPhone and iPad, displayed near the top-left corner of the screen is the Directions icon. Tap on it to enter a Start and End location, and then obtain detailed driving, walking, or public transportation directions between those two points. On the iPhone, this icon looks like a right-pointing arrow. On the iPad, look for the button that says Directions.

NOTE Depending on the two points you enter, walking directions might not be applicable or viable. Currently, if you request public transportation directions between two addresses, you'll be redirected to the App Store to seek out an alternative app.

If you're relying on public transportation to get around a popular city, such as Manhattan, Boston, London, or Paris, download an app specifically designed for that public transportation system. To find one, use the Search option in the App Store. For example, enter the search phrase "London Tube Map" to find a variety of interactive apps to help you navigate your way around London's subway/train system.

Use the Search field located at the top-center of the Maps screen to find and map out any address. You can enter a complete address (house/building number, street, city, state) or provide less specific information, such as just a city, state, or country. Enter United States to see a map of the entire country. Enter California to view a map of the state. You also have the option to enter Los Angeles, California, to view a more detailed map of the city, or you can enter a specific street address located within Los Angeles to view it on a detailed map that shows specific streets (and street names).

This Search field is also used to find businesses, restaurants, points of interest, landmarks, and tourist destinations. When the Maps app finds the location you're looking for, you can zoom in or zoom out manually on that map to see more or less detail. Plus, you can change the Map view and switch between the Standard, Hybrid, Satellite, 3D, and/or Flyover view (each of which will be explained shortly).

TIP In the Search field, enter the name of any contact in the Contacts app to find and display an address for that contact. The app searches the contents of your iOS device (including the Contacts app), followed by a web-based search, if applicable.

Anytime a specific location is specified on the map, such as results of a search, those results are displayed using a virtual red push-pin. Tap on a push-pin to view more details about that location and to access a separate Location screen (iPhone) or window (iPad).

Displayed near the bottom-left corner of the main Maps screen is the My Location icon (it looks like a northeast-pointing arrow). At anytime a map is displayed, tap on this icon to locate and display (or update) your current location on the map. This feature is useful if you look up another destination and then want to quickly see where you're located in comparison to that other location. However, when you're using the Maps app for turn-by-turn directions, your iPhone/iPad keeps track of your location in real time and displays this on the map as you're in motion.

As you're viewing a Standard, Hybrid, or Satellite map, tap on the 3D button that's displayed near the bottom-left corner of the screen to switch to a 3D view. Many people find the 3D view more visually interesting, although it doesn't reveal any new onscreen information that could not be seen using the Maps app's Standard, Hybrid, or Satellite views.

TIP When you're viewing a map of a popular city or metropolitan area, the 3D button is automatically replaced by the Flyover icon. The Flyover feature offers a true, three-dimensional-looking map of the city from the perspective of an airplane cockpit. From this view, use your finger to move around on the screen and see a bird's-eye view of the city, which is visually impressive and highly detailed.

To the right of the 3D button along the bottom of the main Maps screen is a Share button. Tap on this icon to share map details you're currently viewing with others via the Messages, Mail, Twitter, or Facebook app. The Share menu of the Maps app is shown in Figure 6.2.

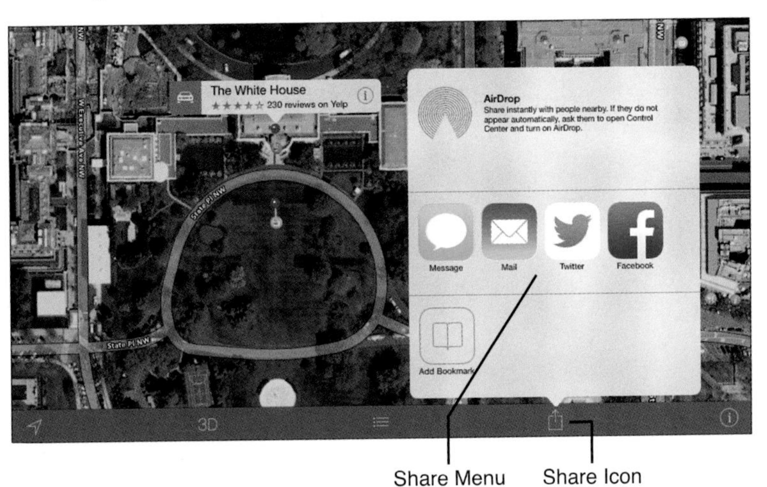

FIGURE 6.2

The Share menu in the Maps app enables you to quickly share details about a location with others, plus create a bookmark for a specific location for later reference.

TIP The newly redesigned Share menu includes an Add Bookmark button. Tap on this to save the currently viewed location as a Maps bookmark for later reference.

From the main Maps screen, look to the upper-right corner to find the Bookmarks option. Just like Safari, the Maps app enables you to store bookmarks for specific locations. When you tap on the Bookmarks option, three command tabs are displayed at the bottom of the screen, labeled Bookmarks, Recents, and Contacts.

Tapping on the Bookmarks tab reveals a list of previously saved bookmarked locations. Tap on the Edit button to edit, delete, or reorder this list, or swipe your finger from right to left across a Bookmark listing to delete it.

Tap on the Recents tab to view a list of recently searched or viewed locations. To clear this list, tap on the Clear button displayed near the top-left corner of the screen.

When you tap on the Contacts tab, the All Contacts listing will be displayed. This shows a comprehensive list of all entries stored in your Contacts database. Whether you're looking at the Bookmarks, Recents, or All Contacts list, tap on one of the listings to view that location on a map.

THE MAPS APP'S INFO SCREEN

The Info icon is displayed near the bottom-right corner of the main Maps screen. When you tap on this circular "i" icon, a new window pops up that enables you to quickly switch between the Standard, Hybrid, or Satellite map view. Simply tap on one of the labeled tabs that are displayed near the top of this window (shown in Figure 6.3).

From the Info window, you can also drop a virtual pin on the map at your current location, wirelessly print a map (if you have an AirPrint-compatible printer linked to your iOS device), and show or hide color-coded traffic details on the map.

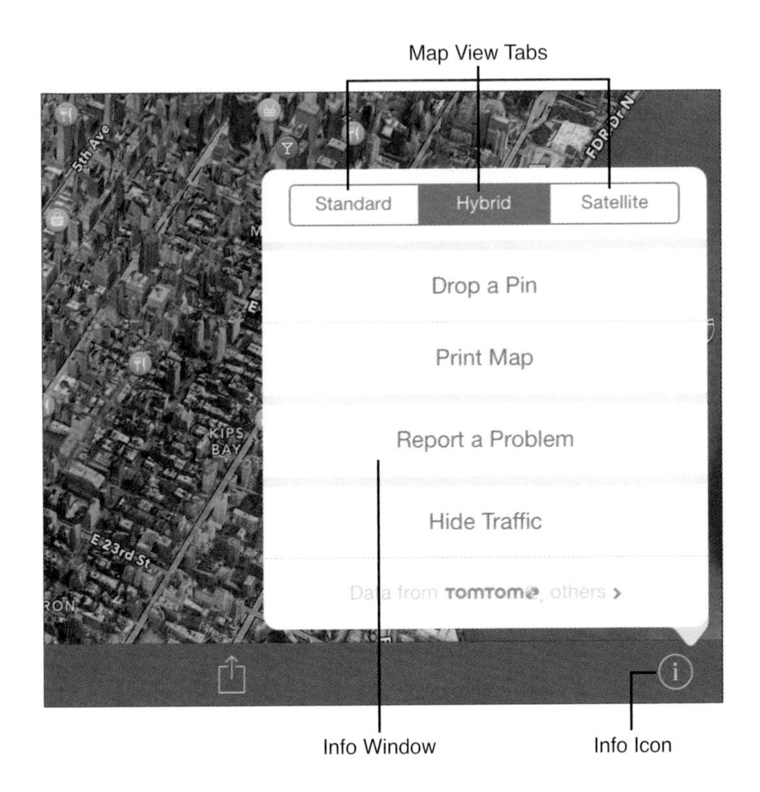

FIGURE 6.3

Tap on the Info icon to reveal this newly designed Info window.

THE DROP A PIN COMMAND

When you tap on the Drop A Pin option, the full Maps screen returns. Tap anywhere on that map to place a virtual push-pin. The new push-pin is displayed in purple instead of red. Once a push-pin is placed, it's possible to view detailed information about that particular location, including its exact address. You can then tap on the displayed Info icon to view a location menu that offers a handful of menu options, including Directions To Here, Directions From Here, Transit Directions, Create New Contact, Add To Existing Contact, Remove Pin, Add Bookmark, or Report a Problem.

THE PRINT MAP COMMAND

If you have a wireless printer linked to your iPhone or iPad via AirPrint, tap on the Print button to create a printout of whatever is displayed on the screen, whether it's a detailed map, a text-based list of turn-by-turn directions to a destination, or a listing of search results (such as restaurants or gas stations in a particular area).

When you tap on the Print button, the Print options screen will be displayed. Select an AirPrint-compatible printer and the number of copies you want printed, then tap on the Print button. If you have a color printer linked to your iPhone or iPad, you can print maps (or color-coded directions) in full color.

THE SHOW/HIDE TRAFFIC OPTION

Regardless of which map view you're looking at, you can have color-coded real-time traffic information superimposed on the map. This feature can help you avoid traffic jams and construction and enables you to seek an alternative route before you get stuck in the traffic.

NOTE Mild traffic is showcased using yellow, while heavy traffic is depicted in red. When construction is being done on a roadway, separate construction icons (in yellow or red) are displayed on the map.

TIP The Show Traffic feature works much better when you're viewing a zoomed-in version of a map that shows a lot of street-level detail. Figure 6.4 shows heavy traffic conditions (a dashed red line) along N. Highland Ave. in Hollywood, California, near the famous TCL (Mann's) Chinese Theatre.

FIGURE 6.4

A red line along a roadway indicates heavy traffic when you have the Show Traffic feature turned on in the Maps app.

THE STANDARD, HYBRID, AND SATELLITE TABS

Displayed along the top of the Maps Info window are the three map view command tabs: Standard, Hybrid, and Satellite. The Standard map view (shown in Figure 6.5) displays a traditional-looking, multicolored map on the screen. Street names and other important information are labeled and displayed on the map.

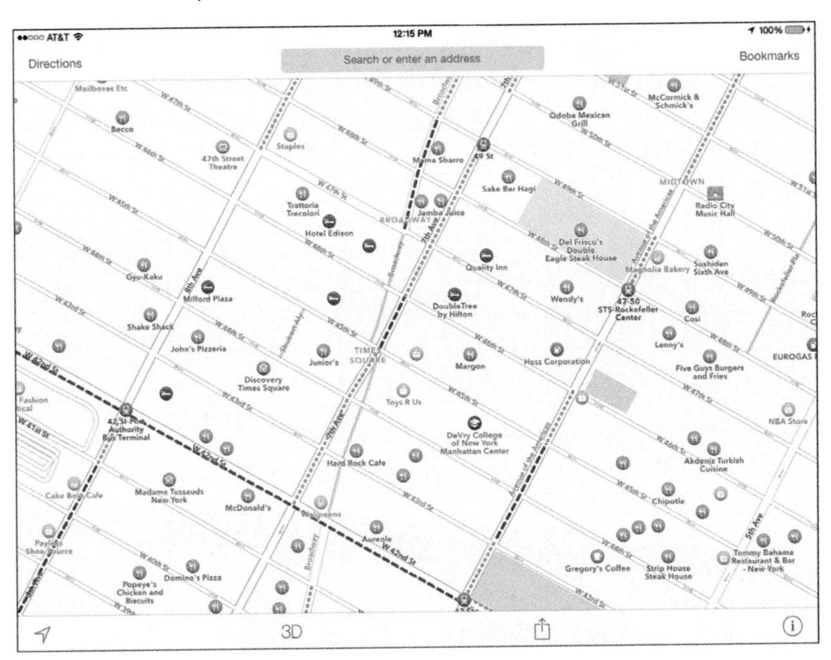

FIGURE 6.5

The Standard map view shows a traditional, multicolored map with street names and other points of interest listed on it.

The Satellite view uses high-resolution and extremely detailed satellite imagery to show maps from an overhead view, while the Hybrid map view (refer to Figure 6.4) showcases the same satellite imagery but overlays and displays street names and other important information, similar to the information you'd see using the Standard view.

TIP Anytime you're viewing a map, you can switch between map views. Then from the main Maps screen, tap on the My Location icon to display your exact location on the map, and/or tap on the 3D icon to add a three-dimensional element to the map. (If a Flyover view is available, the Flyover icon is displayed instead of the 3D icon.)

OBTAIN TURN-BY-TURN DIRECTIONS BETWEEN TWO LOCATIONS

The turn-by-turn directions feature of the Maps app is not only easy to use, it's also extremely useful. Begin using this feature from the main Maps app screen. Tap on the Directions icon near the top-left corner of the screen.

The Start and End fields, as well as the reverse directions, driving, walking, and public transportation icons, are displayed (see Figure 6.6). In the Start field, the default option is your current location. However, to change this, tap on the field and enter any starting address. Then tap on the End field and enter any ending address.

TIP Displayed below the Start and End field are recent locations you've utilized within the Maps app. Scroll up or down this list using your finger, or tap on any entry to use it as your Start or End location.

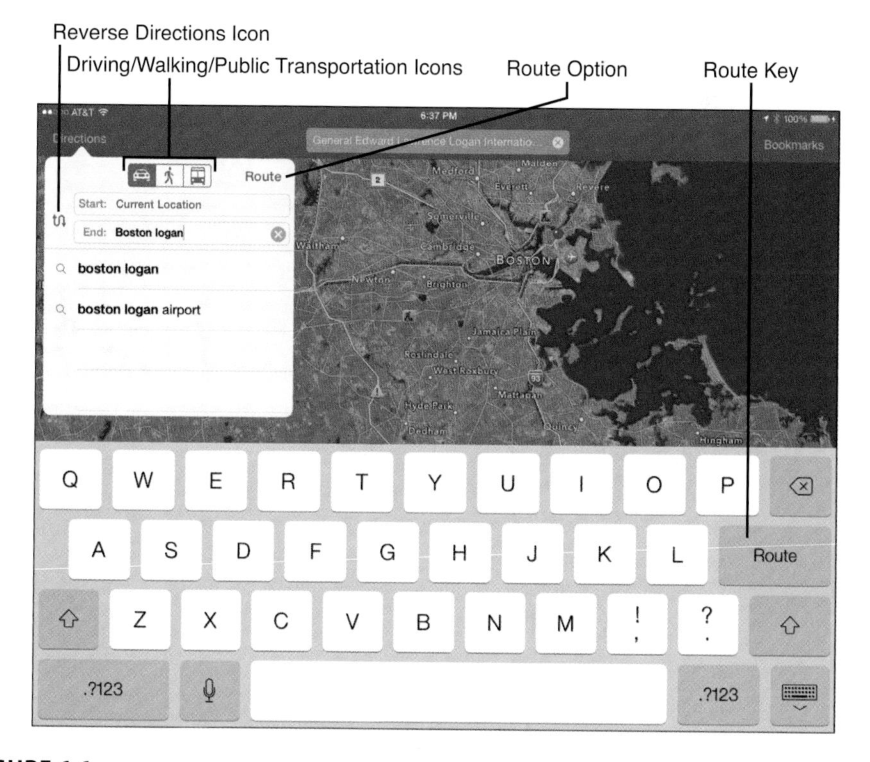

FIGURE 6.6

Fill in the Start and End fields to obtain detailed, turn-by-turn directions between any two locations that you choose.

> **TIP** In the Start and End field, you can enter a contact entry's name, a full address, a city and state, just a state, or just a country. You can use two-letter state abbreviations, and you don't have to worry about using upper- and lower-case letters. For example, you can type "New York, NY," "new york, ny," or "New York, New York" and get the same result. This goes for contacts or business names as well.

When the Start and End fields have been filled in, tap on the car-shaped icon near the top-center of the screen to access detailed driving directions. Or, tap on the person-shaped icon to obtain walking directions between those two locations.

If public transportation is available, tap on the bus-shaped icon. When you seek public transportation guidance, the Maps app refers to you to the App Store and displays several different Routing Map options compatible with public transportation systems in that region, if available.

Next, tap in the Route option near the upper-right corner of the screen. There's also a Route button on the virtual keyboard. A route overview map (shown in Figure 6.7) is displayed. The green push-pin represents your starting location, and the red-push pin represents your ending location. If you select Driving directions, the Maps app displays between one and three possible routes between the Start and End locations.

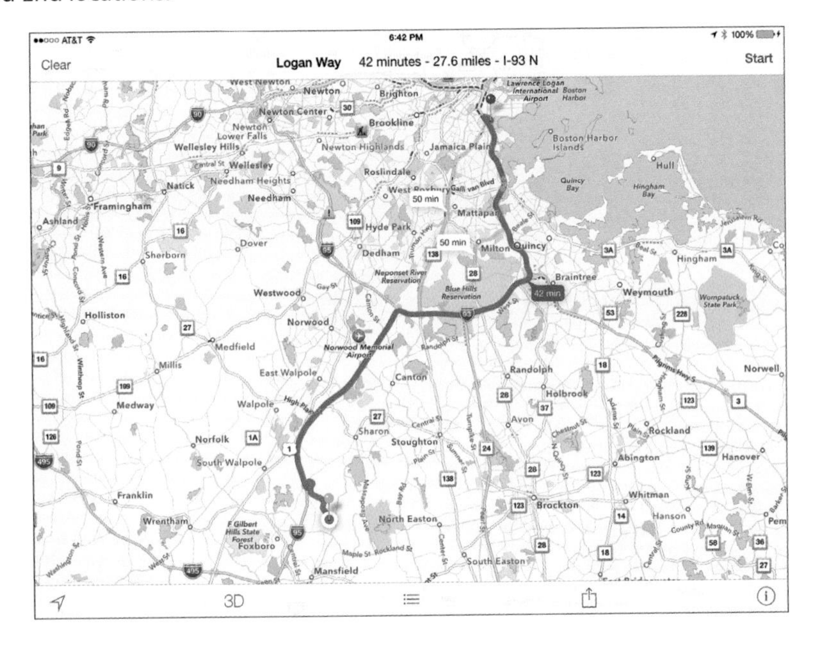

FIGURE 6.7

A sample route overview map shows your Start and End location on one map, plus up to three possible driving routes to get there.

The primary route (Route 1) will be outlined on the route overview map with a dark blue line. If you see a 3 Routes flag along your main route, tap on it to reveal up to two alternative routes. Then, if available, one or two alternative routes will be outlined with light blue lines and be labeled Route 2 and Route 3.

TIP Turn on the Show Traffic option to display current traffic conditions along the three routes, and then choose the one with the least congestion or construction. Tap on the Route 1, Route 2, or Route 3 flag to select your route. (Route 1 is the default selection.)

Tap on the Start button displayed near the upper-right corner of the screen to begin the real-time, turn-by-turn directions. Just like when using a standalone GPS device, a voice guides you through each turn, while also displaying related information on the main map screen (shown in Figure 6.8).

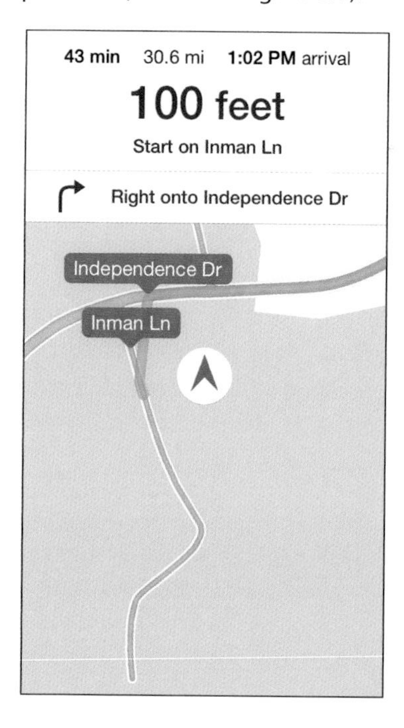

FIGURE 6.8

The Maps app shows detailed turn-by-turn directions on the map screen and speaks to you as you're driving.

While the turn-by-turn directions are being displayed, the Standard map view is used. Your ETA, as well as how much time is left in your trip and the distance from your destination are displayed near the top-center of the screen. At anytime, tap the Overview option to return to the route overview map, or tap the End option to exit out of the turn-by-turn directions feature and return to the main Maps screen.

Follow the voice and onscreen prompts until you reach your destination. If you press the Home button, you can return to the Home screen and launch another app while the Maps feature is still running, and then return to the turn-by-turn directions by tapping on the blue bar that says Touch To Return To Navigation. It's displayed near the top-right corner of the screen. This also works when you launch another app via the multitasking bar.

TIP To view text-based directions to your destination, enter a Start and End location using the Directions feature of the Maps app, but before tapping Start to obtain the directions, tap on the Listing icon displayed at the bottom-center of the screen.

Use your finger to scroll up or down on this list, or tap on one of the individual directions to jump to the map that shows that step.

LOOK UP CONTACT ENTRIES, BUSINESSES, RESTAURANTS, LANDMARKS, AND POINTS OF INTEREST

One of the other primary uses of the Maps app is to find and display addresses, contacts, businesses, points of interest, or landmarks on a map screen. To do this, from the main Maps screen, type what you're looking for into the Search field. In Figure 6.9, Gillette Stadium was entered into the search field.

TIP If you're looking for businesses or services in your immediate area, tap on the My Location icon first, so the iPhone or iPad pinpoints your location, and then enter what you're searching for. No city or state needs to be entered. If you don't tap on the My Location icon first, you must enter what you're looking for, followed by the city, a comma, and the state, to find local search results. Otherwise, the Maps app defaults to the last search location.

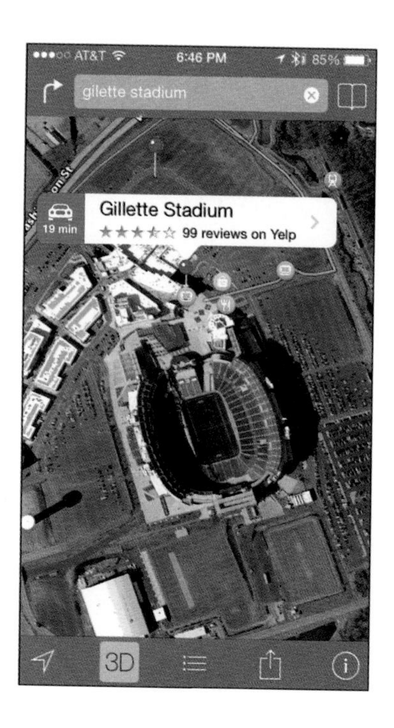

FIGURE 6.9

Gillette Stadium (home of the New England Patriots) in Foxboro, MA, is shown here using the hybrid and 3D map view on an iPhone 5.

USE THE INTERACTIVE LOCATION SCREENS TO FIND MORE INFORMATION

Once search results are displayed on the map in the form of virtual push-pins, tap on any push-pin to view an information banner for a location on a map. In Figure 6.10, a search for Apple Store locations in Los Angeles was performed and displayed on the map.

Tap on one push-pin, and then on tap the left side of the information banner to obtain "quick" turn-by-turn directions from your current location. Or, tap on the Info icon on the right side of the listing to view an interactive Location screen.

FIGURE 6.10

The results of a search for Apple Stores in the Los Angeles area appear as red virtual push-pins on this hybrid view map.

A separate Location screen (shown in Figure 6.11) displays details about that search result using details from the Maps app, the Internet, and from Yelp!. Tap on the Info tab on the Location screen to view the phone number, address, website URL, and other information for that search result. The information displayed depends on whether it's a business, restaurant, point of interest, or tourist attraction.

TIP When looking at multiple search results on a map (refer to Figure 6.10), tap on the Listing icon to view a text-based interactive listing of the search results.

As you scroll down on the Location screen, you'll see a Directions To Here and Directions From Here option (as well as a Transit Directions option). Tap on any of these to obtain directions to or from your current location to the address listed on the screen.

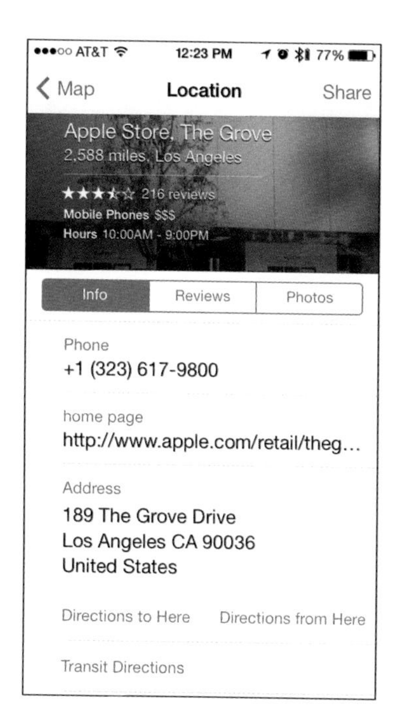

FIGURE 6.11

A detailed Location screen combines location information with details about that location obtained from Yelp!. Information about the Apple Store at The Grove in Los Angeles is shown here.

Tap on the More Info On Yelp! option to launch the Yelp! app or visit the Yelp! website to view more detailed information about that location.

You'll also discover Create New Contact, Add To Existing Contact, Add Bookmark, and Report A Problem options by scrolling down in the Location window, as long as you have the Info tab at the top of the window highlighted.

In the Location window (refer to Figure 6.11), tap on the Reviews tab to view Yelp!-related, star-based ratings and text-based reviews from other Yelp! users, or tap on the Photos tab to view photos of that location, including photos uploaded by other Yelp! users. You can also contribute your own star-based rating, review, or photos for a location.

TIP If you look up information about a restaurant, the Location screen includes Yelp!-related information, including the type of food served, the menu price range (using dollar sign symbols), the hours of operation, and potentially a website link that enables you to view the restaurant's menu. You can also determine whether the restaurant delivers or accepts reservations.

If reservations are accepted, use the optional Open Table app to make reservations online. Activate Siri and say, "Make a reservation for [insert number of people] for [insert day and time]," or initiate a call from an iPhone to the restaurant by tapping on the phone number field.

THE MAPS APP'S FLYOVER VIEW

While the 3D feature makes looking at Standard, Hybrid, and Satellite maps more interesting, the Flyover map view that's available for many major cities is just plain cool, although it doesn't really serve a navigation purpose. This feature, however, can be used to help you get acquainted with the layout of a city and enable you to take a virtual tour of its skyline from your iPhone or iPad.

When it's available, the 3D icon that's normally displayed near the lower-left corner of the Maps screen is replaced with the Flyover icon (which looks like a building). Tap on it to switch to a stunning Flyover map view (shown in Figure 6.12).

FIGURE 6.12

The Flyover view of New York City shown on the iPhone.

TIP When using the 3D or Flyover view, you can zoom in or out on the map, plus change the perspective by placing two fingers on the screen and moving them up or down together. You can also use just one finger to move up, down, left, or right to view a different area of the map and scroll around.

MAPS QUICK TIPS

- To customize a handful of settings related to the Maps app, launch Settings and tap on the Maps option. From the Maps menu screen, it's possible to adjust the navigation voice volume, show distances in miles or kilometers, automatically have the iPhone/iPad translate map labels into English, and adjust whether you prefer driving or walking directions as your default selection.
- As you're viewing a map, it's almost always possible to zoom in or out using either a reverse-pinch or pinch figure gesture, or a double-tap on the area of the map you want to zoom in or out of.
- After tapping the Directions option to obtain directions between two addresses, displayed to the immediate left of the Start and End is a Reverse icon. Tap it to switch the addresses you have in the Start and End fields to obtain reverse directions.
- As the Maps app is giving you real-time turn-by-turn directions, tap on the Overview option displayed near the top-right corner of the screen to switch back to the route overview map. It's then possible to tap on the Listing icon to see a text-based turn-by-turn directions listing. Tap the Resume option to exit out of this view.
- When using your iPhone or iPad and the Maps app for real-time, turn-by-turn directions, the iOS device is in use and accessing the Internet extensively. This drains the device's battery faster. If you use this feature from your car often, consider investing in a car charger that plugs into your car's 12-volt jack. This way, your iPhone/iPad's battery remains charged (and can recharge) while it's being used.
- Using the Maps app for turn-by-turn directions via a cellular data Internet connection requires a significant amount of wireless data usage. Using this feature can quickly deplete your monthly wireless data allocation unless you're subscribed to an unlimited wireless service plan. Also, if you're using international roaming to access the Internet from abroad, using Maps with a cellular data connection can get very expensive.

- When viewing a map, a compass often appears near the upper-right corner of the screen. When you tap on the My Location icon, the Map is displayed using a north-facing orientation. If you double-tap on the My Location icon, the map orientates itself in the direction you're traveling.
- Use Siri to quickly find addresses in your Contacts database or to locate a business or point of interest, and then plug in that information to the Maps app without any manual data entry required.
- As you're looking at the Location screen for a landmark or airport, scroll down and look for the Popular Apps Nearby heading. This lists optional apps that relate to that location. For example, if you select an airport, you can find app icons for airlines and travel apps. Tap on any app icon to launch the App Store and display details about that app.

IN THIS CHAPTER

- Learn to use Facebook and Twitter functionality that's integrated into iOS 7
- Discover how to use the official Facebook and Twitter app
- Discover other online social networking apps for services like YouTube, LinkedIn, Instagram, and Vine

7

MAKE THE MOST OF ONLINE SOCIAL NETWORKING APPS

One of the reasons why online social networking services have become so incredibly popular around the world, allowing them to change the way people stay in touch and communicate with each other, is because access to these services is incredibly easy using a smartphone or tablet, as well as any computer with Internet access.

Available for free from the App Store are official apps from services such as Facebook, Twitter, Instagram, YouTube, Vine, Pinterest, LinkedIn, and countless others that enable you to fully manage your online account, stay in touch with your online friends, and share photos, videos, or other content while you're on the go.

Meanwhile, iOS 7 has Facebook, Twitter, Flickr, and Vimeo integration built in to several of the preinstalled apps. This means you can quickly create and publish app-specific content without actually launching the Facebook, Twitter, Flickr, or Vimeo app.

TIP Almost any iPhone or iPad app that has a Share button now enables you to share app-specific information and publish it on Facebook and/or Twitter from within the app you're using.

To begin using any of the popular online social networking services from your iPhone or iPad, you first must set up a free account with that service. This can be done either by visiting the service's main website (such as www.facebook.com or www.twitter.com) on your primary computer or by clicking on the new account setup-related option in the official iOS mobile app for that service. Figure 7.1 shows the opening screen for the official Facebook app. From here, either sign in using your existing e-mail and password related to your Facebook account, or tap on the Sign Up For Facebook button displayed near the bottom-center of the screen.

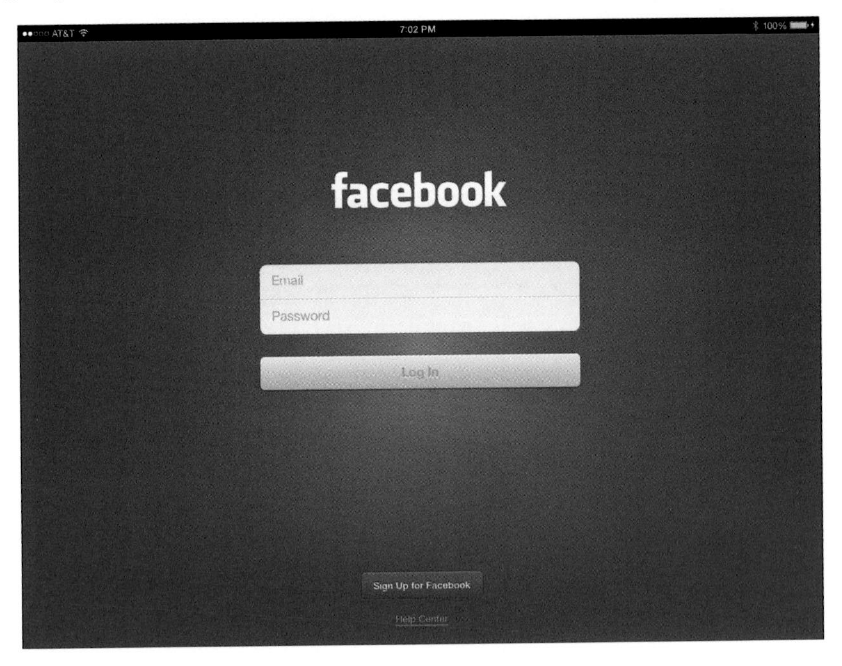

FIGURE 7.1

The opening screen of the Facebook app enables you to set up a new account by tapping on the Sign Up For Facebook button.

After you've set up an account, enter your username and password in the online social networking app you'll be using on your iPhone or iPad.

! CAUTION Many of the online social networking apps automatically tap in to the Location Services function of your iPhone or iPad and will publish your exact location anytime you create a new posting to that service (or upload a new photo or video). To prevent this and protect your privacy, do not grant permission for the online social networking app to access Location Service as you're first setting it up.

Anytime thereafter, it's possible to customize Location Services-related settings for many apps by launching Settings, tapping on the Privacy option, and then tap on the Location Service option. From the Locations Services menu, turn on or off the virtual switch associated with Facebook, Twitter, and other online social networking apps. To further customize these apps, return to the Privacy menu in Settings and tap on the Facebook and/or Twitter options (shown in Figure 7.2). Some services, such as Instagram, enable you to add your location to a posting, but only if you want to.

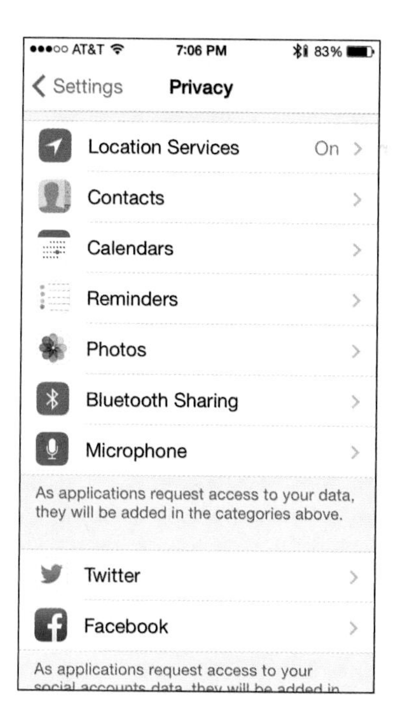

FIGURE 7.2

From the Privacy menu in Settings, you can determine whether Facebook and Twitter can automatically share your exact location whenever you publish content to that service.

FACEBOOK, TWITTER, FLICKR, AND VIMEO INTEGRATION IS BUILT IN TO iOS 7

If you already have a Facebook, Twitter, Flickr, or Vimeo account, you must set up the iOS 7 integration functionality for each of these services separately, plus download and install the official app for each of these services on which you're active.

Setting up account integration with iOS 7 (and many of the apps that come preinstalled on your iOS mobile device) must be done only once per account on each of your iOS mobile devices.

> **NOTE** This integration allows options for the compatible online social networking services to be displayed as part of the Share menu of many apps, including Photos.
>
> If you don't turn on integration with a service, these options will not be accessible from the Share menu of the apps you use.

To set up this integration for each service, follow these steps:

1. Launch Settings from the Home screen.
2. Scroll down to the Twitter, Facebook, Flickr, or Vimeo option that's displayed as part of the main Settings menu. Tap on the app you want to configure.
3. Tap on the Username and Password option and enter the appropriate information (shown in Figure 7.3). The username may be the email address you used to set up the account.
4. Tap on the Sign In option.
5. If you haven't already done so, tap on the Install button displayed next to the app logo for that service to download and install the official app, which gives you full access to your account. Once the app is downloaded, you must sign in to the service from the app, and once again supply your account username and password (this time, within the app).
6. When the app is installed, if applicable, tap on the Settings option below the app icon on the service-specific menu within Settings to customize specific features of the online social networking app.

> **NOTE** Many of the official apps for the various online social networking services have their own Settings or Set Up menu within the app itself. Once the app is installed on your mobile device, access these app-specific menus and adjust the various Privacy options.

FIGURE 7.3

Add your existing Facebook account information to the Facebook menu within Settings, and then tap Sign In to log in to your account. This enables iOS 7 and many apps to include a Share via Facebook option as part of the app's Share menu.

7. Near the bottom of the service-specific menu within Settings, under the heading Allow These Apps To Use Your Account, turn on or off the virtual switches associated with specific apps. Your Calendar and Contacts apps, for example, can synch with your Facebook account if you allow them.
8. When applicable, tap on the Update Contacts button that's also displayed on the service-specific menu within Settings. This enables your iPhone or iPad to access your online account and compare your online friends with the entries you already have within the Contacts app. When appropriate, the Contacts app pulls additional information from services such as Facebook and adds details to each Contacts entry if that person is also an online friend. For example, when you do this for the Facebook app, Contacts adds Profile pictures, birthdays and other information listed on the Facebook profile to your Contacts entry.

TIP If you manage multiple Twitter accounts, repeat the previous listed steps for each account after selecting the Twitter option from the main Settings menu. Later, you can select from which account you publish new content to as you use the Tweet command from within the Share menu of various apps.

From the Share menu of many apps (shown in Figure 7.4), you can now publish new content directly to your compatible online social networking account. However, if you want to fully manage your account and interact directly with your online friends, you must download and install the official app for each other service you're active on, whether it's YouTube, Instagram, Vine, Pinterest, or LinkedIn. Find these apps by performing a search in the App Store or looking in the Social Networking category.

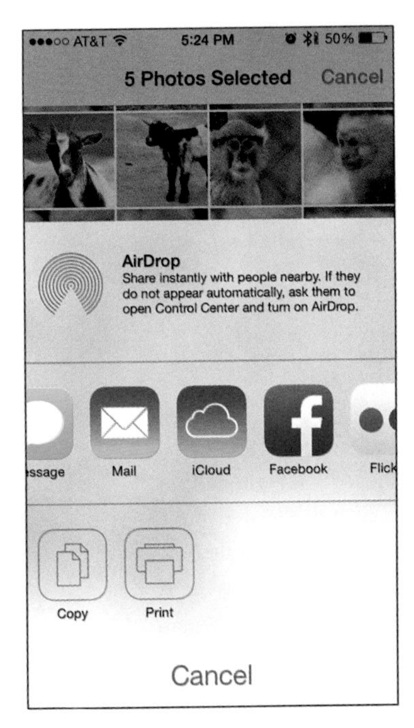

FIGURE 7.4

Once you turn on Facebook, Twitter, Flickr, or Vimeo integration, options for publishing content to these services appear in the Share menu of many compatible apps, including Photos.

MANAGE YOUR FACEBOOK ACCOUNT USING THE OFFICIAL FACEBOOK APP

The official Facebook app offers much of the same functionality for managing your Facebook account as using the web browser on your primary computer to access www.facebook.com. However, the Facebook app is custom-designed to fully utilize the iPhone or iPad's touchscreen and format content for the screen size of the iOS mobile device you're using.

TIP On the iPad, more content is displayed when you use the official Facebook app in landscape mode. When you do this, along the right margin Facebook's real-time Chat feature appears, as well as a listing of your Facebook friends who are currently online. On the iPhone, to access the Chat feature, tap the Chat icon displayed near the top-right corner of the screen.

Displayed along the top of the official Facebook app screen on both the iPhone and iPad is the Menu icon (near the upper-left corner), as well as the Friend Request, Messages, and Notifications icons. In Figure 7.5, the Menu icon has been tapped, so the main menu is displayed, along with the user's News Feed.

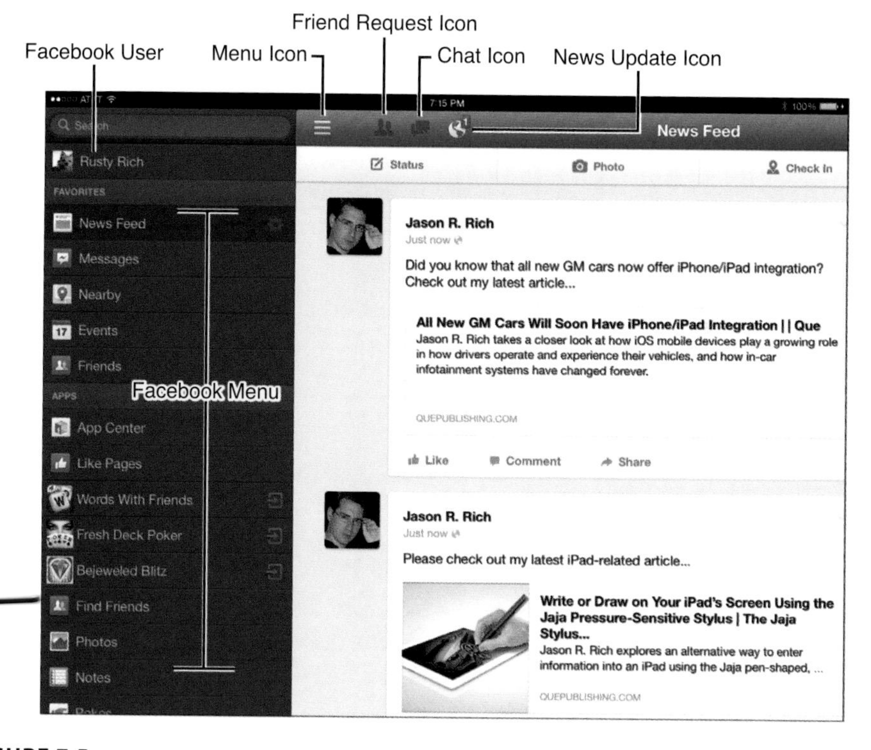

FIGURE 7.5

The official Facebook app shown here on the iPad.

Tap on the Menu icon to access the Facebook app's main menu (shown in Figure 7.6). From here, you can access your own Wall, read your personalized news feed (which includes the status updates from your online friends), see a listing of events you've been invited to, manage your friends, and see which of your friends are close to your current location (based on their last check-in).

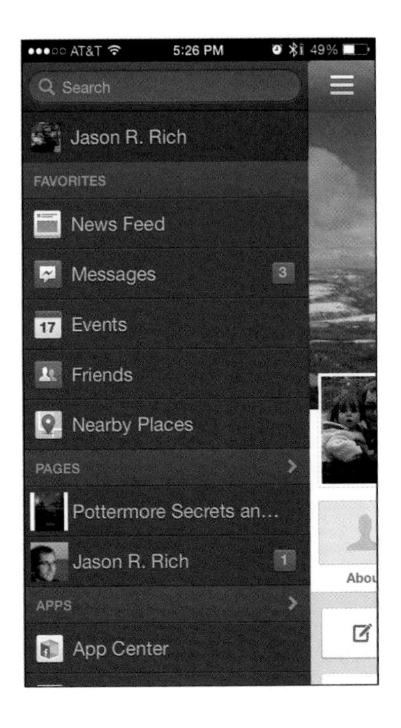

FIGURE 7.6

The official Facebook app's main menu, shown here on the iPhone 5, enables you to manage many aspects of your Facebook account.

From this main menu, a handful of other options for managing all aspects of your Facebook account are available. Meanwhile, near the top of the screen when viewing the News Feed screen, you'll see the Status, Photo, and Check-In options.

PARTICIPATE IN CHATS USING THE FACEBOOK APP

To participate in a real-time, text-based chat with one of your Facebook friends, tap on the Chat icon (iPhone), or tap on their name displayed on the right side of the screen (iPad). A green dot displayed to the left of their name indicates that person is currently online and able to chat. A cell phone icon to the right of their name indicates they're accessing Facebook from their mobile phone. If a time, such as 4m, for four minutes, appears with the phone icon, this tells you the last time they accessed Facebook from their mobile phone.

After tapping on a Facebook friend's name to initiate or return to a chat, a chat window is displayed (shown in Figure 7.7). Text bubbles down the left side indicate what your friend types, while the text bubbles down the right side show what you've typed.

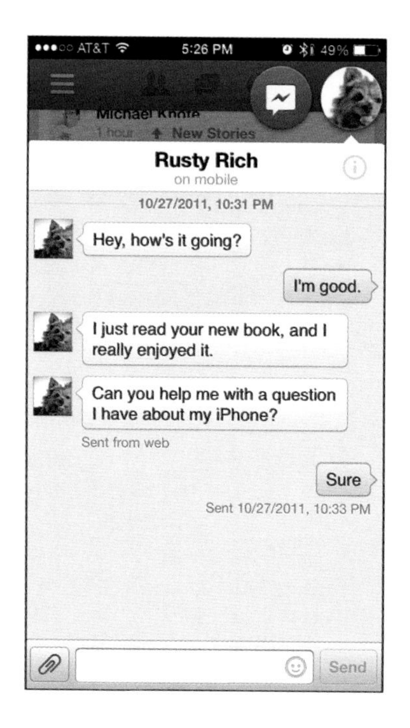

FIGURE 7.7

Participate in real-time text-based chats with your online Facebook friends via the Facebook app.

To enter a new message, tap on the empty field to make the virtual keyboard appear, and type your message. To attach a photo to the message, tap on the paperclip icon. If you want to include an emoticon in the form of a Facebook sticker into your message, tap on the smiley face icon that's displayed on the right side of the empty text field. After you've typed your message, tap the Send button to send it to the other person.

TIP When you're finished with a chat, place your finger on the person's photo icon and drag it toward the "X" icon that appears near the bottom-center of the screen to close the chat. The transcript from the chat, however, is automatically saved, and you can pick up where you left off at anytime later.

READ YOUR NEWS FEED USING THE FACEBOOK APP

From the Facebook app's main menu, tap on the News Feed option to read your continuously updating News Feed and discover what your Facebook friends are up to.

When the News Feed screen is displayed, along the top of the screen, tap the Status option to update your own status and post new information to your Wall. To upload and manage photos to your Facebook account and share them online, tap on the Photo option. The Check-In option enables you to share your current location and details about the activity you're currently engaged in.

Scroll down a bit to read your current News Feed. The postings are displayed in reverse chronological order, with the most recent postings listed first. Just below the person's name who created each post is the time they posted it and their location.

Along the bottom of each posting, you'll discover Like, Comment, and Share icons. Tap Like to "Like" posting. If you want to post a comment related to the update, tap the Comment icon. If you want to share the comment with all of your online friends via your own Facebook Wall, tap the Share icon.

TIP If you're active on several online social networking services and use the official apps for them, be mindful of the permissions you grant to these apps. Many of them are now designed to work together and share information. So, if you post a new tweet on your Twitter account, it can automatically appear on your Facebook Wall or as a Facebook status update, as well. The same is true for Instagram and Facebook, for example. You can customize how these various services interact and what information they share by visiting their main websites (such as www.facebook.com or www.twitter.com) and logging in to your account.

MANAGE YOUR TWITTER ACCOUNT(S) USING THE OFFICIAL TWITTER APP

The official Twitter app enables you to manage one or more Twitter accounts from your iPhone or iPad. Using the app, it's possible to compose and publish new tweets, access your Twitter feed and see what your online friends (the people you're following) are up to, manage your account's followers, send private messages to other Twitter users, and discover content that's of interest to you using the Discover feature with keyword (hashtag) searches and/or tracking what's currently trending on Twitter.

When composing a tweet in the official Twitter app, or by selecting the Twitter option from the Share menu of any compatible app, the Compose Tweet screen (iPhone) or window (iPad) is displayed. Use the virtual keyboard or the Dictation feature to compose an outgoing tweet to publish to your Twitter feed. Of course, it's also possible to use Siri to compose and publish content to either Facebook or Twitter using voice commands.

A tweet can be up to 140 characters in length. Aside from text, you can also attach a photo that's taken using the iPhone or iPad's built-in camera (or that's already stored on your mobile device), include a website URL, or add your exact location to the tweet.

TIP As you're composing a tweet, a character counter is displayed near the bottom-right corner of the Compose Tweet screen/window. Keep in mind, when you attach a photo, website URL, or your location to the tweet, this utilizes some of the 140 characters you have available.

To find and follow your real-life friends who are already active on Twitter, launch the Twitter app, tap on the Discover option, and then scroll down to the Find Friends option. The app then searches through your Contacts database and matches up email addresses in your Contacts entries with active Twitter members and enable you to follow those people by tapping on a Follow button that appears next to each Search result.

One nice feature of the official Twitter app is that you can manage multiple accounts from the same app and quickly switch between accounts. However, as you're composing a tweet, if you have multiple accounts, simply tap on your Twitter username in the Compose Tweet screen/window, and you can choose which of your accounts you want to send the tweet from.

You can create or update your personal profile anytime from within the Twitter app. To do this, launch the Twitter app, tap on the Me option, and then tap on the gear-shaped icon. From the menu that appears, tap on Edit Profile. You can then change your profile photo, Twitter feed header, your name, the optional website URL you associate with your account, and your short (one-sentence) bio or description. Tap the Save button to save your changes.

NOTE Beyond using the official Twitter app to stay active on Twitter from your iPhone or iPad, you can visit the App Store and discover dozens of third-party apps that enable you to easily manage one or more Twitter accounts. Many of these third-party apps, such as Twitterific, TweetCaster, or Tweetbot, are paid apps that offer extra functionality that's not found in the official Twitter app.

DISCOVER THE OFFICIAL APPS FOR OTHER POPULAR ONLINE SOCIAL NETWORKING SERVICES

Official (free) apps from virtually all the popular online social networking services are available from the App Store. You can also find some third-party (paid) apps that offer a different mix of features and functions for managing one or more online social networking accounts.

THE YOUTUBE APP

As an online-based video sharing service, YouTube offers millions upon millions of hours worth of videos you can watch on demand, for free. The official YouTube app enables you to enjoy the service's content from anywhere your iOS mobile device has an Internet connection.

In past versions of iOS, an official YouTube app was included. With iOS 7, however, if you want to access your YouTube account, watch YouTube videos, or upload your own YouTube videos from an iPhone or iPad, the easiest way to do this is using the official YouTube app that's available for free from the App Store.

The interface for the official YouTube app is pretty straightforward. Tap the menu icon displayed near the top-left corner of the screen to sign in to the YouTube service using your established username and password, and then tap the Settings option to customize how the app functions.

> **TIP** When you sign in to the YouTube service from within the app, the YouTube app's main menu adds a My Subscriptions heading. Below it are details about all of the YouTube Channels to which you subscribe. Tap on any of these listings to quickly find the latest videos from your favorite YouTubers.

Displayed under the From YouTube heading of the main menu, tap on the category for videos you're interested in viewing. From the main YouTube screen, tap on the Search icon and then within the Search field, enter any keyword to quickly find videos you might be interested in related to a certain topic.

> **TIP** Look to the immediate right of the Search field and you'll see a microphone icon. Tap on this icon to access Google's own voice-recognition feature that works with the YouTube app.

When you tap on a video listing, what's displayed on the screen (shown in Figure 7.8 and Figure 7.9) is similar to what you'd see when accessing YouTube from your primary computer. This includes a video window in which the YouTube video plays. Tap on the video window to access onscreen controls to play or pause the video, view the time slider, and tap the Full Screen mode icon or the AirPlay icon.

Tap on a video's About tab to view details about the YouTube channel on which the video was published and details about the video itself. You can utilize Like, Dislike, and Share icons, as well as a Subscribe button and Suggested Videos related to the one you're watching.

NOTE Videos you watch using the YouTube app are streamed to your mobile device. These videos are not, however, saved on your device. Thus, to watch them, a continuous Internet connection is required. To avoid quickly using up your monthly cellular wireless data allocation, if applicable, opt to use this app with a Wi-Fi Internet connection.

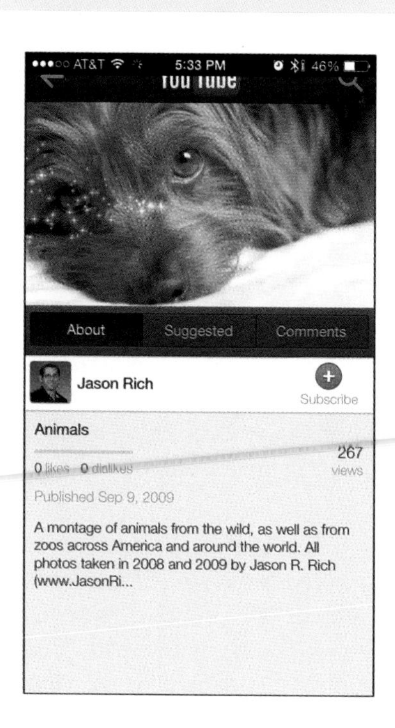

FIGURE 7.8

The official YouTube video enables you to watch unlimited videos for free or manage a YouTube Channel and publish your own videos to share them with others.

FIGURE 7.9

When watching a YouTube video, rotate the iPhone to landscape mode to switch to a full-screen view. Then, tap on the screen to access the onscreen playback controls.

THE VINE APP

Vine is a relatively new online social networking service that enables everyday people to upload and publish videos. These videos, however, can be only 7 seconds long. Think of this service as a cross between YouTube and Twitter. The official Vine app enables you to access your Vine account, upload and publish videos from your mobile device, or watch the videos that have been published by your online friends or other Vine users.

The main menu of this app offers Home, Explore, Activity, and Profile options. To shoot and upload a video using the video camera and microphone built in to the iPhone or iPad, tap the movie camera icon displayed near the top-right corner of the screen.

To view videos from your online friends, tap the Home option and then scroll down. As you watch each video, tap on the Smiley Face icon to "like" a video, the Comment icon to write and publish a public comment, or the Share icon to share someone else's Vine video with your online friends. Tap the More icon to reveal a submenu which offers options that enable you to Report This Post, Share This Post, or Cancel. You can also read the comments related to a video that have been posted by other people.

THE INSTAGRAM APP

Instagram is an online social networking service that enables users to create and share an ongoing stream of individual photos. Each photo can include a caption, keywords, and your location. Unlike other services, the photos you publish can be viewed by your online friends and other Instagram users.

What's cool about this app and service is that instead of using the Camera app to snap pictures, you can use the Instagram app and then use the app's photo editing tools to quickly add a special effect filter and border (shown in Figure 7.10). Unlike other photo sharing services, Instagram crops images into a square shape.

FIGURE 7.10

Snap or select a photo, crop it, and then add a special effect filter and/or border before publishing it on Instagram using the official Instagram app.

Facebook has purchased the Instagram service. Right now, they're being kept separate. However, more and more integration between the two services (and the official apps for them) is being introduced over time.

Instagram offers a fun and easy way to share with others moments of your life, in the form of snapshots taken using the camera that's built in to your iOS mobile device (shown in Figure 7.11).

FIGURE 7.11

Instagram users can share individual photos and manage their online account using the official Instagram app, shown here on an iPad mini.

> **TIP** To view photos posted by strangers, tap on the Explore icon displayed near the bottom of the screen. Then, simply scroll down. You can also use the Search Users and Hashtags feature to quickly find and view images with specific keywords associated with them.

THE LINKEDIN APP

If you're an entrepreneur, business professional, or small business operator, LinkedIn is the online social networking service designed for you. Its focus is specifically on professional networking. Use the service to pinpoint and attract new customers, interact with vendors, seek out expert advice, find employment opportunities, and share information with your online network and/or the service's 225 million members.

The official LinkedIn app enables you to access your online account from anywhere using your iOS mobile device. A separate version of the app is available for the iPhone and iPad. Using the core LinkedIn service is free; however, various subscriptions are available as in-app purchases ($9.99 to $99.00 per month) that offer access to premium content and features.

BECOME A BLOGGER AND START BLOGGING FROM YOUR iPHONE OR iPAD

Although becoming active on Facebook, Twitter, or any of the other popular online social networking services is a form of blogging, if you're interested in launching your own more traditional blog and then being able to update it with new content while on the go, your iPhone or iPad can be used for "mobile blogging" as well.

Many of the most popular blog hosting services, including Wordpress.com, Wordpress.org, Blogger.com, and Tumblr, have their own proprietary apps that enable you to create engaging content using text, photos, and video clips.

What's great about blogging is that you can fully customize your content and you're not constrained by having to stick to a particular format or length for each entry. Whether you're creating and managing a personal blog to be shared with close friends and family or you operate a blog on behalf of your business, the official WordPress and/or Blogger.com apps, for example, allow you to create content, manage your blog account, and track traffic to your blog from virtually anywhere.

ONLINE SOCIAL NETWORKING APP QUICK TIPS

- After you create accounts on the various online social networks, download and install the official app for that service.
- As you're creating posts for Facebook, Twitter, or most other services, keep in mind you can include text, one or more photos, and in some cases short video clips created on your iPhone or iPad. In addition, you can share your exact location where the post is being created.
- Accessing any of the online social networking services via your iPhone or iPad requires a cellular or Wi-Fi Internet connection. However, you're better off using a Wi-Fi connection with services that involve uploading videos to the service or streaming video from the service, such as YouTube and Vine, because this activity will otherwise quickly use up your monthly cellular data allocation (if applicable).

IN THIS CHAPTER

- Use new features iOS 7 brings to the Camera and Photos apps
- Tips and tricks for shooting, editing, and sharing photos and videos
- Take panoramic photos using the iPhone's Camera app

8

SHOOT, EDIT, AND SHARE PHOTOS AND VIDEOS

People love taking photos, and thanks to the two digital cameras built in to the latest iPhones and iPads, plus the improvements and redesign of the Camera and Photos apps in iOS 7, it has never been easier or more fun to shoot, edit, view, print, and share your digital images or video clips.

The iPhone 5, for example, offers an 8MP rear-facing camera, along with the enhanced Camera and Photos apps that come preinstalled with iOS 7. Thus, it's possible to take crystal-clear photos and create large and vibrant, full-color prints from the digital files, or share those images digitally using the Photos app's expanded Share menu.

WHAT'S NEW The iPhone 5S offers a truly state-of-the-art camera system, which includes a better-quality lens, higher-resolution image sensor, and more versatile flash. As a result, a feature that's similar to the HDR shooting mode available to other iPhone users can be automatically utilized when taking pictures using the Camera app on an iPhone 5S.

In addition, when using the iPhone 5S with the Camera app, users can utilize a burst (rapid fire) shooting mode to capture up to 10 images per second in quick succession.

TIP By tapping on the Share icon in the Photo app, you can easily share your images in several ways. It's possible to attach up to five photos to an outgoing email message from within Photos, attach preselected photos to a text/instant message, tweet a photo to your Twitter followers, upload photos directly to your Facebook page, upload photos to your Flickr account, or use the new AirDrop for iOS feature to wirelessly share photos with newer model iPhone, iPad, or iPod touch devices that are in close proximity to you.

It also continues to be possible to sync your images with your primary computer via iTunes Sync, or share your digital images with all your computers and iOS devices by setting up a My Photo Stream or Shared Photo Streams using iCloud.

You can also use your digital images with other apps. For example, you can assign a photo to a contact entry in the Contacts app, use a photo as your Lock screen or Home screen wallpaper, or copy a photo into another app, such as Pages or Keynote.

WHAT'S NEW Depending on which iOS mobile device you're using, the iOS 7 edition of the Camera app now features several shooting modes: still, video, pano (panoramic), square, slo-mo (iPhone 5S only), and burst (iPhone 5S only), which are explained shortly. In addition, the iPhone version of the Camera app offers eight special-effect filters that you can incorporate in real time into your photos as you're shooting.

On either an iPhone or iPad, it's also possible to add filters after the fact when editing your photos using the Photos app.

Meanwhile, the Photos app offers new ways to enhance your images and then organize, view, and share them. Both the Camera and Photos apps have a redesigned look.

The Camera and Photos apps continue to work with many third-party apps, so you can use specialized editing tools or share your photos online in a variety of ways. For example, there's the optional Instagram app for uploading photos and adding special effects to them via your Instagram account. Or, if you want to order prints of photos directly from your iPhone or iPad and have them shipped to your door within a few days, you can use one of several apps (such as FreePrints) that are available from the App Store.

METHODS FOR LOADING DIGITAL IMAGES INTO YOUR iPHONE OR iPAD

Before you can view, edit, print, and share your favorite digital images, you first must shoot them using the Camera app or transfer images into your iOS device.

> **NOTE** Some third-party apps, including Facebook, Twitter, and Instagram, enable you to access and use your iPhone or iPad's built-in cameras without using the Camera app. It's also possible for these apps to access the Camera app's image folders, such as Camera Roll, where newly shot images are stored.

Aside from shooting images using one of your iOS device's built-in cameras, there are several ways to import photos into your iOS device, and then store them in the Photos app:

- Use the iTunes sync process to transfer photos to your device. Set up the iTunes software on your PC or Mac to sync the image folders or albums you want, and then initiate an iTunes sync or wireless iTunes sync from your primary computer. To learn more about the iTunes sync process, visit http://support.apple.com/kb/HT1386.
- Load photos from your My Photo Stream or Shared Photo Stream. Learn how to work with these iCloud features later in this chapter.
- Receive and save photos sent via email. When a photo is embedded in an email, hold your finger on it for a second or two until a menu appears, giving you the option to save the image (in the Camera Roll folder of the Photos app), or copy the image to your device's virtual clipboard (after which you can paste it into another app). This feature, along with other Share options, is shown using the Mail app on an iPad in Figure 8.1.

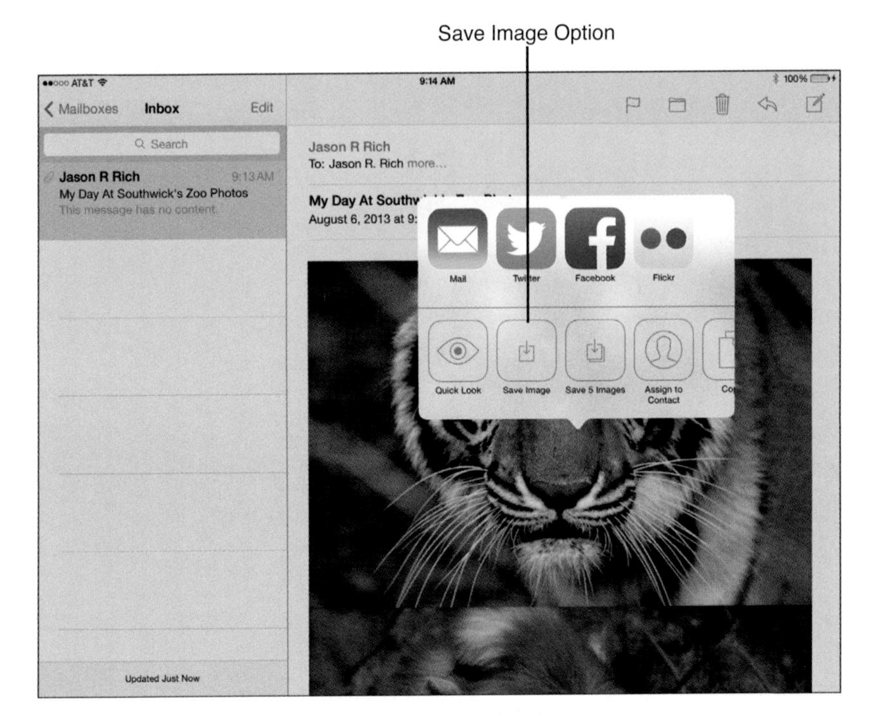

FIGURE 8.1

If you receive a digital photo attached to an incoming email, you can save the image in the Camera Roll by holding your finger on the image thumbnail (in the email), and then tapping on the Save Image option when it appears.

TIP If multiple images are attached or embedded within an incoming email, from the Mail app, when you use your finger and hold it on one of the images, a Save [number] Images option will be displayed in addition to the Save Image option (refer to Figure 8.1). Use the Save [number] Images option to save all of the photos within the email at once to your Camera Roll folder within the Photos app.

- Receive and save photos sent via text/instant message or Twitter. Tap on the image you receive using the Messages app, and then tap on the Copy command. When viewing the image in full-screen mode, tap on the Share button, and then select the Save To Camera Roll option or Open in Photos option, for example.
- Save images directly from a website as you're surfing the Web. Hold your finger on the image you're viewing in a website. If it's not copy-protected,

after a second or two a menu appears, enabling you to save the image or copy it to your device's virtual clipboard (after which you can paste it into another app).

- Accept images sent to your iPhone or iPad wirelessly via AirDrop for iOS from another iOS mobile device user (shown in Figure 8.2). For this feature to work, AirDrop must be turned on, which can be done easily from the new Control Center. Launch Control Center, tap on the AirDrop option, and then select Contacts Only or Everyone. When someone attempts to wirelessly send you one or more images, follow the onscreen prompts to download and store the images in the Camera Roll folder of the Photos app.
- Use the optional Camera Connection Kit ($29, available from Apple Stores or Apple.com) to load images from your digital camera or its memory card directly into your iPhone or iPad.

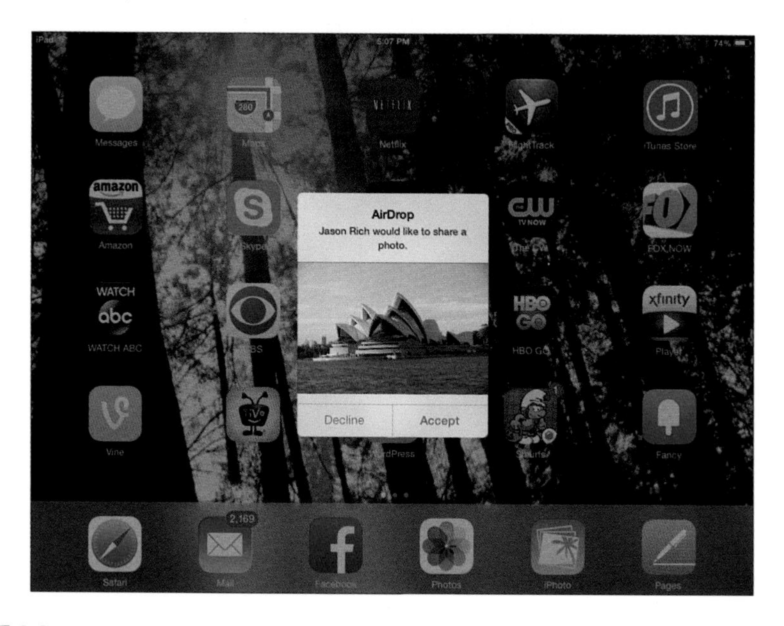

FIGURE 8.2

When someone sends an image via AirDrop to your iPhone or iPad, a pop-up window with an image thumbnail, along with an Accept and Decline button, is displayed.

NOTE When you use the Save Image command, the image is stored in the Camera Roll album of Photos. You can then view, edit, enhance, print, or share it.

THE REDESIGNED CAMERA APP

The Camera app that comes preinstalled with iOS 7 has been redesigned, yet it still remains very easy to use if you want to snap a photo or shoot a video clip. In fact, you can now launch the app and begin snapping photos faster. To begin using the Camera app, launch it from your device's Home screen.

The main camera viewfinder screen (shown in Figure 8.3) appears as soon as you launch the Camera app on an iPhone, iPod touch, or iPad. The main area of the screen serves as your camera's viewfinder. In other words, what you see on the screen is what you'll photograph or capture on video.

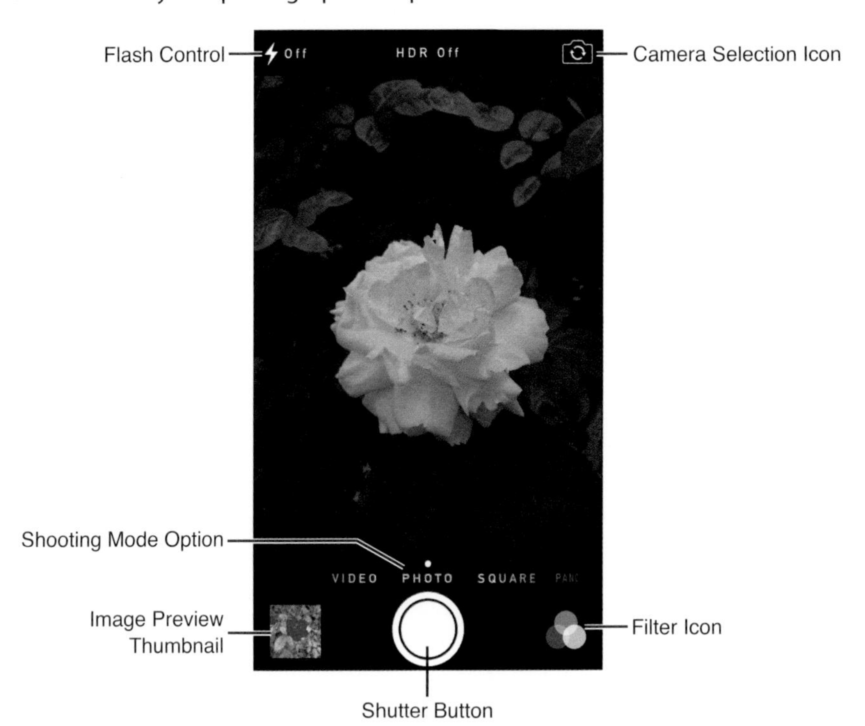

FIGURE 8.3

From the Camera app's main screen (shown here on the iPhone 5), you can snap digital photos or shoot video. The app looks similar on the iPhone and iPad and works pretty much the same way. On the iPhone 5S, additional shooting mode options are listed.

NOTE On the iPad version of the Camera app, filters are not available when shooting, so there's no Filters icon. There's also no Pano (panoramic) shooting option.

Additional features are offered when the Camera app is run on an iPhone 5S. For example, there's a burst shooting mode that allows for up to 10 images per second to be shot in very quick succession. The autofocus sensors and image stabilization features also react much faster, allowing you to more consistently take in-focus shots.

The iPhone 5S's True Tone flash automatically adapts to the lighting situation, enabling the Camera app to more accurately capture colors and skin tones when the flash is used.

Along the bottom of the screen are several command icons and options. A thumbnail image of the last photo or video clip you shot appears in the lower-left corner. Tap on it to view that image or video clip and use some of the Photo app's viewing and editing functions.

At the bottom center of the screen on the iPhone, or on the middle-right side of the screen on the iPad, is the camera's round shutter button. Tap on this to snap a photo or to start and stop the video camera. In Video mode, the shutter button icon transforms from a bright red circle into a red square (pause button) when you tap on it to begin shooting a video clip.

The shooting mode options—Video, Photo, Square, and Pano (iPhone only)—appear just above the shutter button on the iPhone and just below the button on the iPad. Use your finger to scroll left or right, and then tap on your selected option. (The iPhone 5S also offers a Slo-Mo and Burst shooting mode.)

Photo is used to snap regular digital (still) images. Square automatically precrops images as you're shooting to be compatible with services such as Instagram. You wind up with square images.

Pano launches the Camera app's panoramic mode for shooting vast landscapes, skylines, or large groups of people (shown in Figure 8.4). Video is for shooting video and on the iPhone 5S, Slo-Mo is for shooting slow-motion, HD video.

The latest iPhone and iPad models each have two built-in cameras—one in the front, and one on the back of the device. The front-facing camera makes it easier to snap photos of yourself or participate in videoconferences. The rear-facing camera (which enables you to take higher-resolution photos or video) enables you to photograph whatever you're looking at that's facing forward. Tap on the camera-shaped icon located in the upper-right corner of the screen to switch between cameras.

FIGURE 8.4

The Pano (panoramic) shooting mode is ideal for shooting images of vast landscapes, large groups of people or very wide areas, such as the inside of Gillette Stadium in Foxboro, MA during a sporting event (shown here).

When applicable, the HDR button is displayed just above or to the side of the shutter button. Tap it to toggle HDR mode when taking digital photos.

On the iPhone, in the upper-left corner of the main Camera screen, is an icon labeled Auto. It controls whether the iPhone automatically uses the built-in flash when needed as you're shooting photos or video with the rear-facing camera. Tap the icon, then tap the On or Off button to toggle this feature.

MORE INFO The HDR mode in the Camera app stands for High Dynamic Range. It can be used with the rear-facing camera only. When turned on, this feature captures the available light differently and can help you compensate for a photo that would otherwise be over- or underexposed.

When you take a photo with HDR mode turned on, the iPhone or iPad actually captures three separate images and then automatically blends them into a single image. By doing this, it's possible to capture more depth and contrast, plus make better use of available lighting. The result can be more detailed and vibrant photos in many situations.

You can decide whether the original photo and the HDR mode photo are both saved in the Camera Roll of the Photos app, or if just the HDR version of the image is saved. To make this adjustment, launch Settings, tap on the Photos & Camera option, and then set the virtual switch that's associated with the Keep Normal Photo option.

The drawback to using HDR mode is that it takes several extra seconds to store both images each time you snap a photo, and this slows down the Camera app.

iOS 7 **WHAT'S NEW** In low light situations, the iPhone 5S utilizes what equates to HDR mode; however, four images are shot simultaneously and then blended together.

HOW TO SNAP A PHOTO

Snapping a single digital photo using the Camera app is simple. Follow these steps:

1. Launch the Camera app from the Home screen.
2. Make sure the shooting mode is set to Photo or Square.
3. Choose which of your device's two built-in cameras you want to use by tapping on the camera selection icon.
4. Compose or frame your image by holding up your iPhone or iPad and pointing it at your subject.
5. To add a special effect to the image as you're shooting (iPhone only), tap on the new Filter icon and select one of the eight displayed filters by tapping on its preview image (shown in Figure 8.5). The filter thumbnail serves as the shutter button for snapping a photo when you tap on it.

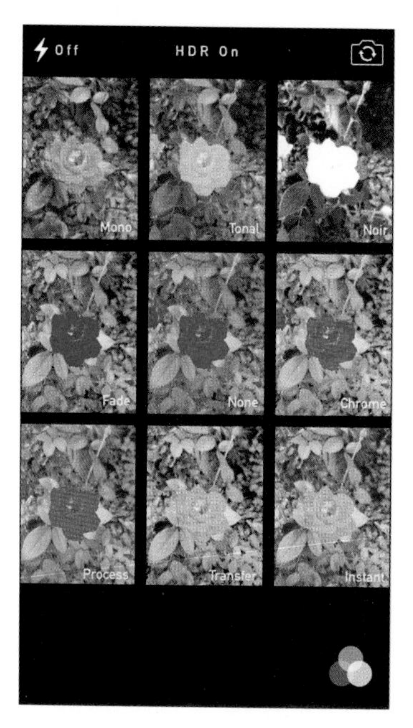

FIGURE 8.5

As you're shooting a photo, you can choose one of the eight image filters and add an effect, such as black and white. Choose None to shoot without using a filter. You can also add a filter later when editing a photo using the Photos app.

6. Select the main subject of your photo, such as a person or an object. Tap your finger on the screen where your subject appears in the viewfinder. An autofocus sensor box appears on the screen at the location you tap. Where this box is positioned is what the camera focuses on (as opposed to something in the foreground, background, or next to your intended subject).

TIP As you're holding your iPhone or iPad to snap a photo or shoot video, be sure your fingers don't accidentally block the camera lens that's being utilized. On the more recent iPhone models, next to the rear-facing camera lens is a tiny flash. Keep your fingers clear of this as well.

NOTE If you're taking a group photo (up to 10 people), the Camera app detects this, and multiple autofocus sensors appear on all of your subjects' faces.

TIP On the iPhone 5S, to use the Burst shooting mode, simply press and hold down the shutter button in the Camera app. You will be able to capture up to 10 images per second. You can later delete the images you don't need but choose the shot that best depicts a specific instant. This shooting mode is ideal for photographing a fast-moving subject.

7. If you want to use the Camera app's zoom feature, use a pinch motion on the screen. A zoom slider (shown in Figure 8.6) appears near the bottom of the screen. Use your finger to move the dot within the slider to the right to zoom in, or to the left to zoom out on your subject.
8. On the iPhone, tap on the Flash icon in the top-left corner of the screen. You have three flash-related options. When turned on, the flash activates for every picture you take. When turned off, the flash does not activate at all, regardless of the lighting conditions. When you select Auto, the Camera app activates the flash when it deems additional light is needed. If you have HDR mode turned on (iPhone only), the flash does not work.
9. When you have your image framed in the viewfinder, tap on the shutter button to snap the photo. Or tap the Volume Up (+) or Volume Down (-) button on the side of your iPhone. You'll see an animation of a virtual shutter closing and then reopening on the screen, indicating that the photo is being taken. At the same time, you'll hear an audio effect.

FIGURE 8.6

As you're framing an image, you can zoom in (or out) on your subject using the onscreen zoom slider. Use a pinch finger gesture on the screen to make this slider appear, and then move the slider to the right or left to increase or decrease the zoom level.

10. The photo will be saved on your device in the Camera Roll album of Photos. You can now shoot another photo or view the photo using the Photos app.

HOW TO SHOOT A PANORAMIC PHOTO (iPHONE ONLY)

To take advantage of the panoramic shooting mode to snap a photo of a landscape, city skyline, or a large group of people, follow these steps:

1. Launch the Camera app.
2. Swipe on the shooting modes to select the Pano shooting mode.
3. Position your iPhone's viewfinder to the extreme left of your wide-angle shot.

TIP If you tap on the large arrow icon in the viewfinder, you can switch the panning direction from right to left, instead of left to right as you're capturing a panoramic shot.

4. Tap the shutter button icon, and then slowly and steadily move your iPhone or iPad from left to right (shown in Figure 8.7). If you go too fast, a message appears on the screen telling you to slow down.

FIGURE 8.7

The Panorama shooting mode is ideal for capturing vast landscapes, city skylines, or large group photos.

5. The panorama slider moves from left to right as you capture your image. You can tap the shutter button again when you're finished, or continue moving the iOS device to the right until the entire length of the image has been captured.
6. The panoramic photo is saved in the Camera Roll folder of the Photos app. You can then view, edit, or share it from within Photos.

> **TIP** When viewing a panoramic photo, hold your iPhone in landscape mode; however, when shooting a panoramic shot, hold it in portrait mode.

TIP As you shoot a panoramic image, it's also possible to move the camera from right to left. To do this, turn on Pano mode and then tap on the white, right-pointing arrow icon. The arrow will now face to the left. Now, when you tap the shutter button, move the camera (iPhone) from right to left, as opposed to from left to right.

HOW TO SHOOT VIDEO

From the Camera app, you can easily shoot video. Follow these basic steps for shooting video on your iPhone or iPad:

1. Launch the Camera app.
2. Swipe on the shooting modes to select the Video shooting mode option.
3. Tap the camera selection icon to choose which camera you want to use. You can switch between the front- and the rear-facing camera at any time.
4. If applicable, tap on the Flash icon that's displayed near the top-left corner of the screen.
5. Hold your iPhone or iPad up to the subject you want to capture on video. Set up your shot by looking at what's displayed on the screen.
6. When you're ready to start shooting video, tap on the shutter button. The red dot turns into a red square. This indicates you're now filming. Your iPhone or iPad captures whatever images you see on the screen, as well as any sound in the area.
7. As you're filming video, notice a timer displayed on the screen (shown in Figure 8.8). Your only limit to how much video you can shoot is based on the amount of available memory in your iOS device and how long the battery lasts. However, this app is designed more for shooting short video clips, not full-length home movies.
8. As you're filming, tap anywhere on the screen to focus in on your subject using the app's built-in autofocus sensor.
9. To stop filming, tap again on the shutter button. Your video footage is saved. You can now view, edit, and share it from within the Photos app or a video app, such as iMovie.

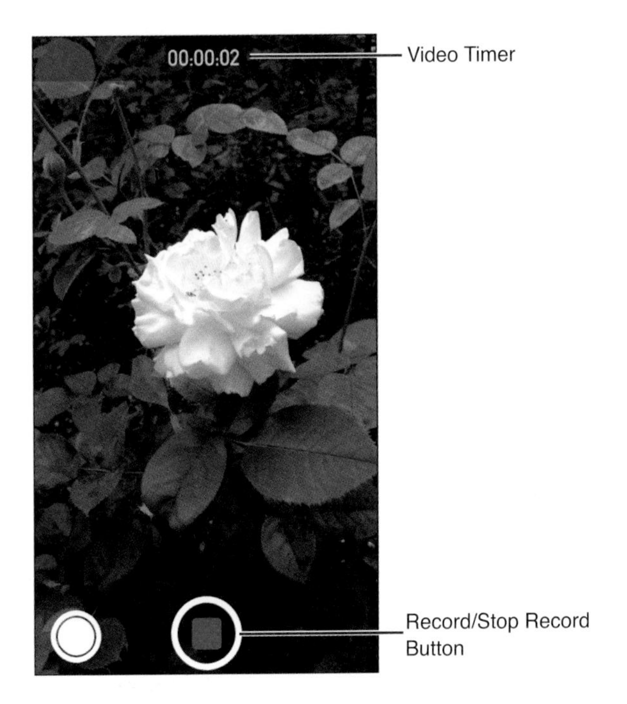

FIGURE 8.8

When shooting video on your iPhone or iPad, make sure the timer is counting up. This indicates you're actually recording.

TIP Although the Photos app enables you to trim your video clips as well as view and share the videos, if you want to edit your videos, plus add titles and special effects, you should purchase and use Apple's feature-packed iMovie app, which is available from the App Store. With all new iOS mobile devices, the iPhoto and iMovie apps are now free. For more information about iMovie, visit www.apple.com/apps/imovie.

iOS 7 WHAT'S NEW iCloud's Shared Photo Stream feature now enables you to include video clips shot on your iOS mobile device (up to 5 minutes in length) in a photo stream that you ultimately share with others.

TIPS FOR SHOOTING EYE-CATCHING PHOTOS

Even though you're using a smartphone or tablet to shoot photos, as opposed to a full-featured, digital SLR or point-and-shoot digital camera, you can still use basic photo composition and framing techniques to snap professional-quality images.

> **TIP** The rear-facing camera built in to your iPhone or iPad offers superior resolution and takes better photos, so use this camera (as opposed to the front-facing camera) as often as possible to get the highest-quality results.

To generate the best possible in-focus, well-lit, and nicely framed images, follow these basic shooting strategies (many of which also apply when shooting video):

- Pay attention to your light source. As a general rule, the light source (such as the sun) should be behind you (the photographer) and shining onto your subject. When light from your primary light source shines directly into your camera's lens (in this case, your iPhone or iPad), you'll wind up with unwanted glares or an overexposed image.
- As you look at the viewfinder screen, pay attention to shadows. Unwanted shadows can be caused by the sun or by an artificial light source. Make sure shadows aren't covering your subject(s).

> **TIP** Shooting indoors using the flash can generate unwanted shadows. Try to keep your subject at least two or three feet away from a wall or backdrop to reduce shadows, and don't get too close to your subject.

- When you're using the flash, red-eye often becomes a problem. To prevent this, try to shine more light on your subject and not rely on the flash. Or step farther away from your subject physically but use the zoom to move in closer.

> **TIP** Like any camera, the flash built in to your iPhone has an optimal range that generates the best lighting results. If you're too close to your subject when using the flash, the photo comes out overexposed. If you're too far away, the photo might turn out underexposed. You can compensate by moving closer or farther away from your subject but then use the zoom feature when necessary.

NOTE When you use the digital zoom built in to the Camera app, a photo's image quality is reduced the further you zoom in. It also becomes even more essential to hold the iPhone steady as you're taking pictures when you use the zoom feature.

- Candid photos of people are great for showing emotion, spontaneity, or true life. The key to taking great candid photos is to have your camera ready to shoot and to be unobtrusive so that your subjects don't become self-conscious when they have a camera aimed at them. Try to anticipate when something interesting, surprising, or funny, or that generates a strong emotion will happen, and be ready to snap a photo. Also, don't get too close to your subject. You're better off being several feet away and using the zoom so that you, as the photographer, don't become a distraction.
- As you get ready to tap the shutter icon and snap a photo, hold your iOS device perfectly still. Even the slightest movement could result in a blurry image, especially in low-light situations.
- If you're shooting in poor light, take advantage of the iPhone's HDR feature by turning it on.

TIP As you're looking at your primary subject through the "viewfinder" (the iPhone or iPad's screen when using the Camera app), tap on the intended subject on the screen once to set the Autofocus. To activate the Auto Exposure Lock, press and hold your finger on the screen for a second or two. A yellow square appears on the screen over your subject. This informs the iPhone or iPad about what you want your primary subject to be, and ensures the best possible focus and available lighting utilization.

One benefit to using the Auto Exposure Lock is that it remains set until it's manually changed, so you can take a handful of photos in succession, without having to refocus on your subject. To turn off the Auto Exposure Lock, tap on the viewfinder screen again.

TIP It's possible to launch the Camera app directly from the Lock screen to save time when you want to shoot a photo. Place your finger on the camera icon that's displayed on the Lock screen, and flick upward to quickly launch the Camera app, then use one of the volume buttons on your device as your shutter button to snap a photo (shown in Figure 8.9).

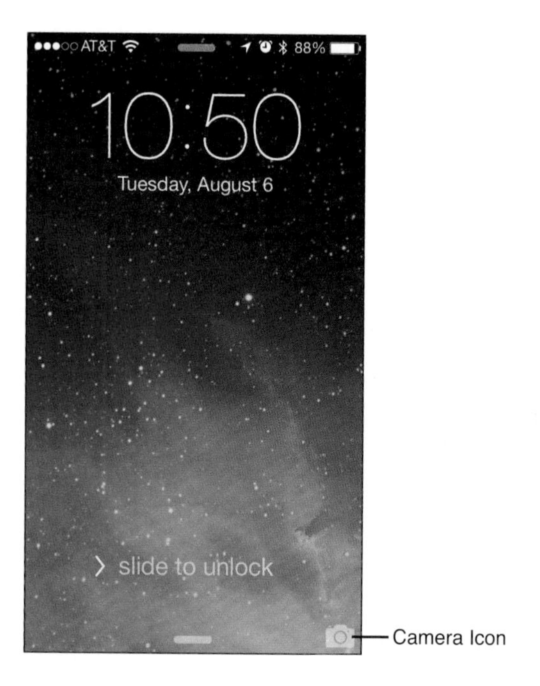

FIGURE 8.9

Launch the Camera app directly from the iPhone or iPad's Lock screen, and start taking photos in seconds.

- As you're framing your subject(s) in the viewfinder, pay attention to what's in the foreground, background, and to the sides of the subject. These objects can often be used to frame your subject and add a sense of multidimensionality to a photo. Just make sure that the autofocus sensor of the Camera app focuses in on your intended subject, and not something else in the photo, to ensure clarity.
- The best way to improve the overall quality of your photos when shooting with your iPhone, iPad, or iPod touch (or any digital camera) is to incorporate the Rule of Thirds when you're framing or composing each shot.

HOW TO USE THE RULE OF THIRDS WHEN SHOOTING

It's a common mistake for amateur photographers to point the camera at the subject head-on, center the subject in the frame, and snap a photo. The result is always a generic-looking image, even if it's well-lit and in perfect focus.

Instead, as you look at the viewfinder screen to compose or frame your image, utilize the Rule of Thirds. This is a shooting strategy used by professional photographers, but it's very easy to take advantage of, and the results will be impressive.

Imagine a tic-tac-toe grid being superimposed on your camera's viewfinder. To make the grid appear in the Camera app's viewfinder, launch the Settings app, select the Photos & Camera option, and then turn on the virtual switch associated with the Grid option (shown in Figure 8.10). The center box in the tic-tac-toe grid corresponds to the center of the image you're about to shoot as you look at the viewfinder screen.

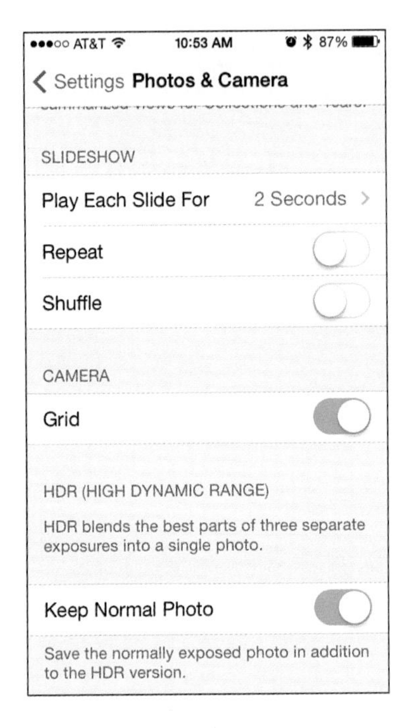

FIGURE 8.10

To turn on the Grid, launch Settings, tap on the Photos & Camera option, and then turn on the virtual switch associated with the Grid feature.

Instead of framing your subject in this center box, reframe the image so your subject is positioned along one of the horizontal or vertical lines of the grid, or so that the main focal point of the image is positioned at one of the grid's intersection points.

MORE INFO In some cases, you might find it easier to use a tripod with your iPhone or iPad to help hold it steady as you're snapping a photo. Joby (http://joby.com/gorillamobile), for example, offers several different mini-tripod and stand products for use with your iOS device.

TIP As you're shooting, instead of holding the camera head-on, directly facing your subject, try shooting from a different perspective, such as from slightly above, below, or to the side of your subject. This will allow you to create more visually interesting images.

Using the Rule of Thirds when framing your images takes a bit of practice, but if you use this shooting technique consistently and correctly, the quality of your images vastly improves. Of course, you also want to take into account lighting, as well as what's in the foreground, in the background, and to the sides of your main subject. And be sure to tap your creativity when choosing your shooting angle or perspective for each shot.

TIP When you're shooting a subject in motion, capture the subject moving into the frame, as opposed to moving out of it, while also taking into account the Rule of Thirds.

MORE INFO To expand the capabilities of the iPhone's Camera app, consider investing in the optional OlloClip 3-in-1 lens ($69.99) or the OlloClip Telephoto + Circular Polarizing Filter Lens ($99.99). These small and lightweight accessories, which are sold separately, clip onto the iPhone over the built-in camera's lens.

The 3-in-1 lens offers a Macro, Wide Angle, and Fisheye lens, while the Telephoto lens doubles the zoom capabilities of the Camera app and offers a polarizing filter which better captures color when taking photos outside. Visit www.OlloClip.com for more information or to order these optional iPhone lenses.

USING THE PHOTOS APP TO VIEW, EDIT, ENHANCE, PRINT, AND SHARE PHOTOS AND VIDEOS

Launch the Photos app from your iOS device's Home screen. First and foremost, use the Photos app to view images stored on your iOS device.

iOS 7 **WHAT'S NEW** Images in the Photos app are now auto-sorted based on when or where they were shot. Years displays thumbnails of all images shot within a particular year and includes details about where those images were shot (shown in Figure 8.11). Collections break down a Years grouping to display images based on when and where they were shot. Moments enable you to display thumbnails of images within a Collection that represent one location or date.

As you're viewing thumbnails in the Moments view, tap on one of them to view a single image. Or, at the bottom of the screen, tap on Photos, Shared, or Albums to view a different set of images stored on your mobile device.

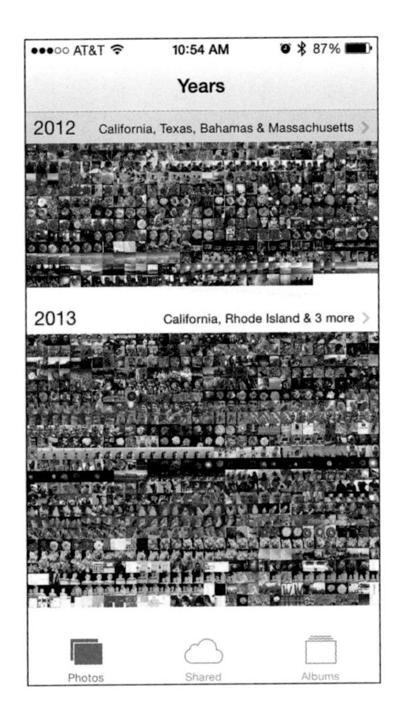

FIGURE 8.11

From the Photos app, you can view tiny thumbnails of all images shot within a particular year. Tap on any thumbnail to view the image in full-screen mode.

On the iPhone, the functionality of the Photos app is almost identical to the iPad version; however, the appearance of some of the screens and the position of certain command icons and menus differs due to the smaller size of the iPhone's screen.

To exit out of the Moments or Collections thumbnail view, use the options displayed at the top-left corner of the screen. From the Years view, tap on a collection (within the main area of the screen) or tap on the Photos, Shared, or Albums icon that's displayed along the bottom of the screen.

When viewing Moments, each group of photos that are shot at the same place and in the same time frame are automatically grouped together into an event. As you're viewing these events, tap on the Share button associated with it to quickly share all images in that event, or select and share specific images from it via AirDrop, Messages, or iCloud. Tap on the Select option at the top-right corner of the screen to choose one or more events or thumbnails. Once selected, tap either the Share or Trash icon in the top-left corner of the screen to manage those images.

VIEW AN IMAGE IN FULL-SCREEN MODE

When viewing thumbnails of your images, tap on any single image thumbnail to view a full-screen version of it. The Edit command is displayed in the upper-right corner of the screen, the Share command icon is displayed in the lower-left corner of the screen, and the Trash icon is displayed near the lower-right corner of the screen (as shown in Figure 8.12).

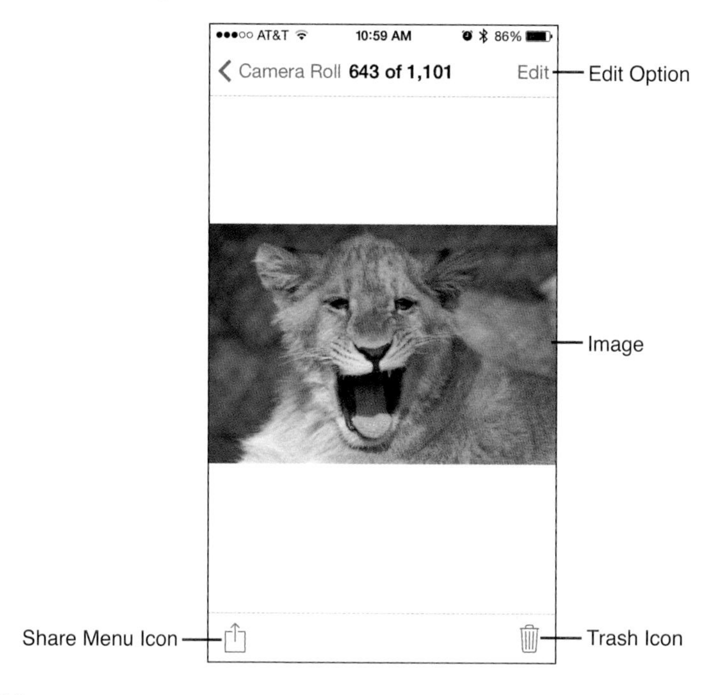

FIGURE 8.12

The Edit, Share, and Trash icons are displayed when viewing a single image on your iPhone or iPad's screen.

As you're viewing a photo, tap on it to hide or show the edit, share and trash-can options, which automatically appear when you first open a photo but then disappear. Tap on the Edit option to reveal the image editing options (shown in Figure 8.13).

FIGURE 8.13

After tapping the Edit option, displayed are the command icons you'll use to ultimately edit and enhance that image.

To exit the single-image view and return to the multi-image thumbnail view, tap anywhere on the screen to make the command icons appear, then tap on the left-pointing arrow-shaped icon displayed in the upper-left corner of the screen.

As you're viewing a single image in full-screen mode, on the iPad along the bottom of the screen will be a filmstrip depiction of all images stored in the current album, or all images stored on your iOS device if you were previously in Photos viewing mode.

EDITING PHOTOS AND VIDEOS

After selecting a single image to view in full-screen mode, tap on the Edit button to access the photo editing commands.

TIP When you tap on the thumbnail for a video clip, you have the option to play that clip in the Photos app. Or you can tap anywhere on the screen (except for the Play icon in the center of the screen) to access the video trimming (editing) feature, as well as the Share icon and the trash can icon (used to delete the video clip from your iOS device).

To trim a video clip, look at the filmstrip display of the clip located at the top of the screen, and move the left or right editing tabs accordingly to define the portion of the clip you want to edit. The box around the filmstrip display turns yellow, and the Trim command icon appears on the right side of the screen. Before tapping on Trim, tap on the Play icon to preview your newly edited video clip. If it's okay, tap on the Trim icon to save your changes. Two additional command icons will appear, labeled Trim Original and Save As New Clip. Trim Original alters the original video clip and replaces the file, whereas the Save As New Clip option creates a separate file and keeps a copy of the original clip.

COMMANDS FOR EDITING PHOTOS

When you tap on the Edit command icon while viewing a single image in full-screen mode, the following command icons are displayed along the bottom of the screen (refer to Figure 8.13). These icons provide the tools for quickly editing and enhancing your image. On the iPhone, these command options are displayed as graphic icons, whereas on the iPad, their purpose is spelled out. The commands include the following:

- **Rotate**—Tap on this icon once to rotate the image counterclockwise by 90 degrees. You can tap the Rotate icon up to three times before the image returns to its original orientation.
- **Enhance**—Tap on the Auto-Enhance feature to instantly sharpen the photo and make the colors in it more vibrant. You should notice a dramatic improvement in the visual quality, lighting, detail, and sharpness of your image. Once you tap the Auto-Enhance feature, it works automatically. Remove the enhancements by tapping on the Enhance option again as you're editing the photo.
- **Filters**—Add one of the new special effect filters available to you after an image has been shot. These filters include Mono, Tonia, Noir, Fade, Chrome, Process, Transfer, and Instant. Each filter gets applied to an entire image and dramatically alters its appearance. Select the None option to turn off the filter option altogether and shoot a normal image.

- **Red-Eye**—If any human subject in your photo is exhibiting signs of red-eye as a result of your using a flash, tap on the Red-Eye icon to digitally remove this unwanted discoloration in your subject's pupils.
- **Crop**—Tap on this icon to crop the image and reposition your subject in the frame. If you forgot to incorporate the Rule of Thirds while shooting a photo, you can sometimes compensate by cropping a photo. You also can cut away unwanted background or zoom in on your subject, based on how you crop it. When the crop grid appears, position your finger in any corner or side of the grid to determine how to crop the image. When you're finished, tap on the Crop icon to confirm your changes.

TIP As you're cropping an image, tap on the Aspect option (displayed near the bottom-center of the screen) to select an image size, such as Original, Square, 3" × 2", 3" × 5", 4" × 3", 4" × 6", 5" × 7", 8" × 10", or 16" × 9". Unless you need the image in a specific size, choose the Original option and then use adjust the crop edges to adjust your image.

TIP If you're cropping an image by moving around the cropping grid using your finger, if you first tap on the Aspect option, this forces the basic dimensions of your image to stay intact. This enables you to make perfectly sized prints later, without throwing off the image dimensions.

- **Undo**—On the iPad, if you tap Undo, the last edit you made to the image is undone but any other edits remain intact. On the iPhone, tap the Cancel button or tap the same edit icon again.
- **Save**—After you've used the various editing commands to edit or enhance your image, tap on the Save command to save your changes.
- **Cancel**—Tap on this icon to exit the photo-editing mode of the Photos app without making any changes to the photo you're viewing.

PRINTING PHOTOS

iOS 7 is fully compatible with Apple's AirPrint feature, so if you have a photo printer set up to work wirelessly with your iOS device, you can create photo prints from your digital images using the Print command in the Photos app. Follow these steps to print an image:

1. Launch the Photos app from the Home screen.
2. From the main View Images screen, tap on any thumbnail to view an image in full-screen mode. You might need to open an album first by tapping on the Album's thumbnail if you have the Albums viewing option selected.
3. Tap on the full-screen version of the image to make the various command icons appear.
4. Tap on the Share icon.
5. From the Share menu, select the Print option.
6. When the Printer Options submenu appears, select your printer, determine how many copies of the print you'd like to create, and then tap on the Print icon.

MORE INFO To print wirelessly from your iOS device using the AirPrint feature, you must have a compatible printer. To learn more about AirPrint, and to configure your printer for wireless printing from your iPhone or iPad, visit http://support.apple.com/kb/HT4356.

TIP Many one-hour photo processing labs (in pharmacies, as well as stores like Wal-Mart or Target) enable you to email photos directly from your iPhone or iPad to their lab, then pick up prints that same day (often within an hour). There are also photo lab services that have special apps which allow you to select photos stored on your iOS mobile device, upload them to a lab, and have prints mailed to you within a few days.

Walgreens for iPad, RitzPix, FreePrints, SnapFish, and Kodak Kiosk Connection are among the apps that allow you to order prints directly from your iPhone or iPad.

TIP When emailing a photo to a lab (or someone who will be printing them on their home photo printer), to achieve the best possible prints, send the images in Full Size mode from your iOS device. To do this, after filling in the Email field and tapping Send, tap on the Actual Size button on the iPhone when the image quality menu appears. On the iPad, tap on the Images option that's displayed to the right of the Front field, and then when the Image Size options appear, tap on the Actual Size tab.

SHARING PHOTOS AND VIDEOS

The iOS 7 version of the Photos app offers a new and expanded Share menu (shown in Figure 8.14). After you have selected one or more images, tap the Share icon (displayed at the bottom-left corner of the screen) to access the Share menu.

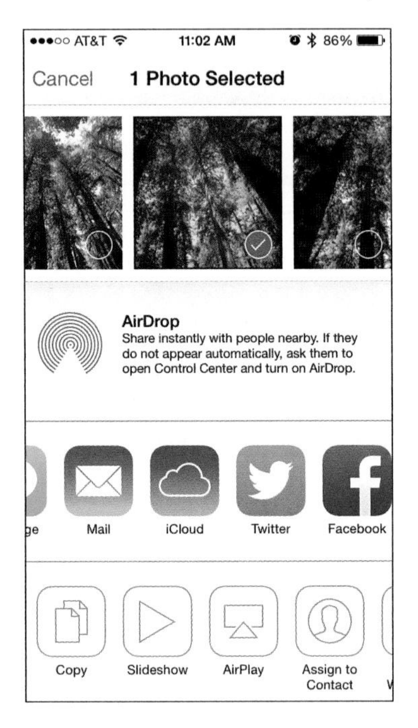

FIGURE 8.14

The Share menu in the iOS 7 version of the Photos app has been greatly expanded.

SEND IMAGES WIRELESSLY VIA AIRDROP

If you're within close proximity to another iPhone 5 (or higher) or fourth-generation iPad (or higher) and you both have the AirDrop feature turned on, you can wirelessly send images from within the Photos app using the AirDrop for iOS feature. This feature becomes active only when others nearby can receive an AirDrop transmission.

SEND IMAGES VIA TEXT/INSTANT MESSAGE

Tap this option to send images via the Messages app. When the New Message window appears, fill in the To field with the recipient's cell phone number or iMessage account username. Tap the plus-sign icon to send the same message to multiple recipients.

You can optionally add text to the photo(s) that are attached to the message. To add more images to the outgoing message, tap on the Camera icon. When you're ready, tap the Send option to send the photos and message.

EMAIL UP TO FIVE IMAGES AT A TIME

From either the iPhone or iPad, when looking at thumbnails for images in an Album, tap on the Edit button to select between one and five images, and then tap on the Share icon.

Select the Mail option and fill in the To field when prompted. If you want, edit the Subject field and/or add text to the body of the email, and then tap the Send button.

When viewing a single image, tap on the Share button, select Mail, fill in the To field, and edit the Subject. If you want, add text to the body of the message (shown in Figure 8.15), and then tap the Send button.

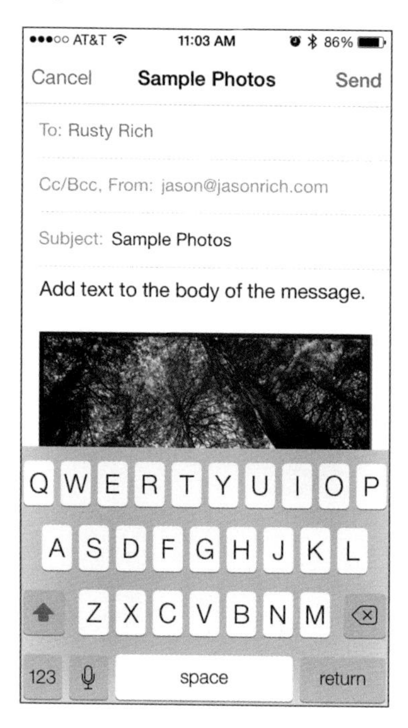

FIGURE 8.15

You can send an email with one to five photos attached to it from within the Photos app.

TWEET A PHOTO TO YOUR TWITTER FOLLOWERS

To tweet a photo, after tapping the Share icon while viewing a single photo in full-screen mode, select the Tweet option. Compose your tweet message (which will already have the selected image attached), and then tap the Send icon.

Keep in mind that it's also possible to tweet photos from the official Twitter app or from a third-party Twitter-related app, such as Twitterific (available from the App Store).

PUBLISH PHOTOS ON FACEBOOK

To publish one or more photos to Facebook with an optional text-based message, tap the Facebook button in the Share menu. From the Facebook window (shown in Figure 8.16), tap the Album option to choose an existing Facebook Photos Album to which the image should be added.

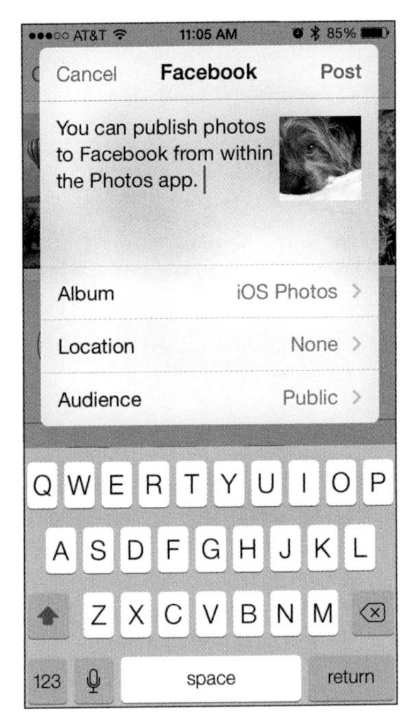

FIGURE 8.16

From the Photos app on your iPhone or iPad, you can send an image directly to your Facebook page as part of a status update.

Next, tap the Location option to publish the location the image was shot on Facebook in conjunction with the photo. Tap on the Audience option to decide who can view the image(s) on Facebook. Your options include Public, Friends, Friends Except Acquaintances, Only Me, Close Friends, or people within a specific Facebook group you've created.

To the left of the photo thumbnail, use the virtual keyboard to enter a caption for the image(s) you're about to upload, and then tap the Post option (displayed at the top-right corner of the Facebook window) to publish the photos.

TIP An alternative to using the Photos app to publish photos to Facebook is to use the official Facebook app. This gives you additional options, such as the ability to tag photos with the names of the people who appear in them. Plus, the Facebook app enables you to add special-effect filters to images before uploading them.

UPLOAD IMAGES TO FLICKR

Flickr is an online-based photo sharing service and photo lab operated by Yahoo!. To upload selected images to your existing Flickr account, select the images from within the Photos app, tap the Share icon, and then tap the Flickr option. You then can choose an album to which your selected images are uploaded.

It's also possible to use the official Flickr app to upload and manage your account from your iPhone or iPad.

COPY AN IMAGE TO ANOTHER APP

From within the Photos app, you can store a photo in your iOS device's virtual clipboard and then paste that photo into another compatible app. To copy a photo into your device's virtual clipboard, follow these steps:

1. From within the Photos app, select a single photo and view it in full-screen mode.
2. Tap on the image to make the various command icons appear.
3. Tap on the Share icon.
4. Tap on the Copy option. The photo is stored in the virtual clipboard.
5. Launch a compatible app and hold your finger down on the screen to use the Paste option and paste your photo from the clipboard into the active app.

CREATE A SLIDESHOW

To create and display an animated slideshow featuring selected images, launch Photos and select a group of images. Next, tap the Share icon and choose the Slideshow option.

From the Slideshow Options screen, choose to display the image on the iPhone (or iPad) or via Apple TV. Select your Transition effect from the menu and decide whether you want music to accompany the presentation. By turning on the virtual switch associated with Play Music, you can choose music that's stored within the Music app of your iOS mobile device. To begin the Slideshow, tap on the Start Slideshow option.

SHOW IMAGE ON A TELEVISION VIA AIRPLAY

Instead of viewing an image in full-screen mode on your iPhone or iPad, tap the AirPlay option, which is part of the Share menu, to wirelessly transmit the image to your HD television set or Mac screen. To use this feature with an HD TV, you'll need the optional Apple TV device. To use the feature with a Mac, be sure AirPlay on your Mac is turned on.

SAVE THE IMAGE TO YOUR CAMERA ROLL FOLDER

If you're viewing images stored in your Photo Stream or a Shared Photo Stream, tap on the Save To Camera Roll option (which appears only when it's available) to store the image in the Camera Roll folder of the Photos app.

ASSIGN IMAGE TO CONTACT

To link an image stored in the Photos app to a specific contact in the Contacts app, follow these steps:

1. From within the Photos app, select a single photo and view it in full-screen mode.
2. Tap on the image to make the various command icons appear.
3. Tap on the Share icon.
4. Tap on the Assign to Contact option.
5. An All Contacts window is displayed. Scroll through the listing, or use the Search field to find the specific entry with which you want to associate the photo.
6. Tap on that person's or company's name from the All Contacts listing.

7. When the Choose Photo window opens, use your finger to move or scale the image. What you see in the box is what will be saved.
8. Tap on the Use icon to save the photo and link it to the selected contact.
9. When you launch Contacts and access that person's entry, the photo you selected appears in the entry.

USE AS WALLPAPER

As you're viewing a photo, you can assign it to be the wallpaper image used on your Home screen or Lock screen by tapping on the Share icon and then choosing the Use As Wallpaper option. When the image is previewed on the screen, tap on the Set button. From the Set Lock Screen, Set Home Screen, or Set Both menu, choose where you want the selected image displayed.

DELETING PHOTOS STORED ON YOUR iOS DEVICE

To delete one image at a time as you're viewing them in full-screen mode, simply tap on the Trash icon displayed near the bottom-right corner of the screen.

To select and delete multiple images at once as you're looking at thumbnails, tap on the Select button. Tap on each thumbnail that represents an image you want to delete. A checkmark icon appears within each image thumbnail indicating that the image has been selected. Tap on the Trash icon to delete the selected images.

EDIT YOUR PHOTOS WITH THIRD-PARTY PHOTOGRAPHY APPS

The latest version of the Photos app enables you to do some basic edits and enhancements to any photo you snap using your iPhone, iPod touch, or iPad, or that you transfer onto your device. If you want vastly more powerful editing tools for your device, acquire the optional iPhoto app from the App Store.

As you explore the Photography section of the App Store, however, you can find literally hundreds of other apps that can be used to shoot, edit, view, achieve, print, and share your digital photos. Some of these apps offer functionality that's not otherwise offered using the Camera, Photos, or iPhoto apps.

The Adobe Photoshop Touch app ($4.99), for example, offers a vast collection of photo editing and enhancement tools that allow you to work with specific areas within an image, rather than applying a filter or edit to an entire image.

CREATE AND MANAGE A PHOTO STREAM VIA iCLOUD

You already know that you can easily transfer images into your iOS device and export them from your device using various methods. One feature of iOS 7 is the capability to create and manage My Photo Stream via iCloud.

My Photo Stream enables you to store a collection of up to 1,000 of your digital images on iCloud, and automatically sync those images with your computer(s) and all of your iOS devices, including Apple TV. Thus, your most recent images are always readily available to you, and you never have to worry about backing them up or manually transferring them to a specific computer or device.

NOTE If you're also using a Mac that's linked to your iCloud account, after each 30-day period, or when you go beyond 1,000 images, My Photo Stream is automatically backed up onto your computer and becomes accessible from there.

To create and use the My Photo Stream feature of iCloud, you must set up a free iCloud account. Then, from within Settings on your iOS device, tap on the iCloud option. Next, tap on the Photos option and then turn on the My Photo Stream option. While you're viewing this menu screen in Settings, also turn on the Shared Photo Stream option. To utilize these features, a Wi-Fi Internet connection is required.

TIP You can store any image from My Photo Stream on your iOS device indefinitely. As you're viewing an image from My Photo Stream, tap on the Share icon and select the Save To Camera Roll option.

CREATE AND MANAGE A SHARED PHOTO STREAM VIA iCLOUD

The Photo Stream feature is designed to sync your photos between your computer and/or devices that are linked to the same Apple ID/iCloud account.

The iCloud Shared Photo Stream feature, however, is a tool that enables you to share groups of photos with other people via the Internet and iCloud. Once you have the Shared Photo Stream feature turned on, as well as an active iCloud account, select the images you want to share from the Photos app.

Next, tap on the Share icon and select the iCloud option. From the iCloud window, add a comment to the image(s) you're about to upload, and then tap on the Stream option to choose the Shared Photo Stream folder to which you want to add the selected images.

To create a new Shared Photo Stream folder (online gallery), tap on the Stream option, and then tap on the New Shared Stream option. You'll be prompted to enter a stream name, which is the title for the Shared Photo Stream. Tap the Next option.

When prompted, enter the email addresses (or names) of the people you want to share the photo stream with (shown in Figure 8.17). If the invitees already have entries in your Contacts database, type their names; otherwise, enter their email addresses into the To field. Tap the Next option to continue.

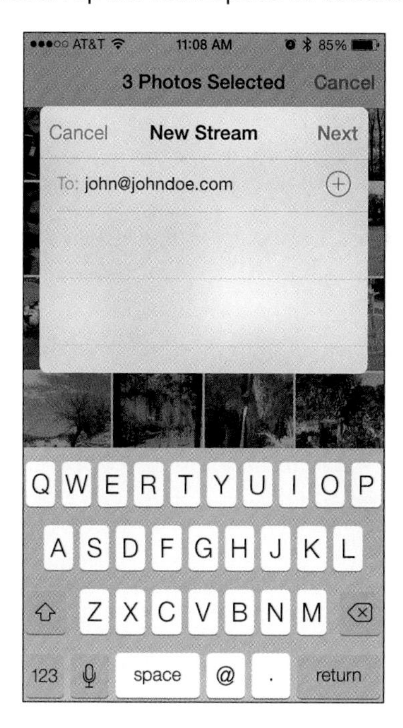

FIGURE 8.17

As you're creating a Shared Photo Stream, you can decide who can see it and send an email to those people containing a special URL to access those photos.

Tap the Post option to upload the images to an iCloud Photo Stream so that they can be viewed by the people you've selected.

If the recipients are iPhoto '11 (Mac) users or iOS device users, they can view your images or download them into their iPhoto '11 software or Photos app. Otherwise, they can view the photos online by visiting the unique URL assigned to your Shared Photo Stream.

You can create and edit as many Shared Photo Streams as you desire, and make each available to different people, if you choose to.

You also can delete a Shared Photo Stream at anytime by tapping on the Photo Stream button in the Photos app, opening a Shared Photo Stream, tapping the Edit button, and then selecting which photos you want to delete. Tap the Delete button to continue. From the Select Photos screen, you can also add photos to an existing Shared Photo Stream.

SHARED PHOTO STREAM QUICK TIPS

- After a Shared Photo Stream is created, to edit or add to the list of invitees who are able to view it, launch Photos, tap on the Shared icon (at the bottom center of the screen). From the Shared Streams menu, tap on one of the listed Shared Photo Stream listings. Thumbnails for the images in that Shared Photo Stream are displayed. Near the bottom of the thumbnail screen, tap on the People tab.

  To remove access for people already invited to view the Shared Photo Stream, tap on their name. (To the right of their name, the Invited status is displayed.) From the Info screen for that person, tap on the Remove Subscriber option. They will no longer be able to view your Shared Photo Stream.

  To add people (subscribers) who can view an already existing Shared Photo Stream you've created, after tapping on the People tab, tap on the Invite People option, and then add the names (or email addresses) to the To field of the Invite People screen.

- If the people you're inviting to view your Shared Photo Stream are Mac or iOS mobile device users, they can subscribe to the Shared Photo Stream and access it as a Shared Album via the iPhoto (Mac or iOS) or Photos (iOS) app.

  For Windows-based users to be able to view your Shared Photo Stream(s), they'll need to use their web browser to view each Shared Photo Stream as an online gallery. For this to work, be sure to turn on the Public Website option when creating the Shared Photo Stream, or after the fact by launching the Photos app, tapping on the Shared option, tapping on a Shared Photo Stream listing, and then tapping on the People tab. Turn on the virtual switch associated with Public Website.

IN THIS CHAPTER

- How to use the calling features you'll find useful
- How to manage Favorites, Recents, Contacts, and Voicemail
- How to participating in conference calls
- How to use the new Reply with Message and Remind Me Later features when receiving a call

MAKE AND RECEIVE CALLS WITH AN iPHONE

Although your iPhone is capable of handling a wide range of tasks, one of its core purposes is to serve as a feature-packed cellphone. Your iPhone makes and receives voice calls using a wireless service provider that you selected when the phone was acquired. The Phone app that comes preinstalled on your iPhone offers a vast selection of calling features that make it easy to stay in touch with people.

TIP If you're an iPad user, you can make and receive Voice over IP (Internet-based) phone calls using Skype or a similar app. These calls can be made to or received from any landline or cell phone. You also can participate in Skype-to-Skype calls for free. In addition to voice-over-IP calls, Skype can be used for free video calls with Mac, PC, iOS mobile device, or Android mobile device users. Using FaceTime for video calls works only with other Mac or iOS mobile device users.

The iPhone or iPad version of Skype is also ideal for saving money when you're making international calls from the U.S., or to avoid hefty international roaming charges when you're calling home to the U.S. when traveling overseas.

After you set up and activate your new iPhone with a wireless service provider and choose a calling plan, it's capable of receiving incoming calls and enables you to make outgoing calls using the Phone app.

In the United States, several wireless service providers now offer iPhone compatibility. When you purchase an iPhone, you must decide in advance which wireless service provider to sign up with (a two-year service agreement with a hefty early termination fee is typically involved). You can, however, purchase an "unlocked" iPhone with no service contract, and then pay a month-to-month fee for service. This requires you to pay an unsubsidized price for the iPhone (around $650), and then pay between $35 and $70 per month for voice, data, and text services.

Choose a wireless service provider that offers the best coverage in your area, the most competitively priced calling plan based on your needs, and the extra features you want or need. When looking at coverage area maps for various service providers, if you have an iPhone 5 or a newer model iPhone, such as the iPhone 5S or iPhone 5C, focus on 4G LTE coverage, as opposed to 3G or plain 4G service.

TIP From Apple's website, you can compare iPhone rate plans for wireless service providers that support the iPhone. In the U.S., visit https://static.ips.apple.com.edgekey.net/ipa_preauth/content/catalog/en_US/index.html.

Not all wireless service providers enable iPhone users to talk and surf the Web at the same time. Likewise, some offer better international roaming coverage than others, while some are more generous when it comes to monthly wireless data allocation. The iPhone hardware is slightly different based on which wireless service provider you choose, so you typically can't switch providers after you've acquired the iPhone.

TIP For your iPhone to make or receive calls, it must be turned on and *not* in Airplane mode. A decent cellular service signal, which is displayed in the upper-left corner of the screen in the form of dots, is also a necessity. The more dots you see (up to five), the stronger the cellular signal (which is based on your proximity to the closest cell towers). For more on Airplane mode, see Chapter 1, "Tips and Tricks for Customizing Settings."

ANSWERING AN INCOMING CALL

Regardless of what you're doing on your iPhone, when an incoming call is received, everything else is put on hold and the Phone app launches, unless the iPhone is turned off, the Do Not Disturb feature is turned on, or in Airplane mode, in which case incoming calls automatically go to voicemail.

To control the volume of the ringer, press the Volume Up or Volume Down buttons on the side of your iPhone; or to turn off the ringer (which causes the phone to vibrate when an incoming call is received), turn on the Mute button on the side of the iPhone.

> **TIP** While your iPhone is still ringing, to silence the ringer and send the incoming call to voicemail after a 5- to 10-second delay, press the Power button or Volume Up or Volume Down button once. To send the incoming call immediately to voicemail, double tap on the Power button or tap the Decline option displayed on the screen.
>
> You also can silence the iPhone's ringer by switching on the Mute button (located on the side of the iPhone, above the Volume Up button). Your phone vibrates instead of ringing when an incoming call is received. To control the Vibrate feature, launch Settings and tap on the Sounds option.
>
> Yet another way to be left alone is to put your phone in Do Not Disturb mode. This can be done automatically at certain predetermined times or manually whenever you want to be left alone.

There are several ways to answer an incoming call. If you're doing something else on your iPhone and it starts to ring, the caller ID for the incoming caller appears, along with a green-and-white Answer button and a red-and-white Decline icon (as shown in Figure 9.1). Tap the Answer button to answer the call. If you tap Decline or wait too long to answer, the call automatically goes to voicemail.

If you're using your iPhone with EarPods, ear buds, or a headset with a built-in microphone, you can answer an incoming call by pressing the Answer button on the headset.

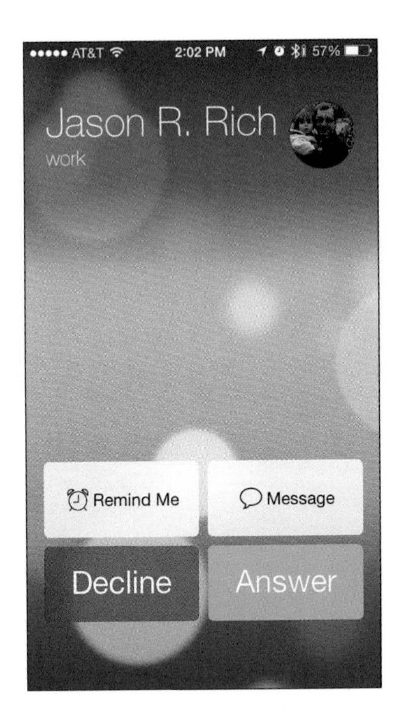

FIGURE 9.1

Your iPhone notifies you when an incoming call is received. You can then answer or decline the call.

TIP When you receive an incoming call, displayed above the Decline and Accept buttons (or the Slide To Answer slider on the Lock screen) are two other options (refer to Figure 9.1) labeled Remind Me and Message.

When you tap on Message, a menu containing four pre-written text messages, along with a Custom button, is displayed. Tap on one of the message buttons to send that message to the caller via text/instant message. Or tap on the Custom button to type a custom message to send to that caller. The incoming call is also transferred to voicemail.

To customize the prewritten messages available from the Message option, launch Settings, tap on the Phone option, and then tap on the Respond with Text option. Displayed on the Respond with Text menu screen are three customizable fields, under the heading, "Can't Talk Right Now." Tap on one of these fields to replace one of the default messages with your own. The new messages display when you access the Message option any time an incoming call is received.

The other option for managing incoming calls is the Remind Me option. When you tap on this button, the incoming call is sent to voicemail, but you can quickly set a reminder (and alarm) for yourself to call that person back in one hour, when you leave your current location, or when you get home. For these last two options to function, Locations Services related to the Phone app must be turned on from within Settings.

If the iPhone is in Sleep mode when an incoming call is received, unlock the phone by swiping your finger from left to right on the Slide to Answer slider, which automatically takes the phone out of Sleep mode, unlocks it, and answers the incoming call. Again, if you ignore the incoming call, it gets sent to voicemail after several rings. You also have access to the Message and Remind Me Later buttons.

TIP If you're too busy to answer an incoming call on your iPhone, you can let the call go to voicemail or set up call forwarding so that the incoming call automatically gets rerouted to another phone number, such as your home or office number. To set up call forwarding and turn this function on or off as needed, launch Settings, and then tap on the Phone option.

From the Phone menu in Settings, you can view your iPhone's phone number, set up and turn on call forwarding, turn on or off call waiting, and decide whether you want your iPhone's number to be displayed on someone's caller ID when you initiate a call.

Also from Settings, you have the option to enable the International Assist feature, which makes initiating international calls much less confusing.

After you answer an incoming call, you have a few options. You can hold the iPhone up to your ear and start talking, or you can tap the Speaker icon to use your iPhone as a speakerphone. You also can use the phone with a wired or wireless headset, which offers hands-free operation. The headset option is ideal when you're driving, plus it offers privacy (versus using the iPhone's speaker phone option).

! CAUTION If you're driving, choose a headset that covers only one ear, or use the Speaker option for hands-free operation. Refrain from holding the phone up to your ear or covering both ears with a headset. (See the section, "A Few Thoughts About Wireless Headsets," for headset considerations.) Make sure you're familiar with state and local laws in your area related to the use of cellphones while driving. Some jurisdictions limit or prohibit using a cellphone while driving, even if the phone is a hands-free model, and many other areas across the country are considering similar legislation.

Many people find it convenient to use a wireless Bluetooth headset with their iPhone. Learn more about headsets later in this chapter. When using a Bluetooth headset, you don't need to hold the phone up to your ear to carry on a conversation. If you're using a headset, tap on the headset's answer button when you receive an incoming call to answer it. There's no need to do anything on your iPhone.

MANAGING THE DO NOT DISTURB FEATURE

To activate and customize the Do Not Disturb feature, launch Settings and tap on the Do Not Disturb option. To later turn on or off the feature, access the new Control Center and tap on the crescent moon-shaped icon (shown in Figure 9.2).

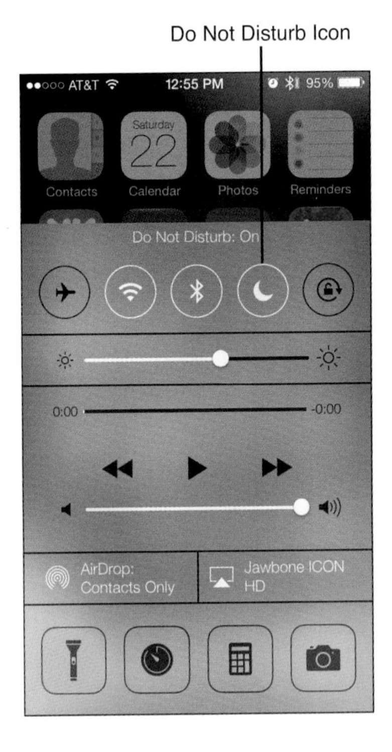

FIGURE 9.2

Accessing the Do Not Disturb feature is now much easier using Control Center in iOS 7.

When turned on, a moon icon is displayed on the iPhone or iPad's status bar, and all calls and alerts are silenced. This feature can be turned on or off at anytime, or you can schedule specific times you want Do Not Disturb to be activated, such as between 11:00 p.m. and 7:00 a.m. on weekdays. From the Do Not Disturb menu in

Settings (shown in Figure 9.3), you can also determine whether certain callers are allowed to reach you when the phone is in Do Not Disturb mode.

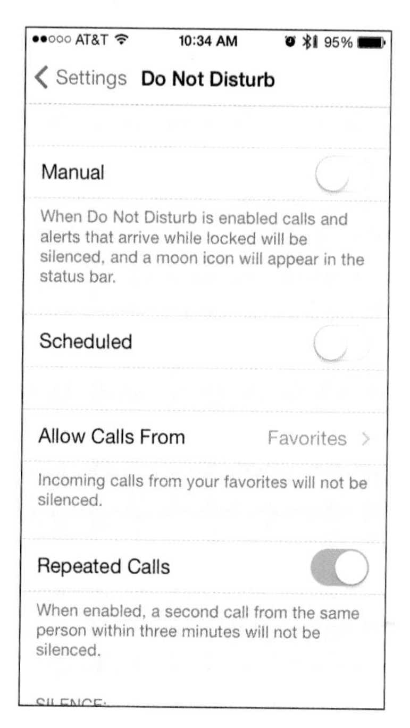

FIGURE 9.3

From the Do Not Disturb menu screen in Settings, be sure to customize this feature so it best meets your needs and schedule, based on when you want to be left alone.

Keep in mind that when your iPhone is turned off, all incoming calls are forwarded directly to voicemail, and it is not possible to initiate an outgoing call. Likewise, incoming text messages, FaceTime calls, and other communications from the outside world are not accepted when an iPhone is turned off. Instead, notifications for these missed messages are displayed in Notification Center, within their respective apps, and potentially on the Lock screen when you turn on the device (depending on how you set up Notification Center).

MANAGE CALLS IN PROGRESS FROM THE CALL IN PROGRESS SCREEN

As soon as you answer an incoming call, the Phone app's display changes to the Call In Progress screen (shown in Figure 9.4). This screen contains several command icons: Mute, Keypad, Speaker, Add Call, FaceTime, Contacts, and End. The caller's information and a call timer are displayed at the top of the screen.

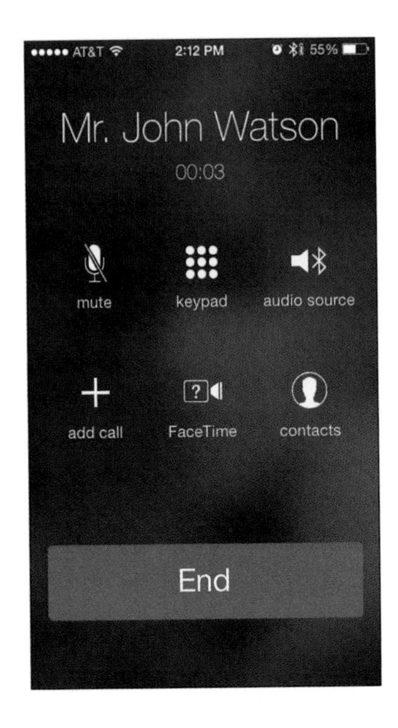

FIGURE 9.4

The main Call In Progress screen on the iPhone appears when you're participating in an incoming or outgoing call.

NOTE When you receive an incoming call, if the caller ID for that caller matches up with a contact stored in the Contacts app, that person's name, which number the call is from (Home, Work, Mobile, and so on), and the caller's photo (if you have a photo of that person linked to the contact) are displayed.

If there's no match in your Contacts database, the regular caller ID data is displayed, which can include the person's name, phone number, and the city and state from which the call is originating. However, not all incoming calls display all this information. You might also receive calls labeled Private or Unknown.

iOS 7 WHAT'S NEW It's now possible to block incoming calls from specific phone numbers. To block a caller, you must first create a new contact in the Contacts app for the person or company you want to block. Then, tap on the Blocked option in the Phone menu of the Settings app (shown in Figure 9.5), followed by the Add New option. Choose a phone number from your Contacts database. Until you manually remove that contact from your Blocked list, no calls, texts, or FaceTime calls will be accepted from that number.

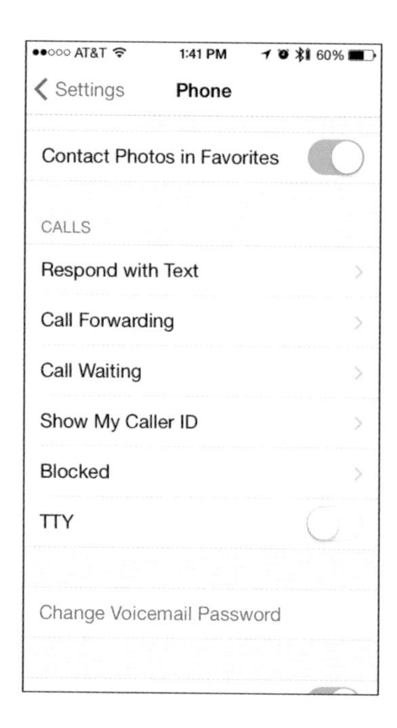

FIGURE 9.5

Customize features of the Phone app from within Settings, like the ability to block certain incoming calls.

Here's a summary of the command icons available to you from the Call In Progress screen during a phone conversation:

- **Mute**—Tap on this icon to turn off your iPhone's microphone. You can still hear what's being said to you, but the person you're speaking with cannot hear you. When you're ready to be heard again, turn off the Mute feature by tapping on this icon again.
- **Keypad**—Replace the current menu screen with the numeric telephone keypad. This is necessary for navigating your way through voicemail trees (for example, when you're told to press 1 for English, press 2 to speak with an operator, press 3 to connect to a call center, and so on).
- **Speaker (or Audio Source)**—Tap the Speaker icon to switch from Handset mode (in which you hold the iPhone up to your ear to have a phone conversation) to Speaker mode, which turns your iPhone into a speakerphone. If you're using your iPhone with a headset, a third Headset option is listed, and this menu feature is labeled Audio Source as opposed to Speaker.
- **Add Call (+)**—During a conversation with someone, you can initiate a conference call and bring a third party into the conversation by tapping on Add Call, as described later in this chapter.

- **FaceTime**—If the person with which you're talking on your iPhone is also calling from an iPhone, and both devices have access to an Internet connection, tap on the FaceTime icon to switch from a traditional phone call to a real-time video call using the FaceTime app.

iOS 7 WHAT'S NEW In addition to being able to launch FaceTime from the Phone app and switch from a normal call to a video call, you can now use the separate FaceTime app to initiate a video call from your iPhone.

NOTE You can participate in FaceTime video calls for free, with iPhone, Mac, iPad, or iPod touch users. For this feature to work, in most cases, your iPhone requires a Wi-Fi Internet connection (although some wireless service providers now allow FaceTime to be used with a cellular data connection). Both parties must have active FaceTime accounts and be able to access the FaceTime service using their computers or iOS mobile devices when a FaceTime call connection is initiated.

- **Contacts**—While you're conversing on the phone, you can access your Contacts database and look up someone's information by tapping on this option.
- **End**—Tap on the large red-and-white End button or tap the end call button on your headset, if applicable, to terminate the call.

TIP Your phone conversation can continue while you're using other apps. Depending on your wireless service provider, you might even be able to participate in a phone conversation and surf the Web at the same time. To launch another app, press the Home button and tap on its app icon from the Home screen. Or to access the multitasking bar, double-tap on the Home button, and then tap on any app icon that appears in the multitasking bar.

When you view the Home screen while still on the phone, a green-and-white banner shows, "Touch to return to call," along with a call timer. Tap on this green bar to return to the Phone app.

RESPOND TO A CALL WAITING SIGNAL WHILE ON THE PHONE

As you're chatting it up on the phone, if someone else tries to call you, you hear a call waiting tone, and a related message appears on your iPhone's screen. You can control the Call Waiting feature from the Settings app.

When a second call comes in, the caller ID information of the new caller is displayed on the screen, along with several command icons and buttons (shown in Figure 9.6). These commands are Answer: End Current Call, Answer: Hold Current Call, and Decline Incoming Call.

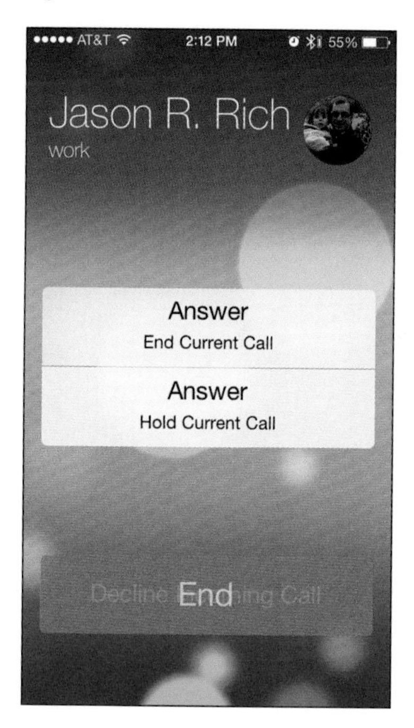

FIGURE 9.6

When you're on a call and you simultaneously receive another incoming call, in addition to hearing the Call Waiting signal, you're given several onscreen options.

As you can see in Figure 9.7, if you place the first call on hold and answer the new incoming call, you'll have the opportunity to merge the two calls and create a conference call or switch between the two calls and speak with each person individually (while the other is on hold).

TIP When the call waiting signal goes off on your iPhone, typically only you hear it. Thus, the person you're speaking with on the other end of the line does not know you've received another call. So before tapping the Answer: End Current Call or Answer: Hold Current Call button, be sure to tell the person you were originally speaking with what's going on.

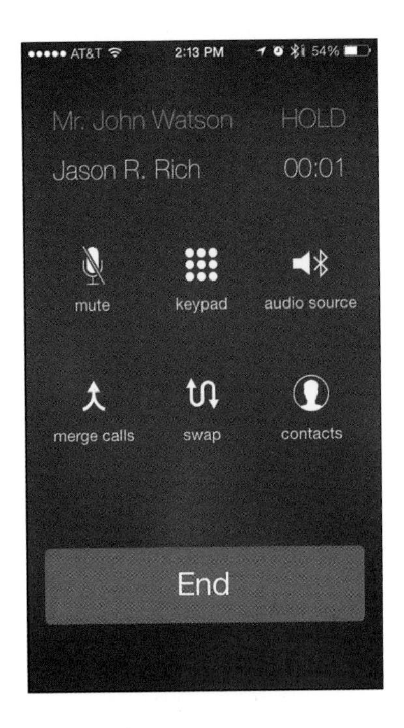

FIGURE 9.7

If you accept a call waiting call, you can merge the two calls together or switch between them.

While engaged in a conference call on your iPhone, the word Conference appears (shown in Figure 9.8). Tap on the circular "i" icon to the right of this information to reveal a new screen that enables you to manage any of the parties involved with the conference call.

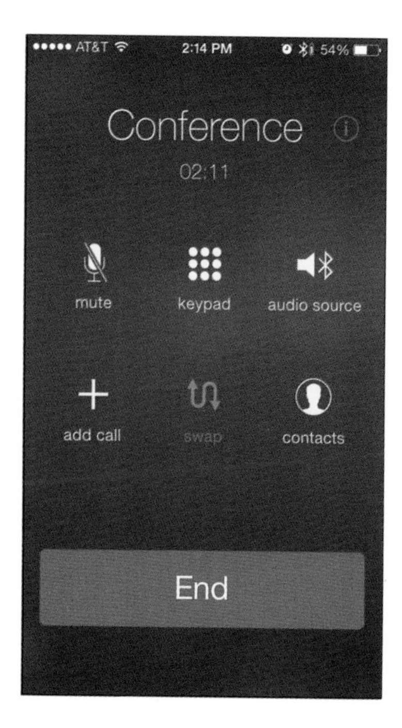

FIGURE 9.8

When you're engaged in a conference call, you can place one party on hold and continue speaking with the other parties by tapping on the circular 'i' icon displayed near names of the people engaged in the call or the word Conference.

While you're engaged in a three-way call (with two other parties), you can tap on the Add Call option again to add more parties to the conference call.

On the secondary Conference Call Info screen (shown in Figure 9.9), next to each name/Caller ID number is an End button and a Private button. Tap on End to disconnect that party, or tap Private to speak with just that party privately and place the other party (or parties) on hold. You can then reestablish the conference call by tapping on the Back button to return to the previous Conference Call screen (refer to Figure 9.7) and then tap on the Merge Calls icon again.

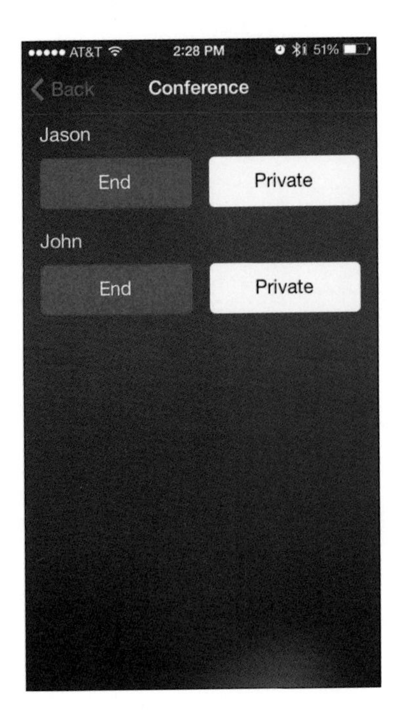

FIGURE 9.9

While engaged in a conference call, you can manage each party from this Conference Info screen in the Phone app.

MAKING CALLS FROM YOUR iPHONE

There are several ways to initiate a phone call from your iPhone; however, you typically must first launch the Phone app. Then, you can do the following:

- Dial a number manually using the keypad.
- Access a listing from your Contacts database (from within the Phone app), choose a number, and dial it.
- Use Siri (which is explained in Chapter 2, "Using Siri, Dictation, and iOS In Your Car to Communicate with Your Mobile Device"). This can be done anytime, regardless of what app is running on your iPhone or whether you're looking at the Home screen.
- Redial a number from the Phone app's Recents call log.
- Select and dial a phone number from the Phone app's Favorites list.
- Redial a number used by someone who left you a voicemail message.

- Dial a number displayed in another compatible app or iOS 7 feature, such as Maps, Mail, Safari, Contacts, or the Notification Center window. When you tap on the phone number, it dials that number and initiates a call using the Phone app.

MANUAL DIALING

To initiate a call by manually dialing a phone number, follow these steps:

1. Launch the Phone app from the Home screen.
2. Tap on the Keypad icon displayed at the bottom of the screen (as shown in Figure 9.10).

FIGURE 9.10

A telephone numeric keypad appears when you tap on the Keypad option (displayed at the bottom of the screen) in the Phone app.

3. Using the numeric phone keypad, dial the number you want to reach, including the area code. If you're making an international call, include the country code as well.
4. If you make a mistake when entering a digit, tap the small "X" icon that's displayed near the top-right corner of the screen (refer to Figure 9.10).

5. When the phone number is entered and displayed at the top of the screen, tap the green-and-white Call button to initiate the call.
6. The display on the iPhone changes to display a "Calling" message until the call connects, at which time the Call Menu screen is displayed.

TIP You can use Siri to dial a phone number. To do this, activate Siri and say, "Dial 2 1 2 5 5 5 1 2 1 2," speaking each digit.

NOTE As you enter a phone number using the keypad, if that number is already stored in your Contacts database (within the Contacts app), the person's name automatically displays at the top of the screen, just below the phone number you entered.

You can also use the Cut, Copy, and Paste features of iOS 7 to copy a phone number displayed in another app, and then paste it into the phone number field on the Keypad screen. Or, if you tap on a phone number that's displayed in the Contacts app or while surfing the Web using Safari, for example, the Phone app automatically launches and a call to that number is initiated.

DIALING FROM A CONTACTS ENTRY IN THE PHONE APP

From within the Phone app, it's possible to look up any phone number stored in your personal contacts database that's associated with the Contacts app. The Phone and Contacts apps work nicely together on your iPhone. To use this feature, follow these steps:

1. Launch the Phone app from the Home screen.
2. Tap on the Contacts icon displayed at the bottom of the screen.
3. An alphabetized listing of the contacts stored in the Contacts app is displayed. At the top of the screen is a blank Search field. Using your finger, either scroll through the alphabetized list of contacts or use the iPhone's virtual keyboard to find a stored listing.
4. Tap on any listing to view its complete Contacts entry. This might include multiple phone numbers, such as Home, Work, and Mobile. From a contact's entry screen, tap on the phone number you want to dial.
5. The display on the iPhone changes. A "Calling" message is displayed until the call connects, at which time the Call Menu screen is displayed.

USE SIRI TO INITIATE CALLS

After you have added entries into your Contacts database using the Contacts app, you can use Siri to dial someone's phone number by speaking into the iPhone. More information about using Siri with the Phone app can be found earlier in this chapter, as well as in Chapter 2.

INITIATING A CONFERENCE CALL

During a typical phone conversation with one other person, you can initiate a conference call and bring a third party into the call. To do this, from the Call In Progress screen, tap on the Add Call (+) icon. The Call In Progress screen is replaced by the All Contacts screen (which includes a listing of all contacts stored in your Contacts database), as well as a blank Search field. You can either look up the phone number you want to add to your conference call or tap on the Keypad icon (displayed at the bottom of the screen) to manually enter the phone number.

MANAGING YOUR VOICEMAIL

Your unique iPhone phone number comes with voicemail, which enables people to leave you messages if you're not able to speak with them when they call.

Just as with any voicemail service, you can record your outgoing message, play back missed messages from your iPhone, or call your iPhone's voicemail service and listen to your calls from another phone.

RECORD YOUR OUTGOING MESSAGE

To record your outgoing voicemail message, which is what people hear when they call your iPhone and you don't answer, follow these steps. Or you can have a computer-generated voice instruct callers to leave a message.

1. Launch the Phone app from the Home screen.
2. Tap on the Voicemail icon, displayed in the lower-right corner of the screen.
3. In the upper-left corner of the Voicemail screen, tap on the Greeting option.
4. From the Greeting screen (shown in Figure 9.11), tap on the Default option to skip recording a message and have a computer voice use a generic message. Or tap on the Custom option to record your own outgoing voicemail message.

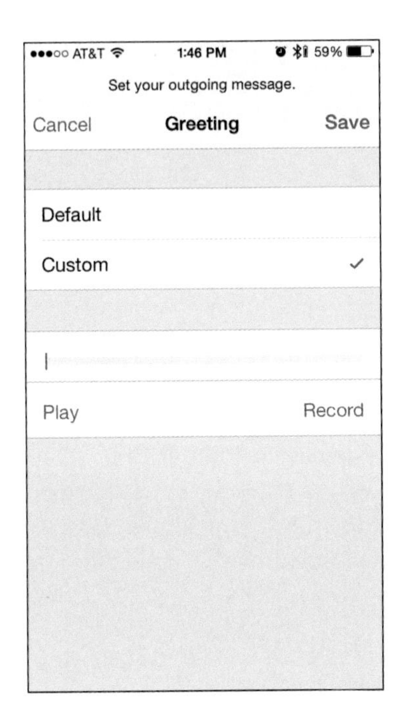

FIGURE 9.11

The Greeting screen in the Phone app. From here, you can record an outgoing greeting.

5. After you tap the Custom option, tap on the Record option that's also displayed on the Greeting screen. Hold the phone up to your mouth and begin recording your message.
6. When you're finished recording, tap on the Stop option. You can now play back your message by tapping on the Play option, or tap on the Save option to save your message and activate it.

HOW TO PLAY AND DELETE VOICEMAIL MESSAGES

It's possible to listen to voicemail messages either from your iPhone or by calling your iPhone's voicemail from another phone.

LISTEN TO VOICEMAIL FROM YOUR iPHONE

From your iPhone, to listen to and then save or delete an incoming voicemail message, follow these steps:

1. Launch the Phone app from the Home screen.
2. Tap on the Voicemail icon that's displayed in the bottom-right corner of the screen.

3. Under the Voicemail heading seen at the top of the screen is a listing of missed voicemail messages. Tap on a message to highlight it.

NOTE When you see a blue dot to the left of a voicemail message listing, this indicates it's a new, unheard message. After you listen to the message, the blue dot disappears. When you tap on the message to listen to it, the blue dot changes into a Pause/Play icon.

4. After a message is highlighted, tap on the small play/pause icon. The message begins playing. It might, however, take a few seconds for the message to load. A brief pause should be expected.
5. Near the bottom of the voicemail listing is a slider that depicts the length of the message, along with Call Back and Delete options. As your message plays, the thin blue line on the timer slider moves to the right. You can listen to parts of the message again by moving this slider around with your finger.
6. When you're finished listening to the message, you can leave the listing alone (which keeps the message saved on your phone) or tap the Delete option to erase it. You also have the option of calling back the person who left the message by tapping on the Call Back option.
7. To exit the voicemail options, tap on any of the other command icons displayed at the bottom of the Phone app's screen, or press the Home button on your iPhone.

TIP You might find it easier to listen to your voicemail messages via speaker phone, by first tapping on the Speaker or Audio option that's displayed below the timer slider.

TIP If you accidentally delete an important voicemail, don't panic. From the voicemail screen, scroll to the very bottom of your voicemail message list and tap on the Deleted Messages icon. Tap on the message you want to undelete to highlight it, and then tap on the Undelete icon.

LISTEN TO YOUR iPHONE'S VOICEMAIL FROM ANOTHER PHONE

You also have the option of using another phone to call your iPhone's voicemail service and listen to the messages that were left. Follow these steps:

1. From any other phone besides your iPhone (including a landline or another cellphone), dial your iPhone's phone number.
2. When your iPhone's voicemail picks up, press the * key on the phone from which you're calling.
3. When prompted by the computer voice, enter the numeric password that's associated with your voicemail.

> **TIP** To set or change your voicemail password, launch the Settings app and tap on the Phone option. From the Phone menu in Settings, scroll down to the Change Voicemail Password option and tap on it. When the Password screen appears, use the keypad to create and enter a password. To change a password, first enter your current password, tap Done, and then enter a new voicemail password.

4. Follow the voice prompts to listen to or delete your messages.
5. As you're listening to your messages, you can press certain keys to manage specific functions. These options vary based on your cellular service provider, but might include the following:
   - Press 1 to play back your messages.
   - Press 5 to hear details about a message, including the incoming phone number and the time/date it was recorded, as well as the message length.
   - Press 7 to delete the current message.
   - Press 9 to save the message.
   - Press # to skip the current message.
   - Press 0 for more options.
6. Hang up when you're finished listening to your voicemail messages.

CREATE AND USE A FAVORITES LIST

From within the Phone app, you can create a Favorites list, which is a customized list of your most frequently dialed contacts. To access this list, launch the Phone app, and then tap on the Favorites icon that's displayed near the bottom-left corner of the screen.

To add a contact to the Favorites list, tap on the plus-sign (+) icon that you see in the upper-right corner of the screen. Select any listing from your Contacts database and tap on it. When the complete listing for that entry appears, tap on the specific phone number you want listed in your Favorites list. The newly created Favorites listing appears at the end of your Favorites list.

> **TIP** Each favorites entry can have one name and one phone number associated with it. So, if a Contact entry has multiple phone numbers listed, choose one. If you want quick access to someone's home, work, and mobile numbers from your Favorites list, create three separate entries for that person. When you create the entry in Favorites, the type of phone number (Home, Work, Mobile, iPhone, and so on) is displayed to the right of the person's name. A Favorites listing can also relate to someone's FaceTime identifier (their iPhone number, Apple ID, or the email address they used to set up their FaceTime account).

To edit the contacts already listed in your Favorites list, tap on the Edit option in the upper-left corner of the screen. After tapping Edit, you can change the order of your Favorites list by holding your finger on the rightmost icon next to a listing, and then dragging it upward or downward to the desired location. Or you can delete a listing by tapping on the red-and-white negative-sign icon displayed to the left of a listing. When you're finished making changes, tap on the Done icon that's displayed in the upper-left corner of the screen.

> **TIP** As you're viewing your Favorites list, tap on the Info ('i') icon, shown to the right of each listing. This enables you to view that person's entire entry from within your Contacts database.

To dial a phone number listed in your Favorites list, simply tap on its listing. The Phone app automatically dials the number and initiates a call.

ACCESSING YOUR RECENTS CALL LOG

The Phone app on your iPhone automatically keeps track of all incoming and outgoing calls. To access this detailed call log, launch the Phone app from the Home screen, and then tap on the Recents command icon displayed at the bottom of the screen.

At the top of the Recents screen are two command tabs, labeled All and Missed, along with an Edit option. Tap on the All tab to view a detailed listing of all incoming and outgoing calls, displayed in reverse-chronological order. Missed incoming calls are displayed in red. Tap on the Missed tab to see a listing of calls you didn't answer. Tap on the Edit option to delete specific calls from this listing, or tap on the Info ("i") icon to view more details about that caller, including their recent call history with you.

TIP Missed calls are also displayed in the Notification Center window on your iPhone or as an icon badge or alert on your Home screen, depending on how you set up Notifications for the Phone app within the Settings app. To customize the Notifications options for the Phone app, launch Settings from the Home screen and tap on the Notifications option. From the Notifications screen in Settings, tap on the Phone option. You can adjust how your iPhone alerts you to missed calls by personalizing the options on this Phone screen.

Each listing in the Recents call log displays the name of the person you spoke with (based on data from your Contacts database or the Caller ID feature) or their phone number. If it's someone from your Contacts database, information about which phone number (home, work, mobile, or such) the caller used appears below the name.

If the same person called you, or you called that person, multiple times in a row, a number in parentheses indicates how many calls were made to or from that person. This is displayed to the right of the name or phone number.

On the right side of the screen, with each Recents listing, is the time the call was made or received. To view the Contacts entry related to that person, tap on the right-pointing blue-and-white arrow icon associated with the listing. At the top of a contact's entry screen are details about the call itself, including its time and date, whether it was an incoming or outgoing call, and its duration.

To call someone back who is listed in the Recents list, tap anywhere on that listing, except for on the blue-and-white arrow icon.

DO YOU TALK TOO MUCH? KEEPING TRACK OF USAGE

Some iPhone voice plans come with a predetermined number of talk minutes per month. Some plans offer unlimited night and weekend calling, but calls made or received during the day count against your monthly minute allocation.

> **CAUTION** Contact your wireless service provider (or read your service agreement carefully) to determine the time period that's considered prime daytime, versus night or weekend, because it varies greatly. Unlimited night and weekend calling does not start until 9:00 p.m. with some wireless service providers. If you have a truly unlimited calling plan, however, this is not a concern.

If your plan does have a monthly allocation for talk minutes, if you go over your monthly minute allocation, you will be charged a hefty surcharge for each additional minute used.

> **TIP** Each wireless service provider that supports the iPhone offers a free app for managing your wireless service account. It's available from the App Store. Use it to manage all aspects of your account, pay your monthly bill, and view your voice, data, and text-messaging use at any time. You can also set the alert option in the app to remind you each month when the bill is due for payment.

CUSTOMIZING RINGTONES

Thanks to the iTunes Store, you can purchase and download custom ringtones for your iPhone. You can use one ringtone as your generic ringtone for all incoming calls, or you can assign specific ringtones to individual people.

> **TIP** iOS 7 comes with more than two dozen preinstalled ringtones. To shop for ringtones, launch Settings, select Sounds, and from the Sounds menu screen, tap on the Ringtone option. Tap on the Store option that's displayed near the top-right corner of the Ringtone menu screen (within Settings).
>
> When you purchase and download a new ringtone, it becomes available on your iPhone's internal ringtones list. Most ringtones from the iTunes Store cost $1.29 each.

To choose a default ringtone for all your incoming calls, launch Settings and select the Sounds option. From the Sounds menu screen, scroll down to the Ringtone option and tap on it. A complete listing of ringtones stored on your iPhone is displayed.

CUSTOM RINGTONES FOR SPECIFIC CONTACTS

To assign a custom ringtone to a specific person so that you hear it when that person calls your iPhone, follow these steps:

1. Launch the Contacts app from the iPhone's Home screen.
2. From the All Contacts screen, find the specific contact with whom you want to link a custom ringtone. You can scroll through the listing or use the Search field to find a contact.
3. When the contact is selected and you're looking at that Contacts entry, tap the Edit option that's displayed in the upper-right corner of the screen.
4. From the Info screen that displays that contact entry's data, scroll down to the Ringtone field and tap on it (shown in Figure 9.12).

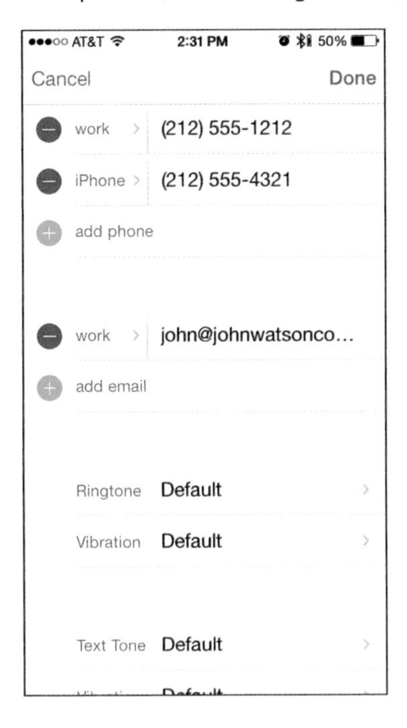

FIGURE 9.12

It's possible to choose a custom ringtone from each entry within the Contacts app.

5. When the Ringtone screen appears, select a specific ringtone from the list that you want to assign to the contact and tap on it. You can choose a specific song (purchased from iTunes) or ringer sound that reminds you of that person.

6. Tap on the Done icon to save your selection and return to the contact's Info screen.
7. When that contact calls you, you will hear the ringtone you just linked to that contact (as opposed to the default ringtone).

A FEW THOUGHTS ABOUT WIRELESS HEADSETS

Many states have outlawed using a cellphone while driving unless you have a wireless headset or hands-free feature on your phone. Although the speakerphone feature of your iPhone counts as a hands-free feature, to ensure the best possible call quality while you're driving, invest in a wireless Bluetooth headset.

Not only can you use a wireless Bluetooth headset while driving, but you can keep it on your person throughout the day and use it whenever you make or receive calls using your iPhone. This enables you to keep your hands free while you're talking or to easily access other apps or iPhone features during a phone conversation. If you invest in only one accessory for your iPhone, and you plan to use the iPhone to make and receive phone calls, a wireless Bluetooth headset is a worthwhile investment (although a good-quality iPhone case is also highly recommended).

Bluetooth wireless headsets are priced as low as $20 but can cost as much as $200. If you want to ensure the highest-quality phone conversations possible, so that people can hear you and you can hear them, even if there's background noise present, invest in a good-quality Bluetooth wireless headset that includes a noise-canceling microphone and a good-quality speaker. Plus, choose a headset that's comfortable to wear and that has a long battery life.

Although you have literally hundreds of wireless Bluetooth headsets to choose from, some of the best ones on the market, that work perfectly with an iPhone, are available from a company called Jawbone (www.Jawbone.com). Jawbone has several wireless Bluetooth headset models available, including the Jawbone Era ($129.99) and Jawbone Icon ($99.99). Both models are available online, at stores like Best Buy, or wherever cellphone accessories are sold.

IN THIS CHAPTER

- How to use FaceTime for video phone calls
- How to use the Skype service (with the Skype app) to make and receive voice-over-IP calls and participate in free video phone calls

10

VIDEO PHONE CALL STRATEGIES USING FACETIME

All of the more recent iPhone, iPad, and iPod touch models have a front-facing camera enabling you to shoot digital images or video clips (using the Camera app). These same cameras, along with your device's built-in microphone and speaker (or an optional headset), can be used for real-time video phone calls.

iOS 7 comes with the FaceTime app preinstalled. When your iOS device is connected to the Internet via a Wi-Fi connection, the FaceTime app enables you to participate in real-time video calls with other FaceTime users.

NOTE Making and receiving calls using FaceTime and participating in video calls is free via a Wi-Fi Internet connection. You can make or receive an unlimited number of calls and stay connected for as long as you'd like. Depending on your cellular service provider and your data plan, you might be allowed to use FaceTime with a cellular Internet connection. Using your cellular data plan with FaceTime can result in extra charges, however, if you exceed your monthly data allotment.

The first time you use FaceTime, you must set up a free account. If you're using an iPhone, by default, your account utilizes your iPhone's unique 10-digit phone number. However, on an iPhone or iPad, you can also opt to use your Apple ID or a different email address to be your FaceTime identifier.

When you make or receive a call using the Phone app, if your iPhone determines that the person you're connecting with also has FaceTime available, simply tap on the FaceTime icon to launch the FaceTime app and convert the traditional call into a video call.

TIP Your iPhone's phone number, the Apple ID, or the email address you link to your FaceTime account serves as your unique identifier when you're using FaceTime. It enables others to initiate a FaceTime connection with you when you both have FaceTime running on your devices. Likewise, if you want to call another FaceTime user with this app, you must know the email address that the user has associated with FaceTime or her iPhone phone number. It is now possible to associate an iPhone number and an email address, as well as an Apple ID account username, to the same FaceTime account. This makes it easier for people to connect to you via the FaceTime service if you use an iPhone, iPad, or Mac.

After the FaceTime app setup process is complete (it takes less than a minute), as long as you have FaceTime running and your iOS mobile device is connected to the Internet, you can initiate or receive calls and participate in video calls.

iOS 7 **WHAT'S NEW** The iOS 7 edition of FaceTime allows for full-screen mode. When you're engaged in a video call, all command icons temporarily disappear, allowing you more onscreen real estate to view the person with whom you're conversing. Tap on the screen at any time during a FaceTime call to make the Camera Selection, End, and Mute buttons appear.

HOW TO USE FACETIME FOR VIDEO PHONE CALLS

To launch the FaceTime app, first look near the upper-left corner of your iOS device's Home screen, and make sure it is connected to the Web using a Wi-Fi connection. The Wi-Fi signal strength icon is displayed if a Wi-Fi connection exists.

LAUNCH FACETIME ON YOUR iPHONE

On the iPhone, FaceTime can be launched through the Phone app or using the standalone FaceTime app. When you initiate a call with another iPhone user, on the main phone screen after a call is connected, the FaceTime icon becomes active, meaning that if you tap on it, a video call connection will be made.

You can also look up contacts listed in your Contacts database from the Phone app by tapping on the Contacts icon. If the contact entry you're looking at can also connect to FaceTime, the FaceTime icon becomes active and a tiny video-camera icon appears in it.

Finally, if you receive an incoming call from another FaceTime user, your phone rings but you're notified that the call is a FaceTime request, as opposed to a regular incoming call. If you accept the request, a FaceTime connection is automatically established between the two devices and a video call begins via the FaceTime app.

NOTE After a FaceTime video call connection is made between your iPhone or iPad and another FaceTime user, the main FaceTime screen looks identical, regardless of which device you're using. See the section "Participating in a FaceTime Call."

When you launch the FaceTime app on the iPhone, three command buttons display at the bottom of the screen: Favorites, Recents, and Contacts. Use one of these three options to choose with whom you want to initiate a FaceTime call. As soon as you tap on one of the listings, a FaceTime call is initiated and, assuming the other party is available, a videoconference begins within a few seconds.

LAUNCH FACETIME ON YOUR iPAD

As soon as the FaceTime app is launched, the device's forward-facing camera turns on, and you should see yourself on your iPad's screen. On the right side of the screen, a window requests that you enter your Apple ID and password to sign in (as shown in Figure 10.1). Enter this information using the virtual keyboard, and then tap the Sign In icon that's displayed below the username and password fields. Or you can tap on the Create New Account option to set up a free Apple ID account from within the FaceTime app.

FIGURE 10.1

On the iPad, you must sign in to your FaceTime account before a video call can be established.

You're now ready to initiate or receive FaceTime calls and participate in video calls via the Web. Displayed at the lower-right corner of this app screen are three command icons labeled Favorites, Recents, and Contacts (as shown in Figure 10.2).

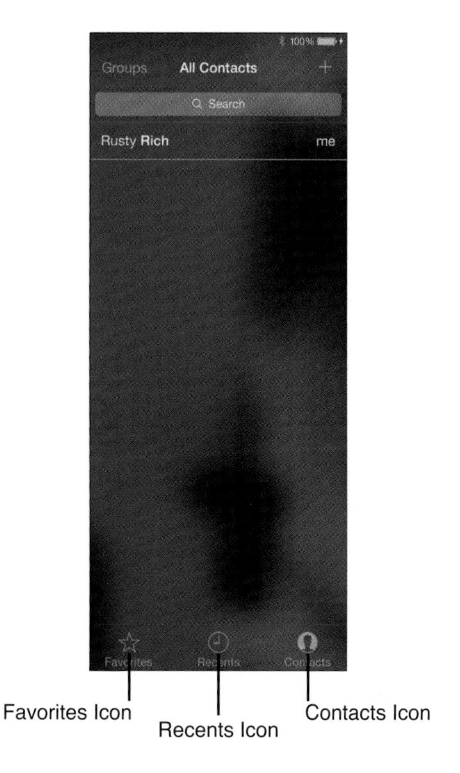

FIGURE 10.2

You can decide whom to FaceTime video call with using the Favorites, Recents, or Contacts icon displayed at the bottom of the FaceTime screen when it's used with an iPad.

CREATE A FACETIME FAVORITES LIST

A Favorites list in FaceTime is a list you can customize to include the people with whom you FaceTime video call the most. In essence, this Favorites option serves as a one-touch speed-dial list. Tap on the Favorites option to access it.

NOTE On the iPhone, your Favorites list can be maintained as part of the Phone app, but you can also maintain a separate Favorites list within the FaceTime app that's specific to FaceTime.

The entries within your Favorites list can include either a contact's iPhone phone number (to initiate a FaceTime call) or the FaceTime account username they've used to set up their FaceTime account. This could be their Apple ID or an email address.

To add a contact in your Favorites list, tap on the plus sign icon that's located in the upper-right corner of the Favorites screen (iPhone) or window (iPad). When the All Contacts screen appears, select a contact entry from your Contacts database.

TIP In the Contacts entry for each person, if that person is an iPhone user, be sure to associate his mobile phone number with the iPhone label, as opposed to the mobile phone label, so that the FaceTime app can easily identify and connect with him.

USE FACETIME'S AUTOMATIC RECENTS LIST

When you tap on the Recents icon while using the FaceTime app, you see a list of people with whom you've already communicated using FaceTime. Tap on any of the contacts in this list to video call with that person again.

If this is the first time you're using the FaceTime app, the Recents list will be empty, except for the All and Missed tabs displayed near the top of the screen/window. After you begin using the app, the All tab displays all FaceTime video calls you've participated in, as well as any incoming missed calls you didn't answer. Tap on the Missed tab to see a list of just the incoming FaceTime calls you didn't answer.

CHOOSE A CONTACT FROM YOUR CONTACTS DATABASE

The Contacts option that's displayed near the bottom of the FaceTime screen enables you to select and call a fellow FaceTime user who is listed in your Contacts database.

Remember that FaceTime works only with other compatible iOS devices or Mac users. As long as someone's device or Mac is turned on and connected to the Internet (via Wi-Fi or, in some cases, a cellular data connection), the person can automatically receive incoming FaceTime calls.

HOW TO INITIATE A FACETIME CALL

To initiate a call with someone who also has FaceTime installed and operating on his computer or iOS device, select that person from your Contacts list, and tap on the email address or iPhone phone number that he used to register with FaceTime. If a connection can be made, a FaceTime icon automatically appears next to the person's name in the FaceTime app.

When you initiate a call, the front-facing camera of your iPhone or iPad turns on, and you should see yourself if you're holding the camera up to your face. The message "FaceTime..." and the person's name is also displayed.

Meanwhile, along the bottom of the screen is the End icon, which you can tap at any time to terminate the connection. To the left of the End button is the camera selection switch, and to the right of the End icon is the Bluetooth icon (if applicable).

PARTICIPATING IN A FACETIME CALL

When a FaceTime connection is established with another party, your own image is displayed on the screen as a video thumbnail. The rest of the FaceTime screen displays the video feed from the person you're now connected with using FaceTime.

> **TIP** Once the FaceTime connection is established, to move the video thumbnail that shows your video feed (what you're sending to the person you're conversing with) around on the screen, place and hold your finger on the video thumbnail and drag it to any of the screen's other corners.

Notice that near the very bottom of the screen are three command icons (as shown in Figure 10.3) labeled Mute, End, and Switch Camera. These command icons are used for the following purposes:

- Tap on the Mute button to retain the video connection but mute your iOS device's built-in microphone so that the person you're communicating with can see you but not hear you.
- Tap on the End button to terminate the FaceTime connection and promptly end the call.
- Tap on the Switch Camera icon to alternate between the two cameras built in to your iOS device. Use this to show the person with whom you're speaking other things in the area using the camera on the back of your device.

> **NOTE** When using FaceTime, while you're engaged in a call, if you temporarily exit out of FaceTime to use another app, the audio connection remains active but your video feed is temporarily paused until you return to the FaceTime app by tapping on the green-and-white Touch To Resume FaceTime bar displayed near the top of the screen. You also have the option of tapping on the FaceTime icon displayed on the Home screen.

FIGURE 10.3

When a FaceTime video call is underway, your own video feed appears in a small window. The person you're talking with is displayed in the main area of the FaceTime screen, and several command icons are displayed near the bottom center of the screen.

ANSWERING AN INCOMING FACETIME CALL

When you receive an incoming FaceTime call while the iPhone or iPad is in Sleep mode, a Slide To Answer option is displayed, along with a Remind Me Later or Respond with Text option (shown in Figure 10.4). To ignore the call, double-press the iPhone's Power button quickly.

If your iPhone or iPad is already turned on and being used when an incoming FaceTime call is received, a large green-and-white Answer button, a large red-and-white Decline button, and the Remind Me and Message options appear on the screen (shown in Figure 10.4).

> **TIP** While using any iPhone or iPad app, if you receive an incoming FaceTime call from someone, the FaceTime app launches automatically. The app you were using continues running in the background. If you decline or later end the FaceTime call, your device switches back to that app. You can also return to the app while engaged in a FaceTime call using iOS 7's multitasking mode.

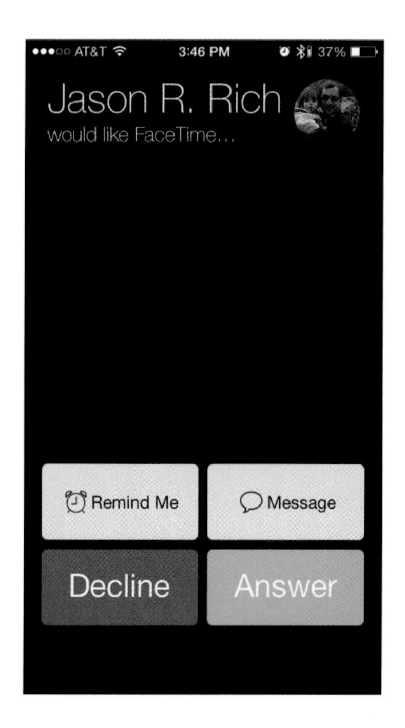

FIGURE 10.4

If you're actively using any app on your iPhone or iPad, this is what the screen looks like when you receive an incoming FaceTime call.

Tap on the Message button to send the caller a pre-written or custom text message that informs him that you're unavailable and will call him later, for example. Or, tap on the Remind Me button to set up a reminder for yourself to return the call at a later time.

FACETIME QUICK TIPS

Here are a few basic strategies for improving the quality of your FaceTime connection, which helps to ensure that you see and hear the person you're video phone calling and that the other person can see and hear you.

> **TIP** These strategies should be implemented by both you and the person with whom you're video phone calling.

- Use a Wi-Fi Internet connection that has a strong signal. If necessary, move closer to the wireless Internet router.

- Participate in a FaceTime video call from a quiet location so that your iPhone or iPad's microphone doesn't pick up background noise that might distort or drown out your voice. Turn off any nearby televisions or radios, for example.
- Make sure that the primary lighting in the area is shining on your face and is not behind you. If too much light is behind you, the person you're video phone calling with will see your silhouette (as opposed to the detail of your face). Try to position the main light source in front of you so that your face is evenly lit. A light shining from overhead, for example, often causes shadows to appear on your face, which might make you look older or ill.
- While video phone calling, refrain from excessive movement. The real-time video image remains clearer if you're sitting or standing still. Try propping your iPhone or iPad on a table using a stand so that the device remains steady and pointed at your face during a FaceTime call.
- When participating in a video call, it's common to forget that the camera is turned on after a while. Refrain from doing anything that you don't want the other person to see and/or hear.
- To improve the audio quality of a FaceTime call, consider using a headset that offers a noise-cancelling microphone and noise-reduction speakers.

NOTE The most confusing aspect of FaceTime is making that initial connection with someone else and setting your iOS device to initiate a call to the proper iPhone number, Apple ID, or email address that's associated with that person's FaceTime account. After a connection is established once, future connections can be made with a single tap on the screen.

USE SKYPE TO MAKE AND RECEIVE VOICE AND/OR VIDEO CALLS VIA THE INTERNET

Skype is a Voice-over-IP (VoIP) phone service that enables you to make and receive calls over the Web (as opposed to a cellular phone network or traditional telephone landline). In addition to working with the iPhone and iPad, what makes Skype appealing is that the service also works with PCs and Macs, as well as Android-based smartphones and tablets. Unlike FaceTime, you're not limited to conversing only with Apple users.

The Skype service transforms a computer, smartphone, or tablet into a virtual speakerphone, enabling users to make and receive calls that originate from the Internet. Thus, your iPad can be used to make and receive calls, as long as an Internet connection is available. The Skype app on either the iPhone or iPad can also be used to participate in real-time videoconferences with other Skype users for free.

> **NOTE** There is a free Skype app designed for the iPhone, as well as a separate iPad-specific Skype app. Both are available from the App Store, and the latest version of these apps enable users to engage in real-time videoconferences, as well as voice-only calls.
>
> Either version of the Skype app takes advantage of your iOS device's Internet connection, built-in speaker, microphone(s), and cameras to transform the iPhone or iPad into a full-featured telephone or video phone call tool.
>
> You can also use Skype with an optional headset, which is recommended to improve the audio quality of calls and get rid of ambient noise. Using a headset also increases your level of privacy by helping to prevent unwanted eavesdroppers.

Making unlimited Skype-to-Skype calls (including video calls) is always free; however, there is a very low per-minute fee to make calls to a landline or cellular telephone from Skype. This per-minute fee is typically just pennies per minute, even if you're traveling overseas and make a call back to the United States. You can also save a fortune on international calling from the United States when making calls to any other country. When you're traveling abroad, making and receiving calls on a cell phone (such as an iPhone) costs anywhere from 50 cents to $3 per minute because international roaming fees apply. However, with Skype, that same call costs just 2.3 cents per minute, or you can pay a flat fee of less than $20 per month to make and receive unlimited domestic and international calls via Skype from your iOS device.

> **NOTE** Although Skype calls originate from the Internet, calls can be made to (or received from) any landline or cellphone. Thus, your iPhone or iPad, when connected to the Internet via a cellular data or Wi-Fi connection, can be transformed into a full-featured telephone, complete with caller ID, conference calling, a mute button, and one-touch dialing.

> **! CAUTION** Skype works much better (and with no limitations) when used with a high-speed Wi-Fi Internet connection. When used with a cellular data connection, it requires a significant amount of 3G or 4G (LTE) data usage and can quickly deplete your monthly cellular data allocation from your wireless service provider or result in high international wireless data roaming fees if used abroad.

Through Skype, you can obtain your own unique telephone number (for an additional fee of $6 per month or $60 per year), which comes with call forwarding, voicemail, and other features, so you can manage incoming calls whether or not Skype is activated and your iPhone or iPad is connected to the Web.

When you have your own Skype phone number, people without their own Skype account can reach you inexpensively by dialing your unique Skype phone number from any phone, regardless of where you're traveling. You can, however, initiate calls without paying for a unique phone number.

NOTE In terms of call quality, as long as you're within a cellular data coverage area or a Wi-Fi hotspot provides a strong and stable connection to the Internet, calls will be crystal clear.

The Skype app is easy to use and enables you to maintain a contacts list of frequently called people (although it also links with the Contacts database associated with the Contacts app). You can also dial out using a familiar telephone touchpad display and maintain a detailed call history that lists incoming, outgoing, and missed calls.

If you opt to establish a paid Skype account (to have your own unique phone number or make non-Skype-to-Skype calls), setting up the account takes just minutes when you visit www.Skype.com, and all charges are billed to a major credit card or debit card.

TIP If you experience poor call clarity and you're using a Wi-Fi Internet connection with your iOS device, move closer to the wireless router to enhance the signal strength and improve call clarity.

When you don't have Skype activated, if you have your own Skype phone number, you can automatically forward incoming calls to another number or have them go directly to your Skype voicemail account.

When you're online with the Skype service, you can have your status displayed so other Skype users will be able to find and call you via the Skype network. If you don't want to be disturbed by incoming calls, access the My Info screen and tap on the Status option. From the Status window, select Do Not Disturb or Invisible.

TIP Beyond using FaceTime or Skype for video calls or videoconferencing, other online-based videoconferencing services offer proprietary iPhone and iPad apps. For example, ooVoo Video Chat enables users to engage in videoconferences, for free, with multiple people at once. There's also the GoToMeeting service, which is fee-based.

To make and receive VoIP calls, the Line2 app for the iPad transforms your tablet into a full-featured telephone with its own phone number. This is a fee-based service. The Beeztel: Free Calls & SMS enables you to make and receive VoIP calls for free.

To discover additional services (and apps) for making and receiving Internet-based calls and for videoconferencing, use the Search field in the App Store and enter the search phrase "VoIP" or "videoconferencing."

IN THIS CHAPTER

- How to send and receive emails using the Mail app
- How to add your existing email accounts to the Mail app
- How to send and receive text messages on your iPhone using your cellular service provider's text-messaging service or the iMessage service

11

SEND AND RECEIVE EMAILS, TEXT, AND INSTANT MESSAGES WITH THE MAIL AND MESSAGES APPS

If you're someone who's constantly on the go, being able to send and receive emails from virtually anywhere there's a cellular or Wi-Fi Internet connection enables you to stay in touch, stay informed, and be productive from wherever you happen to be. Managing one or more email accounts from an iPhone or iPad is more practical than ever, thanks to the improvements made to the Mail app that comes preinstalled with iOS 7.

The Mail app offers a comprehensive set of tools, features, and functions to help you compose, send, receive, and organize emails from one or more existing accounts. From your iPhone or iPad, you can simultaneously manage your personal and work-related email accounts, as well as the free email account that's provided to you when you set up an iCloud account.

Before you can begin using the Mail app, it's necessary to set up your existing email accounts from within Settings.

> **NOTE** If you don't yet have an email account, there are several ways to get one. You can sign up for a free Apple iCloud account, which includes an email account. In addition, Google offers free Gmail email accounts (http://mail.google.com), and Yahoo! offers free Yahoo! Mail accounts (http://features.mail.yahoo.com), both of which are fully compatible with your iOS device's Mail app.

HOW TO ADD EMAIL ACCOUNTS TO THE MAIL APP

To initially set up your iOS device to work with your existing email account(s), launch Settings from the Home screen. This process works with virtually all email accounts, including Yahoo! Mail, Google Gmail, AOL Mail, iCloud Mail, Microsoft Exchange, and other email accounts established using industry-standard POP3 and IMAP email services.

If you have an email account through your employer that doesn't initially work using the setup procedure outlined in this chapter, contact your company's IT department or Apple's technical support for assistance.

> **NOTE** The process for setting up an existing email account to use with your iPhone or iPad and the Mail app must be done only once per account.

Follow these steps to set up your iOS device to work with each of your existing email accounts:

1. From the Home screen, launch Settings.
2. Tap on the Mail, Contacts, Calendars option.
3. When the Mail, Contacts, Calendars menu screen appears, tap on the Add Account option displayed near the top of the screen, below the Accounts heading.
4. From the Add Account screen, select the type of email account you have. Your options include iCloud, Microsoft Exchange, Google Gmail, Yahoo! Mail, AOL Mail, Microsoft Outlook.com, and Other (shown in Figure 11.1). Tap on the appropriate option. If you have a POP3 or IMAP-compatible email account that doesn't otherwise fall into one of the provided email types, tap on the Other option, and follow the onscreen prompts.

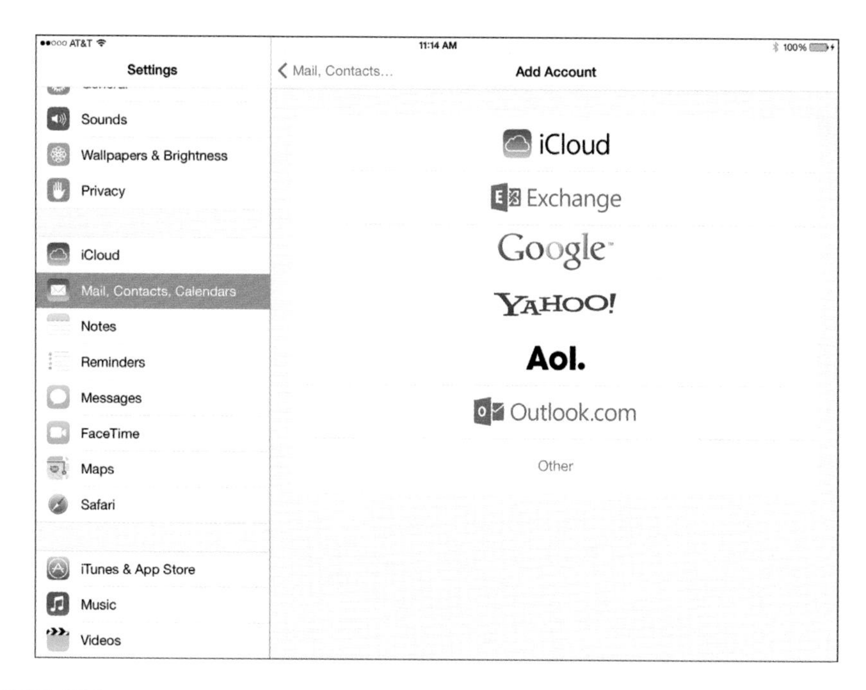

FIGURE 11.1

Choose the type of email account you'd like to add by tapping on the appropriate menu option.

If you have an existing Yahoo! email account, for example, tap on the Yahoo! icon. When the Yahoo! screen appears (shown in Figure 11.2), use the iPhone or iPad's virtual keyboard to enter your account name, email address, password, and a description for the account.

TIP As you're adding an email account from within Settings, the account name should be your full name or whatever you want to appear in the From field of outgoing emails (alongside your email address) that you compose and send using that email account. You can opt to use just your first name, a family name (such as "The Anderson Family"), or a nickname, based on what you want to share with the recipients of your emails. The Description can be anything that helps you personally differentiate that account from your other accounts, such as Home email, Work email, or Yahoo! email. The email account description is something that you see only on your device.

5. Tap on the Next button located in the upper-right corner of the window. Your iOS device connects to the email account's server and confirms the account details you've entered. The word Verifying appears on the screen.

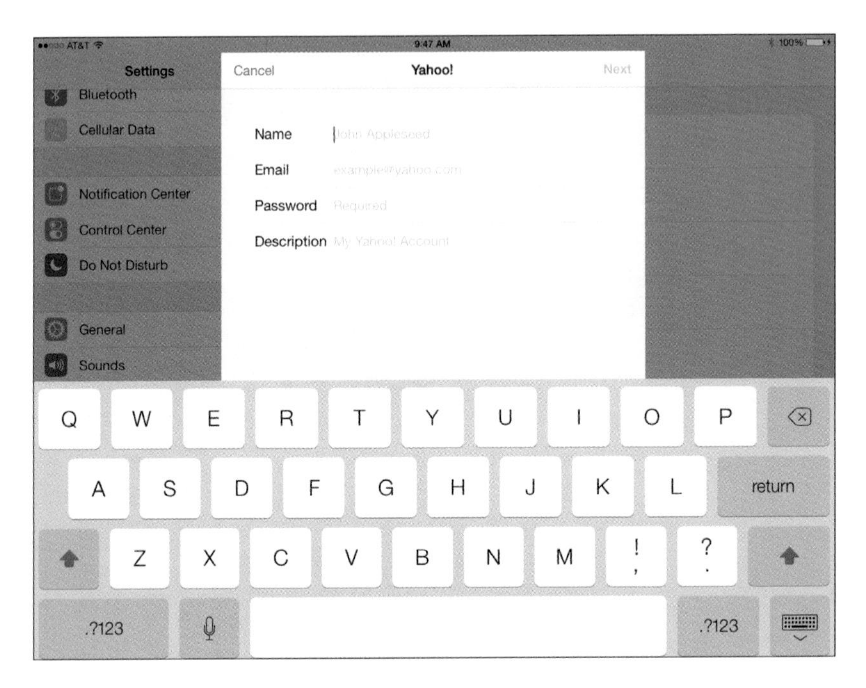

FIGURE 11.2

If you're setting up a Yahoo! Mail account, tap on the Yahoo! option, and then fill in your account information.

6. After the account has been verified, a new window with options is displayed. They're probably labeled Mail, Contacts, Calendars, Reminders, and Notes, although depending on the type of email account you're setting up, not all of these options might be available. Each option has a virtual on/off switch associated with it. The default for many of these options is On. They're used to determine what additional app-specific data can be linked with the Mail account, such as your Contacts database, the schedule from your Calendar app, your to-do list from the Reminders app, or your notes from the Notes app.

! CAUTION If you're already syncing app-specific data for Contacts, Calendar, Reminders, and/or Notes with iCloud, do not also sync them with Yahoo!, Google, or a Microsoft Exchange–compatible account, or you could wind up with duplicate records or entries in each app. Likewise, if you're already syncing your app-specific data with Google, don't also sync this information using iCloud.

7. Tap on the Save button located in the upper-right corner of this window. An Adding Account message is briefly displayed, and details about the email account you just set up are added to your iOS device and become immediately accessible via the Mail app.
8. If you have another existing email account to set up, from the Mail, Contacts, Calendars screen in the Settings app, tap on the Add Account option again, and repeat the preceding procedure. Otherwise, exit the Settings app and launch the Mail app from the Home screen.

Depending on the type of email account you're setting up, the information for which you're prompted varies slightly. For example, to set up an existing Microsoft Exchange email account, the prompts you need to fill in during the email setup procedure include Email Address, Domain, Username, Password, and a Description for the account. To set up an existing iCloud email account, you only need to enter your existing Apple ID and password.

TIP If you plan to set up a POP3 or IMAP email account, in addition to your existing email address and password, you are prompted to enter your host name [mail.example.com] and outgoing mail server information [smtp.example.com]. Obtain this information from your email account provider or the IT department at your company before attempting to set up this type of account on your iPhone or iPad.

After the account is set up, it is listed within Settings under the Accounts heading when you tap on the Mail, Contacts, Calendars option.

TIP When you purchase a new iOS device, it comes with free technical support from AppleCare for 90 days. If you purchased AppleCare+ with your iOS device, you have access to free technical support from Apple for two years. This includes the ability to make an in-person appointment with an Apple Genius at any Apple Store and have someone set up your email accounts on your iPhone or iPad for you.

To schedule a free appointment, visit www.apple.com/retail/geniusbar. Or call Apple's toll-free technical support phone number and have someone talk you through the email setup process. Call 800-APL-CARE (275-2273).

HOW TO CUSTOMIZE MAIL OPTIONS FROM SETTINGS

To customize options available in the Mail app, launch Settings and select the Mail, Contacts, Calendars option. On the Mail, Contacts, Calendars screen (shown in Figure 11.3) are a handful of customizable features pertaining to how your iOS device handles your email accounts.

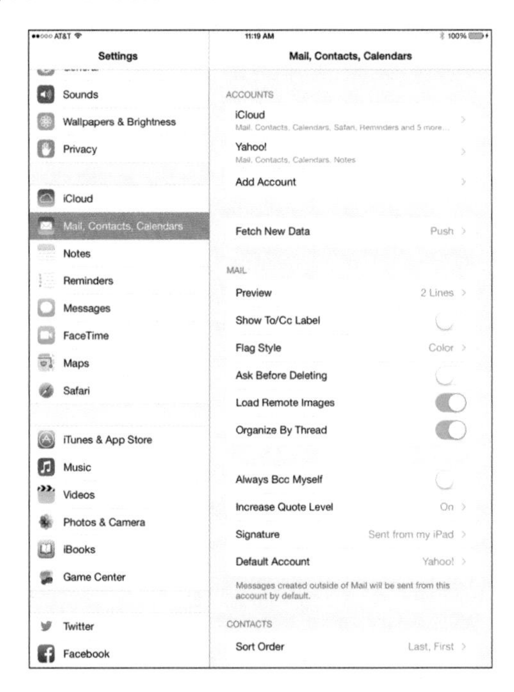

FIGURE 11.3

From Settings, you can customize a handful of settings relating to the Mail app.

iOS 7 WHAT'S NEW It is now possible to customize each email account separately. This includes how your iOS device displays new incoming email details in the Notification Center window, as well as uses alerts or banners for each account. To set this up for each account, launch Settings, tap on Notification Center, select the Mail option, and then one at a time, tap on the listing for each of your email accounts. There's also a separate listing for VIP, which enables you to set separate alerts for important incoming emails from people on your VIP list.

At the top of the Mail, Contacts, Calendars screen is a listing of the individual email accounts you have already linked with the Mail app. Below this is the Fetch New Data option. Use this to determine how often your iOS device automatically accesses the Internet to check for and download new incoming email messages from each email account's server.

TIP From the Fetch New Data screen, you can enable or disable the Push feature. When turned on, your iPhone or iPad automatically accesses and displays new incoming emails as they arrive on your email account's server. When the Push feature is turned off, you can select how often you want your iOS mobile device to check for new emails. Your options include Every 15 Minutes, Every 30 Minutes, Hourly, or Manually. You can customize this setting separately for each of your email accounts.

The benefit of using the Fetch feature set to Manually is that you can greatly reduce the amount of wireless data usage you utilize. This is important if you have a monthly cellular data allocation through your wireless service provider. If you have an account that offers unlimited wireless data or you utilize a Wi-Fi connection, this is not a concern.

By scrolling down on the Mail, Contacts, Calendars menu screen, you see the Mail heading. Below this heading is a handful of customizable options relating to how the Mail app manages your email accounts and email messages:

- **Preview**—As you look at your Inbox (or any mailbox) using the Mail app, you can determine how much of each email message's body text is visible from the mailbox summary screen, in addition to the From, Date/Time, and Subject. You can choose None or between one and five lines of the email message.

TIP The Preview option also impacts the email-related notifications that appear in the Notification Center if you assign it to continuously monitor the Mail app. You can adjust this in Settings by tapping on the Notification Center option under the main Settings menu.

- **Show To/Cc Label**—Decide whether to view the To and Cc fields when viewing the preview screen for emails.
- **Flag Style**—When you flag an email as important, the Flag style determines whether the Mail app displays a flag-shaped icon or a colored dot next to the flagged email message.

- **Ask Before Deleting**—This option serves as a safety net to ensure that you don't accidentally delete an important email message from your iOS device. When this feature is turned on, you're asked to confirm your message deletion request before an email message is actually deleted. At least until you become comfortable using the Mail app, it's a good idea to leave this feature turned on. Keep in mind that, by default, you cannot delete email messages stored on your email account's server. When you delete a message from the Mail app, it is deleted from only your iPhone or iPad but is still accessible from other devices. On your iOS device, it might also appear in the Trash folder that's related to that email account, depending on how it is set up.
- **Load Remote Images**—When an email message has a photo or graphic embedded in it, this option determines whether that photo or graphic is automatically downloaded and displayed with the email message. You can opt to have your iOS device refrain from automatically loading graphics with email messages. This reduces the amount of data transferred to your iPhone or iPad (which is a consideration if you're connected to the Internet via a cellular data network). You still have the option to tap on the placeholder icon in the email message to manually download the graphic content in a specific message, including photos.

NOTE In addition to reducing your cellular data usage, disabling the Load Remote Images option can help you cut down on the amount of spam (unsolicited emails) you receive, because remote image loading can be tracked by the senders of spam and used to verify valid email addresses.

However, when turned off, displaying images embedded within an email requires an additional step on your part because you now must tap the image icon to load the image if you want to view it.

- **Organize by Thread**—This feature enables you to review messages in reverse chronological order if a single message turns into a back-and-forth email conversation in which multiple parties keep hitting Reply to respond to messages with the same subject. When turned on, this makes keeping track of email conversations much easier, especially if you're managing several email accounts on your iPhone or iPad. If it's turned off, messages in your Inbox are displayed in reverse chronological order as they're received, not grouped by subject.
- **Always Bcc Myself**—To ensure that you keep a copy of every outgoing email you send, turn on this feature. A copy of every outgoing email is sent to your Inbox if this feature is turned on. Typically, all outgoing messages

automatically get saved in a Sent folder that's related to that account. If your email account type does not enable you to access sent emails from another computer or device, using the Bcc Myself option compensates for this. When you send an email message from your iPhone/iPad, using this feature also ensures that the message becomes accessible from your primary computer.

- **Increase Quote Level**—When turned on, anytime you reply to a message or forward a message, the contents of that original email appear indented, making it easier to differentiate between the message you add and the original message being replied to or forwarded. This option impacts message formatting, not actual content.
- **Signature**—For every outgoing email that you compose, you can automatically add an email signature. The default signature is "Sent from my iPhone" or "Sent from my iPad." However, by tapping on this option within Settings, you can use the virtual keyboard to create customized signatures for each email account. A signature might include your name, mailing address, email address, phone number(s), and so forth.
- **Default Account**—If you're using the Mail app to manage multiple email accounts, when you reply to a message or forward a message, it is always sent from the email account to which the message was originally sent. However, if you tap on the Compose New Email icon to create a new email from scratch, the email account that message is sent from is whichever you have set up as the Mail app's default account. If you wish to change this account for a specific email, simply tap on the From field as you're composing a new email and select one of your other accounts.

After you make adjustments to the Mail app–related options from within Settings, exit Settings by pressing the Home button to return to the Home screen. You're now ready to begin using the Mail app to access and manage your email account(s).

TIPS FOR VIEWING YOUR INCOMING EMAIL

When you launch the Mail app on your iPhone or iPad, the Inbox for your various email accounts is displayed. You can opt to display incoming messages for a single email account, or display the incoming messages from all of your email accounts by selecting the All Inboxes option.

Even though Mail enables you to simultaneously view incoming emails from multiple accounts within a single listing, behind the scenes, the app automatically keeps your incoming and outgoing emails, and your various email accounts, separate. So if you opt to read and respond to an email from your work-related Inbox, for example, that response is automatically sent out from your work-related email account and saved in the Sent Folder for that account.

TIP The Mail app is fully compatible with Siri. Be sure to refer to Chapter 2, "Using Siri, Dictation, and iOS In Your Car to Interact with Your Mobile Device," for more information.

Viewing all the Inboxes for all of your accounts simultaneously makes it faster to review your incoming emails, without having to manually switch between email accounts.

If you have multiple email accounts being managed from your iOS device, to view all of your Inboxes simultaneously, or to switch between Inboxes, follow these steps:

1. Launch the Mail app.
2. The Inbox you last looked at is probably displayed.
3. Tap on the left-pointing, arrow-shaped Mailboxes icon displayed in the upper-left corner of the screen to select which Inbox you want to view.
4. From the menu that appears, the first option displayed is All Inboxes. Tap on this to view a single listing of all incoming emails. Or tap on any single email account that's listed on the Mailboxes screen.

TIP Tap on the VIP mailbox listing to view only emails from your various inboxes that have been received from people you've added to your VIP List. When you tap on the VIP option, these emails are displayed in a single mailbox, although the list is comprised of VIP messages from all the accounts you're managing on your iPhone or iPad. You learn more about using the VIP List feature of the Mail app shortly.

Below the VIP listing under the Inboxes heading is a Flagged listing. This enables you to view a separate mailbox comprised of only emails you've previously flagged as being important. Again, this is a comprehensive listing of flagged incoming emails from all the accounts you're managing on your iPhone or iPad. In reality, however, the Mail app keeps the messages sorted behind the scenes, based on which email account each is associated with.

COMPOSING AN EMAIL MESSAGE

In the Mail app, you can easily compose an email from scratch and send it to one or more recipients. To compose a new email, tap on the Compose icon. On an iPhone, the Compose icon can be found in the lower-right corner of the screen in the Mail app. On an iPad, the Compose icon is displayed in the upper-right corner of the screen.

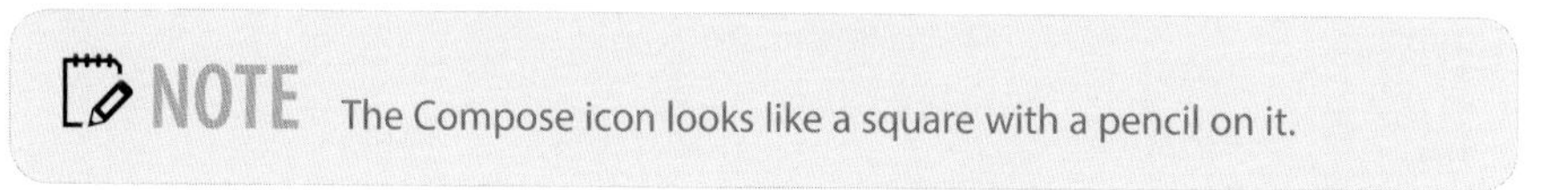

NOTE The Compose icon looks like a square with a pencil on it.

When you tap on the Compose icon, a blank New Message email message template appears on the iPhone or iPad's screen. On the iPhone, a New Message screen is displayed. On the iPad, a New Message pop-up window appears. Using the virtual keyboard, fill in the To, Cc, Bcc, and/or Subject fields (as shown in Figure 11.4). At the very least, you must fill in the To field with a valid email address for at least one recipient. The other fields are optional.

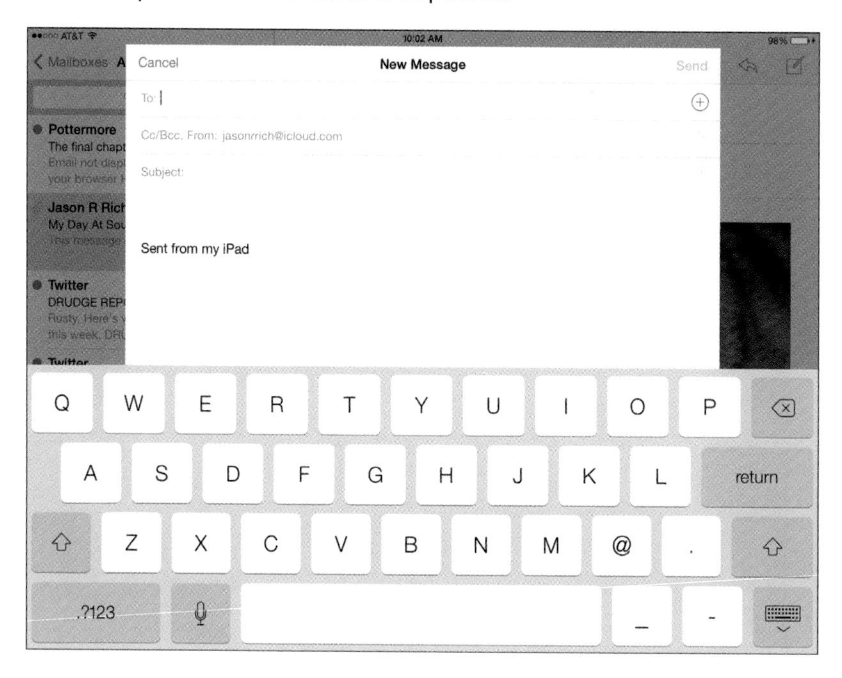

FIGURE 11.4

Tap on the Compose icon to create an email from scratch and send it from your iOS device.

You can send the same email to multiple recipients by either adding multiple email addresses to the To field or by adding additional email addresses to the Cc and/or Bcc fields.

If you're managing one email account from your iOS device, the From field is automatically filled in with your email address. However, if you're managing multiple email addresses from the iPhone or iPad, tap on the From field to select which email address you want to send the message from. The default account is otherwise used.

TIP As you fill in the To field when composing an email, the Mail app automatically accesses your Contacts database and matches up entries based on what you type in the To field. This can save you time because you don't have to manually enter email addresses. If you know that the person you're sending an email to already has an entry including their email address in your Contacts database, you can type that person's name in the To field.

Next, tap on the Subject field and use the virtual keyboard to enter the subject for your message. As you do this, the subject appears at the very top center of the Compose window (replacing the New Message heading).

TIP When using almost any app with a Share menu, to compose and send an email that contains app-specific content without first launching the Mail app, tap on the Share icon, and then select Mail. Keep in mind that sending or receiving email with large attachments can deplete your monthly data allotment from your wireless provider, unless you are connected to the Internet via Wi-Fi when you send/receive the mail.

A New Message screen appears with the related app-specific content already attached to that outgoing email message. Use the virtual keyboard to compose your email, and then tap on the Send icon. The email message is sent and you are returned to the app you were using.

Meanwhile, as you're viewing a Contact's entry in the Contacts app, if you tap on an email address within that entry, a New Message screen (iPhone) or window (iPad) appears, and you can compose and send an email message to that person from within the Contacts app.

To begin creating the main body of the outgoing email message, tap in the main body area of the message template on the screen, and begin using the virtual keyboard (or the external keyboard you're using with your iPhone or iPad) to compose your message. You also have the option of tapping on the Dictation key and then dictating your message using iOS 7's Dictation feature.

! CAUTION If you have the Auto-Capitalization, Auto-Correction, and/or Check Spelling feature(s) turned on, as you type, the iPhone or iPad automatically corrects anything that it perceives as a typo or misspelled word. Be very careful when using these features because they are notorious for plugging the wrong word into a sentence. Especially if you're creating important business documents and emails, make sure you proofread whatever you type on your iPhone or iPad carefully before sending it. Typically, these features are helpful, but they do have quirks that can lead to embarrassing and unprofessional mistakes.

To control the Auto-Capitalization, Auto-Correction, and Check Spelling features, launch the Settings app, tap on the General option, select the Keyboard option, and then turn on or off the virtual switch that's associated for each option that's displayed within the Keyboard menu screen.

The signature you set up from within Settings for the selected From account is automatically displayed at the bottom of the newly composed message. You can return to Settings to turn off the Signature feature, or change the signature that appears. A signature can also be edited or added manually directly from the Compose screen as you create or edit each message.

When your email is fully written and ready to be sent, tap on the blue-and-white Send button in the upper-right corner of the Compose window. In a few seconds, the message is sent from your iOS device, assuming that it is connected to the Internet. A copy of the message appears in your Sent or Outbox folder.

As a message is being sent, a "Sending" notification appears near the bottom of the Mail app's screen.

NOTE The Mail app enables you to format your outgoing email messages and include **bold**, *italic*, and/or underlined text (as well as combinations, like ***bold-italic*** text).

To format text in an email message you're composing, type the text as you normally would using the virtual keyboard. After the text appears in your email, hold your finger on a word to make the Select, Select All, Paste, Insert Photo or Video, and Quote Level command tabs appear above that word.

Tap on Select, and then use your finger to move the blue dots that appear to highlight the text you want to modify. When the appropriate text is highlighted in blue, tap the right-pointing arrow that appears above the text (next to the Cut, Copy, and Paste commands), and then tap on the **B**/*I*/U option. A new menu appears above the highlighted text with three options, labeled Bold, Italics, and Underline. Tap on one or more of these tabs to alter the highlighted text (as shown in Figure 11.5). On the iPad, all options are listed and no scrolling is required.

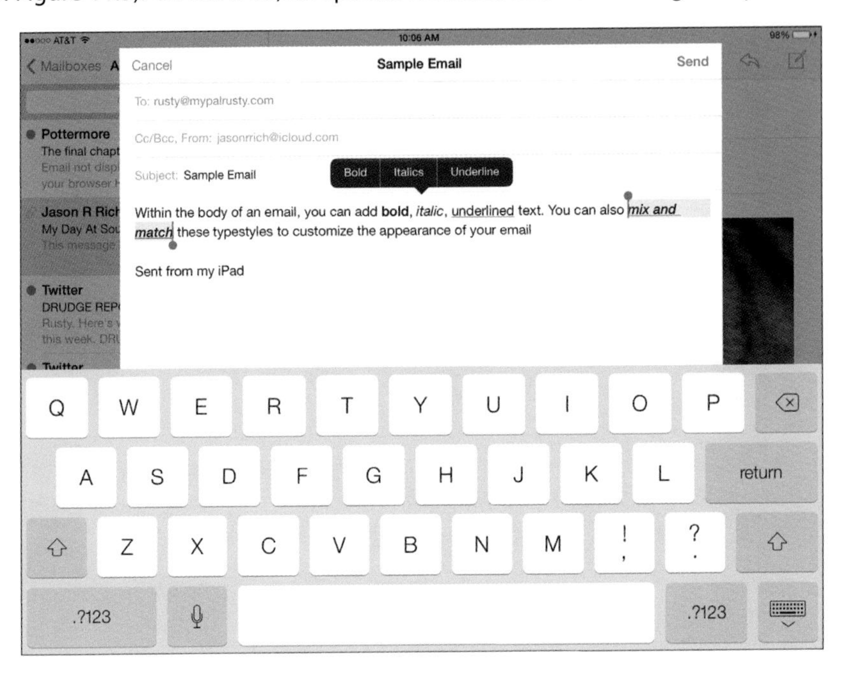

FIGURE 11.5

Mail enables you to use bold, italic, and/or underlined text in the body of your outgoing email messages.

INSERT A PHOTO OR VIDEO INTO YOUR OUTGOING EMAIL

As you're composing an outgoing email, if you want to insert a photo or video clip that's stored on your iPhone or iPad into that email, place and hold your finger anywhere in the body of the email where you want to embed the photo or video.

> **NOTE** On the iPhone, tap on the right-pointing arrow displayed to the right of the Select, Select All, and Paste commands to access the Insert Photo or Video option.

When the Insert Photo or Video tab is displayed, tap on it. The Photos screen (iPhone) or window (iPad) appears. Select the photo you want to insert into the email by selecting an album and then tapping on an image or video thumbnail. The photo/video you selected is previewed in the Choose Photo window. Tap on the Use button to insert the photo or video into your email.

You can repeat this process to include multiple images within an email (up to five), keeping in mind that the overall file size associated with the outgoing email is often limited by your email service.

TIP When you insert a photo into an outgoing email on the iPad, to the right of the Cc/Bcc, From: field a new option that says Images: [file size] is displayed. To alter the image file size (and by default, the resolution) of the attached photo(s), tap on the Images option. Under the From field, an Image Size option appears. To the right of this option are four command tabs: Small, Medium, Large, and Actual Size. Each is accompanied by the file size of the image(s) you're sending. Tap on one of these options.

On the iPhone, when you tap the Send button, you might be asked to select an image resolution for the photo(s) you've attached to the outgoing email.

If you know the photo(s) will be made into prints later, send the images using the Actual Size option. This, however, has a greater impact on your wireless data use if you're using a cellular data connection and have a monthly usage allocation.

USING SELECT, SELECT ALL, CUT, COPY, AND PASTE

The iOS operating system offers Select, Select All, Cut, Copy, and Paste commands, which are accessible from many iPhone or iPad apps, including Mail. Using these commands, you can quickly copy and paste content from one portion of an app to another, or from one app into another app, whether it's a paragraph of text, a phone number, or a photo.

To use these commands, use your finger to hold down on any word or graphic element on the screen for one or two seconds, until the Select and Select All tabs appear above that content. To select a single word or select what content you want to copy or cut, tap on the Select tab. Or to select all the content on the screen, tap the Select All tab.

After text (or a graphic element, such as a photo) is selected, tap on the Cut tab to delete that selected content from the screen (if this option is available in the app you're using), or tap the Copy tab to save the highlighted content in your iPhone or iPad's virtual clipboard.

Now, move to where you want to paste that saved content. This can be in the same email or document, for example, or in another app altogether. Choose the location on the screen where you want to paste the content, and hold your finger on that location for two or three seconds. When the Paste tab appears, tap on it. The content you just copied is pasted into that location.

TIP In the Mail app, as you use the Select, Select All, Cut, Copy, and Paste commands, notice a Quote Level option that appears on the menu above the highlighted text or content you select. Tap on this to increase or decrease the indent of that content, which impacts how it's formatted on the screen.

HOW TO SAVE AN UNSENT DRAFT OF AN EMAIL MESSAGE

If you want to save a draft of an email without sending it, as you're composing the email message, tap on the Cancel button that appears in the upper-left corner of the Compose message window. Two command buttons appear: Delete Draft and Save Draft. To save the unsent draft, tap on Save Draft. You can return to it later to modify and/or send it. To do this, from the main Inbox screen in Mail, tap on the left-pointing Mailboxes icon that looks like an arrow displayed at the upper-left corner of the screen. From the Mailboxes screen, scroll down to the Accounts heading and tap on the listing for the email account from which the email draft was composed.

When you see a list of folders related to that email account, tap on the Drafts folder. Tap on the appropriate listing to open that email message. You can now edit the message or send it.

TIPS FOR READING EMAIL

After you launch the Mail app, you can access the Inbox for one or more of your existing email accounts, compose new emails, or manage your email accounts. Just like the Inbox on your main computer's email software, the Inbox of the Mail app (shown in Figure 11.6 on an iPhone, and Figure 11.7 on an iPad) displays your incoming emails.

TIP As you're looking at the inbox for any of your email accounts (or the All Inboxes mailbox), to the left of each email message preview you might see a tiny graphic icon (refer to Figure 11.6 and Figure 11.7). A blue dot represents a new and unread email (or an email that has been marked as unread). A solid blue star represents a new and unread email from someone on your VIP list, while a gray star icon represents a read email from someone on your VIP list.

An orange flag-shaped icon displayed to the left of an email preview means that you have manually flagged that message (or message thread) as urgent. Instead of a flag icon, a blue dot with an orange circle can be displayed indicating a message is urgent and unread. Just an orange dot will appear after it's read. You can choose between a flag or a dot icon from Settings.

A curved, left-pointing arrow icons means that you have read and replied to that message, while a right-pointing arrow icon means you've read and have forwarded that message to one or more people.

If no tiny icon appears to the left of a email preview listing, this means the message has been read and is simply stored in that inbox (or mailbox).

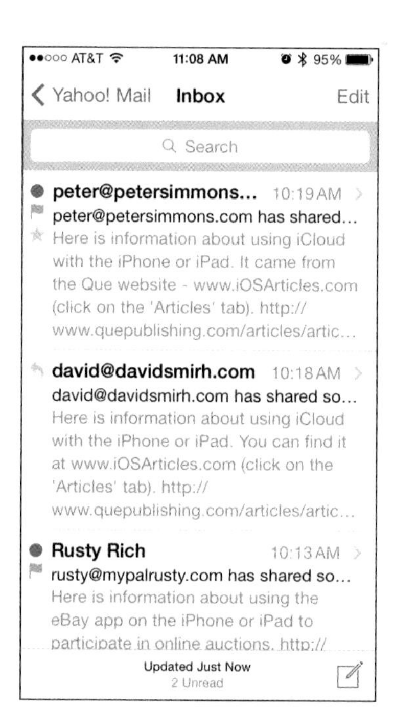

FIGURE 11.6

The Inbox screen of the Mail app displays a listing of your incoming emails on the iPhone 5.

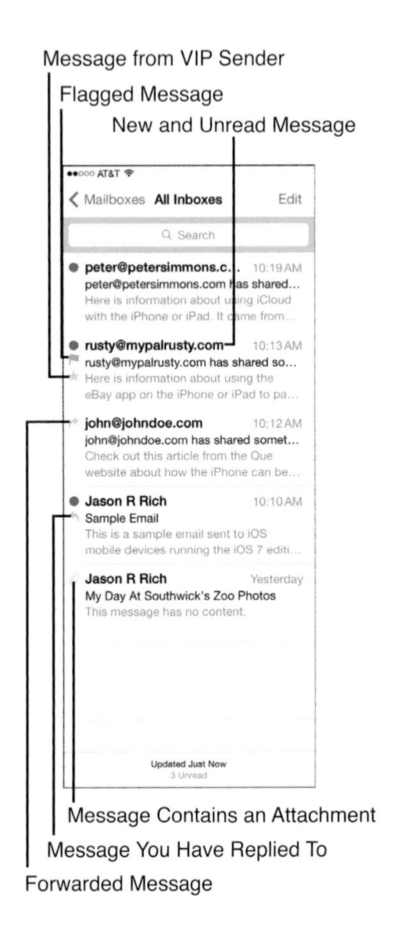

FIGURE 11.7

On the iPad, the Inbox provides a listing of your incoming emails.

THE MAIL APP'S INBOX

When you're viewing your Inbox(es), a list of the individual emails is displayed. Based on the customizations you make from the Settings app that pertain to the Mail app, the Sender, Subject, Date/Time, and up to five lines of the message's body text can be displayed for each incoming message listing.

On the iPhone, when viewing your Inbox and the listing of incoming (new) email messages, tap on any message listing to read that message in its entirety. When you do this, a new message screen appears. At the bottom of this screen is a series of command icons for managing that email.

On the iPad, the email message that's highlighted in gray on the left side of the screen is the one that's currently being displayed, in its entirety, on the right side of the screen. Tap on any email listing on the left side of the screen to view the entire message on the right side of the screen. Icons at the top of the screen are used for managing that email.

At the top of the Inbox message listing are two command icons, labeled Mailboxes (or the name of the mailbox you're viewing) and Edit.

Just below the Inbox's heading is a Search field. You might need to swipe your finger downward along the Inbox to reveal it. Tap on this Search field to make the virtual keyboard appear, enabling you to enter a search phrase and quickly find a particular email message. You can search the content of the Mail app using any keyword, a sender's name, or an email subject, for example.

THE EDIT BUTTON

Located on top of a mailbox's message listing (to the right of its heading) is a command button labeled Edit. When you tap on this button, you can quickly select multiple messages from a mailbox, such as your inbox, to delete or move to another mailbox (or folder) (as shown in Figure 11.8).

iOS 7 WHAT'S NEW After tapping the Edit button, you can manually select one or more message listings to move or delete, or tap on the new Mark All option to select all the messages within that Inbox. You can then Flag or Mark As Read/Unread all of the selected messages.

TIP If you tap on the Mark button that's displayed to the right of the Trash and Move buttons, you can then flag them or mark one or more emails as read or unread at the same time. You can also move selected messages to your Junk folder.

After you tap the Edit button, an empty circle icon appears to the left of each email message preview listing. To move or delete one or more messages from the current mailbox's listing (which could be your Inbox, VIP, Archive, or Junk mailbox), tap on the empty circle icon for that message. The folders listed vary based on your email account. A blue-and-white check mark fills the empty circle icon when you do this, and the Trash and Move command icons displayed at the bottom of the screen become active. For some types of email accounts, a Delete All button is also displayed, enabling you to select and delete all messages within that mailbox at the same time.

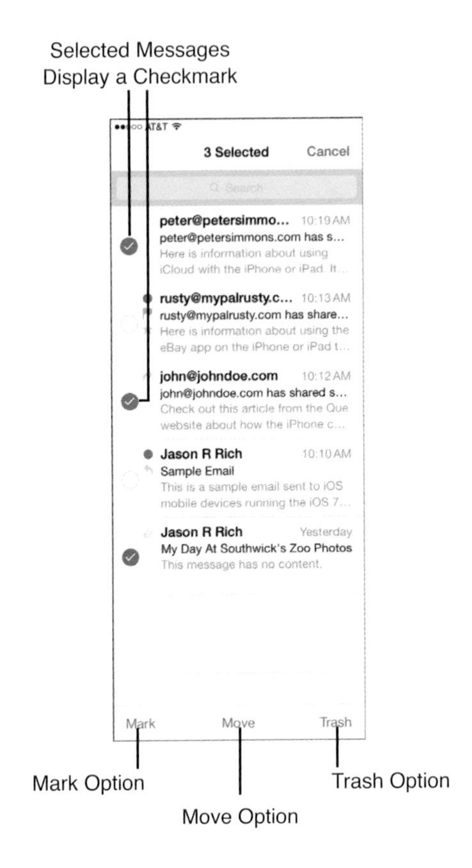

FIGURE 11.8

Tap the Edit button to manage your incoming messages, delete them in quantity, or move them to the Junk folder.

After you've selected one or more messages, tap the Trash button to quickly delete one or more messages simultaneously from the mailbox (which sends them to the Trash folder), or tap the blue-and-white Move button, and then select to which folder you want to move those email messages.

To exit this option without doing anything, tap on the blue-and-white Cancel button displayed at the top of the Inbox listing, to the right of the Inbox heading.

HOW TO DELETE INDIVIDUAL INCOMING MESSAGES

On your iPhone or iPad, as you're looking at the listing of messages in your Inbox (or any mailbox), you can also delete individual messages, one at a time. Swipe your finger from right to left over a message listing. Tap on the red-and-white

Trash button that appears on the right side of that email message listing (shown in Figure 11.9) to delete the message.

FIGURE 11.9

Swipe your finger from right to left over a single email message listing to make the More and Trash options appear.

WHAT'S NEW If you've been using iOS 5 or iOS 6 and recently upgraded to iOS 7, note that the swipe motion to delete a single message from an inbox is now reversed. Swipe from right to left, not from left to right. Also, a new More option appears, enabling you to transfer the message from its current Inbox to another folder without opening that message first. Other options available from the More menu enable you to reply, forward, flag, or mark the message as unread.

TIP Another way to delete a message from your Inbox, or any mailbox, is to tap on a message listing to view that message. To then delete the message, tap on the Trash icon. On the iPhone, the Trash icon is displayed at the bottom center of the screen. On the iPad, it's displayed near the upper-right corner of the screen.

HOW TO VIEW YOUR EMAILS

When a single email message is selected from the Inbox listing, that message is displayed in its entirety. At the top of the message, see the From, To, Cc/Bcc (if applicable), Subject, and the Date/Time it was sent.

In the upper-right corner of the email message is a blue Hide command. If you tap on this, some of the message header information will no longer be displayed. To make this information reappear, tap on the More option.

As you're reading an email, tap on the flag icon to flag that message and mark it as urgent, or mark the email as unread. These options appear within a pop-up menu. When you flag a message, an orange flag (or an orange dot) becomes associated with that message, which is displayed in the message itself (to the right of the date and time), and in the inbox (mailbox) in which the message is stored. Plus, from your Inboxes menu, if you tap on the Flagged option, you can view a separate mailbox that contains only flagged (urgent) messages.

TAKE ADVANTAGE OF THE MAIL APP'S VIP LIST FEATURE

In addition to flagging individual messages as important, you can have the Mail app automatically highlight all emails sent from particular senders, such as your boss, important clients, close friends, or family members. Once you add a sender to your VIP List, all of their incoming emails are marked with a star-shaped icon instead of a blue dot icon that represents a regular, new incoming email.

To add someone to your VIP List, as you're reading an email from that person, tap on the From field (their name/email address). A Sender screen (iPhone) or window (iPad) appears. At the bottom of this window, tap on the Add To VIP button. This adds and keeps that sender on your custom VIP list until you manually remove them.

To later remove someone from your VIP list, read any of their email messages and again tap on the From field. When the Sender window appears, tap on the Remove From VIP button (which has replaced the Add To VIP button).

Now, as you're reviewing your Inbox for a specific email account, the All Inboxes mailbox, or any other mailbox for that matter, any messages from people on your VIP list have a star displayed to the left of their email listings.

> **TIP** From the Mailboxes menu, you can also tap on the VIP listing to view a special mailbox that displays only incoming emails from people on your VIP list. Using the VIP List feature helps you quickly differentiate important emails from spam and less important incoming emails that don't necessarily require your immediate attention.

HOW TO DEAL WITH INCOMING EMAIL MESSAGE ATTACHMENTS

The Mail app enables you to access certain types of attachment files that accompany an incoming email message. Dozens of different file formats are compatible with the Mail app. As you add third-party apps that support other file formats, they become recognized by the Mail app. This includes files related to text, photos, audio clips, video clips, PDFs, and eBooks, as well as iWork and Microsoft Office documents and files.

To open an attached file using another app, in the incoming email message, tap and hold down the attachment icon for one to three seconds. If the attachment is compatible with an app that's installed on your iPhone or iPad, you're given the option to transfer the file to that app or directly open or access the file using that app.

If an incoming email message contains an attachment that is not compatible or accessible from your iOS device, you can't open or access it. In this case, you must access this content from your primary computer.

ORGANIZE EMAIL MESSAGES IN FOLDERS

Email messages can easily be moved into another folder, enabling you to better organize your emails. Here's how to do this:

1. From the Inbox listing, tap the Edit button that's located above the Inbox listing. Or, if you're viewing an email message, swipe your finger from right to left across the message listing.
2. Tap the More option. A menu that offers various folders and options available for that email account are displayed (shown in Figure 11.10).
3. Tap on the Move Message option, and then tap on the mailbox folder to which you want to move the message. The email message is moved to the folder you select.

TIP As you're managing incoming and outgoing emails, the Mail app uses the default mailboxes that are already associated with that email account, such as Inbox, Drafts, Sent, Trash, and Junk. For some accounts, you are limited to only these default mailboxes. However, for many types of email accounts, you can create additional mailboxes and then move messages into those mailboxes to organize them.

To create a custom mailbox (assuming that your account allows for this feature), from the Inbox, tap on the Mailboxes icon. When the Mailboxes screen appears, under the Accounts heading, tap on the account for which you want to create a mailbox. A listing of the existing mailboxes for that account is displayed.

Tap on the Edit button at the top of the screen. Then, tap on the New Mailbox icon that appears at the bottom of the screen. Enter the name of the mailbox you want to create, and then tap on the Save button. Your new mailbox is now displayed with that email account. The process works the same on the iPhone and iPad, but the position of the icons varies slightly.

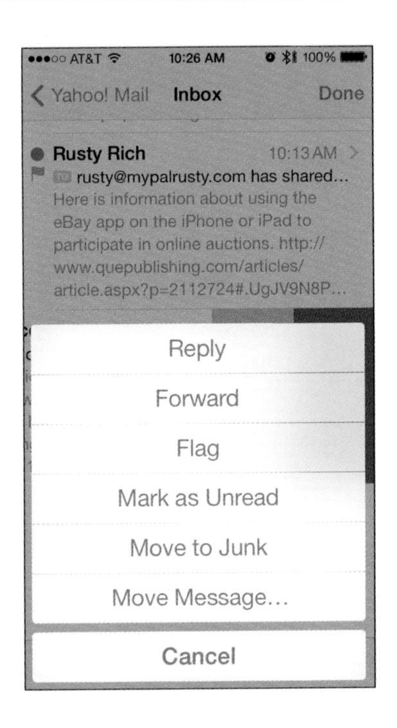

FIGURE 11.10

To move an email message between folders, tap on the Move Message option, and then tap on the name of the folder to which you want to move the message.

FORWARDING, PRINTING, AND REPLYING TO MESSAGES

From the Mail app, you can forward an incoming message to someone else, reply to the message, or print the email by tapping on the left-pointing, curved-arrow icon that's displayed when you're viewing an email. On an iPhone, the curved-arrow icon is displayed at the bottom of the screen. On an iPad, it can be found in the upper-right corner of the main Inbox screen (next to the Trash icon).

When you tap on this icon, as you're reading any email message, a menu offers the following three options: Reply, Forward, and Print.

To reply to the message you're reading, tap on the Reply icon. An email message template appears on the screen that already contains the content of the message you're replying to. Refer to the "Composing an Email Message" section for details on how to write and send an email message from the Mail app.

To forward the email you're reading to another recipient, tap on the Forward icon. If an attachment is associated with the email, you're asked, "Include attachments from original email?" with two options displayed on the screen, Include and Don't Include. Tap on the appropriate response.

When you opt to forward an email, a new message template appears on the screen. However, the contents of the message you're forwarding appears in the body of the email message. Start the message-forwarding process by filling in the To field. You can also modify the Subject field (or leave the message's original subject), and then add to the body of the email message with your own text. This text appears above the forwarded message's content.

TIP To forward an email to multiple recipients, enter each person's email address in the To field of the outgoing message, separating each address with a comma (,). Thus, you'd type **Jason@JasonRich.com, JasonRich77@yahoo.com** in the To field to forward or send the message to these two recipients simultaneously. Or tap on the plus icon (+) that appears to the right of the To field to add more recipients.

When you're ready to forward the message, tap on the blue-and-white Send button that appears, or tap the Cancel button to abort the message-forwarding process.

If you have an AirPrint-compatible printer set up to work with your iOS device, you can tap the Print icon that appears when you tap the left-pointing curved-arrow icon as you're reading an email.

MAIL APP QUICK TIPS

- To refresh your Inbox, swipe your finger downward on the inbox screen (iPhone) or within the inbox column on the left side of the Mail app's screen (iPad).
- As you're reading email, if the text is difficult to see, you can automatically increase the size of all text displayed in the Mail, Contacts, Calendar, Messages, and Notes apps by adjusting the Accessibility option within Settings. To make this font size adjustment, launch Settings. Select the General option, and then tap on the Accessibility option. From the Accessibility menu screen, tap on the Large Text option. You can now select

the font size you'd like your iOS device to use when displaying your emails and other content from various apps.

- As you're reading emails, all of the touchscreen finger motions you've learned work on the section of the iOS device's screen that's displaying the actual email messages. You can scroll up or down and/or zoom in or out.

COMMUNICATE EFFECTIVELY WITH APPLE'S iMESSAGE SERVICE

Although text and instant messaging has been around for decades, today's tweens and teens now commonly use it as a primary form of communication. Most young people are equipped with a state-of-the-art cell phone or smartphone these days. But, instead of talking with their friends over the phone (and using up minutes of their airtime plan), or even conversing face to face, they often "talk" via text messaging and instant messaging.

Using short, text-based messages, and a special "language" composed of abbreviated terminology, such as LOL (meaning "laugh out loud") or BRB (meaning "be right back"), people of all ages have begun to rely on text messaging and instant messaging as a convenient way to communicate (as shown in Figure 11.11).

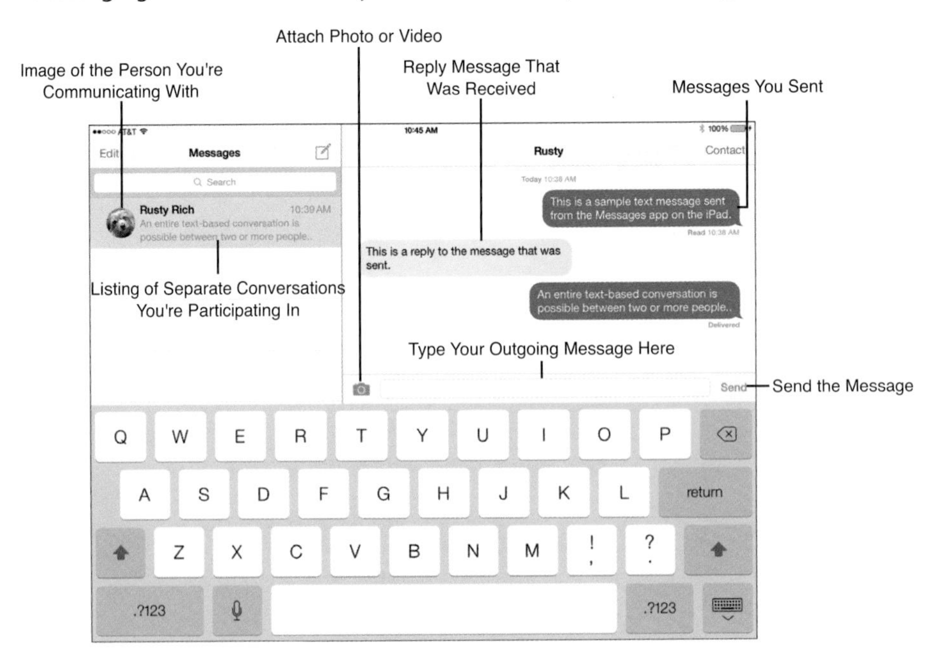

FIGURE 11.11

Text/instant messaging is done using the Messages app. Text-based conversations are formatted to be easy to read and follow.

NOTE On the iPad, if the person you're communicating with via the Messages app has an entry in your Contacts app database, and that entry contains their photo, it is displayed in the Messages app; otherwise, the person's initials are displayed by default if their entry contains no photo. Or, if there's no Contacts entry at all for the person, a generic head graphic is used. On the iPhone, only the person's name or phone number is displayed.

Most iPhone service plans have three components: voice, data, and text messaging. Upon signing up with a wireless service, you can choose a paid text-messaging plan that allows for the sending or receiving of a predetermined number of text messages per month or pay extra for an unlimited text-messaging plan. If your plan has no text messaging component, you will be charged for every text message you send or receive. These days, most shared family plans come with unlimited text messaging, however.

Text messaging using the service offered by your wireless service provider enables you to send and receive messages and converse with any other cell phone user, regardless of which service provider their phone is registered with. So if you use AT&T Wireless, you can easily communicate with a cell phone user (even if it's not an iPhone) who uses Verizon Wireless, Sprint PCS, or T-Mobile as a cellular service provider.

There are different types of text messages. There are text-only messages (SMS, or Short Message Service), as well as text messages that can contain a photo or video clip (MMS or Multimedia Messaging Service). Also, these messages can be sent to one or more people (within a group you create) simultaneously.

On the iPhone, the process of composing, reading, sending, and receiving text messages is done using the Messages app. The Messages app can also be used with Apple's own iMessage service.

NOTE iMessage is a free text-messaging service operated by Apple that utilizes the Internet and allows iOS mobile device and Mac users to communicate with other iOS device and Mac users, as long as the devices have access to the Internet. This means you can send an iMessage even if you are connected to the Internet via Wi-Fi, unlike an SMS or MMS text message, which requires a cellular network connection.

TIP It's possible to use Siri to dictate and send text messages using your voice. To do this, activate Siri and say something like, "Send text message to Rusty Rich." When Siri says, "What would you like it to say?," speak your message, and then confirm it (as shown in Figure 11.12). When prompted, tell Siri to send the text message you dictated. This feature works best if details about the person to which you're sending a text message are already stored in your Contacts database.

Siri can also be used to read your newly received text messages, without having to look at or touch the iPhone's screen.

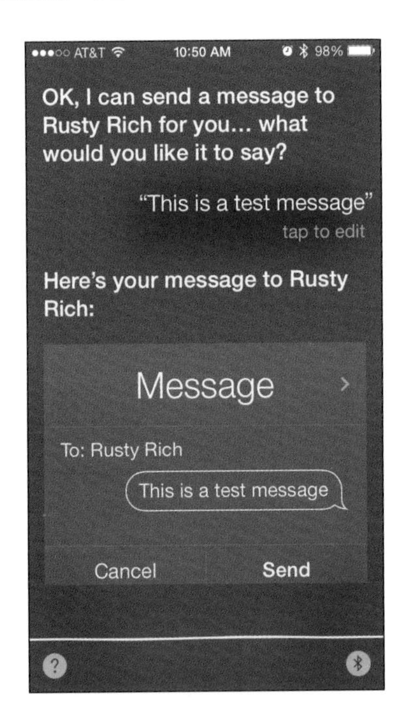

FIGURE 11.12

Siri on an iPhone can be used to compose and send text messages using your voice.

CAUTION This should be common sense, but if you look around as you're out and about, you'll see it clearly isn't. Under no circumstances should you drive and use text messaging on your iPhone or iPad at the same time. Likewise, as you're walking down the street or crossing a busy intersection, don't try multi-tasking by also sending or reading text messages. Every day, numerous accidents happen (some very serious) as a result of people sending or reading text messages when they should be focused on something else.

QUICK START: APPLE'S IMESSAGE SERVICE

Whether your iPhone or iPad is connected to the Internet via a Wi-Fi or cellular data connection, using iMessage with the Messages app that comes preinstalled on your device, you now can communicate via instant messages with other Macs and iOS mobile device users. Unlike the text-messaging services available through wireless service providers, Apple's iMessage service is free of charge, and it allows for an unlimited number of text messages to be sent and received. (When using iMessage via a Cellular data connection, this uses some of your monthly data allocation, if applicable.)

The service also taps into your iPhone or iPad's other functions and allows for the easy sharing of photos, videos, locations, and contacts; plus, it works seamlessly with Notification Center.

TIP When the iMessage service is used with the Messages app, it enables you to send the same text message to multiple recipients. It uses a feature referred to as *group messaging* that enables everyone in that group to participate in the same text-message–based conversation. Messages can also be sent to groups using SMS messaging, if not everyone you're conversing with is using Apple equipment that's compatible with iMessage.

iMessage enables you to participate in text-based, real-time conversations. When someone is actively typing a message to you during a conversation on iMessage, a bubble with three periods in it appears. You can view and respond to the message a fraction of a second after it is sent.

SET UP A FREE IMESSAGE ACCOUNT

Because traditional text messaging is tied to a cell phone, which has a unique phone number, there is no need to have a separate username or account name when using the text-messaging feature through your cellular service provider. If you know someone's cell phone number, you can send a text message to that person from your cell phone (and vice versa). However, because iMessage is web-based, before using this service, you must set up a free iMessage account.

The first time you launch the Messages app to use it with the iMessage service, you're instructed to set up a free account using your existing Apple ID. Or, instead of using your Apple ID, tap on the Create New Account option to create an account that's linked to another existing email address.

NOTE iPhone users can associate their cell phone numbers with their iMessage accounts to send and receive text messages using this service. However, an Apple ID or existing email address can be used as well.

TIP If you've upgraded your iPhone to iOS 7, when you first launch Messages, you might discover the app automatically uses your existing Apple ID to establish your free iMessage account. You can modify this in Settings by selecting the Messages option from the main Settings menu, if you want to create a separate Apple ID account for use with these services.

One reason to use multiple Apple ID accounts is to link one with your online purchases and another with iMessage. This is useful if your kids or spouse also use an Apple computer or device and you want to share purchased content with them without giving them access to your other data.

To do this, you must complete the information requested from the New Account screen. When the requested New Account information is entered, tap on the blue-and-white Done icon in the upper-right corner of the New Account window. Keep in mind that if you simply enter your existing Apple ID information to set up your iMessage account, and then tap on the Sign In icon, the initial process for establishing an iMessage account is quick.

TIP Just as when you're using FaceTime, the unique Apple ID, email address, or iPhone phone number you use to set up your iMessage account is how people find you and are able to communicate with you. So if you want someone to be able to send you messages via iMessage, that person must know the iPhone phone number, Apple ID, or email address you used to set up the account. Likewise, to send someone a text message via iMessage, you need to know the iPhone phone number, Apple ID, or email address the recipient used to set up his or her iMessage account.

PROS AND CONS OF USING iMESSAGE

The biggest benefit to using iMessage over other text-messaging services is that it's free, and you can send/receive an unlimited number of messages. The Messages app itself also nicely integrates with other features, functions, and apps on your iPhone or iPad.

If you're away from your iPhone or iPad when an incoming text message arrives, don't worry. The Notification Center app can continuously monitor the Messages app and inform you of any missed messages in the Notification Center window.

Another convenient feature of iMessage is that you can begin a text-message–based conversation using your iPhone, for example, and switch to using your iPad or Mac and continue that conversation using the iMessage service. This feature is not available if you're using the Messages app for SMS text messaging via your cellular service provider.

All messages that are sent and received are saved in reverse chronological order and categorized by the person you communicated with. Until you manually delete the conversation, you always have a record of what was said, accompanied by the time and date messages were sent/received.

Currently, one potential drawback to the iMessage service is that to find and communicate with someone, you must know the Apple ID or email address used to set up the person's iMessage account. Thus, you must know beforehand whether they're a Mac, iPhone, or iPad user. However, after you know this, sending and receiving text messages with that person becomes a straightforward process. You can store the person's account information in your Contacts database (which links to the Messages app).

TIPS AND TRICKS FOR USING THE MESSAGES APP

The Messages app on the iPhone has two main screens: a summary of conversations labeled Messages, and an actual conversation screen labeled at the top of the screen using the name of the person(s) with whom you're conversing. Both of these screens have a handful of icon-based commands that give you access to the app's features and functions.

On the iPad, the Messages screen is divided into two main sections. On the left is a listing of your previous conversations. When Messages is running, the right side of the iPad screen is the active conversation window. From here, you can initiate a new conversation or respond to incoming messages, one at a time.

> **NOTE** When you need to type messages, the iPhone or iPad's virtual keyboard appears. To give you more onscreen real estate to reread a long conversation, tap on the Hide Keyboard key that always appears near the lower-right corner of the virtual keyboard when it's visible.

CREATE AND SEND A TEXT MESSAGE

The first time you launch Messages on the iPad, the New Message screen is visible, the cursor flashes on the To field, and the virtual keyboard is displayed. If you have contact information stored in the Contacts app, as soon as you start typing in the To field, Messages attempts to match up existing contacts with the name, cell phone number, or email address you're currently typing. When the intended recipient's name appears, tap on it.

TIP To initiate a conversation with someone else, tap on the New Message icon that appears in the upper-right corner of the Messages screen on the iPhone or next to the Messages heading on the upper-left side of the iPad's screen.

To quickly search your Contacts database to find one or more recipients for your text messages, you can also tap on the blue-and-white plus icon in the To field as you're composing a new message. A scrollable list of all contacts stored in Contacts displays, along with a Search field you can use to search your contacts database from within the Messages app.

TIP If you're using an iPhone, to use your cellular service provider's SMS text-messaging service to send a message to another cell phone user, enter the recipient's cell phone number in the To field of a new message. This applies if the person doesn't have an entry in your Contacts database.

If you're using an iPhone or iPad to send a message to another iOS mobile device or Mac user via iMessage, in the To field, enter the recipient's Apple ID or the email address the user has linked with his iMessage account. If the person is using an iPhone, his iMessage account might be associated with his iPhone's phone number, based on how he initially set up the account.

In your Contacts database, you can create a separate field for someone's iMessage username, or when viewing the person's Contacts listing, simply tap on the appropriate contact information based on how you want to send the text message.

After filling in the To field with one or more recipients, if you have the Subject feature turned on in Settings, tap on the optional Subject field to create a subject for your text message, and then tap on the blank field located to the left of the Send icon to begin typing your text message. On the iPhone, a blank field for the body of your text message is available, displayed to the left of the Send icon.

If you're sending only text in your message, enter the text and then tap on the blue-and-white Send icon. Or to attach a photo or video clip to your outgoing text message, tap on the camera icon displayed to the left of the field where you're typing the text message.

TIP When you tap on the camera icon as you're composing a text message, two command options are displayed (shown in Figure 11.13). Tap on the Take Photo or Video option to launch the Camera app from within Messages, and quickly snap a photo or shoot a video clip using your iPhone or iPad's built-in camera.

If you already have the photo or video clip stored on your phone or tablet that you want to share, tap on the Choose Existing option to launch the Photos app in Messages, and then tap on the thumbnail for the photo or video clip you want to attach to the message.

When the photo or video clip has been attached to the outgoing text message, and you've typed any text that you want to accompany it, tap on the Send key to send the message.

FIGURE 11.13

After tapping on the camera icon, choose to take a photo using your device's built-in camera, or select a photo or video clip that's already stored on your iPhone or iPad (shown here).

PARTICIPATING IN A TEXT-MESSAGE CONVERSATION

As soon as you tap Send to initiate a new text-message conversation and send an initial message, the New Message window transforms into a conversation window, with the recipient's name displayed at the top center. Displayed on the right side of the conversation window are the messages you've sent. The responses from the person you're conversing with are left-justified and displayed in a different color on the screen with text bubbles.

As the text-message–based conversation continues and eventually scrolls off the screen, use your finger to swipe upward or downward to view what's already been said.

> **TIP** Whenever there's a pause between the sending of a message and the receipt of a response, the Messages app automatically inserts the date and time in the center of the screen so that you can later easily track the time period during which each conversation took place. This is particularly helpful if there are long gaps and the conversation did not take place in real time.

To delete or forward part of a text message, press and hold down that section of the message. A Copy and More option will be displayed. Copy enables you to transfer the selected content to your device's virtual clipboard and then copy it elsewhere. The More option enables you to select more of the text message conversation and then delete or forward it by tapping on the trashcan or Forward icon.

> **TIP** From the Messages conversation screen on an iPad, tap on the Contact icon displayed in the upper-right corner of the conversation window to view the complete Contacts database entry for the person with whom you're conversing.

To delete entire conversations in the Messages app, press and hold one section of the message conversation, and then tap on the More option. Next, tap on the Delete All option to delete the entire conversation. Or from the Messages screen which lists the individual conversations you've had or are engaged in, swipe your finger across a listing from right to left, and then tap on the Delete option.

RESPONDING TO AN INCOMING MESSAGE

Depending on how you set up the Messages app in Settings, you can be notified of an incoming message in a number of ways. For example, notification of a new text message can be set to appear in the Notification Center window. Or, if the

Messages app is already running, a new message alert is heard and a new message listing appears on the Messages screen (iPhone) or under the Messages heading on the left side of the iPad screen. If you already have the conversation screen open and a new message from that person you're conversing with is received, that message appears on the conversation screen.

TIP When a new message arrives, a blue dot appears to the left of the new message's listing (under the Messages heading on the iPad or on the Messages screen on the iPhone). The blue dot indicates it's a new, unread message.

To read the incoming message and enter into the conversation window and respond, tap on the incoming message listing. If you're looking at the listing in the Notification Center window, for example, and you tap on it, the Messages app launches and the appropriate conversation window automatically opens.

After reading the incoming text message, use the virtual keyboard to type your response in the blank message field, and then tap the Send icon to send the response message.

RELAUNCH OR REVIEW PAST CONVERSATIONS

From the Messages screen on the iPhone, or from the left side of the screen on the iPad when the Messages app is running, you can view a listing of all saved conversations. Each listing displays the person's name, the date and time of the last message sent or received, and a summary of the last message sent or received. The Messages app automatically saves all messages until you manually delete them. Tap on any of the listings to relaunch that conversation in the Conversation window. You can either reread the entire conversation or continue the conversation by sending a message to that person.

TIP By tapping on one conversation listing at a time, you can quickly switch between conversations and participate in multiple conversations at once.

On the iPhone, to exit the conversation screen you're currently viewing, tap on the left-pointing arrow icon that's displayed in the upper-left corner of the screen, labeled Messages.

On the iPad, to exit a conversation, tap on one of the other listings under the Messages heading on the left side of the screen.

To exit the Messages app altogether, press the Home button.

From the Messages screen on the iPhone (or the Messages listing on the iPad that's displayed on the left side of the screen), tap on the Edit icon to quickly delete entire conversations with specific people. To do this, tap on the red-and-white icon that's displayed next to the listing under the Messages heading once you tap the Edit icon.

CUSTOMIZE THE MESSAGES APP

In Settings, you can customize several settings related to the Messages app. To do this, launch Settings from the Home screen, and then tap on the Messages option that's displayed in the main Settings menu.

In the Messages setup window, you can turn on or off the iMessage service altogether, plus make adjustments that are relevant to sending and receiving messages from your iOS 7 device.

For example, by adjusting the virtual switch associated with the Send Read Receipts option to the on position, your contacts are notified when you read their messages.

On the iPhone, you can also set preferences for using text messages (SMS and MMS messages) versus iMessage. On the iPad, the customizations available in Settings pertain exclusively to the iMessage service.

Also from the Messages submenu in Settings on the iPhone, if you turn on the virtual switch associated with character count, as you're composing a new message, the number of characters it contains is automatically displayed.

By tapping on the Blocked option, it's possible to create a list of people from your Contacts database that you do not want to receive messages from. The people you add to the Blocked list will be prevented from sending you messages via the Messages app.

IN THIS CHAPTER

- How to use new features in the iOS 7 version of Safari
- How to create and use offline Reading Lists
- How to use Safari Reader
- How to sync open browser windows with the iCloud Tabs feature

12

SURF THE WEB MORE EFFICIENTLY USING SAFARI

Chances are, if you know how to use a Mac or PC, you already know how to surf the Web using a browser such as Safari, Microsoft Internet Explorer, Firefox, or Google Chrome on your computer.

The Safari web browser on your iPhone (shown in Figure 12.1 with the www.google.com website displayed) or iPad (shown in Figure 12.2) offers the same basic functionality as the web browser for your desktop or laptop computer, but it's designed to maximize the iPhone or iPad's touchscreen and screen size.

With the release of iOS 7, Apple once again enhanced the Safari app, giving it a handful of new features that make web surfing a more enjoyable, secure, and efficient experience.

iOS 7 WHAT'S NEW In addition to having a new look, Safari on the iPhone and iPad now features a single smart Search field, as well as a new tabbed view so you can see all of the browser windows currently open. There's also no limit to how many browser windows can be open.

The Reading List feature is now easier to use and enables you to read everything in your reading list at once or read each article separately. One of the most useful new features is iCloud Keychain, explained shortly.

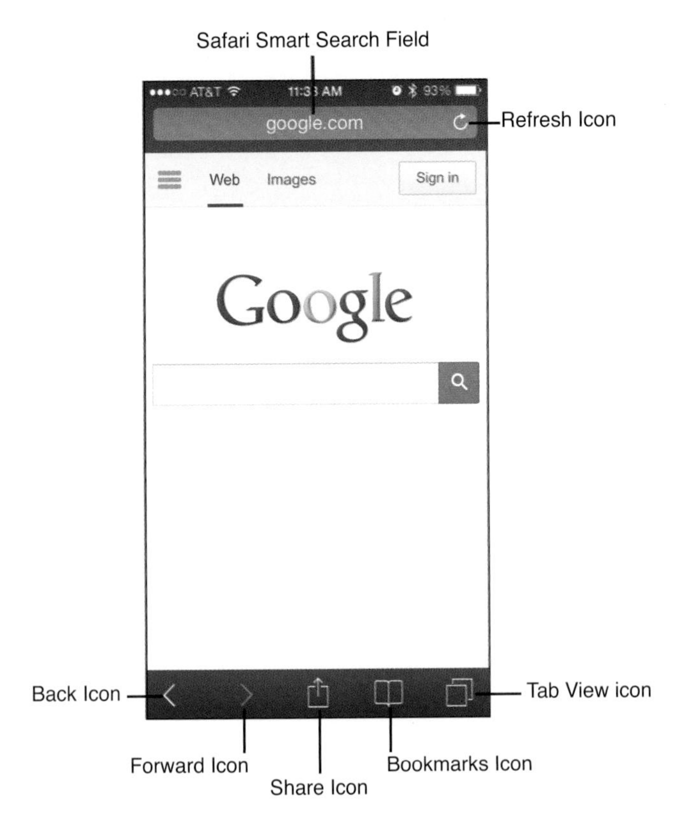

FIGURE 12.1

The main screen of the Safari web browser on the iPhone 5.

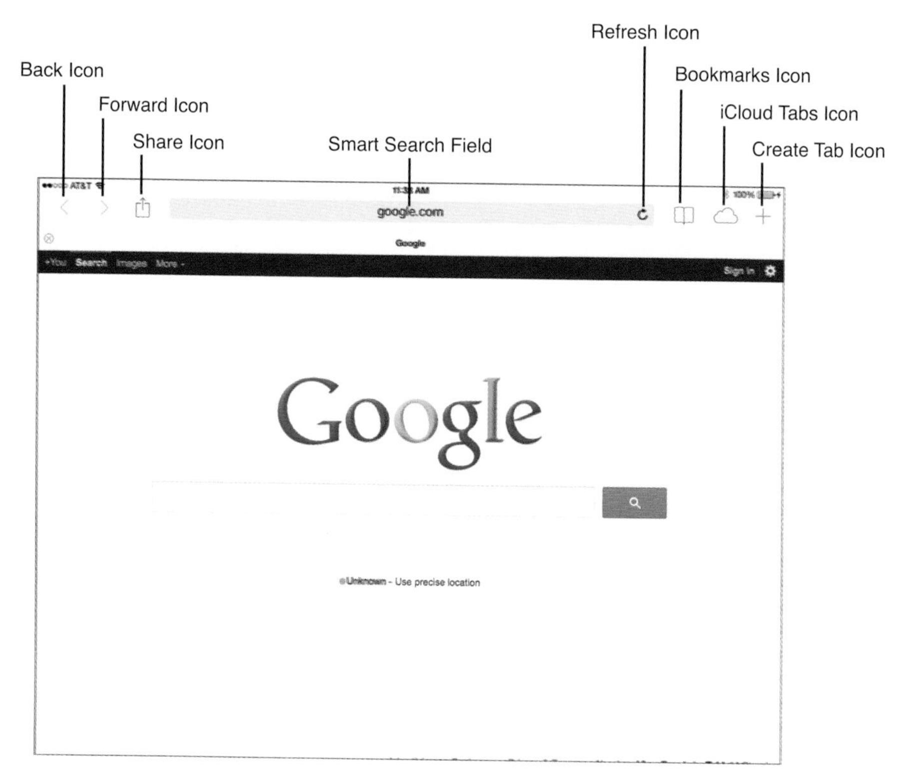

FIGURE 12.2

The main screen of the Safari web browser on the iPad.

As you'd expect from your iPhone or iPad, surfing the Web using the Safari app is a highly customizable experience. For example, you can hold your device in Portrait or Landscape mode while surfing.

On most websites, you can also zoom in on or zoom out of specific areas or elements, such as a paragraph of text or a photo, using the reverse-pinch finger gesture (to zoom in) or the pinch gesture (to zoom out), or by double-tapping on a specific area of the screen to zoom in or out.

CUSTOMIZE YOUR WEB SURFING EXPERIENCE

To customize your web surfing experience using Safari, launch Settings, and then tap on the Safari option. The Safari menu screen appears (as shown in Figure 12.3) with a handful of customizable menu options. Here's a summary of what each is used for:

- **Search Engine**—The new smart Search field is used to enter specific website URLs (addresses) and to find what you're looking for on the Web via a search engine, such as Google, Yahoo!, or Bing. This option enables you to select your default (favorite) Internet search engine. So if you select Google as your default, whenever you perform a search using Safari's Search field, the browser automatically accesses Google to obtain your search results.

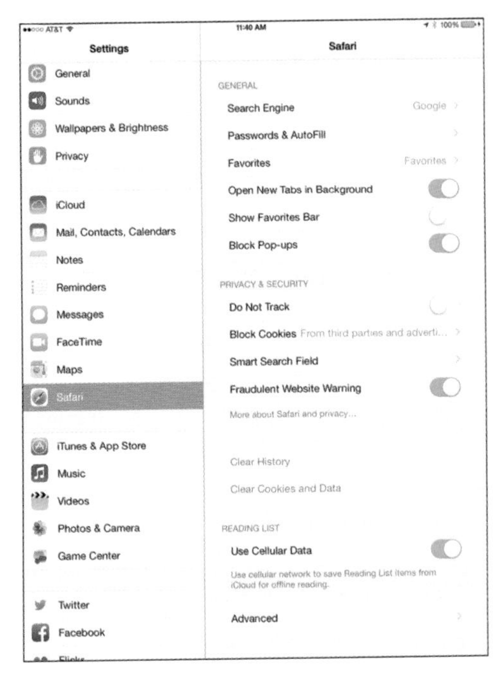

FIGURE 12.3

Customize your web surfing experience when using Safari from within Settings on your iOS device.

> **TIP** Regardless of which Internet search engine (Google, Yahoo!, or Bing) you select to be your default in the Settings app, you can always add the other two (or any other search engine) to your Bookmarks or Favorites Bar, so that you can access the other search engines directly, by pointing Safari to www.Google.com, www.Yahoo.com, www.Bing.com, and so on.

- **Passwords & AutoFill**—One of the more tedious aspects of surfing the Web is constantly having to fill in certain types of data fields, such as your name, address, phone number, email address, and website-related passwords.

When turned on, this feature remembers your responses and automatically inserts the data into the appropriate fields. It also pulls information from your own entry in the Contacts app. To customize this option and link your personal contact entry to Safari, tap on the Passwords & AutoFill option, turn on the Use Contact Info option, and then tap on My Info to select your contact entry. You can also set whether Safari remembers names and passwords for specific websites you visit, as well as credit card information that you use to make online purchases. This functionality is part of what Apple calls iCloud Keychain.

- **Favorites**—This feature serves as a shortcut for accessing websites you frequently visit. As you begin typing a website address or website name into the Search field, Safari accesses your Favorites list and auto-inserts the appropriate website URL. When you tap on the Search field, a screen with icons representing sites in your Favorites list is displayed.
- **Open Links (iPhone only)**—Anytime a new web page opens as a result of you tapping on a link, this feature determines whether the new browser window is opened as the new active browser window or whether it opens in the background.
- **Open New Tabs in Background (iPad only)**—Anytime a new web page opens as a result of you tapping on a link, this feature determines whether the new browser window is opened as the new active browser window or whether it opens in the background.
- **Block Pop-Ups**—When turned on, this feature prevents a website you're visiting from creating and displaying extra windows or opening a bunch of unwanted browser pages. The default for this option is turned on because this makes for a more enjoyable web surfing experience.
- **Do Not Track**—By default, when you surf the Web using Safari, the web browser remembers all the websites you visit and creates a detailed History list that you can access to quickly revisit websites. By turning on the Do Not Track feature, Safari does not store details about the websites you visit.
- **Block Cookies**—Many websites use cookies to remember who you are and your personalized preferences when you're visiting that site. Cookies contain data that gets saved on your iPhone or iPad and is accessible by the websites you revisit. When this option is turned on, Safari does not accept cookies from websites you visit. Thus, you must reenter site-specific preferences and information each time you visit that site. The Blocked Cookies submenu offers three options: Always (meaning all cookies are blocked), From Third Parties and Advertisers (meaning cookies unrelated to websites you purposely visit are blocked), and Never (meaning no cookies are blocked).

- **Smart Search Field**—Tap on this option to reveal a submenu that enables you to turn on or off the Search Engine Suggestions and Preload Top Hit options. This determines whether Safari makes suggestions as you use the Search field to find information on the Web.
- **Fraudulent Website Warning**—This feature helps prevent you from visiting impostor websites designed to look like real ones, which have been created for the purpose of committing fraud or identity theft. It's not foolproof, but keeping this feature turned on gives you an added level of protection, especially if you use your iOS device for online banking and other financial transactions.
- **Clear History**—Using this feature, you can delete the contents of Safari's History folder that stores details about all the websites you have visited.
- **Clear Cookies and Data**—Use this command to delete all cookies related to websites you've visited that Safari has stored on your iOS device.
- **Use Cellular Data**—This option enables your iPhone or iPad to use the cellular data service (as opposed to a Wi-Fi Internet connection) to download Reading List information to your device from your iCloud account so that it can be read offline. Although this feature is convenient, it also utilizes some of your monthly cellular data allocation, which is why an on/off option is associated with it.
- **Advanced**—From this submenu, you can view details about website-specific data that Safari has collected. If you choose, you can manually delete this information. You also can enable or disable the JavaScript feature.

HOW TO USE TABBED BROWSING WITH SAFARI

Safari's main screen contains the various command icons used to navigate the Web. On the iPhone, these icons are displayed along the bottom of the Safari screen, while the new smart Search field is displayed along the top of the screen.

The command icons along the bottom of the Safari screen when using the iPhone include Back, Forward, Share, Bookmark, and Tab View.

If you're using Safari on an iPad, the Title bar displays all of Safari's command icons along the top of the screen. Immediately below the Title bar, if you have the option turned on, your personalized Favorites Bar is displayed. Below the Favorites Bar, the Tabs bar becomes visible if you have more than one web page loaded in Safari at any given time.

SWITCHING BETWEEN WEB PAGES ON AN iPHONE

The iPhone version of tabbed browsing involves Safari opening separate browser windows for each active web page. By tapping on the new Tab View icon at the bottom-right corner of the Safari screen, you can quickly switch between browser windows (shown in Figure 12.4).

FIGURE 12.4

Safari's new Tab View is shown here on the iPhone. To open a new page, tap on the "+" option near the bottom-center of the screen.

When you're viewing the Tab View screen, tap on the New Page icon (which looks like a plus sign) to create a new (empty) browser window, and then manually surf to a new website (by typing a URL or search term into the unified smart search field selecting a favorite icon, or selecting a bookmark).

TIP When viewing the Tab View in Safari, tap on the Private option to turn on the Private web surfing mode. This prevents Safari from storing details about the websites you visit and syncing this information with your iCloud account.

To switch between active (viewable) browser windows that are open, simply tap on one of the tabs displayed. You can scroll through them using an upward or downward swipe motion with your finger as needed.

Tap the Done button (in the lower-right corner of the screen) to exit the Tab View screen and return to the main Safari web browser screen. Or tap on one of the web page thumbnails as you scroll through them on the Tab View screen.

TABBED BROWSING ON THE iPAD

When you tap on a link in a web page that causes a new web page to automatically open, a new tab in Safari is created and displayed, assuming you have the Open New Tabs in Background option (in Settings) turned off. Tabs are shown in Figure 12.5.

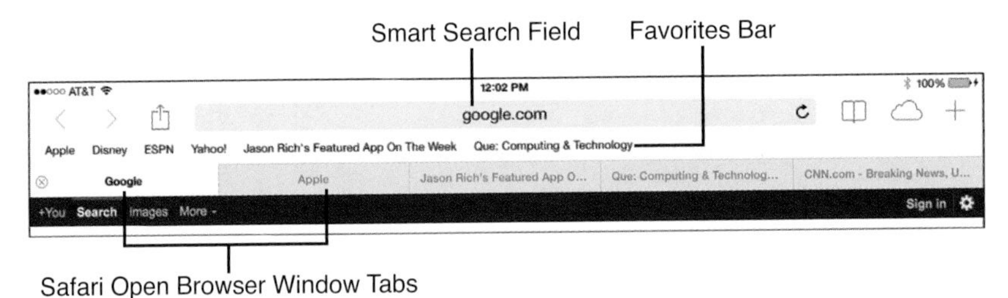

FIGURE 12.5

Instead of separate windows, Safari on the iPad uses onscreen tabs that enable you to instantly switch between web pages that are simultaneously open.

> **TIP** On the iPad, in addition to showing open browser windows as tabs, you can display the Favorites Bar (refer to Figure 12.5), which you can also fully customize. From the Safari menu in Settings, you can determine whether browser tabs and/or the Favorites Bar are displayed.

As you're viewing a web page, you can simultaneously open another web page by tapping on the plus sign icon displayed in the top-right corner of the Safari screen. When you do this, a new tab is created, and you can visit a new web page without closing the previous page.

Along the Tab bar on the iPad, you can have multiple web pages accessible at once. You can instantly switch between web pages simply by tapping on a tab.

To close a tab, tap on the small x that appears on the left side of that tab.

TAKE ADVANTAGE OF THE iCLOUD TABS FEATURE OF SAFARI

You already know that iCloud can be set up to sync app-specific data between your iPhone, iPad, Mac(s), and PC(s) that are linked to the same iCloud (Apple ID) account. In addition to syncing your Safari Bookmarks, Bookmarks Bar, and Reading List information, the iOS 7 version of Safari also syncs, in real time, your open Safari browser windows.

Thus, if you're surfing the Web on your Mac and have one or more browser windows open, you can pick up your iPad, tap on the iCloud Tabs option (the icon that looks like a cloud), and then open that same browser window(s) on your mobile device (or vice versa), without having to reenter the web page's URL.

On the iPhone, to access the iCloud Tabs feature and view the browser windows open on your computer(s) and/or other mobile devices that are linked to the same iCloud account, access the Tab View screen and scroll down to the bottom of it. A listing of open tabbed browser windows on your other Macs and iOS mobile devices that are linked to the same iCloud account is displayed. Tap on any listing to open that browser window on your iPhone.

On the iPad, the iCloud icon is displayed along the Title Bar, in between the Bookmarks and New Tab icons (refer to Figure 12.2). When you tap on the iCloud Tabs option, a separate window appears that lists open browser windows or tabs on each computer or device. Tap on a listing to open that page on the device you're using.

> **! CAUTION** With this feature turned on, as you're surfing the Web on your iPhone or iPad, someone can literally follow along and see what web pages you're visiting in real time online by tapping on the iCloud Tabs option while using Safari on your computer (if they're signed in using your account). To prevent this, activate Safari's Private Browsing feature.

REMOVE SCREEN CLUTTER WITH SAFARI READER

Safari Reader works on the iPhone and iPad and enables you to select a compatible website page; strip out graphic icons, ads, and other unwanted elements that cause onscreen clutter; and then read just the text (and view related photos) from that web page on your iOS device's screen.

The Safari Reader works only with compatible websites, including those published by major daily newspapers and other news organizations. If the feature is available while you're viewing a web page, a newly designed Reader icon (as shown in Figure 12.6) is displayed next to that web page's URL in Safari's Smart Search field.

WHAT'S NEW The Reader button in the iOS 7 version of Safari now looks like a series of horizontal lines that appears on the edge of the smart search field. It no longer actually says "Reader."

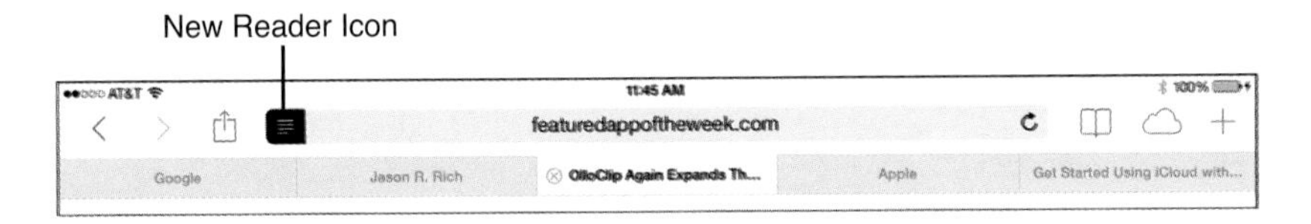

FIGURE 12.6

When you see a Reader icon appear in the smart search field in Safari, you can open that content in the Reader window and view it clutter free.

When you see the Reader icon displayed, tap on it. An uncluttered screen (iPhone) or window (iPad) that contains just the article or text from that web page, along with related photos, is displayed. Use your finger to scroll up or down.

To exit the Reader window and return to the main web page, tap anywhere in the margins of the screen outside the Reader window.

CREATE AND MANAGE READING LISTS

As you're surfing the Web, you might come across specific web pages, articles, or other information that you want to refer to later. In Safari, you can create a bookmark for that website URL and have it displayed in your Bookmarks list or on your Favorites Bar, or you can add it to your Reading List, which is another way to store web page links and content that's of interest to you.

NOTE The iOS 7 version of Safari enables the Reading List feature to download entire web pages for offline viewing, as opposed to simply storing website addresses that you can refer to later. Although this feature downloads text and photos associated with a web page, it does not download animated graphics, video, or audio content associated with that page.

To add a website or web-based article to your personalized Reading List for later review, tap on the Share icon, and then tap on the Add to Reading List button displayed as part of Safari's newly expanded Share menu. Figure 12.7 shows an example of a Reading List, which you can access by tapping on the Bookmarks icon in Safari and then tapping on the Reading List tab (which looks like eyeglasses).

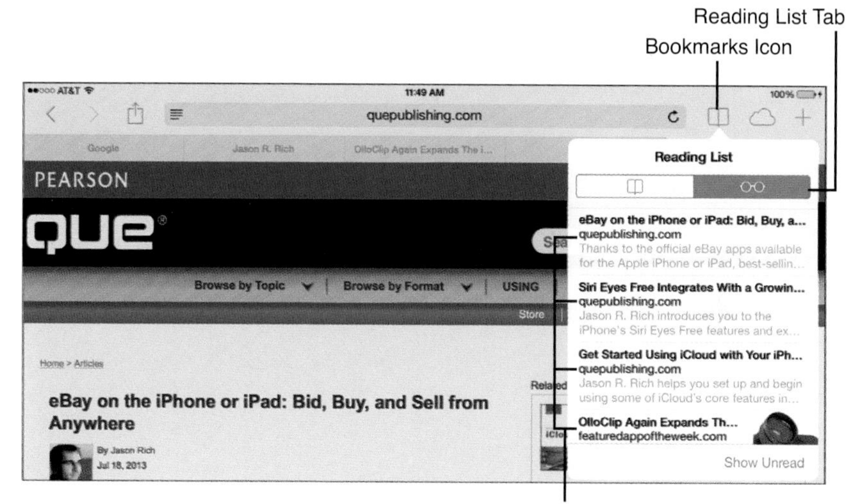

FIGURE 12.7

Creating a Reading List is another way to store links related to specific content on the Web that you want to easily be able to find again and access later. (Shown here on the iPad.)

When you want to refer to items stored in your Reading List, from Safari, tap on the Bookmarks icon, and then tap on the Reading List tab. A listing of your saved web pages or articles previously saved to your Reading List is displayed.

TIP Like your Bookmarks list and Favorites Bar, the items stored in your Reading List can automatically be saved to iCloud and almost instantly made available on any other computer or iOS device that's linked to your iCloud account. See the section, "Create, Manage, and Sync Safari Bookmarks," for details on setting up these features for backup to iCloud.

NEW OPTIONS FOR SHARING WEB CONTENT IN SAFARI

There are probably times when you're surfing the Web and come across something funny, informative, educational, or just plain bizarre that you want to share with other people, add to your Bookmarks list, or print. The iOS 7 version of Safari makes sharing web links extremely easy, plus it now gives you a handful of new options.

Anytime you're visiting a web page that you want to share with others, tap on the Share icon to reveal a newly expanded Share menu (as shown in Figure 12.8).

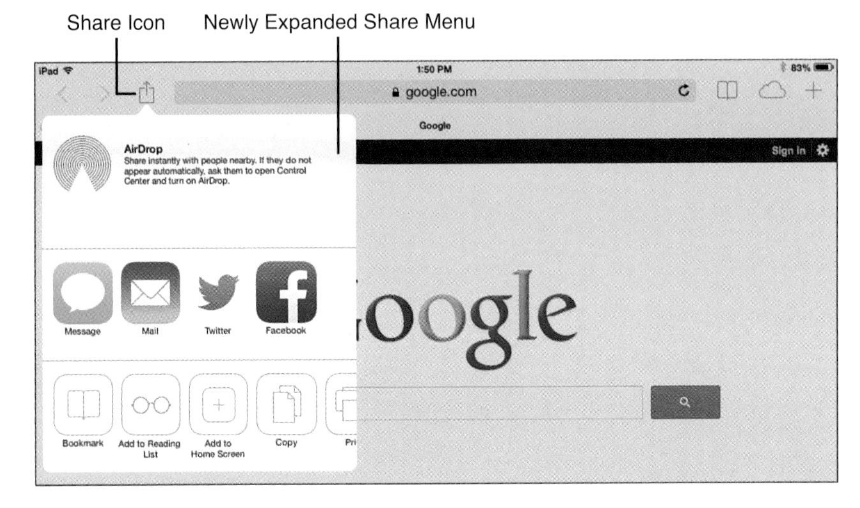

FIGURE 12.8

Safari's Share menu offers a handful of ways to store and share web page content.

On the iPhone, the Share icon is displayed near the bottom center of the Safari screen. On the iPad, the Share icon can be found to the immediate left of the smart search field.

iOS 7 WHAT'S NEW If you have the new AirDrop for iOS feature turned on, when you access the Share menu in Safari, an AirDrop option is also available. This enables you to wirelessly share content with nearby (compatible) iPhone, iPad, or iPod touch users. Some older models don't offer AirDrop, even with iOS 7 installed.

To turn on AirDrop for iOS, open Control Center and tap on the AirDrop button. Then choose whether you want to communicate wirelessly with Contacts Only or all AirDrop users in your immediate vicinity. If AirDrop is not turned on, this feature will not appear in the Share menu.

The following options are available from the Share menu:

- **Message**—Send details about the web page you're currently viewing to one or more other people via text or instant message using the Message app (without having to leave Safari). Tap on Message, fill in the To field, and then tap the Send button. The website URL is automatically embedded within the text or instant message.

- **Mail**—To share a website URL with others via email, as you're looking at the web page or website you want to share, tap on the Share icon and select the Mail option from the Share menu. In Safari, an outgoing email window appears.

  Simply fill in the To field with the recipient's email address, and tap the Send icon (as shown in Figure 12.9). The website URL automatically is embedded within the body of the email, with the website's heading used as the email's subject. Before sending the email, you can add text to the body of the email message or change the subject.

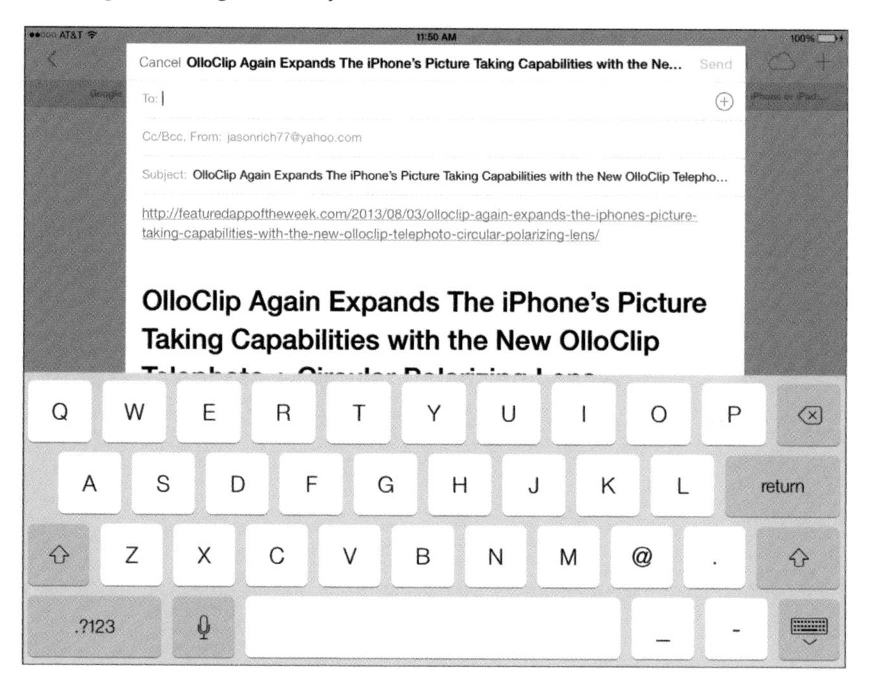

FIGURE 12.9

In Safari, you can email information about a website to one or more recipients without first having to exit Safari.

- **Twitter**—If you have an active Twitter account that's set up for use with iOS 7, tap on the Twitter option from the Share menu to create an outgoing tweet that automatically has the website URL attached.

  When the Tweet window appears (shown in Figure 12.10), enter your tweet message (up to 140 characters, minus the length of the automatically shortened version of the website URL). Tap the Send icon when the tweet message is composed and ready to share with your Twitter followers.

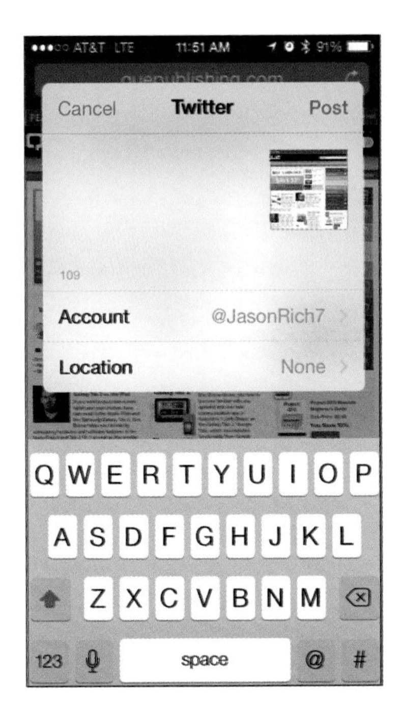

FIGURE 12.10

Send out a tweet to your Twitter followers from within Safari, and automatically include a link to the web page you're viewing.

> **TIP** If you're managing multiple Twitter accounts from your iOS device, in the outgoing tweet window, tap on the From field, and then select from which of your Twitter accounts you want to send the tweet you're composing.

- **Facebook**—Thanks to Facebook integration within iOS 7, when you tap on the Facebook option, you can update your Facebook status and include details about the web page you're currently viewing in Safari.
- **Bookmark**—Tap on this option to add a bookmark to your personal Bookmarks menu or Favorites Bar that's stored in Safari. You can later access your bookmarks and/or Favorites by tapping on the Bookmark icon.

  When you opt to save a bookmark, an Add Bookmark window appears (as shown in Figure 12.11). Here, you can enter a title for the bookmark and decide whether you want to save it as part of your Bookmarks menu or in your Favorites Bar. It's also possible to create separate subfolders in your Bookmarks menu to organize your saved bookmarks.

FIGURE 12.11

You can save a website URL as a bookmark in your Bookmarks menu or to be displayed as part of Safari's Favorites Bar.

- **Add to Reading List**—Instead of adding a web page URL to your Bookmarks list or Favorites Bar, you can save it in your Reading List for later reference. (It will be downloaded to your iPhone or iPad for later viewing, even if no Internet connection is later available.) To access your Reading List, tap on the Bookmarks icon, and then tap on the Reading List tab.
- **Add to Home Screen**—In addition to saving a website URL in the form of a bookmark or in your Reading List, another option is to save it as a Home screen icon. This feature is explained later, in the "Launch Your Favorite Websites Fast with Home Screen Icons" section.
- **Copy**—Use this command to copy the web page URL you're looking at to the virtual clipboard that's built in to iOS 7. You can then paste that information into another app.
- **Print**—In Safari, you can wirelessly print a website to any AirPrint-compatible printer that's set up to work with your iOS device. To print a web page, tap on the Print command. From the Printer Options screen, select the printer you want to use, and then choose the number of copies you want printed. Tap the Print icon at the bottom of the Print Options window to send the web page document to your printer.

TIP To access your Bookmarks list, tap on the Bookmarks icon displayed next to the Share icon in Safari on the iPhone (or to the immediate right of the smart search field on the iPad), and tap on the Bookmarks tab to view your personalized list of saved website bookmarks.

NOTE When using Safari on the iPhone, you can maintain a Favorites Bar (if you sync this data from a computer or other iOS device); however, to conserve onscreen space, the Favorites Bar is not displayed across the top of the Safari screen like it is on an iPad. Instead, on an iPhone, the Favorites Bar is displayed as an additional Bookmark folder when you tap on the Bookmarks icon.

CREATE, MANAGE, AND SYNC SAFARI BOOKMARKS

Thanks to the fact that Safari is fully integrated with iCloud, if you have an active iCloud account, your iOS device automatically syncs your Bookmarks and related Safari data with your other iOS devices, as well as the compatible web browsers on your primary computer(s).

To activate this iCloud sync feature, launch Settings from the Home Screen, and then tap on the iCloud option. When the iCloud menu screen appears, make sure your iCloud account is listed at the top of the screen, and then make sure the virtual on/off switch associated with the Safari option is turned on.

Your Bookmarks list, Favorites Bar, open browser windows (tabs), and Safari Reading List are automatically continuously synced with your iCloud account. Thus, when you add a new bookmark while surfing the Web on your iPad, within seconds that same bookmark will appear in your Bookmarks list on your iPhone and on Safari that's running on your Mac, for example.

SYNC USERNAMES AND PASSWORDS USING iCLOUD KEYCHAIN

Another new feature in the iOS 7 version of Safari that also utilizes iCloud is called iCloud Keychain. When this feature is turned on (on each of your iOS mobile devices and Macs), anytime you enter a username and password for a website you visit, Safari stores that information and syncs it with iCloud. Then, anytime you revisit that website on any of your Macs or iOS mobile devices that are linked to the same iCloud account, your username and password for that website are remembered and you're automatically logged in.

NOTE iCloud Keychain also remembers credit card information you use when making online purchases from a website. All usernames, passwords, and credit card details are stored using 256-bit AES encryption to maintain security.

To turn on and begin using iCloud Keychain, launch Settings and tap on the iCloud option. Then, from the iCloud Control Panel, turn on the virtual switch that's associated with the iCloud Keychain option. Follow the on-screen prompts that walk you through the feature's built-in security precautions. Next, return to the main Settings menu and tap on the Safari option. Tap on the Passwords & AutoFill option. From the Passwords & AutoFill menu, turn on the virtual switch associated with the Names and Passwords option if you want iCloud Keychain to remember the usernames and passwords you use to access various websites you visit.

Some online banking and financial websites do not automatically support iCloud Keychain. To ensure that Safari stores all of your website-related usernames and passwords, also turn on the virtual switch associated with the Always Allow option. However, when using this feature, it's a good strategy to also activate the Passcode Lock feature of your iOS mobile device to prevent unauthorized people from accessing personal information when using your iPhone or iPad to surf the Web.

If you also want iCloud Keychain to store your credit card details for when you shop online, turn on the virtual switch associated with the Credit Cards option. Then, tap on the Saved Credit cards option and enter your credit card details. This needs to be done only once.

Using iCloud Keychain, you no longer need to remember the unique usernames and passwords that you associate with each of the websites you frequently visit. Plus, to make your web surfing experience even more secure, you can use the Password Generator feature that's built in to Safari to create highly secure passwords for you (which the web browser then remembers).

LAUNCH YOUR FAVORITE WEBSITES QUICKLY WITH HOME SCREEN ICONS

If you regularly visit certain websites, you can create individual bookmarks for them. However, to access those sites, you still must launch Safari from your iPhone or iPad's Home screen, tap on the Bookmarks icon, and then tap on a specific bookmark listing to access the related site.

A time-saving alternative is to create a Home screen icon for each of your favorite websites (as shown in Figure 12.12).

FIGURE 12.12

Create Home screen icons for your favorite websites so that you can launch them directly from your iOS device's Home screen with a single tap.

To create a Home Screen icon, surf to one of your favorite websites using Safari. After it loads, tap on the Share icon, and tap on the Add to Home Screen button from the Share menu.

A new Add to Home window appears. It displays a thumbnail image of the website you're visiting and enables you to enter the title for the website (which is displayed below the icon on your device's Home screen). Keep the title short. When you've created the title (or if you decide to keep the default title that Safari creates), tap on the Add option in the upper-right corner of the window.

NOTE When you use the Add to Home feature in Safari, if you're creating a shortcut for a website designed to be compatible with an iPhone or iPad, a special website-related icon (as opposed to a thumbnail) is displayed. The CNN logo icon displayed in Figure 12.12 is an example of this. Otherwise, a thumbnail of the home page is displayed (as seen in the Jason R. Rich icon in the same figure).

Safari closes, and you are returned to your device's Home screen. Displayed on the Home screen will be what looks like a new app icon; however, it's really a link to your favorite website. Tap on this icon to automatically launch Safari from the Home screen and load your web page.

After a Home screen icon is created for a web page, it can be treated like any other app icon. You can move it around on the Home screen, add the icon to a folder, or delete the icon from the Home screen.

NOTE Although many improvements have been made to the web-surfing capabilities of Safari on the iPhone and iPad, what's still missing is Adobe Flash compatibility. Adobe Flash is a website programming language used to generate many of the slick animations you see on websites. Unfortunately, these animations are not visible when you access a Flash-based website using the iOS version of Safari.

If you want limited Flash compatibility on your iPhone or iPad, try using a third-party web browser app, such as Photon Flash Web Browser for iPhone ($3.99) or Photon Flash Web Browser for iPad ($4.99). Both versions are available from the App Store and offer compatibility with some (but not all) Flash-based content on the Web.

IN THIS CHAPTER

- Get acquainted with the Calendar and Contacts apps
- Discover strategies for staying organized, on time, and productive with your iOS device
- How to keep your app data synced between your iOS mobile devices, computer(s), online apps and iCloud

13

CALENDAR AND CONTACT MANAGEMENT STRATEGIES

Veteran iPhone or iPad users should immediately discover that the Contacts and Calendar apps that come bundled with iOS 7 have the same core functionality as before, but both apps have been given a rather significant makeover.

In keeping with iOS 7's theme of inter-app integration, the Calendar and Contacts apps are fully compatible with iCloud, which makes synchronizing your app-related data a straightforward process. You can also more easily synchronize data with online-based calendars or contact management apps related to Microsoft Exchange, as well as Google, Yahoo!, or Facebook. Plus, Calendar can easily be set up so all of your alerts, alarms, reminders, and notifications are consistently displayed in one place—the Notification Center—that's constantly available to you.

NOTE The features and functions offered by the Calendar and Contacts apps are virtually identical on the iPhone, iPad, and iPod touch. However, due to varying screen sizes, the location of specific command icons, options, and menus sometimes varies. However, after you get to know how each app functions in general, you can easily switch between using them on your iPhone, iPad, Mac, or the iCloud.com website without confusion.

On the iPad, all information relevant to a specific app or function is typically displayed on a single screen. On the iPhone, however, that same information is often split up and displayed on several separate screens.

GET ACQUAINTED WITH THE CALENDAR APP

With its multiple viewing options for keeping track of the scheduling information stored in it, the iOS 7 version of the Calendar app for the iPhone or iPad is a highly customizable scheduling tool that enables you to easily sync your scheduling data with your primary computer's scheduling software (such as Microsoft Outlook on a PC or the Calendar app on a Mac) or an online-based scheduling application (from Google, Yahoo!, Facebook, or Microsoft Exchange-compatible).

SYNC APP-SPECIFIC DATA WITH ONLINE-BASED APPS

To sync your calendar or contacts data with Yahoo!, Google, or Microsoft Exchange–compatible software, instead of using iCloud, launch Settings and tap on the Mail, Contacts, Calendars option. Under the Accounts heading, tap on Add Account. Then, choose which type of account you want to sync data with, such as Microsoft Exchange, Gmail (Google), Microsoft Outlook, or Yahoo!.

When prompted, enter your name, email address, password, and an account description (as well as any other information related to your account that's requested). After your account is verified, a menu screen in Settings related to that account lists app-specific options, such as Mail, Contacts, Calendars, Reminders, and/or Notes. Turn on the virtual switch associated with any or all of these options. Your iPhone or iPad can automatically and continuously sync your app-specific data on your iOS device with your online-based account. So, if you turn on the virtual switch associated with Calendars, your event data is continuously synchronized.

To sync scheduling and/or contact-related data with Facebook, launch Settings and tap on the Facebook option. When prompted, enter your Facebook username and password. Then, near the bottom of the Facebook menu screen in Settings, turn on the virtual switch that's associated with Calendar and/or Contacts. Periodically tap on the Update All Contacts option as you add new online Facebook friends. Calendar and/or contacts data is imported from Facebook and incorporated into your Calendar and/or Contacts apps.

Both the Calendar and Contacts apps also work seamlessly for syncing data between your iOS mobile devices, Mac(s), and PC(s) that are linked to the same iCloud account. To set up this feature, launch Settings, tap on the iCloud option, and then turn on the virtual switch associated with Calendar and/or Contacts. This needs to be only done once on each device or computer that's linked to the same iCloud account. Your app-specific data automatically remains synced.

From within Calendar, you can also share some or all of your schedule information with colleagues and maintain several separate, color-coded calendars to keep personal and work-related responsibilities, as well as individual projects, listed separately, while still being able to view them on the same screen.

MORE INFO For details about syncing Calendar data with a Yahoo! account, visit http://help.yahoo.com/kb/index?locale=en_US&page=content&id=SLN4922. For directions on how to sync the Calendar app with a Google account, visit https://support.google.com/a/users/answer/138740.

CONTROLLING THE VIEW

Launch Calendar from your iOS device's Home screen, and then choose in which viewing perspective you'd like to view your schedule data. Regardless of which view you're using, tap on the Today option to immediately jump back to the current date on the calendar. The current date is always highlighted with a red dot.

On the iPad, switching between Calendar views is as easy as tapping on the Day, Week, Month, or Year tab displayed near the top center of the Calendar app screen. On the iPhone, however, the Calendar app opens on the Day view. At the top of the screen is a calendar for the week and below that is your hour-by-hour schedule for the highlighted day. It's possible to scroll up and down in this schedule, or scroll horizontally to move forward or backward by a week.

To switch to the Week view, rotate your iPhone to landscape mode by turning it sideways. In portrait mode, however, to switch to the Month or Year view from the Day view, tap on the Month option displayed near the top-left corner of the screen (accompanied by a left-pointing arrow icon). Tapping the month switches from the Day view to the Month view.

Tap on the Year option (which replaces the month option near the top-left corner of the screen) to switch to the Year view. From the Year view, to switch back to the Month view, tap on any Month calendar that's displayed to view that month's calendar. Then, to switch to the Day view, tap on a day.

As you're viewing the Week view, scroll up and down to view each entire day's hour-by-hour schedule, or scroll left or right to move backward or forward by a week. From the Month view, it's possible to scroll up or down to move between months. You can also scroll up or down as you're viewing the Year view.

Your Calendar view options include the following:

- **Day**—This view displays your events individually, based on the time each item is scheduled for (as shown in Figure 13.1).

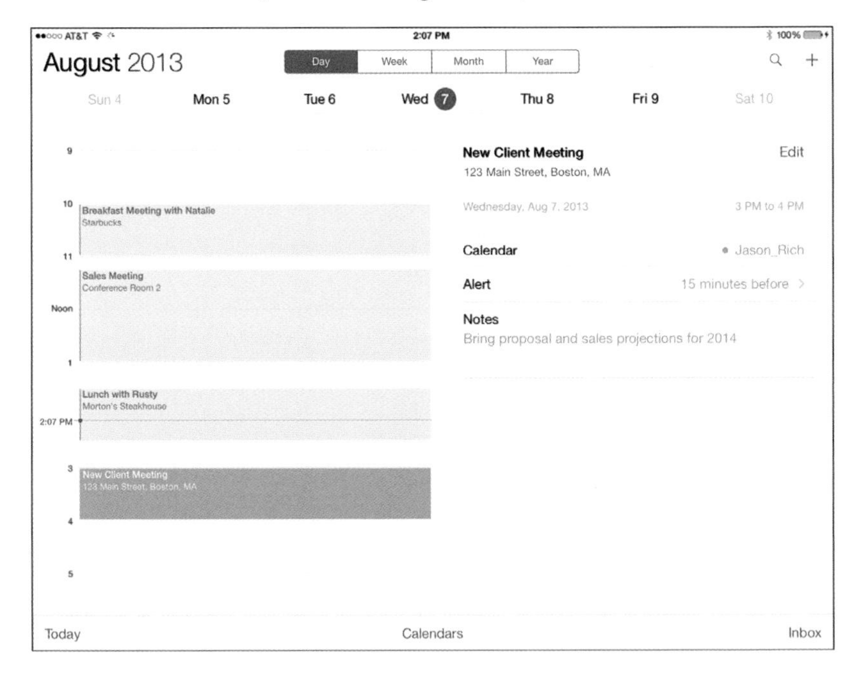

FIGURE 13.1

The Day view of the Calendar app lets you see your schedule broken down one day at a time, in one-hour increments. (Shown here on the iPad.)

On the iPhone, the Day view displays a week's worth of calendar dates near the top of the screen. Below that, the selected date is displayed, followed by an hour-by-hour rundown of your events.

On the iPad, the Day display is split into two sections. The selected date, along with a week's worth of calendar dates, is displayed at the top of the screen, followed by a summary listing of appointments and/or events displayed on the left side of the screen. Details about one selected appointment or event are displayed on the right side of the screen.

TIP Use the Day view of the Calendar app to see a detailed outline of scheduled events for a single day. Swipe your finger to scroll up or down to see an hour-by-hour summary of that day's schedule.

Scroll right or left along the week's worth of calendar days to see upcoming or past dates and to view another day's schedule. Tap on a specific day to switch to that date's day view.

TIP To quickly find an event, tap on the Search icon and then enter any relevant text to help you find the item you're looking for that's stored in the Calendar app. You can enter a date, time, name, business, meeting location, or other pertinent information. Tap on a search result to view that event listing in detail in the Calendar app.

You can also use Siri to quickly find an upcoming event. Activate Siri and say, "When is my next appointment with [name]?", "When am I meeting with [name]?", or "What does my schedule look like for [date]?".

- **Week**—This view uses a grid format to display the days of the week along the top of the screen and time intervals along the left side (shown in Figure 13.2). With it, you have an overview of all events scheduled during a particular week (Sunday through Saturday).

  Scroll along the dates displayed near the top of the screen to quickly view your schedule for past or future weeks.

- **Month**—This view enables you to see a month's worth of events at a time. On the iPhone, tap any single day to immediately switch to the Day view to review a detailed summary of events slated for that day. Use your finger to scroll up or down to look at past or future months. On the iPad, use the Day, Week, Month, or Year tabs near the top of the screen to switch Calendar views.

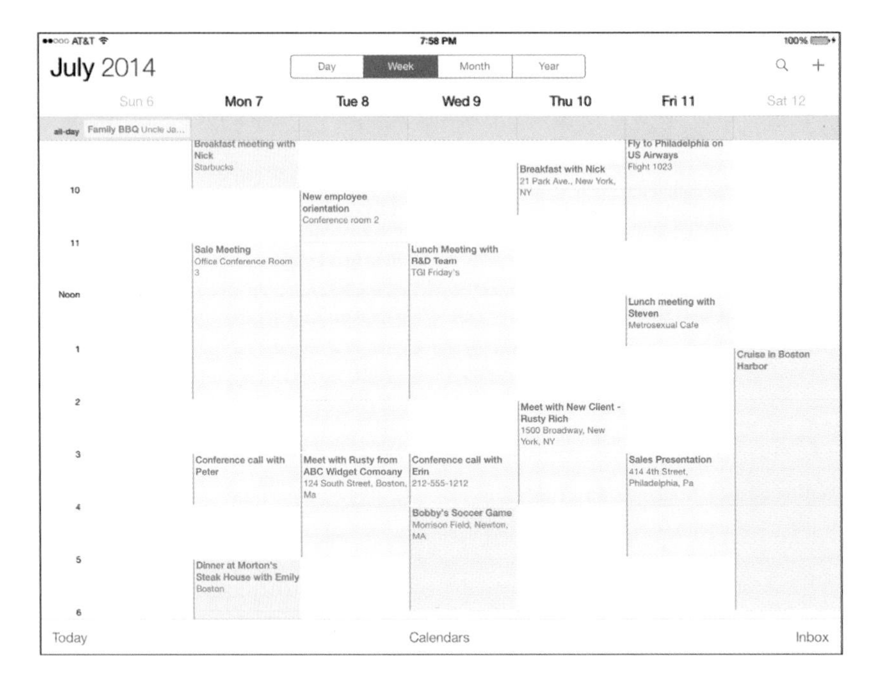

FIGURE 13.2

The Calendar app's Week view shown here on the iPad. To view it on the iPhone, rotate the device to landscape mode. Three separate color-coded calendars are displayed here simultaneously.

- **Year**—This Year view in Calendar enables you to look at 12 mini-calendars and see a color-coded preview of your schedule (with minimal detail displayed). For example, use this view to block out vacation days, travel days, and so on, and get a comprehensive view of your overall annual schedule. To view it on the iPhone, keep tapping on the "<" icon that's displayed near the upper-left corner of the Calendar app screen to switch from the Day to Week to Month to Year views. On the iPad, simply tap on the Year tab near the top center of the screen.

TIP Regardless of which Calendar view you're looking at, with the exception of the Week view on the iPhone, the Calendars option is displayed near the bottom center of the screen. Tap on this to determine which of your separate, color-coded calendars you wish to view on the screen. You can opt to view just one specific calendar (such as your work calendar) or display multiple calendars simultaneously.

Tap on the Inbox option, displayed near the bottom-right corner of the screen, to view invites for events from other people that you might want to import into one of your calendars.

HOW TO ENTER A NEW EVENT

Regardless of which calendar view you're using, follow these steps to enter a new event:

1. Tap the plus sign icon in the upper-right corner of the screen. This causes an Add Event window to be displayed (shown in Figure 13.3).

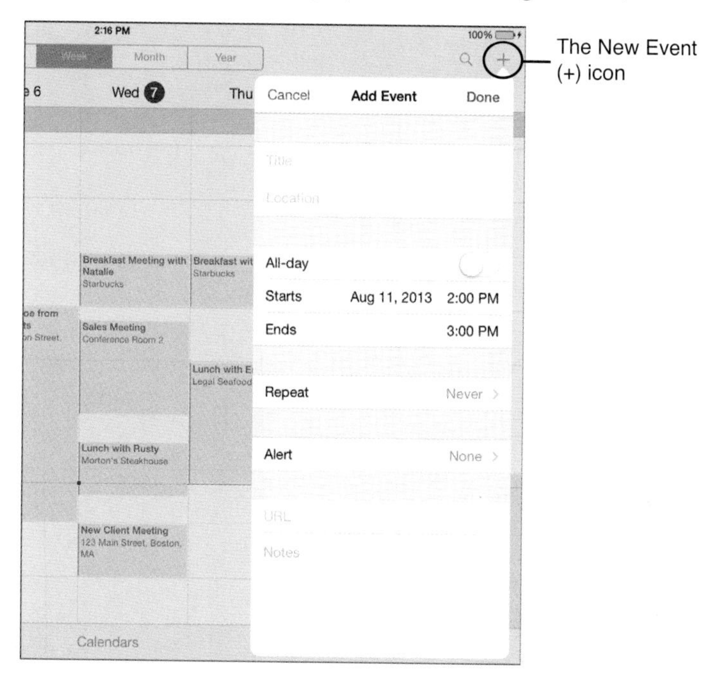

FIGURE 13.3

Add a new event to the Calendar app from the Add Event screen (iPhone) or window (iPad).

> **NOTE** When you're using the Calendar app, all appointments, meetings, and other items you enter are referred to as "events."

2. The first field in the Add Event window is labeled Title. Using the virtual keyboard, enter a heading for the event, such as "Lunch with Rusty," "Ryan's Soccer Practice," "Call Email," or "Mandatory Sales Meeting at Work."
3. If a location is associated with the event, tap the Location field located below the Title field, and then use the virtual keyboard to enter an address or a location. Entering information into the Location field is optional. You can be as detailed as you want when entering information into this field.

4. If the appointment lasts the entire day, tap the All-Day virtual switch, moving it from the off to the on position. Otherwise, to set the time and date for the new appointment to begin and end, tap the Starts field.
5. Use the scrolling Date, Hour, Minute, and AM/PM dials to select the start time for your event.
6. After entering the start time, scroll down and tap on the Ends option, and again use the scrolling Date, Hour, Minute, and AM/PM dials to select the end time for your appointment.

   If the event you're entering repeats every day, every week, every two weeks, every month, or every year, tap the Repeat option, and choose the appropriate time interval. The default for this option is Never, meaning that it is a nonrepeating, one-time-only event.
7. To invite other people to the event, tap on the Invitees option and, when prompted, fill in the To field with the invitees' names or email addresses. Use their name if they already have a contact entry in the Contacts app; otherwise, enter an email address for each person separated by a comma. The people you add as invitees are sent an email allowing them to respond to the invite. The Calendar app keeps track of RSVPs for event attendees and displays this information in the app.
8. To set an audible alarm for the event, tap the Alert option displayed below the Repeat option in the Add Event window. The Event Alert window temporarily replaces the Add Event window.
9. In the Event Alert window, tap to specify when you want the audible alarm to sound to remind you of the appointment. Your options are None (which is the default), At Time of Event, 5 minutes before, 15 minutes before, 30 minutes before, one hour before, two hours before, one day before, two days before, or one week before. Once you tap a selection, you are returned to the Add Event window.

TIP After you've added an alert, a Second Alert option displays in the Add Event screen/window. If you want to add a secondary alarm to this event, tap the Second Alert option, and when the Event Alert window reappears, tap on the interval when you want the second alarm to sound. This is useful if you want to be reminded of an appointment or deadline several hours (or days) before it's scheduled to occur, and then again several minutes before, for example.

10. When you return to the Add Event window, tap on the Calendar option and select the appropriate color-coded calendar if you're maintaining several separate calendars in the Calendar app.

11. Tap the Done option to save the new appointment information and have it displayed in your calendar. Tap the Cancel icon in the upper-left corner of the window to exit without saving any new information.

> **TIP** Scroll down in the Add Event window to access optional Show As, URL, and Notes fields. Tap on Show As to determine how you want the times you schedule events to be displayed within Calendar. Tap on the URL field to manually enter a website URL that corresponds to the event. Likewise, tap on the Notes field and type notes pertaining to the appointment (or paste data from other apps into this field).

USE SIRI TO ENTER NEW EVENTS INTO THE CALENDAR APP

Instead of manually entering event information into your iPhone or iPad using the virtual keyboard, or importing/syncing scheduling data from another computer or device, you always have the option to use Siri. Refer to Chapter 2, "Using Siri, Dictation, and iOS In Your Car to Interact with Your Mobile Device," for more information.

VIEWING INDIVIDUAL APPOINTMENT DETAILS

From any view in the Calendar app, tap an individual event to display the details related to that item.

When you tap on a single event listing, a new window opens. Tap the Edit icon in the upper-right corner to modify any aspect of the event listing, such as the title, location, start/end time, alert, or notes.

To delete an event entry entirely, tap the red-and-white Delete Event option at the bottom of the Edit window. Or when you're finished making changes to an event entry, tap on the Done option in the upper-right corner of the window.

> **TIP** The Calendar app works with several other apps, including Contacts and Notification Center. For example, in Contacts, you can enter someone's birthday in a record, and that information can automatically be displayed in the Calendar app.
>
> To display birthday listings in Calendar, tap the Calendars button displayed near the bottom center of the screen in the Calendar app, and then tap on the Birthdays option to add a check mark to that selection. All recurring birthdays stored in Contacts appear in Calendar.

QUICKLY FIND APPOINTMENT OR EVENT DETAILS

In addition to viewing the various calendar views offered within the Calendar app, use the in-app or Spotlight Search options to find individual events.

The in-app Search button can be found near the top-right corner of the Calendar app screen. Use the virtual keyboard to enter any keyword or phrase associated with the event you're looking for.

Or from the iPhone or iPad's Home screen, swipe your finger from the middle of the screen in a downward direction to access the Spotlight Search screen (assuming you have not manually disabled this function in Settings). In the Search field that appears, enter a keyword, search phrase, or date associated with an event. When a list of relevant items is displayed, tap the event you want to view. This launches the Calendar app and displays that specific event.

> **TIP** Using Siri, say something like, "When is my next appointment with [name]?" You can also say, "Show me my schedule for Wednesday," or ask, "What's on my calendar for July 7?" to quickly find an event stored in the Calendar app. If you enter information into the Location field as you're creating events in the app, you can later ask Siri, "Where is my next meeting?".

VIEWING ONE OR MORE COLOR-CODED CALENDARS

One of the handy features of the Calendar app is that you can view and manage multiple color-coded calendars at once on the same screen, or you can easily switch between calendars.

To decide which calendar information you want to view, tap the Calendars option near the bottom center of the screen. When the Show Calendars window appears, select which calendar or calendars you want to view on your device's screen by tapping on their listings.

Each calendar is color-coded, so you can tell entries apart when looking at multiple calendars on the screen at once. If you're using color-coding on your Mac with the Calendar app, this coding transfers to your iOS device when you sync Calendar data. Otherwise, each time a new Calendar is created in the Calendar app, a color is assigned to it by the app.

CUSTOMIZING THE CALENDAR APP

There are many ways to customize the Calendar app beyond choosing between the various calendar views. For example, you can set audible alerts and/or use onscreen alerts and banners to remind you of events. You can also display Calendar-related information in the Notification Center.

> **TIP** To customize the audio alert generated by the Calendar app, launch the Settings app, and then select the Sounds option. Tap on the Calendar Alerts option and choose a sound from the menu. To purchase and download additional sounds, tap on the Store option. Choose the None option from the Calendar Alerts menu to set up Calendar so it never plays audible alerts or alarms.

If you want to be able to receive event invites from others, tap on the Mail, Contacts, Calendars option in the Settings app. Then scroll down to the Calendars heading and make sure the New Invitations Alerts option is turned on.

Also from this screen, under the Calendars heading, determine how far back in your schedule you want to sync appointment data between your primary computer and your iOS device. Your options include Events 2 Weeks Back, Events 1 Month Back, Events 3 Months Back, Events 6 Months Back, and All Events.

ADJUSTING TIME ZONE SUPPORT

When the Time Zone Support option is turned on and you've selected the major city that you're in or near, all alarms are activated based on that city's time zone. However, when you travel, turn off this option. With Time Zone Support turned off, the iPhone or iPad determines the current date and time based on the location and time zone you're in (when it's connected to a cell network or the Internet), and adjusts all your alarms to go off at the appropriate time for that time zone.

To access the Time Zone Support feature, follow these steps:

1. Launch the Settings app.
2. Select the Mail, Contacts, Calendars option.
3. Scroll down to the options listed under Calendars, and then tap on Time Zone Support.
4. When the Time Zone Support screen appears, set the virtual switch. When it's turned on, below the switch is a Time Zone option. Tap it, and then choose your home city (or a city in the time zone you're in).

When turned off, Time Zone Support displays event times in your Calendar and activates alarms based on the time zone selected. So if New York City (Eastern Time Zone) is selected, and you have an appointment set for 2:00 p.m. with an accompanying alarm, you see that appointment listed at 2:00 p.m. and hear the alarm at 2:00 p.m. Eastern Time, regardless of where, or in what time zone, you're actually physically located.

> **TIP** Just as with Contacts, Reminders, and Notes, you can sync your app-specific Calendar data with iCloud so that your schedule becomes accessible on all of your iOS mobile devices, as well as your Mac(s) or PC(s) that are linked to the same account. When you do this, you can also visit www.iCloud.com, log in using your Apple ID and password (or iCloud username and password), and then use the online-based version of the Calendar to view your scheduling data from any computer or Internet-enabled device.

To set up the Calendar app to work with iCloud, launch Settings, tap on the iCloud option, make sure your iPhone or iPad is logged in to your iCloud account (or sign in to the account as prompted), and then turn on the virtual switch associated with the Calendars option.

USE CONTACTS TO KEEP IN TOUCH WITH PEOPLE YOU KNOW

The art of networking is all about meeting new people, staying in contact with them, making referrals and connections for others, and tapping the knowledge, experience, or expertise of the people you know to help you achieve your personal or career-related goals.

In addition to the contacts you establish and maintain within your network, your personal contacts database might include people you work with, customers, clients, family members, people from your community with whom you interact (doctors, hair stylist, barber, dry cleaners, and so on), your real-world friends, and your online friends from Facebook, for example.

> **NOTE** Contacts is a powerful and customizable contact management database program that works with several other apps that also came preinstalled on your iPhone or iPad, including Mail, Calendar, Safari, FaceTime, and Maps, as well as optional apps, like the official Facebook and Twitter apps.

THE CONTACTS APP IS HIGHLY CUSTOMIZABLE

Chances are, the same contacts database that you rely on at your office or on your personal computer at home can be synced with your iPhone or iPad and made available to you using the Contacts app. Of course, Contacts can also be used as a standalone app, enabling you to enter new contact entries as you meet new people and need to keep track of details about them on your iOS device.

The information you maintain in your Contacts database is highly customizable, which means you can keep track of only the information you want or need. For example, in each contact entry, you can store a vast amount of information about a person, including the following:

- First and last name
- Name prefix (Mr., Mrs., Dr., and so on)
- Name suffix (Jr., Sr., Ph.D., Esq., and so on)
- Phonetic first, middle, and last name
- Nickname
- Job title
- Department
- Company
- Multiple phone numbers (work, home, cell, and so on)
- Multiple email addresses
- Multiple mailing addresses (work, home, and so on)
- Multiple web page addresses
- Facebook, Twitter, Skype, Instant Messenger, or other online social networking site usernames

> **NOTE** To include some of these fields in a Contacts entry, you must use the Add Field option and select the field type from the submenu.

You can also customize your contacts database to include additional information, such as each contact's photo, spouse's and/or assistant's names, birthday, as well as detailed and freeform notes about the contact.

When you're using the Contacts app, your entire contacts database is instantly searchable using data from any field within the database, so even if you have a database containing thousands of entries, you can find the person or company you're looking for in a matter of seconds.

THE CONTACTS APP WORKS SEAMLESSLY WITH OTHER APPS

After your contacts database has been populated with entries, Contacts works with other apps on your iPhone and/or iPad in the following ways:

- When you compose a new email message in Mail, you can begin typing someone's full name or email address in the To field. If that person's contact information is already stored in Contacts, the relevant email address automatically displays in the email's To field.
- If you're planning a trip to visit a contact, you can pull up someone's address from your Contacts database and obtain driving directions to the person's home or work location using the Maps app.
- If you include each person's birthday in your Contacts database, that information can automatically be displayed in the Calendar app to remind you in advance to send a card.
- As you're creating each Contacts entry, you can include a photo of that person—by either activating the Camera app from the Contacts app to snap a photo or using a photo that's stored in the Photos app—and link it with the entry. You also can insert photos of Facebook friends into the app automatically. See the section called, "How to Add a Photo to a Contacts Entry," later in this chapter.
- In FaceTime, you can create a Favorites list of people you videoconference with often, compiled from entries in your Contacts database.
- From the Messages app, you can access your Contacts database when filling out the To field as you compose new text messages to be sent via iMessage, text message, or instant message.
- If you're active on Facebook or Twitter, you have the option of adding each contact's Facebook username or Twitter username in their Contacts entry. When you do this, the app automatically downloads each entry's Facebook profile picture and inserts it into your Contacts database.

When you first launch the Contacts app, its related database is empty. However, you can create and build your database in two ways:

- You can sync the Contacts app with your primary contact management application on your computer, network, or online (cloud)-based service, such as iCloud.
- You can manually enter contact information directly into the app.

As you begin using this app and come to rely on it, you can enter new contact information or edit entries either on your iOS device or in your primary contact management application, and keep all the information synchronized, regardless of where the entry was created or modified.

WHO DO YOU KNOW? HOW TO VIEW YOUR CONTACTS

From the iPhone or iPad's Home Screen, tap the Contacts app to launch it.

On the iPhone, the All Contacts screen displays an alphabetical listing of your contacts. Along the right side of the screen are alphabetic tabs, and a Search field is located near the top of the screen.

> **NOTE** If you've used the Contacts app previously and it has been running in the background, the last contact entry you viewed will be displayed when you relaunch the app.

On the iPad, in the middle of the screen are alphabetic tabs. The All Contacts heading is near the upper left of the screen. Below it is a Search field. After you have added entries in your contacts database, they are listed alphabetically on the left side of the screen, below the Search field (as shown in Figure 13.4).

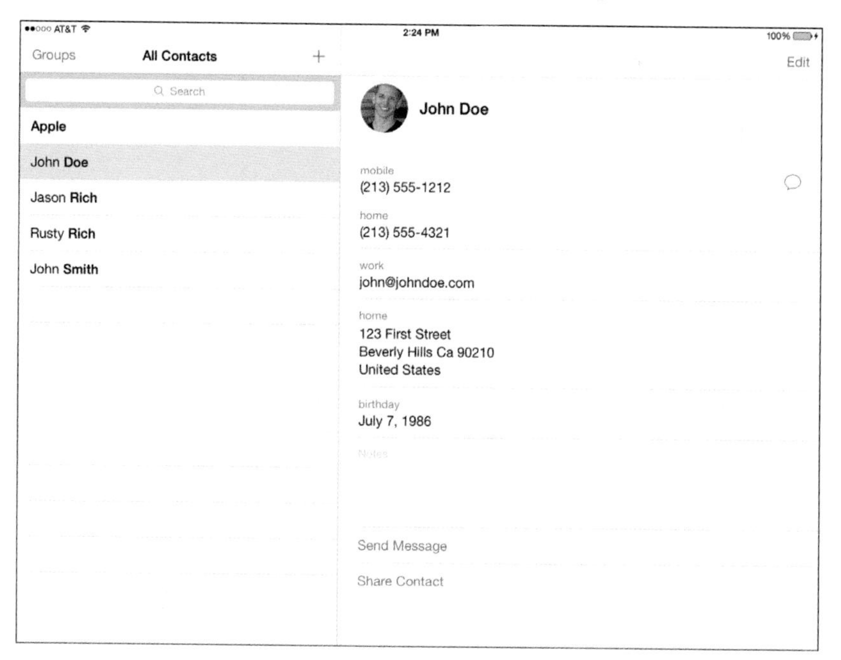

FIGURE 13.4

On the iPad, the All Contacts listing and individual listings are shown on the left and right side of the screen, respectively. On the iPhone, this information is divided into two separate screens.

TIP If you tap the Search field, you can quickly find a particular entry by entering any keyword associated with an entry, such as a first or last name, city, state, job title, or company name. Any content in your Contacts database is searchable from this Search field.

You can also tap a letter tab on the screen to see all entries "filed" under that letter by a contact's last name, first name, or company name, depending on how you set up the Contacts app in the Settings app's Mail, Contacts, Calendars option.

On the iPhone, to see the complete listing for a particular entry, tap on its listing from the All Contacts screen. A new screen shows the specific contact's information (shown in Figure 13.5).

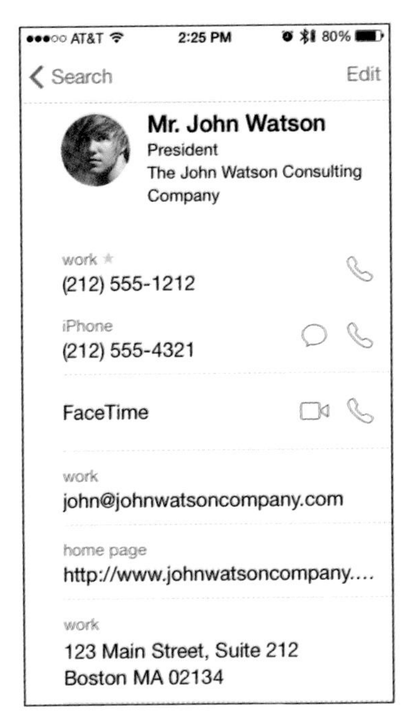

FIGURE 13.5
A sample contact entry from the Contacts app displayed on the iPhone.

On the iPad, to see the complete listing for a particular entry, tap on it from the All Contacts display on the left side of the screen. That entry's complete contents are then displayed on the right side of the screen.

TIP In addition to using the search field in the Contacts app, you can quickly find information by accessing the Spotlight Search from your iPhone or iPad's Home screen.

If you're using Siri, you can quickly find and display any contact in your Contacts database by activating Siri and saying, "Find [name] within Contacts."

MEET SOMEONE NEW? CREATE A NEW CONTACTS ENTRY

To create a new Contacts entry, tap the plus icon. On the iPhone, it's displayed in the upper-right corner of the All Contacts screen. On the iPad, the plus icon can be found near the top center of the Contacts screen.

After tapping on the plus icon, the main Contacts screen is replaced by a New Contact screen.

NOTE As you're creating each Contacts entry, you can fill in whichever fields you want. You can always edit a contact entry to include additional information later.

In the New Contact screen (iPhone) or window (iPad) are several empty fields related to a single Contacts entry, starting with the First Name field (shown in Figure 13.6).

Some fields, including Phone, Email, and Mailing Address, enable you to input multiple listings, one at a time. So you can include someone's home phone, work phone, and mobile phone numbers in the entry. Likewise, you can include multiple email addresses and/or a home address and work address for an individual.

Begin by filling in one field at a time. To jump to the next field, tap it. So, after using the virtual keyboard to fill in the First Name field, tap on the Last Name field to fill it in. For each type of field, the virtual keyboard modifies itself accordingly, giving you access to specialized keys, as necessary.

One of the available fields is Add Related Name. Use this field to add the names of your contact's mother, father, parent, brother, sister, child, friend, spouse, partner, assistant, manager, or other. You can also add your own titles for the Related People field.

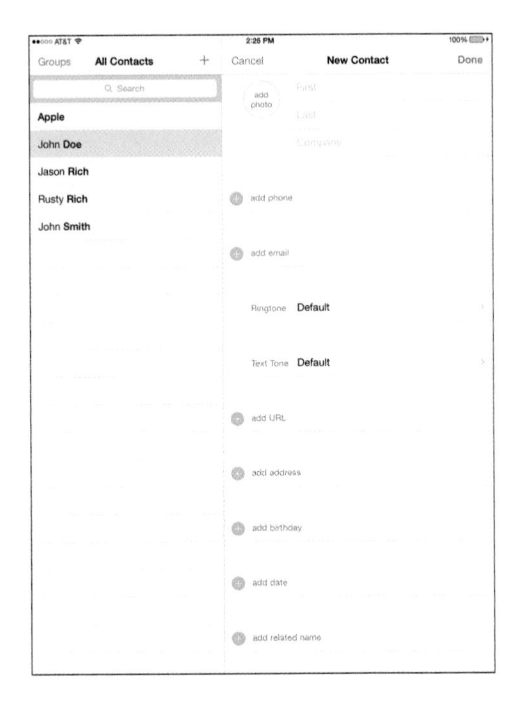

FIGURE 13.6

From this New Contact screen, you can create a new contact and include as much information pertaining to that person or company as you want.

TIP You can change the label associated with certain fields (which are displayed in blue) by tapping the field label itself. This reveals a Label menu, offering selectable options for that field. For example, the Label options for the Phone Number field include Mobile, iPhone, Home, Work, Main, Home Fax, Work Fax, Pager, and Other. At the bottom of this Label window, you can tap the Add Custom Label option to create your own label if none of the listed options applies.

Tap the label title of your choice. A check mark appears next to it, and you are returned to the Info window.

At the bottom of the New Contact screen is an Add Field option. Tap it to reveal a menu containing a handful of additional fields you can add to individual Contacts entries as applicable, such as a middle name, job title, and nickname (as shown in Figure 13.7 on the iPad).

If there's a field displayed that you don't want to utilize or display, simply leave it blank as you're creating or editing a Contacts entry.

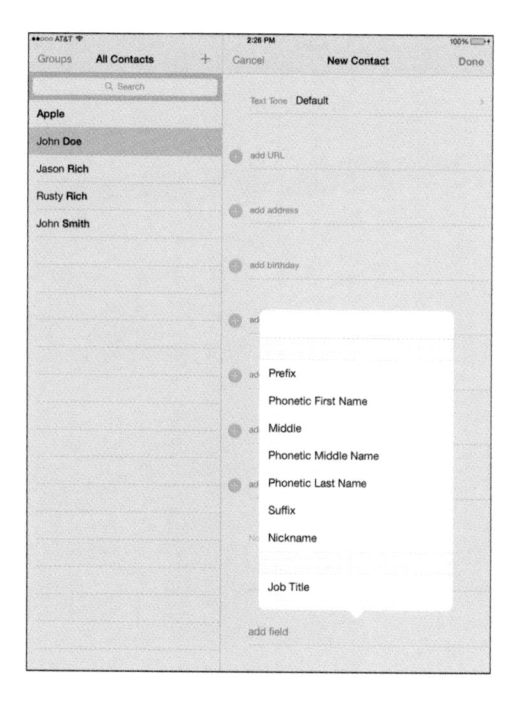

FIGURE 13.7

From the Add Field option, choose what additional information you want to include in a particular contact's entry.

Each time you add a new mailing address to a contact's entry from within the Info screen, the Address field expands to include a Street, City, State, ZIP, and Country field.

After you have filled in all the fields for a particular entry, tap the Done option, which is displayed in the upper-right corner of the New Contact screen (iPhone) or window (iPad). Your new entry gets saved and added to your contacts database.

HOW TO ADD A PHOTO TO A CONTACTS ENTRY

To the immediate left of the First Name field is a circle that says Add Photo. When you tap this field, a submenu with two options—Take Photo and Choose Photo—is displayed.

Tap Take Photo to launch the Camera app from within the Contacts app and snap a photo to be linked to the Contacts entry you're creating. Or tap on the Choose Photo option. In this case, the Photos app launches so that you can choose any digital image that's currently stored on your iOS device. When you tap the photo of your choice, a Choose a Photo window displays on the Contacts screen, enabling you to move and scale the image with your finger.

TIP As you're previewing the image (shown in Figure 13.8), use a pinch or reverse-pinch finger motion to zoom in or out, and then hold your finger down on the image and reposition it within the frame.

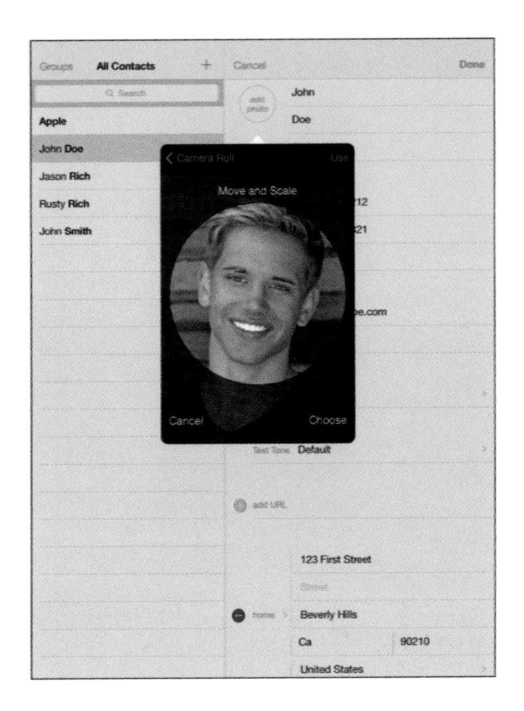

FIGURE 13.8

Linking a photo with someone's Contacts entry enables you to visually identify the person as you're reviewing your contacts.

After cropping or adjusting the photo selected, tap the Use icon displayed in the upper-right corner of the Choose Photo window to link the photo with that contact's entry (as shown in Figure 13.8).

TIP If you use an iPhone, or FaceTime on your iPhone or iPad, from the Ringtone option in the Info window, you can select the specific ringtone you hear each time that particular contact calls you. Your iPhone or iPad has 25 preinstalled ringtones. From the iTunes Store, you can purchase and download thousands of additional ringtones, many of which are clips from popular songs.

EDITING OR DELETING AN ENTRY

To edit a contact, tap on its listing from the All Contacts screen to display the contact details, then tap on the Edit button in the upper-right corner of the screen. Tap any field to modify it using the virtual keyboard. Delete a field(s) by tapping on the red-and-white minus sign icon associated with it, and then tap the Delete button that appears to the right of the entry.

You can also add new fields in an entry by tapping any of the green-and-white plus sign icons and then choosing the type of field you want to add.

When you're finished editing a Contacts entry, again tap the Done option.

TIP To delete an entire entry from your Contacts database, as you're editing a contact entry and looking at the Info window for that entry, scroll down to the bottom of it and tap the Delete Contact option.

Keep in mind that if you have your Contacts database autosyncing via iCloud, the contact you delete is removed from all your computers and devices that are connected to the Internet within seconds.

HOW TO LINK CONTACT ENTRIES TOGETHER

Depending on how you use the Contacts app, you might find it useful to link contacts based on relationships. For example, you might have duplicate listings that contain different information for the same person. Linking these contacts makes it easier for you to organize people who have separate entries, such as for the Home and Work information. When you do this, all entries for that person appear as one single entry in the Contacts app, and their combined information can be viewed on a single screen.

NOTE Duplicate entries can occur if you use Facebook integration with iOS 7 (with the official Facebook app), for example, and you sync your Facebook friends with your Contacts database.

If the Contacts entry and Facebook contact data don't match perfectly, because someone uses a middle name or maiden name, for example, a second entry is created for that person in your Contacts database. To keep things simple, you can then link those two contact entries. If the contact data is the same between your Contacts database and the online service, the Contacts app links those contacts automatically.

When you're in edit mode, modifying content in a contact's entry, scroll down to the bottom of the window or screen to link contact entries.

On the iPhone, tap on the Link Contact icon that's displayed under the Linked Contacts heading, and then choose one or more contact entries to link to the one you're editing.

On the iPad, link contacts by scrolling down below the red-and-white Delete contact icon when editing an entry. Tap on the small icon with a silhouette of a head with a plus sign next to it to link this contact with one or more other contacts already in your database.

SHARING CONTACT ENTRIES

From the main Contacts screen, tap a contact about which you want to share details. When the contact's entry is displayed, scroll down toward the bottom of the entry until you see the Share Contact option. Tap it. You can then choose to share the contact's details with someone else via AirDrop, text/instant message (via the Message app), or email (via the Mail app).

If you choose Mail, an outgoing email message form displays on your iPhone or iPad's screen. Fill in the To field with the person or people you want to share the contact info with. The default subject of the email is Contact. However, you can tap this field and modify it using the virtual keyboard.

If you choose Message, an instant/text message screen (iPhone) or window (iPad) is displayed, enabling you to fill in the To field with the names or text/instant message usernames or mobile phone numbers for the people with whom you want to share the information.

The Contacts entry you selected (stored in .vcf format) is already embedded in the outgoing email or text/instant message. When you've filled in all the necessary fields, tap the blue-and-white Send icon. Upon doing this, you are returned to the Contacts app.

The recipient(s) quickly receives your email or message. When he/she clicks on the email's attachment (the contact entry you sent), it can automatically be imported into their contact management application as a new entry, such as in the Contacts app on their Mac, iPhone, or iPad. If the recipient doesn't have a compatible app, they can simply view the contact information using compatible software.

CONTACTS APP QUICK TIPS

- If someone shares a Contacts entry with you via email, when you're viewing the incoming email on your iPhone or iPad, tap the email's attachment. The Contacts entry that was emailed is displayed in a window. At the bottom of this window, as the recipient of the contact's information, tap the Create New Contact or Add to Existing Contact option to incorporate this information into your Contacts database.

- To add a contact entry to your Phone or FaceTime app's Favorites list, when you're viewing any single contact, scroll downward. Tap the Add to Favorites button, and then choose a phone number or FaceTime address that's associated with that contact to feature within your Favorites list.
- As you're creating or editing a contact entry, in the Notes field, you can enter as much information pertaining to that contact as you want using freeform text. It's also possible to paste content from another app into this field using the iOS's Select, Copy, and Paste commands, and using the multitasking capabilities of your iPhone or iPad to quickly switch between apps.
- If you use Contacts on your Mac and Contacts on your iPhone and/or iPad, syncing your contacts is most easily done using iCloud as long as all of the computers and mobile devices are linked to the same iCloud account. In Settings on the iOS device, select the iCloud option and then turn on the virtual switch associated with Contacts that's part of the iCloud submenu. Be sure to do this on each of your iOS mobile devices. On each of your Macs, launch System Preferences, click on the iCloud icon, and then add a checkmark to the Contacts checkbox.
- When creating or editing contacts, it's extremely important to associate the correct labels with phone numbers, email addresses, and address data. For each phone number you add to a contact's entry, for example, it can include a Home, Work, Mobile, iPhone, or Other label (among others). For many of the features of iOS 7 that utilize data from your Contacts database to work correctly, it's important that you properly label content you add to each Contacts entry. This is particularly important if you'll be using Siri.
- If you opt to use Facebook or Twitter integration with iOS 7, it's possible to sync your Contacts database with your online Facebook or Twitter friends data. To do this, launch Settings, scroll down and tap on the Facebook or Twitter option, and then from the Facebook or Twitter submenu, tap on Update All Contacts. You should repeat this process every few weeks, as you add and remove online friends from these services.
- If you use a Mac, you can use the Groups feature in the OS X Contacts app to help organize your entries, such as family members or employees within the same company. Groups can then be synced with an iOS mobile device. While you can view groups on your iOS device, however, you cannot create them on the device.

IN THIS CHAPTER

- Play your digital music using the Music app
- Watch music videos, TV shows, and movies with the Videos app
- Acquire new content from the iTunes Store
- Listen to streaming music using iTunes Radio

14

GET ACQUAINTED WITH THE MUSIC, VIDEOS, AND iTUNES STORE APPS

What do eight-track tapes, vinyl records, cassettes, and CDs have in common? These are all outdated methods for storing music that have been replaced by digital music players, such as Apple's iPods. The music in your personal library can now be kept in a purely digital format, transferred via the Internet, and listened to on a digital music player.

iOS 7 comes with the newly redesigned Music app preinstalled. This app serves as your digital music player and transforms your iPhone or iPad into a full-featured iPod. However, before playing your music or audio content, you first must load digital music files into your iPhone or iPad. There are several ways to do this, including the following:

- Purchase digital music directly from the iTunes Store (using the iTunes Store app) on your iPhone or iPad. An Internet connection is required. Your purchases are billed to the credit or debit card that's linked to your Apple ID.

- You can purchase music using the iTunes software on your primary computer (used to connect to the iTunes Store), and then transfer music purchases and downloads to your iPhone or iPad using the iTunes Sync process or through iCloud.
- You can "rip" music from traditional CDs and convert it to a digital format using your primary computer, and then transfer the digital music files to your iOS device. For this, the free iTunes software on your computer, or other third-party software, is required.
- You can upgrade your iCloud account by adding the optional iTunes Match service, for $24.99 per year, and access your entire digital music library via iCloud, whether that music was purchased from the iTunes Store, ripped from your own CDs, or purchased/downloaded from another source. To learn more about iTunes Match, visit www.apple.com/itunes/itunes-match.
- You can shop for and download music from another source besides the iTunes Store, load that music into your primary computer, convert it to the proper format, and then transfer it to your iPhone or iPad using the iTunes Sync process.

NOTE The Apple iTunes Store offers an ever-growing selection of more than 20 million songs available for purchase and download, including all the latest hits and new music from the biggest bands and recording artists, as well as up-and-coming and unsigned artists/bands. You can also find classic songs and oldies from all music genres.

The Music app is used for playing digital music, audiobooks, and other audio content that you load into your iPhone or iPad. If you want to watch videos, TV show episodes, or movies that you've purchased and/or downloaded from the iTunes Store, use the Videos app, which also comes preinstalled with iOS 7.

WHAT'S NEW One of the new features added to the Music app is iTunes Radio. This is an online-based streaming music service that enables you to listen to music for free via the Music app when your mobile device has Internet access. This service is similar to Pandora. Learn more about it later in this chapter.

To experience the free podcasts available from the iTunes Store, you must download and install Apple's optional Podcast app, or to utilize the vast collection of educational and personal enrichment content available from the Apple iTunes U service, download and install the free iTunes U app.

Another option for watching video or listening to audio content (including music videos, TV show episodes, movies, radio stations, and so on) is to stream it directly from the Internet.

NOTE When you stream content from the Internet, it gets transferred from the Internet directly to your iOS device. However, your iPhone or iPad does not save streamed content, just as your standalone television set doesn't record the shows you watch (unless you have a DVR or another recording device hooked up to it).

Streaming content from the Internet requires a specialized app, which is provided by the source of the content. Later in this chapter, you'll discover which apps to use to access specific on-demand television programming, movies, videos, radio stations, and other content that gets streamed (not downloaded) to your iPhone or iPad.

TIPS FOR USING THE MUSIC APP

The Music app displays the music in your digital music library that's currently stored on your device (as shown in Figure 14.1 on the iPad). It enables you to play one song at a time, listen to entire albums, or create personalized playlists that can provide hours' worth of music listening without your having to tinker with the app.

If you have the Music app set up to work with iCloud, all the music you've purchased from the iTunes Store (in addition to what's stored on your iOS device) is displayed. Songs that are accessible to you for download via iCloud have an iCloud icon displayed next to their listings. Tap on the iCloud icon to download the song (or album) from iCloud and store it on your iPhone or iPad.

TIP To initially set up the Music and iTunes Store apps to work with iCloud, launch Settings and tap on the iTunes & App Store option. Near the top of the iTunes & App Store submenu, enter your Apple ID and password. This needs to be done only once.

NOTE When you download music (or other iTunes Store content) to your iPhone or iPad, you are using storage space that could otherwise be used to hold more apps, photos, or other types of data, but your music is then accessible at anytime, without the need for an active Internet connection.

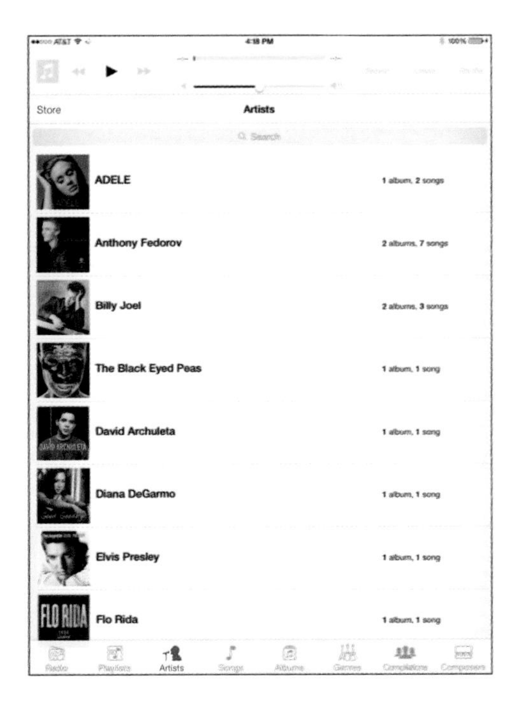

FIGURE 14.1

The main Artists screen of the Music app on the iPad. On the iPhone, the same features and functionality are available from the Music app, but the menu layout is different due to the phone's smaller screen size.

> **TIP** The Music app works nicely with Siri. Use your voice to command Siri to play music from a specific artist, a specific playlist, or to play a specific song, just by speaking its title. This applies to music stored on your iPhone or iPad. For example, if you want to hear "Rolling in the Deep" from Adele, and it's stored on your iOS device, activate Siri and say, "Play Rolling in the Deep." Or to play a Lady Gaga song, say "Play a song from Lady Gaga." It's also possible to use Siri to pause, restart, skip, or shuffle your music.

Thanks to iOS 7's multitasking capabilities, you can play music from the Music app while using other apps on your iPhone or iPad. When music is playing, you can even place your iOS device into Sleep mode, and the music continues playing unless you pause it first.

TIP Music app controls are also accessible from the Lock screen or the Control Center. To activate these controls, swipe your finger upward from the bottom of the screen to display the Control Center. Using these Music app controls, you can play, pause, fast forward, or review the last song, playlist, or album (or audiobook) that was loaded into the Music app (as shown in Figure 14.2). These controls also work with iTunes Radio, as well as other apps that are capable of playing in the background, such as the Podcast player, Pandora, or Spotify.

To access Control Center from the Lock screen, it's necessary to turn on this feature. To do this, launch Settings, tap on Control Center, and then turn on the virtual switch associated with the Control Center option.

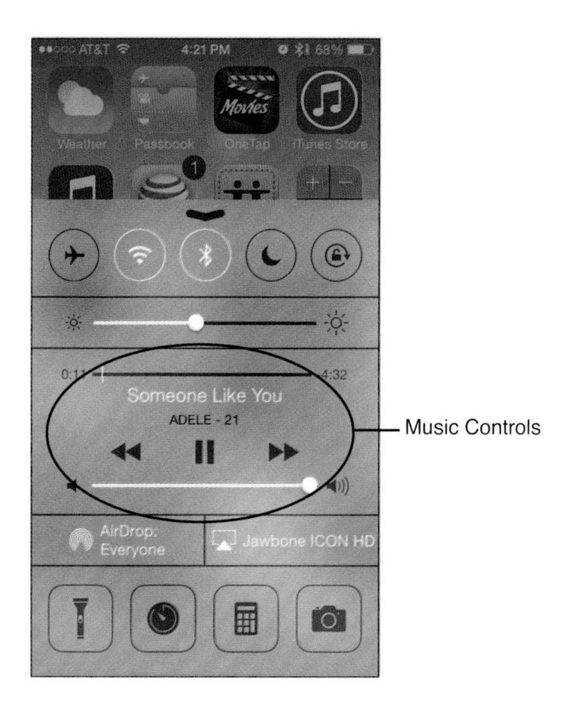

FIGURE 14.2

You can access the Music app controls from the iPhone or iPad's Control Center, and then play, pause, fast forward, rewind, move between music tracks, and adjust the volume.

Keep in mind that it's also possible to control the Music app from the controls found on the cord of the Apple EarPods or Apple's original ear buds, as well as on some other optional corded headphones.

To fully manage your digital music library, create playlists, and play songs or albums using the Music app, launch the app from the Home screen. Displayed along the bottom of the screen are various icons for selecting music-related options.

NOTE From Settings, it's possible to customize some of the Music app–related options available to you. To do this, launch Settings, and then select the Music option. In addition to turning on or off the iTunes Match service (if you've subscribed to it) and the Home Sharing feature (which is one way to share your digital music library with your primary computer or Apple TV via a wireless network), you can tinker with the EQ (to adjust how the audio sounds) or impose a maximum volume limit when listening to music (shown in Figure 14.3).

It's also possible to display song lyrics for some songs and/or to group music by album and artist, based on how you adjust settings offered as part of the Music submenu in Settings.

If you want your iPhone or iPad to download music from iTunes and/or iCloud only when you're connected to the Internet using a Wi-Fi connection (as opposed to a cellular data connection, which uses up some of your monthly wireless data allocation), from Settings, select the iTunes & App Stores option. Then, adjust the virtual on/off switch associated with the Use Cellular Data option, and turn off this feature. When you do this, iCloud and iTunes Match functionality are disabled in the Music app unless a Wi-Fi connection is present.

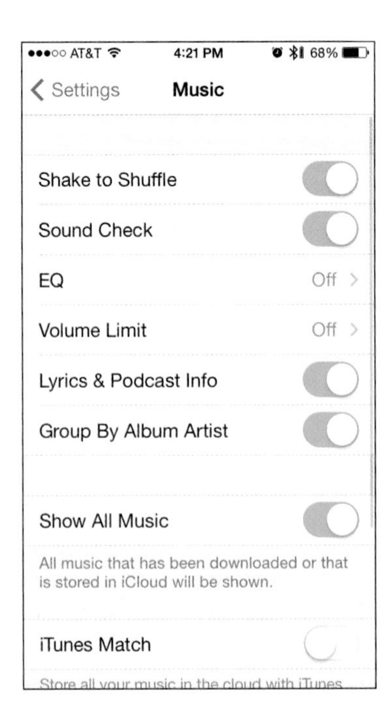

FIGURE 14.3

You can adjust Music app–related options from within Settings (shown here on the iPhone).

TIP Quickly find any song stored on your iPhone or iPad by using a keyword search. In the Search field, enter a song title (or a portion of a title), an artist's name, an album title, or any other keyword that's relevant to your music to find specific music content stored on your iOS device.

The Search field appears at the top of the Artists, Songs, or Albums lists. Tap on the Search field to make the virtual keyboard appear. Enter your keyword or search phrase, and then tap the Search key on the keyboard to see the results. Tap on the search result of your choice to select a specific song, album, or artist.

You can also use the Spotlight Search feature from the Home screen to locate music that's stored on your iOS mobile device.

MUSIC APP CONTROLS ON THE iPHONE

When you launch the Music app on your iPhone, you can then tap on the Playlists, Artists, Songs, or Albums buttons that are displayed along the bottom of the screen. The Store button is displayed in the upper-left corner of the screen. Tap on it to launch the iTunes Store app via the Internet and shop for new music.

At the bottom of the Music app's screen are five command buttons (shown in Figure 14.4), as follows:

- **Radio**—Access the online-based iTunes Radio streaming music service and listen to music for free.
- **Playlists**—Create and manage personalized playlists in the Music app. A playlist is a "digital mix tape" that you manually compile from music that's in your music library.

NOTE An iCloud icon displayed to the right of a song listing (refer to Figure 14.4) indicates that you own the music but it's not currently stored on your device. Tap the iCloud icon to download it from your iCloud account.

- **Artists**—View an alphabetized listing of all recording artists and music groups whose music you own. Tap on an artist's name or graphic to view the albums or individual songs you own from that artist, music group, or band.
- **Songs**—View a complete alphabetical listing of all songs stored in your iOS device, sorted by song title.

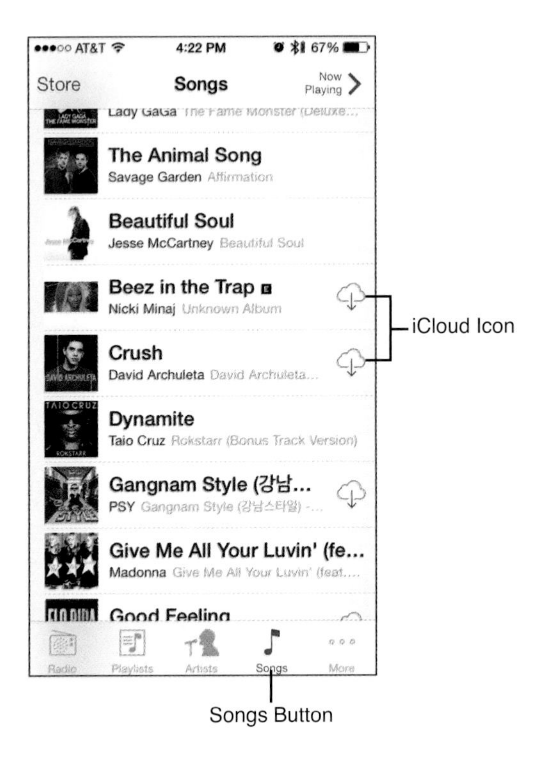

FIGURE 14.4

When you tap on the Songs button at the bottom of the Music app, you'll see an alphabetized listing of songs you own.

> **TIP** If you rotate your iPhone to view the Music app in landscape mode, you can browse through your music by viewing album cover artwork using the Cover Flow menu (shown in Figure 14.5). Swipe your finger from left to right, or from right to left, across the screen to view album artwork. Tap on the album cover to view the songs you own from that album, and then tap on a song listing to play it.

- **More**—Beyond music, you can access audiobooks you've purchased by tapping on the More option. Plus, you can view a listing of songs sorted by Albums, Compilations, Composers, or Genres.

FIGURE 14.5

The Cover Flow menu on the iPhone enables you to scroll through the music you own on your iPhone.

> **TIP** You can change the menu buttons that are displayed along the bottom of the Music app's screen. Instead of displaying, from left to right, the Playlists, Artists, Songs, Albums, and More buttons, you can swap out the Playlists, Artists, Songs, or Albums button with Audiobooks, Compilations, Composers, and/or Genres buttons, plus change the positions of these menu buttons. To do this, launch the Music app, tap on the More button, and then tap on the Edit button at the top-left corner of the screen.
>
> From the Configure screen that's displayed, one at a time, drag one of the command buttons shown at the top of the screen to the desired location along the menu bar that the Music app displays along the bottom of the screen. As you do this, keep in mind that the More button remains constant. Tap the Done option when you're finished.
>
> Your new selection of command buttons are displayed at the bottom of the Music app screen.

CREATE A MUSIC APP PLAYLIST

Playlists are personalized collections of songs that you can group together and then play at any time. Each playlist is given its own title and can include as many songs from your personal music collection as you wish.

You can create separate playlists for working out, to enjoy while you drive, to listen to when you're depressed, or to dance to when you feel like cutting loose. There is no limit to the number of separate playlists you can create and store on your iOS device. Here's how to create a playlist:

> **TIP** When listening to a playlist, you can play the songs in order or have the Music app randomize the song order (using the Shuffle command). A playlist can also be put into an infinite loop, so it continuously plays until you press Pause. This can also be done when listening to an album or other grouping of songs.

1. Launch the Music app, and tap on the Playlist button at the bottom of the screen.
2. To create a new playlist, tap on the New Playlist (+) button near the top left of the screen on the iPhone, below the Store button, or on the upper-right corner of the screen on the iPad.
3. Enter a title for your new playlist, such as Workout Music or Favorite Songs, and tap the Save option.
4. When the Songs screen appears, one at a time, tap on the red-and-white plus sign icon that's associated with each song you want to add to your playlist, as shown in Figure 14.6. All songs currently stored on your device (or available to you from iCloud) are listed in the Songs screen. Tap the Done option to save your selections.

After you finish creating your playlist, it automatically appears on your screen (shown in Figure 14.7). The name of your new playlist displays near the top of the screen with the songs it contains listed below.

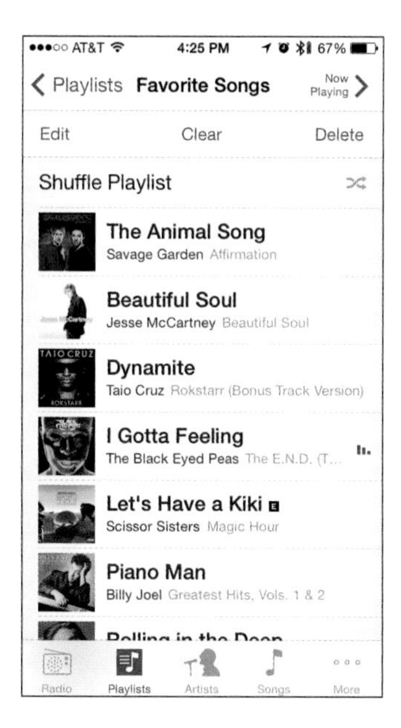

FIGURE 14.6

Choose the songs you want to add to your playlist, based on the listing of all songs stored on your iPad or in your iCloud account. Tap the + icon (on the right) to add each song.

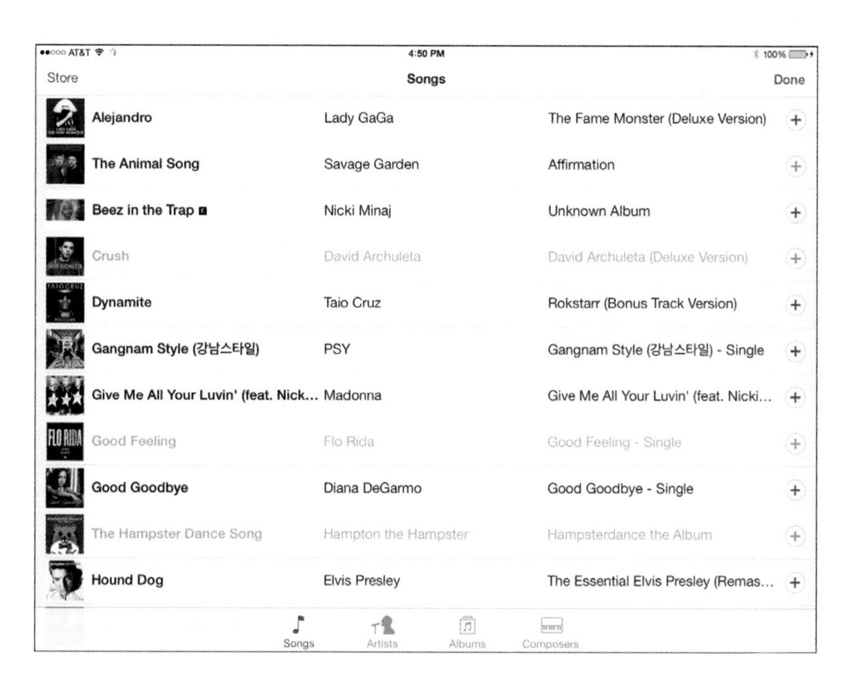

FIGURE 14.7

A sample playlist screen shown here on the iPhone.

Use the Edit, Clear, or Delete buttons below the playlist title to manage your newly created playlist. Tap the Edit button to delete individual songs from the playlist or change the order of the songs, as shown in Figure 14.8. To delete a song, tap on the negative sign icon. To move a song, place your finger on the Move icon displayed to the right of a song's title (it looks like three horizontal lines) and drag it up or down to reposition that song in the playlist's order. Tap the Done button when you're finished editing your playlist.

FIGURE 14.8

The Playlist screen of the Music app enables you to play, edit, or manage a selected playlist. It's shown here in Edit mode. From here, you can delete songs or arrange them.

Tap the Clear button to keep the master playlist file but remove all the songs from it. Or tap the Delete button to delete the playlist altogether from your iOS device.

NOTE If you notice an iCloud icon displayed at the bottom of the playlist, this means one or more of the songs you've selected is stored on your iCloud account but not on your iPhone or iPad. Tap the iCloud icon to download that music from your iCloud account and add it to your playlist. Because you own the music, you are not charged to download it again.

To listen to your newly created playlist, return to the main Playlist screen by tapping on the Playlists button at the bottom of the screen (if you're not already there), and tap on the playlist title of your choice. Next, tap on a song from that playlist and begin listening. To start the playlist from the beginning, tap on the first song listed. Tap on the Shuffle option to continue playing the playlist in a random order.

FIND YOUR WAY AROUND THE NOW PLAYING SCREEN

The Music app's Now Playing screen (shown in Figure 14.9) shows what song is currently playing. You'll also see commands to play or pause the music and rewind or fast forward. A volume slider, for adjusting the music's volume, is also displayed.

FIGURE 14.9

Use the command icons on the Now Playing screen to control the current song or move to the previous/next track.

If you press and hold the rewind or fast forward icon, you can move backward or advance within the song that's currently playing. However, if you tap on one of these two icons, you jump to the previous track or advance to the next track in your playlist, respectively.

Displayed along the top of the screen is a left-pointing arrow icon that enables you to return to the previous screen you were viewing. In the upper-right corner of the screen is an icon that enables you to view a text-based listing that includes additional information about the song or album that's playing.

Album- or artist-related artwork is displayed in the upper portion of the Now Playing screen and, below that, the song's title that's currently playing is displayed, along with the artist's name and the album name with which the song is associated. (Refer to Figure 14.9 to see an example of the Now Playing screen.)

Just above the song title information is the song's time slider. Use your finger to move this slider right to advance within the song, or left to move back in the song manually. On the left of this slider, a timer shows how much of the song you've already listened to. On the right side of the slider is a timer that shows how much of the song is remaining.

If you are listening to a playlist, displayed along the bottom of the Now Playing screen are three additional options: Repeat Playlist, Create, and Shuffle. Repeat Playlist allows music in that Playlist to keep repeating until it's manually paused. Use the Create option to create a new Playlist from scratch. Tap on the right-most shuffle icon to shuffle the order of the songs in the playlist or album you're listening to.

If available, the AirPlay icon can also be seen on this screen. It enables you to stream the music you're listening to from your iOS device to your home theater system or television speakers (via Apple TV) or to AirPlay-compatible external speakers.

When music is playing, you can control the volume from the onscreen volume slider, using the Volume Up or Volume Down buttons on the side of your iOS device, or using the controls found on the cord of your Apple earbuds or Apple EarPods.

Also while music is playing, you can exit out of the Now Playing screen and access other areas of the Music app, use another app altogether (thanks to the multitasking feature of your iPhone or iPad), or you can place your device into Sleep mode and continue listening to the music.

MUSIC APP CONTROLS ON iPAD

When you launch music on your iPad (shown in Figure 14.10), the Store option appears near the upper-left corner of the screen. Tap it to access the iTunes Store via the Internet to shop for new music using the iTunes app.

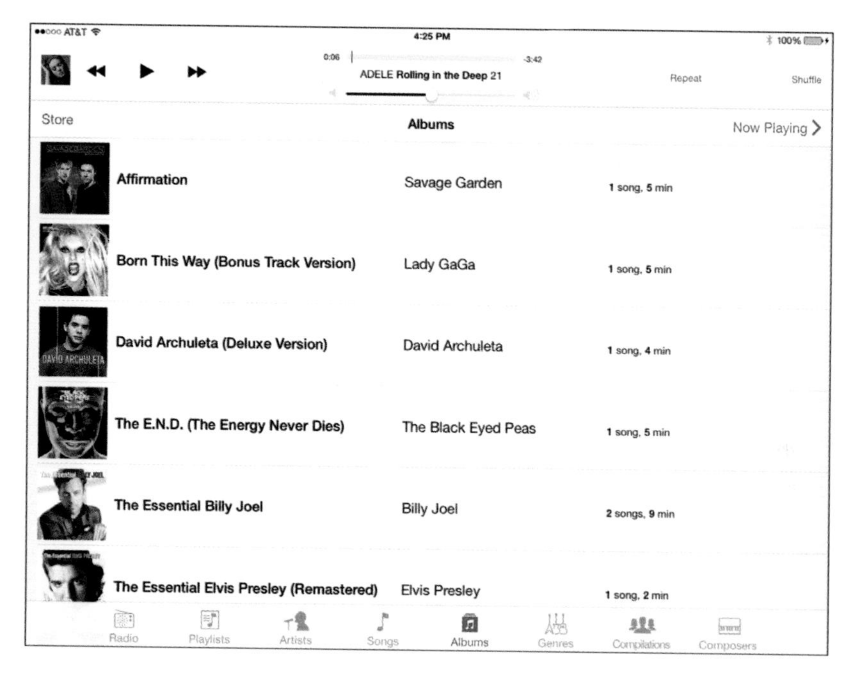

FIGURE 14.10

This is what the Music app looks like on the iPad when the Albums button (located near the bottom center of the screen) is selected.

TIP Have you ever been listening to the radio, watching TV, or riding in an elevator and want to know the name of a song that's playing so you can purchase it? Well, there's an app for that. Download the free Shazam app from the App Store. When you hear a song you want to identify, launch the app. It "listens" to what's playing, and then identifies the song for you, complete with its title and artist. It then launches the iTunes Store app, giving you the option to purchase the song. This is one of the most popular, free iPhone/iPad apps of all time. Another similar app is called SoundHound.

Also near the bottom of the screen are eight additional command buttons labeled Radio, Playlists, Artists, Songs, Albums, Genres, Compilations, and More. These command buttons function just like on the iPhone, as described earlier in this chapter. Tap on a listing to access the music controls and begin playing a song.

When the music controls are displayed, near the upper-left corner are the Rewind, Play/Pause, and Track Forward icons. Near the top center of the screen, the song's time slider, song title, artist information, and volume slider are displayed. Look near the top-right corner of the screen to find the Repeat and Shuffle All options.

Move the volume slider to the right to increase the volume or to the left to decrease it. You can also use the volume control buttons on the side of your iPad for this purpose, or, if applicable, the volume control buttons on the cord of your headset. If available, the AirPlay icon is displayed on the Music app screen, as well.

MORE MUSIC APP FEATURES

After music is playing on your iPhone or iPad, you can exit the Music app and use your iOS device for other purposes. The music keeps playing. It automatically pauses, however, if you receive an incoming call on your iPhone or an incoming FaceTime call on your iPhone or iPad.

After you purchase a song from iTunes, it gets downloaded to the computer or device from which it was purchased, and is also instantly made available at no extra charge to all of your iOS devices via iCloud.

As you're looking at a song listing or album graphic in the Music app (after tapping on the Songs, Artists, or Albums button), you can delete that content from your iOS device. If it's a song listing, swipe your finger across that listing, from right to left. When the Delete button appears (as shown in Figure 14.11), tap on it.

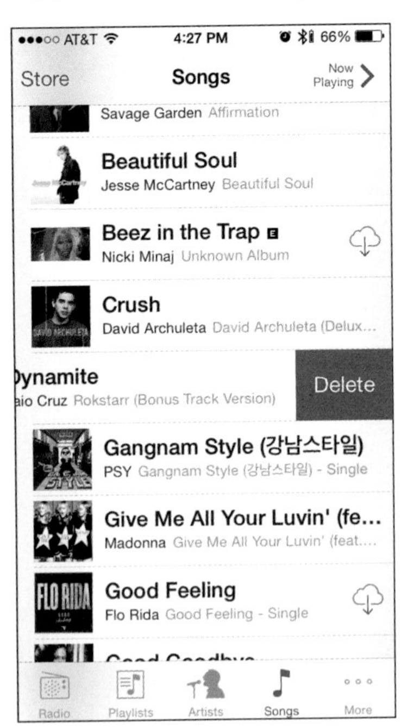

FIGURE 14.11

You can delete one song at a time from your iOS device by swiping your finger from right to left across the listing, and then tapping on the Delete button.

Keep in mind that when you delete a song or album from your iOS mobile device, that music remains in your iTunes library (and stored on iCloud), so you can re-download it at anytime, as long as your iPhone or iPad has Internet access.

TIP After you've downloaded one or more singles (individual songs) from an artist or band's album, you can later purchase the rest of the album and get credit for the eligible song(s) you've already purchased by tapping on the Complete My Album option as you're shopping for music from the iTunes Store.

To use the Complete My Album feature, launch the iTunes Store app, tap on the Music icon (displayed at the bottom of the screen), and then access the listing for the Album you want to purchase. You can use the Search field to find the album quickly. If you already own songs from that album, the Price icon automatically displays a lower price than the regular price, and it has a Complete My Album label next to it. The prorated price that's displayed for the album is based on how many songs you already own from it.

Apple wants you to shop for your music from the iTunes Store, for obvious reasons; however, you do have other options. From your primary computer, you can shop for (or otherwise download) music from other sources, import the music files into the iTunes software, and then perform an iTunes Sync. Or you can upgrade to the iTunes Match service and gain access to your entire digital music library via iCloud.

Some other sources for legally buying and downloading music include the Amazon MP3 music store (www.amazonmp3.com), Napster (www.napster.com), eMusic (www.eMusic.com), and Rhapsody (www.rhapsody.com).

STREAM MUSIC TO YOUR iPHONE OR iPAD USING iTUNES RADIO

While the iTunes Store enables you to purchase and then download music, Apple's new iTunes Radio service enables you to stream music from the Internet to your iOS mobile device and listen to it as you would listen to a traditional radio station. However, instead of being beamed over radio waves, iTunes Radio programming is sent from the Internet to your mobile device and played using the Music app.

iTunes Radio is a free way to hear new music from popular and up-and-coming artists, listen to songs from your favorite artists that you don't own, or enjoy a selection of songs from a specific music genre or era (such as the 70s or 80s).

iTunes Radio programming does include some commercials (unless you're an iTunes Match subscriber, in which case the programming is commercial free); however, it is fully customizable. You can choose your favorite artists, bands, music genres, or eras, and then hear music that's custom programmed to your liking. As you're listening to a station, you can also pause and then resume the music at anytime.

As long as your mobile device has Internet access (Wi-Fi is preferred), you can control and stream iTunes Radio from the Music app by tapping on the Radio icon that's displayed at the bottom of the app screen.

TIP When listening to iTunes Radio, if you hear a song you like and want to buy and immediately download it from the iTunes Store, tap on the price icon displayed near the top-right corner of the screen.

The first time you use iTunes Radio, you're given the options to Learn More or Start Listening. Tap Start Listening to get started with iTunes Radio (shown in Figure 14.12), then choose from one of the hundreds of pre-created stations, or tap on the Add a Station icon to create your own custom station from scratch.

FIGURE 14.12

From the main iTunes Radio screen, select a Featured Station or create your own.

After selecting or creating a station, the music controls are displayed near the top of the screen. These include a Play/Pause icon as well as a Fast Forward icon. Instead of a Rewind icon, however, there's a star-shaped Favorite icon. When you hear a song you like, tap on this icon. A submenu appears with three options: Play More Like This, Never Play This Song, and Add To iTunes Wish List.

By tapping on the Play More Like This option, iTunes Radio learns about your music preferences over time and fine tunes the custom programming it offers so that the songs played are always to your liking.

If a song does play that you don't like, tap on the Fast Forward icon to skip to the next song on the station's playlist. There's also a Never Play This Song option, which prevents it from being added to future programming you listen to.

TIP As music is playing via iTunes Radio, tap on the Info icon (a lowercase "i" in a circle) to display more information about the artist or band, purchase their song or album, or create a new custom iTunes Radio station based around that artist, group, song, or music genre.

In addition to iTunes Radio, there are several other popular streaming music services with their own proprietary apps for the iPhone and iPad. For example, there's Pandora, iHeartRadio, and Spotify. Many traditional radio stations, as well as NPR and Sirius/XM Satellite Radio, also have their own apps that enable you to stream live and on-demand audio programming from the Internet to your mobile device. Some of these other services either charge to hear ad-free programming or have a subscription fee associated with them.

USE THE VIDEOS APP TO WATCH TV SHOWS, MOVIES, AND MORE

After you purchase and download TV show episodes, movies, or music videos from the iTunes Store, that video-based content can be enjoyed on your iPhone and/or iPad using the Videos app. It can also be viewed on your primary computer using the iTunes software and shared between devices via iCloud. If you have Apple TV, you can also stream videos to your home theater system.

After you've downloaded or transferred iTunes Store video content to your iPhone or iPad, it is accessible from the Videos app.

When you launch the Videos app on your iPhone or iPad, you'll see multiple tabs on the screen, based on the types of video content stored on your device (as shown in Figure 14.13). These tabs are labeled TV Shows, Rentals, Movies, and/or Music Videos. On the iPhone, they're displayed near the bottom of the screen, whereas on the iPad, they're displayed near the top center.

NOTE If you have movies rented from iTunes, as opposed to movies you own stored on your iOS device, a tab labeled Rentals is displayed in addition to or instead of a tab labeled Movies.

FIGURE 14.13

The Videos app shows what video content you have stored on your device. Content is categorized based on whether it's a TV show episode, movie, movie rental, or music video. Here, the TV Shows tab (near the top center of the screen) is selected.

When you tap on the TV Shows, Movies, Rentals, or Music Videos tab, thumbnail graphics representing that video content is displayed. To begin playing a video, tap on its thumbnail graphic.

If an iCloud icon appears near the lower-right corner of the graphic, it means you own that content but it is not currently stored on your mobile device. By tapping on the cloud icon, you can automatically download the video from your iCloud account and then store it on the device you're using.

> **TIP** When looking at the graphic thumbnails for TV shows you own, the number displayed in a blue circle near the top-right corner indicates how many episode of that particular TV series you own. Tap on the thumbnail to see a listing of specific episodes and then view them.

To delete video content from your iPhone, access the listing for that particular TV show episode, movie, or music video, and then swipe your finger from right to left across the listing. Tap the Delete button to confirm your decision.

On the iPad, to delete movies, tap on the Edit button near the top-right corner of the screen, and then tap on the "X" icon that appears on the movie thumbnail listing(s) you want to delete. You can use this same method to delete TV show episodes or entire seasons.

After you delete iTunes Store–purchased content from your iPhone or iPad, you can always redownload it from your iCloud account for free.

To shop for additional video content from the iTunes Store while using the Videos app, tap on the Store button displayed in the upper-left corner of the screen.

To play a video, tap on a thumbnail representing the video that you want to watch. If you've downloaded a TV show, for example, a new screen appears listing all episodes from that TV series currently stored on your iOS device (as shown in Figure 14.14). Tap on the episode of your choice to begin playing it. You can also tap on the Play icon.

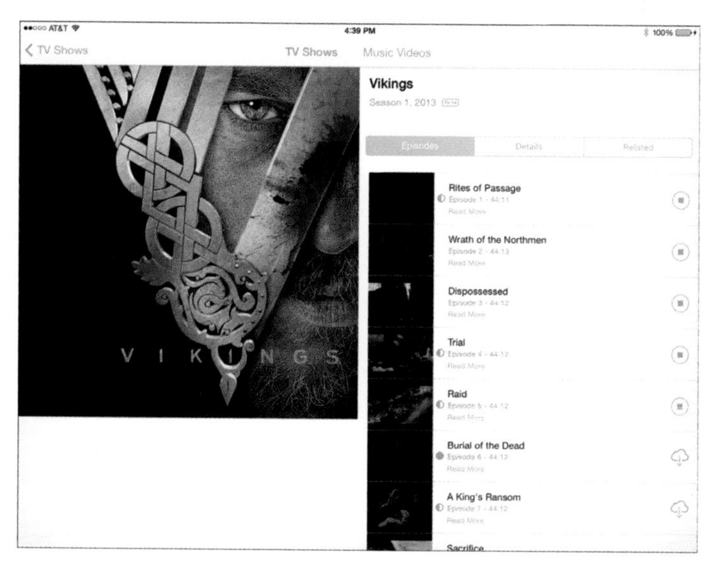

FIGURE 14.14

Multiple episodes of a TV series are grouped together for easy access and viewing.

For music videos or movies, a similar information screen pertaining to that content is displayed. Tap on the Play icon to begin watching your movie or music video.

> **TIP** When playing video content, you can hold your iPhone or iPad in either portrait or landscape mode. However, the video window is significantly larger if you position your iOS device sideways and use landscape mode.
>
> If applicable based on the video content you're watching, you can instantly switch between full-screen mode and letterbox mode as your onscreen viewing option by tapping the icon displayed in the upper-right corner of the screen.

While video content is playing on your iPhone or iPad, it displays in full-screen mode. Tap anywhere on the screen to reveal the onscreen command icons used for controlling the video as you're watching it. These controls are identical on the iPhone and iPad (shown in Figure 14.15). When a video is playing, these controls disappear from the screen automatically after a few seconds. Tap anywhere on the screen to make them reappear.

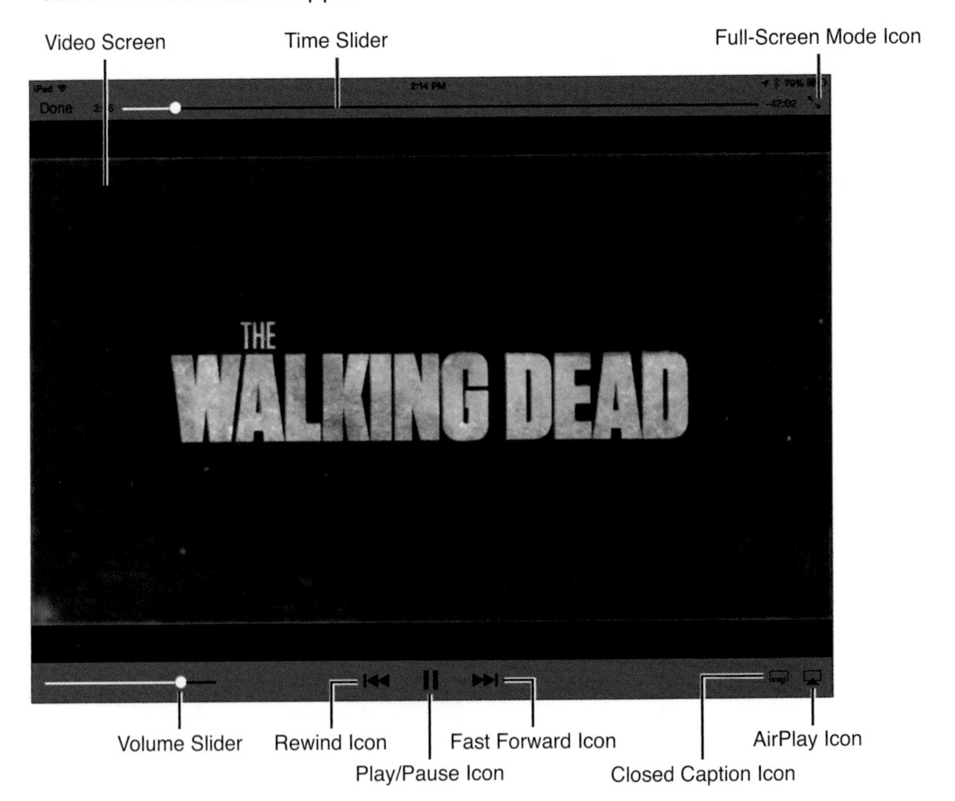

FIGURE 14.15

The onscreen icons for controlling the video you're watching on your iOS device.

Along the top center of the screen is a time slider. On either end of this slider are timers. To the left is a timer that displays how much of the video you've already watched. On the right of the slider is a timer that displays how much time in the video remains. Tap on the Done button in the upper-left corner of the screen to exit the video you're watching.

TIP To manually fast-forward or rewind while watching a video, place your finger on the dot icon that appears on the timer slider. Move it to the right to advance within the video, or move it to the left to rewind within the video.

Near the bottom center of the screen as you're watching video content are the Rewind and Fast Forward icons. Tap on the Rewind icon to move back by scene or chapter, or tap the Fast Forward icon to advance to the next scene or chapter in the video (just as you would while watching a DVD). Press and hold the Rewind or Fast Forward icon to rewind or fast forward while viewing the onscreen content. You can rewind or advance by a few seconds at a time.

Tap the Play icon to play the video. When the video is playing, the Play icon transforms into a Pause icon, used to pause the video.

NOTE If you pause a video and then exit the Videos app, you can pick up exactly where you left off watching the video when you relaunch the Videos app. This information is automatically saved.

To the left of these three icons is the volume control slider. Use it to manually adjust the volume of the audio. You can also use the volume control buttons located on the side of your iPhone or iPad or, if applicable, the volume control buttons on the cord of your headset (such as the Apple EarPods).

Located near the lower-right corner of the screen while a video is playing (when the controls are visible) are the Captions and AirPlay icons. Tap on the Captions icon to adjust captions and/or switch between audio languages, if the video content you're watching supports these features. If not available, the text-bubble icon will not be visible.

Tap on the AirPlay option to stream the video from your mobile device to your television set or home theater system when using an Apple TV. If you have Bluetooth- or AirPlay-compatible speakers, you can stream just the audio from a TV show or movie, for example, to external speakers or wireless headphones.

NOTE You must use Wi-Fi to stream video from your iOS mobile device to your HD television via Apple TV. Both the iOS mobile device and Apple TV must be linked to the same wireless network.

TIP From the iTunes Store, it's possible to purchase TV show episodes (or entire seasons from your favorite series), as well as full-length movies. In addition, you can rent certain movies.

When you rent a move from the iTunes Store, it remains on your device for 30 days before it automatically deletes itself, whether or not the content has been viewed. However, after you press Play in the Videos app and begin watching rented content, you have access to that video for only 24 hours before it deletes itself. During that 24-hour period, you can watch and rewatch the movie as often as you'd like.

The first time you tap Play to watch a rented movie, you're prompted to confirm your choice. This starts the 24-hour clock and allows the rented movie to begin playing.

Unlike movies you purchase from iTunes (that you can load into all of your computers and/or iOS mobile devices that are linked to the same Apple ID account), rented movies can be stored on only one computer, Apple TV, or iOS mobile device at a time. You can, however, transfer unwatched rented movies between devices.

USE THE iTUNES STORE APP TO ACQUIRE NEW MUSIC, TV SHOWS, MOVIES, AND MORE

The redesigned iTunes Store app comes preinstalled with iOS 7 and is used to acquire music, movies, TV shows, audiobooks, and ringtones.

To utilize the iTunes Store app (shown in Figure 14.16), your iOS mobile device will need Internet access. For smaller-sized files, such as songs, albums, or ringtones, a cellular data connection can be used. However, for larger-sized files, such as TV show episodes and movies, you must use a Wi-Fi Internet connection.

NOTE You can access the iTunes Store using the iTunes Store app by launching it from the Home screen or directly from the Music or Videos app by tapping on the Store button.

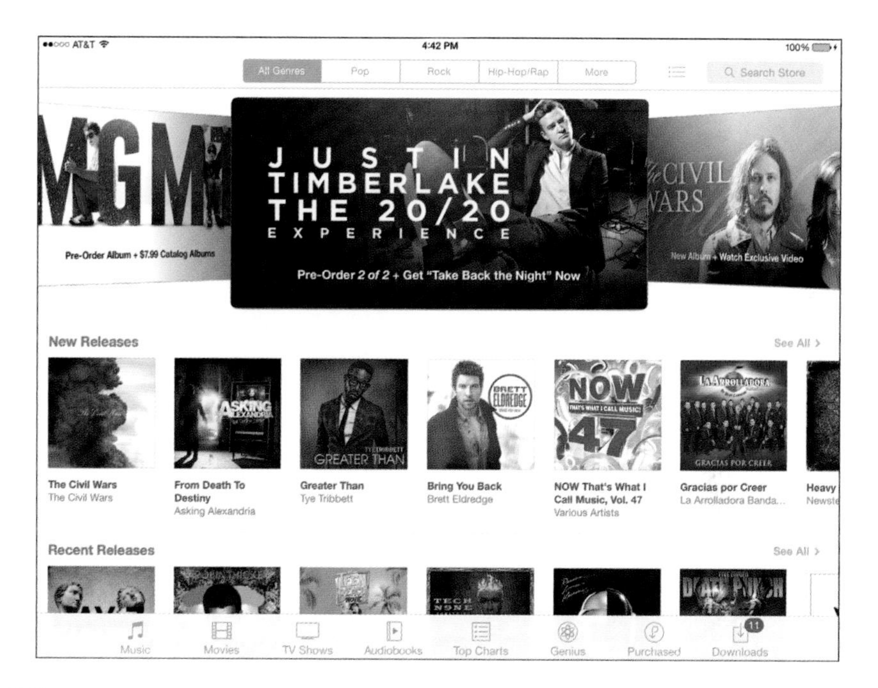

FIGURE 14.16

The iTunes Store app is used to purchase content and acquire free music and videos.

Displayed along the bottom of the iTunes Store screen are five command icons: Music, Movies, TV Shows, Search, and More. To shop for music (or acquire free music), tap on the Music icon. Likewise, to purchase or rent movies, tap on the Movies icon. For TV shows (either individual episodes or entire seasons of a show), tap on the TV Shows icon.

Use the Search feature to quickly find audio or video content using keywords. Tap on the More icon to shop for ringtones or audiobooks.

> **TIP** After you tap on the More icon, tap Purchased to view all past purchases from the iTunes Store. You can also track the download progress of new content you've acquired by tapping on the Downloads option. If a download gets halted for some reason, tap on the Downloads option, and then tap on the Resume icon that's displayed to the right of the listing for the content being downloaded.

Just like when using the App Store to acquire new apps for your mobile device, when you make a purchase from the iTunes Store, all charges are automatically billed to the credit or debit card you have linked with your Apple ID or offset against any credit your account might have from redeemed gift cards.

TIP You can redeem an iTunes Gift Card and add the credit to the Apple ID account used for making online purchases from the iTunes Store, App Store, iBookstore, or Newsstand. When you select the Redeem option, it's now possible to scan the physical gift card using the camera that's built in to your iOS mobile device so you don't have to manually type the long redemption code.

When you make a purchase from your iPhone or iPad, it immediately gets downloaded to that mobile device and, at the same time, gets stored in your iCloud account. Thus, that same content can then be downloaded and experienced on your other Macs and iOS mobile devices that are linked to the same iCloud account.

TIP The iTunes Store offers a Complete My Season feature for TV show seasons. If you purchase one or more single episodes of a TV series (from a specific season), you can later return to the iTunes Store and purchase the rest of the episodes from that season at a reduced price (based on how many episodes from that season you already own). This feature works just like the Complete My Album feature but relates to TV shows.

NOTE If you're interested in purchasing and listening to audiobooks on your iOS mobile device, thousands of titles are available from the iTunes Store and can be played using the Music app. However, the Audible.com service also offers a vast and ever-growing audiobook library. Individual audiobook titles can be purchased online and enjoyed using the free Audible app that's available from the App Store.

QUICKLY FIND TV EPISODES YOU WANT TO PURCHASE ON iTUNES

When shopping for TV show episodes to purchase and watch using the iTunes Store app, tap on the TV shows button that's displayed near the bottom of the screen. Shows are displayed by series name. The search results display the TV show by season number and by available episodes.

Tap on the TV series artwork icon that's associated with the season from which you want to purchase episodes to reveal a listing of individual episodes from that season, in chronological order, based on original airdate. The most recently aired episodes are toward the bottom of the list, so scroll down.

At the top of the screen, you also have the option of purchasing the entire season at a discounted rate, plus choosing between high definition (HD) or standard definition (SD) video quality.

To save money, purchase an entire season of your favorite show's current season. This is called a Season Pass. Then, when a new episode airs each week and becomes available from the iTunes Store (about 24 hours later), it can automatically be downloaded to your iOS device and made available to you via iCloud using a Wi-Fi Internet connection. You'll also receive a weekly email from Apple telling you when each new episode in your Season Pass is available.

When you shop for TV episodes from the iTunes Store (via the iTunes app), those files get downloaded and stored on your iPhone or iPad. They're commercial free and available to watch whenever you wish. They're also permanently accessible via your iCloud account to be downloaded to any computer, iOS device, or Apple TV device that's linked to the same iCloud account. Once an episode is download to your iPhone or iPad, an Internet connection is no longer needed to watch it.

NOTE Keep in mind that, without commercials, a one-hour program appears in the iTunes Store (and in the Videos app) as being between 42 and 44 minutes long, while a half-hour program appears as between 21 and 24 minutes long.

STREAMING VIDEO ON YOUR iOS MOBILE DEVICE

To stream video content to your iPhone or iPad from the Internet, you must use a specialized app, based on where the content is originating from on the Internet.

Whenever you're streaming video content from the Internet, you can pause the video at any time. Depending on the app, you also can exit the app partway through a video and resume watching it from where you left off when you relaunch the app later.

CAUTION The capability to stream content from the Internet and experience it on your iPhone or iPad gives you on-demand access to a wide range of programming; however, streaming audio or video content requires a tremendous amount of data to be transferred to your iOS device. Therefore, if you use a cellular data connection, your monthly wireless data allocation will quickly get used up. So, when you're streaming Internet content, it's best to use a Wi-Fi connection.

Not only does a Wi-Fi connection often allow data to be transferred to your iPhone or iPad at faster speeds, there's also no limit as to how much data you can send or receive. Plus, when streaming video content, you can often view it at a higher resolution using a Wi-Fi connection.

The following sections describe some of the popular apps for streaming TV shows, movies, and other video content directly from the Internet. Keep in mind that many cable television service providers (such as Xfinity/Comcast and Time Warner) and satellite TV service providers, as well as individual television networks (ABC, NBC, CBS, The CW, USA Network, Lifetime, SyFy, and so on), and even specific TV shows, often have their own proprietary apps available for streaming content from the Internet directly to your iPhone and/or iPad. There are also paid streaming services, such as Netflix and Hulu Plus, that offer vast libraries of TV shows and movies available for streaming.

When you stream TV episodes from the Internet using a specialized app, this programming does not get stored on your iOS device and is available only when your iPhone or iPad has a constant connection to the Internet while you're watching that content. In many cases, a Wi-Fi connection is required.

NOTE As a general rule, free streamed programming from a television network app (from ABC, NBC, or CBS, for example) includes commercials. Programming from a premium cable network that you're already paying for through your cable TV service (such as HBO or Showtime) is commercial free, as are streamed TV shows or movies accessed through a paid service, such as Netflix or Hulu Plus. When you purchase TV show episodes from the iTunes Store, they are ad free.

WATCH ABC

The ABC Player is a free app from the ABC Television Network that enables you to watch full-length episodes of your favorite ABC-TV dramas, reality shows, sitcoms, game shows, and soap operas, for free. The episodes are streamed to your iPhone or iPad and can be watched using this app. The shows are advertiser supported, so you must watch ads during the programs you stream. In some areas, ABC is streaming live programming via the Watch ABC app, as well as offering on-demand episodes of popular series.

The Watch ABC app is separate from the free ABC News app, which enables you to watch news coverage from the network.

TIP All the major TV networks offer free apps for streaming full-length episodes on an on-demand basis, seeing previews of upcoming shows, and keeping track of your favorite shows. Using these apps, you can watch your favorite shows whenever you want. However, the selection of available episodes at any given time can be limited.

HBO GO

If you're already a paid subscriber to HBO, you can download the free HBO Go app and watch every episode of every HBO original series on-demand, as well as an ever-changing lineup of movies, comedy specials, sports programs, and documentaries.

After you set up a free online account with your local cable or satellite television provider, sign in to the app and select the programming you want to watch. Begin playing a TV episode or movie with the tap of a finger, or create a queue of shows to watch at your leisure. Movies and TV episodes can be paused and resumed later.

One great feature of the HBO Go app is that HBO sometimes releases episodes on this app one week before they air on television. Plus, you can access behind-the-scenes content of popular HBO series, like *Game of Thrones*.

! CAUTION Most of the streaming video apps for the iPhone and iPad work only in the United States. If you try to access HBO Go from abroad, for example, the app will not work.

HULU PLUS

Full-length and commercial-free episodes from thousands of current and classic TV series (as well as an ever-growing library of movies) are available on your iOS device using the Hulu Plus app. However, although the app itself is free, the Hulu Plus service requires you to pay a flat monthly subscription fee ($7.99) to access and view content.

Hulu Plus members can access season passes to current TV shows airing on ABC, FOX, and NBC, for example, or pick and choose from thousands of episodes from classic TV series. A Wi-Fi connection is recommended, although the app does work with a 3G or 4G Internet connection.

The Hulu Plus app enables you to pause programs and resume them later, plus create a queue of shows to watch on your tablet.

MORE INFO Visit www.hulu.com/plus to subscribe to the Hulu service and browse available programming.

XFINITY TV

If Xfinity (Comcast) is your cable TV provider, use this app to watch a wide range of free, on-demand programming, including TV shows and movies. The free TWCable TV app from Time Warner Cable offers similar functionality. If you subscribe to another cable TV or satellite TV service, check the App Store to see whether a similar app is available.

One benefit to the Xfinity app is that you can download and save certain programs to your mobile device so you can watch that content later, without an Internet connection.

MAX GO

This free app works just like the HBO Go app but enables you to watch Cinemax programming on demand from your iOS device. The content is free, as long as you're already a paid Cinemax subscriber.

NOTE There's also a free Showtime app, called Showtime Anytime, available for the iPhone and iPad if you're a paid Showtime subscriber with AT&T U-verse, Verizon FiOS, Comcast Xfinity, DirecTV, or Optimum. This app offers on-demand programming from the Showtime network, including original TV series such as *Dexter*, as well as an ever-changing selection of movies. For Xfinity and Time Warner cable subscribers, on-demand Showtime programming is available from the Xfinity or TWC TV apps. For Xfinity cable subscribers who pay for Showtime, that network's programming is also available through the Xfinity app on an on-demand basis.

NETFLIX

Netflix is a subscription-based service that enables you to watch thousands of movies and TV show episodes via the Internet on your Internet-enabled television, on your computer screen, from a video game console (such as Xbox 360, Xbox

One, PlayStation 3, or PlayStation 4), using Apple TV, using a DVR (such as TiVo), or directly on your iPhone or iPad (when you use the free Netflix app). The subscription fee for Netflix is a flat $7.99 per month for unlimited access.

You can watch as much streaming content as you'd like per month from any compatible computer or iOS mobile device. Simply browse the Netflix Instant Watch library, and tap on the Play button when you find the movie or TV show episode you want to watch. You can also create and manage an Instant Queue, which is a personalized listing of shows or movies from Netflix that you'd like to watch in the future or that you consider a Favorite.

YOUTUBE

The official YouTube app (free) is available for the iPhone and iPad from the App Store. This app enables you to watch unlimited streaming videos produced and uploaded by everyday people, companies, television networks, and other organizations. In addition to millions of entertaining videos and video blogs, YouTube features free educational content and how-to videos. All YouTube content is free of charge to watch. Some of it is advertiser supported, however.

TIP In addition to streaming videos, TV shows, and movies to watch on your iPhone or iPad, you can stream audio programming from AM, FM, and satellite-based radio stations and radio networks, as well as Internet-based radio stations. Some of the apps available for doing this are Pandora Radio, TuneIn Radio Pro, Spotify, iHeartRadio, and SiriusXM. A monthly fee applies to stream SiriusXM programming.

NOTE Using specialized apps from TV networks and cable channels, in addition to watching on-demand programming of shows that have already aired, in some cases it's becoming possible to stream live television programming as well. This is now possible using the CNN app, for example. Live television streaming will become more prevalent in 2014 and beyond.

IN THIS CHAPTER

- How to use iBooks to access iBookstore and shop for eBooks
- How to access and read PDF files on your iPhone or iPad using iBooks
- Use the Newsstand app to read digital editions of newspapers and magazines

15

CUSTOMIZE YOUR READING EXPERIENCE WITH iBOOKS AND NEWSSTAND

When it comes to reading eBooks, Apple has a solution to meet every person's reading habits and taste. Thanks to Apple's own iBooks app, eBooks can easily be read on any iOS mobile device.

If you have a Mac, iPhone, and/or an iPad, you can use iCloud to sync your eBook library and related bookmarks between devices automatically, so your books, even if you've acquired hundreds of them, are available to you regardless of which computer or iOS mobile device you're using.

Anything having to do with shopping for, downloading, installing, and then reading eBooks on your iPhone or iPad is done using the iBooks app, which does not come preinstalled on your device. However, as soon as you begin using a new or newly upgraded iPhone or iPad, you're automatically prompted to download and install Apple's latest edition of the iBooks app from the App Store.

TIP You also have the option to download and use other third-party eBook reading apps with your iOS device. These apps, which include the Amazon Kindle and Barnes & Noble Nook apps, are discussed later in this chapter.

iBooks has two main purposes. First, it's used to access Apple's online-based iBookstore. From iBookstore, you can browse an ever-growing collection of eBook titles (including traditional book titles from bestselling authors and major publishers that have been adapted into eBook form). Although some eBooks are free, most must be paid for.

TIP As with purchases from the iTunes Store, App Store, or Newsstand, eBook purchases made from iBookstore get charged to the credit or debit card associated with your Apple ID. iBookstore and Newsstand purchases can also be paid for using prepaid iTunes gift cards.

After you've downloaded eBooks to your iOS device, the iBooks app is used to transform your mobile device into an eBook reader, which accurately reproduces the appearance of each page of a printed book on your device's screen. So reading an eBook is just like reading a traditional book in terms of the appearance of text, photos, or graphics that would otherwise appear on a printed page.

One advantage to reading an eBook, as opposed to a traditionally printed book, is that the iBooks app enables you to customize the appearance of a book's pages. For example, you can select a font that is appealing to your eyes, choose a font size that's comfortable to read, and even change the background color of the screen to a Sepia or Night theme, which some people find less taxing on their eyes.

iBooks offers many features that make reading eBooks on your iOS device a pleasure. For example, when you stop reading and exit the iBooks app (by pressing the Home button), the app automatically saves the page you're on using a virtual bookmark and later reopens to that page when the iBooks app is restarted. It can sync your bookmarks and eBook library with iCloud and your other iOS mobile devices automatically.

NOTE Thanks to iCloud, you can begin reading a book on one computer or iOS mobile device, and then pick up exactly where you left off on another, simply by opening the iBooks app. You are allowed to install copies of your eBooks on all computers and devices that are linked to the same iCloud account, so you do not have to purchase the same eBook multiple times.

CUSTOMIZE iBOOKS SETTINGS

To customize settings related to iBooks, launch Settings and tap on the iBooks option. You can turn on or off Full Justification and/or Auto-Hyphenation, as well as the Both Margins Advance feature (which, when turned on, enables you to tap the left or right margin of the screen to turn a page, instead of using a horizontal finger swipe).

To turn on the iCloud syncing functions for iBooks, turn on the virtual switches associated with Sync Bookmarks and Sync Collections. If you turn on the Show All Purchases option, all of the eBooks you own are displayed on the Library screen, even if they're not currently stored on the device you're using. To then download one of the eBooks you own from iCloud, simply tap on the iCloud icon associated with that eBook listing.

You must customize the settings associated with iBooks only once, but you can return to Settings at any time to adjust the customizable options as you see fit.

NOTE eBook publishers can update content in their titles after they've been purchased by iBookstore customers. From the iBooks menu in Settings, turn on the virtual switch that's associated with the Online Content option to enable your iOS device to download updated content automatically (and for free), when applicable.

iBooks enables you to store and manage a vast library of eBooks on your iOS device, the size of which is limited only by the storage capacity of the device itself. Plus, all of your iBookstore purchases automatically get saved to your iCloud account. Thus, you can easily download eBook titles you've previously purchased via iCloud when you want to access a particular eBook that is not currently stored on your device. If you have the Show All Purchases option turned on, tap on the eBook's iCloud icon that appears in the Library screen to download the book. Otherwise, return to iBookstore and tap on the Purchased icon displayed at the bottom of the screen to download a previous eBook purchase.

TIP Your iPhone or iPad needs Internet access to browse or shop for eBooks via iBookstore. However, you do not need Internet access to read your books when they are stored on your device. Thus, you can read an eBook while on an airplane, for example, with your iPhone or iPad in Airplane mode, as long as you preload the eBook(s) you want to read onto your device before your flight.

THE iBOOKS MAIN LIBRARY SCREEN

When you launch iBooks for the first time, the app's main Library screen is displayed. However, the Library screen, which looks like a virtual bookshelf, will be empty. From the Library screen, tap on the Store button to access Apple's iBookstore to browse and shop for eBooks. An Internet connection is required for this.

TIP If you've already purchased eBooks from iBookstore using another computer or device, from the iBooks app, tap on the Store icon to access the iBookstore. Then, tap on the Purchased button that's displayed near the bottom of the screen. A listing of all eBooks you own and that are formatted to be read with iBooks is displayed. Near the top of the screen, tap on the Not on This iPhone or Not on This iPad tab to see the list of eBooks you own but that are not currently stored on the device you're using.

Next, tap on the iCloud icon for each book and download it to your iPhone or iPad. If you have the Sync Collections option turned on in Settings, this happens automatically.

On the iPhone, the Store button is located in the upper-right corner of the Library screen. On the iPad, the Store button can be found in the upper-left corner of the Library screen.

NOTE Throughout this chapter, the term *purchased* eBooks refers to eBook titles you already have purchased from iBookstore, as well as free eBooks you download through iBookstore. These are eBooks already stored in your iCloud account or that are displayed when you tap on the Purchased Books option or have the Sync Collections option in Settings turned on.

It is possible to download and read eBooks acquired from sources other than iBookstore using iBooks; however, the eBooks must be a compatible file format. The iBooks app works with PDF files (or eBooks in PDF format), as well as eBooks created in the industry-standard ePub format.

Typically, the Library screen displays all the eBook titles currently stored on your device (as shown in Figure 15.1). From this screen, you can manage your eBook library, access iBookstore, or access PDF files stored on your device.

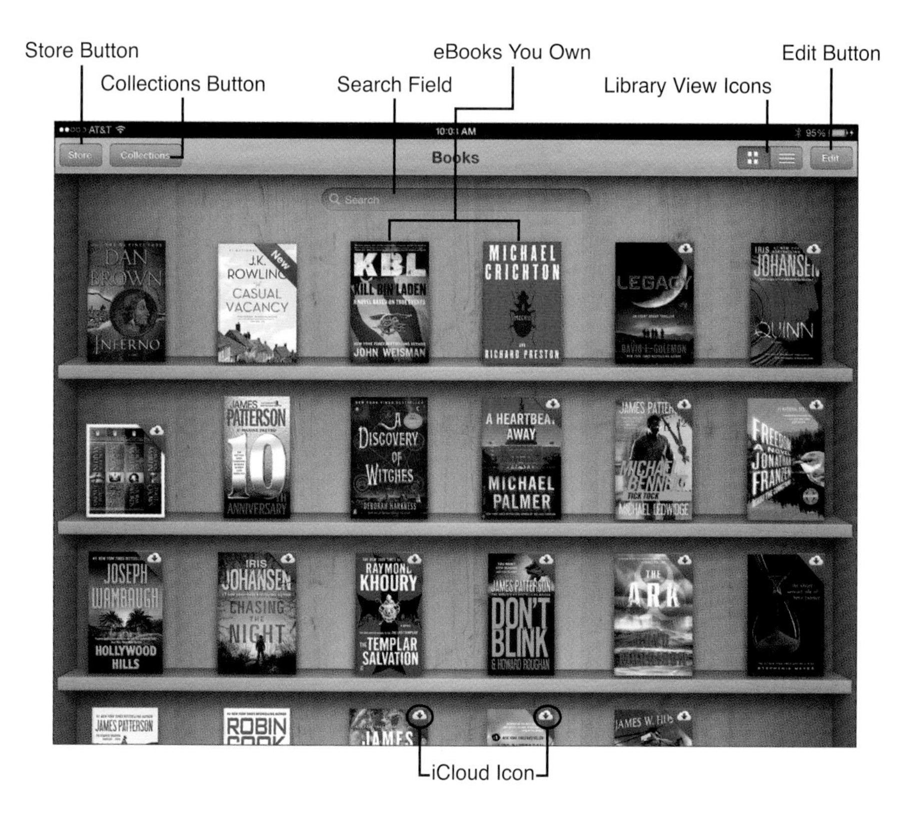

FIGURE 15.1
Shown here is the Library screen on an iPad, with a collection of eBooks stored on the tablet.

> **NOTE** As you look at Figure 15.1, when you see book covers that have an iCloud icon near their top-right corner, it indicates that you own the eBook but it's not currently stored on the device you're using. Tap the icon to download it from iCloud.

As you add books to your library, the cover art for each title is displayed on the Library screen.

To see an alternative listing view of the Library screen, on the iPhone, when viewing the Library screen, swipe your finger downward from the center of the screen. The app's Search field, along with the Thumbnail view and Listing view icons, are displayed. On the iPad, these two icons can be found near the top-right corner of the Library screen. (However, to access the Search field on the iPad, you must swipe your finger downward.)

To utilize the Listing view, tap the icon that's comprised of three horizontal lines (shown in Figure 15.2). To return to the default Thumbnail view, tap the icon showing four squares.

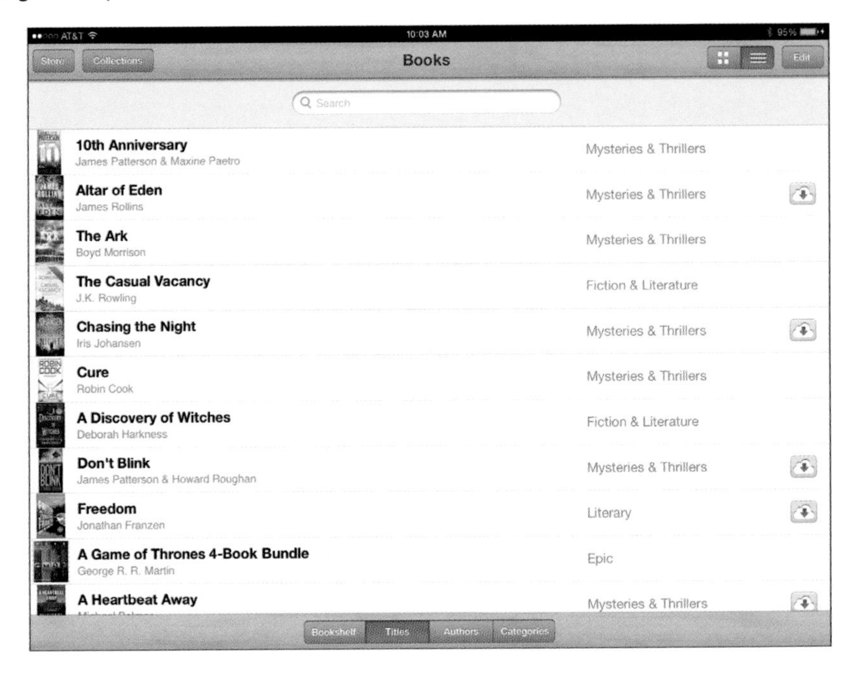

FIGURE 15.2

Sort and then view your eBook collection using this alternative listing format, as opposed to viewing eBook covers on a virtual bookshelf.

TIP From the bottom of the Library screen's Listing view screen, tap on the Bookshelf, Titles, Authors, or Categories tab (displayed at the bottom center of the screen) to sort your eBook collection.

MANAGING YOUR EBOOK COLLECTION FROM THE LIBRARY SCREEN

While looking at the Library screen, it's possible to sort and manage your eBook collection. To do this on the iPhone, tap on what by default is labeled the Books button displayed near the top center of the screen. On the iPad, tap on the Collections button displayed near the top-left corner of the screen.

By default, the Collections screen (iPhone) or window (iPad) is comprised of the Books, Purchased Books, PDFs, and Favorites folders (also called Collections).

By tapping on the New button, you can create additional folders (Collections) with custom names, and then place one or more eBooks into those folders. From the Library screen, tap the Edit button to delete or rearrange the order in which the folders are displayed.

Once folders are created, from the main Library screen, tap on the Edit button to select eBooks (by tapping on their covers). Then, tap on the Move button to move those selected eBook titles from the main Library screen into a specific folder (Collection). Tap the Done button when you're finished organizing your eBook collection.

TIP You can create separate eBook folders (Collections) for specific book series, authors, various subject matters, or based on whether the books are related to work, pleasure, or personal enrichment, for example.

To free up internal storage space on your iPhone or iPad, it's possible to delete one or more eBooks that aren't currently being read. To do this, tap the Edit button, select the eBooks you wish to delete, and then tap the Delete button. The eBooks are removed from your device, but they remain available to you via iCloud and can quickly be reloaded anytime (as long as an Internet connection is available). You can access iBookstore using a cellular or Wi-Fi Internet connection.

BROWSE AND SHOP FOR EBOOKS VIA iBOOKSTORE

When you're ready to begin browsing the vast eBook selection offered by iBookstore, make sure your iPhone or iPad is connected to the Internet, and then tap on the Store button. The interface and layout of iBookstore are similar to those of the App Store and Newsstand; however, what's offered here are exclusively eBooks.

TIP You also have the option to shop for eBooks using the new iBooks software on your Mac. As soon as you make an eBook purchase, it is added to your iCloud account, so you can then download it to your iOS device.

You can browse through iBookstore's offerings by subject, book title, an author's name, by viewing bestseller lists, or using various other methods. When you access iBookstore, you see the main screen, which on the iPhone looks like what's shown in Figure 15.3.

FIGURE 15.3

The iPhone version of the iBookstore. The Featured button displayed at the bottom of the screen has been selected. From here, you can begin browsing for eBooks to purchase and download (or download for free in some cases).

Figure 15.4 shows the main iBookstore screen on an iPad. Although browsing and shopping from iBookstore are basically the same on the iPhone and iPad, the main command icons vary slightly between an iPhone versus an iPad.

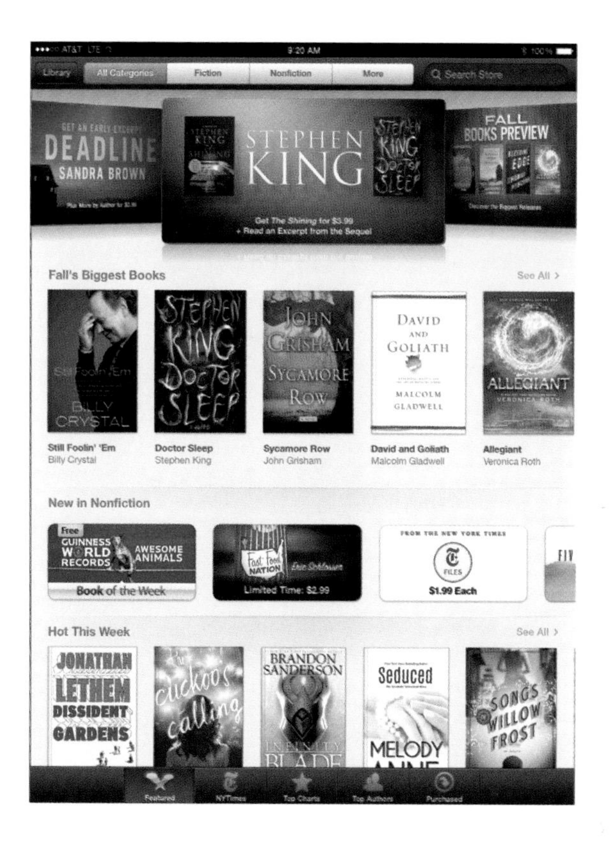

FIGURE 15.4

When you browse iBookstore using an iPad, more content can be displayed on the screen at once. For example, the Categories tabs are displayed near the top center of the screen.

USING THE iBOOKSTORE OPTIONS

At the top of the iBookstore screen are a Categories button (labeled All Categories on the iPad) and a Library button. Along the bottom of the screen are five additional command buttons. Here's a summary of how these features work:

- **Categories**—View eBooks by category, such as Arts & Entertainment, Business & Personal Finance, Fiction & Literature, Nonfiction, and Reference. There are 24 categories to choose from within iBookstore; they become accessible on the iPad (shown in Figure 15.5) when you tap on the More button. Some categories also contain subcategories.

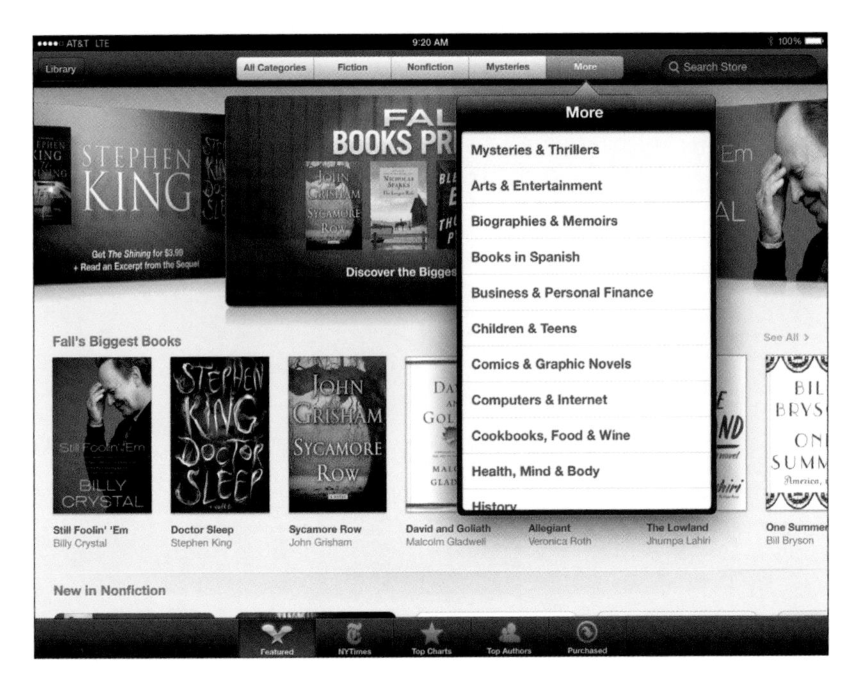

FIGURE 15.5

Tap on the More button displayed near the top of iBookstore's Featured screen to view all of the store's Categories.

- **Library**—Tap this button to exit iBookstore and return to the Library screen of the iBooks app.
- **Featured**—View a selection of what Apple decides are "featured" eBook titles currently available from iBookstore. Under each heading, such as New In Fiction or New In Nonfiction, are a selection of eBook listings. Scroll horizontally through the listings below each heading, or tap on the corresponding See All option to view a separate screen that displays all eBook listings that fall under that heading.
- **Top Charts**—View Bestseller charts relating to paid and free eBooks available from iBookstore. The Books lists are compiled based on sales or downloads from iBookstore. On the iPad, a NYTimes button appears to the left of the Top Charts button listing the current *New York Times* Bestsellers. Figure 15.6 shows the Top Charts screen on an iPhone 5, while Figure 15.7 shows the same screen, but with more information, on the iPad.

FIGURE 15.6

The Top Charts screen on the iPhone 5. Notice the Books and NYTimes tabs near the top center of the screen, which are used to determine which Top Charts chart you view.

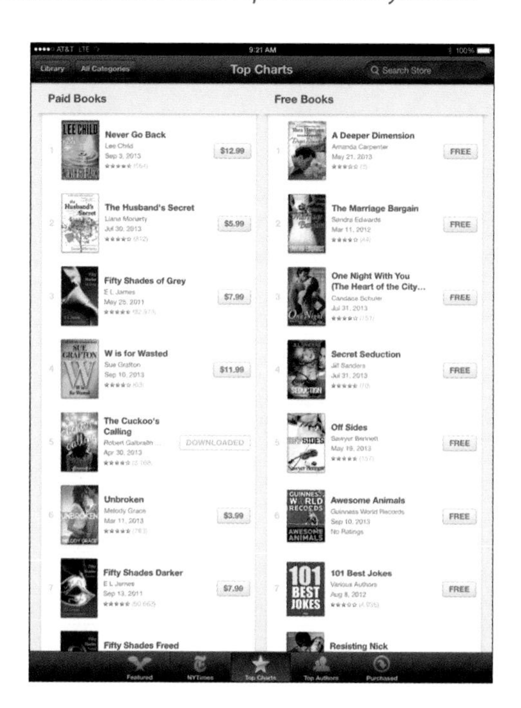

FIGURE 15.7

Discover the bestselling books on iBookstore by tapping on the Top Charts button.

TIP After tapping on the Top Charts icon at the bottom of the screen, and then tapping on the Books tab (displayed near the top of the screen), each chart displayed is comprised of bestselling or popular eBooks from all categories. To narrow down the list and see charts for a specific category, tap on the Categories button, and then choose a category. The Paid Books and Free Books charts are compiled based on books from the selected category.

- **Top Authors**—This option displays an alphabetical listing of popular authors. You can narrow down your search by tapping on the Top Paid or Top Free tab displayed near the top center of the screen. Or, to quickly find an author without having to scroll through a list, tap on the Search button.
- **Search**—This option appears at the bottom of the screen on the iPhone and in the top-right corner on the iPad. When you tap on this button on the iPhone, a blank search field is displayed at the top of the screen. Enter the book title, author name, subject, or any keyword associated with an eBook title or description that you're looking for. Then, tap the Search key on the virtual keyboard to initiate the search and view the results. A selection of eBook listings is displayed. Tap on a listing to display the Description screen for the selected eBook.
- **Purchased**—This command icon enables you to access your iCloud account and load any previously purchased eBooks to your iPhone or iPad, regardless of which computer or iOS mobile device the eBooks were originally purchased from. Tap the All tab to view all the eBook titles you own, or tap on the Not On This Phone [iPad] tab to view eBooks you own that are not installed on the iPhone you're using. To download one of the eBooks listed, tap on the iCloud icon displayed to the right of its listing.

Use the Books, NYTimes, Top Charts, Top Authors, Search, or Purchased options to find, purchase (if applicable), and download eBooks. What you initially see are eBook listings that include the book's cover artwork, title, and author. Tap on the eBook's cover to reveal a more detailed description screen for a book.

TIP After tapping on the Featured button at the bottom of the screen, scroll downward to access the Quick Links section. Here are buttons for browsing eBooks that fall into a handful of specialized themes or categories that change regularly.

Below the Quick Links section is the Apple ID [Your Username] button, the Redeem button, and the Send Gift button. Tap on the Apple ID button to manage your Apple ID account. Tap on the Redeem button to redeem iTunes Gift Cards and add credit to your Apple ID account. Tap Send Gift to send someone you know an eBook as a gift. You'll need to know the recipient's email address that's associated with their Apple ID.

HOW TO FIND A SPECIFIC EBOOK—FAST

Although you can use the various command buttons and spend hours browsing through eBook titles, just as you can spend an equal amount of time perusing the shelves of a traditional bookstore, here are some simple strategies for quickly finding a specific eBook title you're looking for.

As soon as iBookstore loads, use the Search field to enter the eBook title, author's name, subject, or keyword that's associated with what you're looking for. Entering a specific book title reveals very specific search results. However, entering a keyword relating to a topic or subject matter reveals a selection of eBook suggestions that somehow relate to that keyword.

Tap on any listing to reveal a more detailed description relating to a particular eBook. As you review a description screen (iPhone) or window (iPad) for an eBook, look carefully at its ratings and its written reviews, especially if it's a paid eBook.

LEARN ABOUT AN EBOOK FROM ITS DESCRIPTION

A typical eBook listing includes the eBook's cover artwork, its title, and author. An eBook's description screen (iPhone) or window (iPad) is divided into several sections. Tap on the Details, Ratings and Review, or Related tabs to view all information pertaining to a specific eBook.

On both an iPhone and iPad, displayed near the upper-left corner of a typical eBook description, as shown in Figure 15.8, is the eBook's cover artwork.

To the right of this is a text-based summary of the book, including its title, author, the book's publication date and publisher, its average star-based rating, the number of ratings it has received, and the book's length. The page length of the printed edition of the book is also displayed.

The book's price button and Sample button are also displayed near the top of the description screen/window.

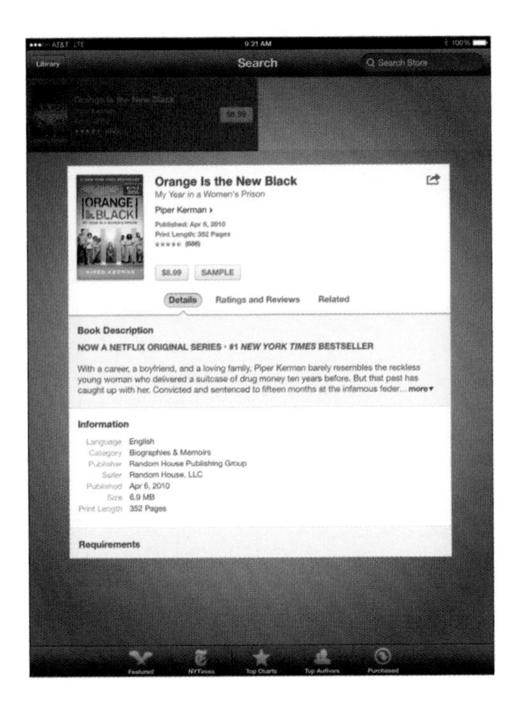

FIGURE 15.8

Read a detailed description of an eBook before making your purchase and/or downloading it.

A Share icon appears at the upper-right corner of an eBook description, including options for Mail, Message, Twitter, Facebook, and Copy Link.

> **TIP** You can preview an eBook before paying for it. On each book's description screen/window is a Sample button. Tap on it to download a free sample of that eBook. The length of the sample varies and is determined by the eBook's publisher. It is usually between a few pages and a full chapter.

Tap on the Details tab to view a detailed description or summary of the book, as well as the Information section. The Information section displays the Language, Category, Publisher, Seller, Publication Date, File Size, and Print Length of the book (refer to Figure 15.8).

Tap on the Ratings and Reviews option (shown in Figure 15.9) to access the iBookstore Ratings chart, which showcases the book's average star-based rating and how many ratings the book has received. Below the star-based ratings are more detailed, text-based reviews written by other iBookstore customers.

FIGURE 15.9

From the Ratings and Reviews section of an eBook's Description screen/window, you can see the book's star-based ratings, more detailed reviews, "Like" the book on Facebook, and/or create your own rating or review.

Also on the Ratings and Reviews screen/window is the Facebook Like button. Tap on it to like the book and share details about it with your Facebook friends. This feature works only if you have Facebook integration turned on in your iPhone or iPad. From this same window/screen, you can also add your own star-based rating and/or tap on the Write a Review button to compose and publish your own review of that book, which will then appear on iBookstore.

Tap on the Related option to view other books by that same author or similar books that Apple recommends.

To exit an eBook description screen on the iPhone, tap on the left-pointing arrow icon in the upper-left corner of the screen. The label on this icon depends upon the screen from which you entered the eBook description screen, such as Books or Featured. On the iPad, tap anywhere on the tablet's screen that is outside the Description window.

eBooks available from iBookstore are rated in much the same way apps are reviewed in the App Store. As a result, don't just pay attention to an eBook's average star-based rating. Also, pay attention to how many people have rated that eBook. After all, it's harder to get a good idea of a book's true quality if it has a five-star rating but has been rated by only a small number of people, versus a book with dozens or hundreds of five-star ratings.

To help make a purchase decision, scroll down below the customer ratings and take a look at the more detailed text-based customer reviews. Here, people who have theoretically read the book have written their own (sometimes lengthy) reviews.

PURCHASING AN EBOOK

To quickly purchase and download an eBook, tap on the price button displayed in its description. When you tap on a price button, it changes to a Buy Book button. Tap this button to confirm your purchase decision. You then need to enter your Apple ID password to begin the download process.

If you're downloading a free eBook, tap on the Free button that is displayed instead of a price button. Then, instead of a Buy Book button, a Get Book button appears. Tap on it, enter your Apple ID, and download the free eBook. Even though you must enter your Apple ID, you are not charged to download a free eBook.

It typically takes between 10 and 30 seconds to download a full-length eBook to your iPhone or iPad, depending on the speed of your Internet connection and the size of the eBook's digital file. As soon as it's downloaded and ready to read, the book's front cover artwork is displayed as part of the Library screen in the iBooks app.

USING iCLOUD WITH iBOOKS

As you know by now, all of your iBookstore purchases are automatically stored in your iCloud account and become accessible from all of your iOS devices that are linked to that same account. This means that you can purchase an eBook on your iPad, for example, but also download and read it on your iPhone, without having to repurchase that title.

Adjust the customizable options in Settings that relate to the iBooks app to turn on or off specific iCloud-related features and functions related to how eBooks are synced with iCloud. See the section, "Customize iBooks Settings," found earlier in this chapter.

HOW TO RELOAD A PREVIOUSLY PURCHASED EBOOK

Here's one way to manually load a previously purchased or downloaded eBook from iCloud (if you have the Sync Collections feature in Settings turned off):

1. Launch the iBooks app from the Home screen.
2. From the Library screen, tap on the Store button.
3. Tap on the Purchased button displayed near the bottom of the iBookstore screen.
4. When the Purchased screen appears, either use the Search field to type the title of the eBook you want to load, or scroll through the list of already purchased eBook titles that are not currently stored on your device.
5. When the listing for the pre-purchased eBook you want to load is displayed, tap on the iCloud icon that's displayed to the right of that listing.
6. The selected eBook is transferred from iCloud to your device and displayed on the iBooks Library screen. A blue-and-white New label appears across the book's cover, indicating that the eBook has just been added to your device and has not yet been accessed or read.
7. From the iBooks app's Library screen, tap on the eBook's cover to launch the eBook reader functionality of the app and begin reading your eBook.

iBOOKSTORE QUICK TIPS

- If you're looking for a book in a specific genre, such as a romance novel, tap on the Top Charts button, tap on the Categories button, and then select the Romance option from the Categories listing.
- A selection of enhanced, full-color, interactive eBooks are also available from iBookstore. For example, some popular children's books fall into this category, as do some cookbooks, textbooks, and reference books. These enhanced eBooks include animations, interactive elements, "pop-up" graphics (which replace traditional pop-up book pages), and sound, plus they take full advantage of the iPhone or iPad's full-color, high-definition Multi-Touch display.
- For students, the iBookstore now offers a Textbooks section. Apple is working with many of the leading textbook publishers to make "enhanced," interactive versions of commonly used textbooks available for iBooks.
- If you're interested in reading eBooks about digital photography, for example, but you don't know any specific book titles or authors who have written such books, simply enter the keywords "digital photography" into the Search field. A series of individual eBook listings that relate to digital photography

are displayed in the main part of the iBookstore screen. Some of these are paid books, whereas others are free publications.

- While exploring iBookstore, to return to the main Library screen of iBooks, tap on the Library button that's displayed near the top of the screen.
- Before purchasing any eBook, you can download and read a free sample of it by tapping on the Sample button that's displayed as part of each book's description.

CUSTOMIZE YOUR EBOOK READING EXPERIENCE USING iBOOKS

From the Library screen of iBooks, tap on a book cover thumbnail to open an eBook and start reading it. While reading eBooks, hold the iPhone or iPad in portrait or landscape mode. As you're reading an eBook, tap anywhere on the screen to make the various command icons and buttons appear (shown in Figure 15.10).

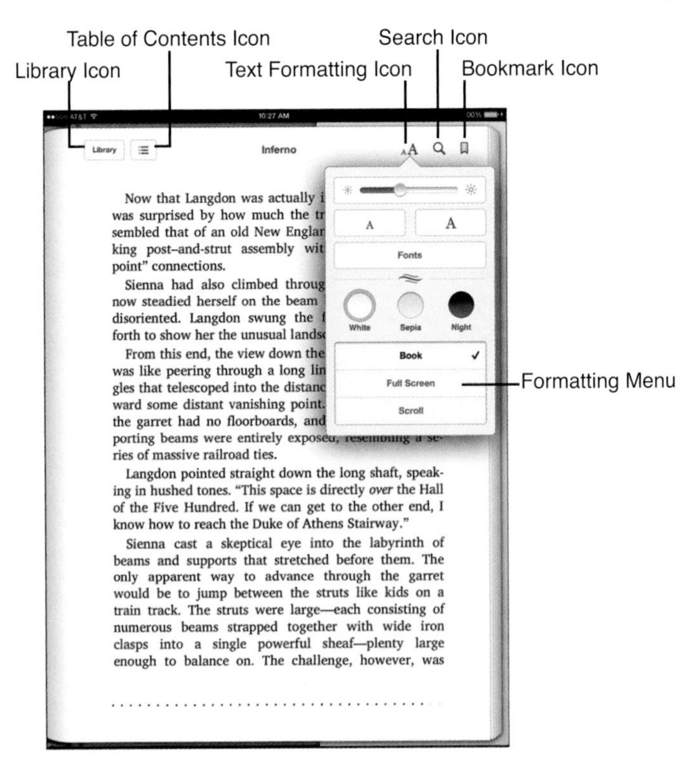

FIGURE 15.10

Tap on the "aA" icon to customize the appearance of the text in the eBook you're reading. In this example, the Themes button that initially appears in this menu window has been tapped to reveal the additional menu options.

TIP Tap on the Library button that's displayed near the upper-left corner of the screen to bookmark your location in that eBook and return to the iBooks Library (Bookshelf) screen.

Located to the right of the Library button is the Table of Contents icon. Tap on it to display an interactive table of contents for the eBook you're reading (as shown in Figure 15.11).

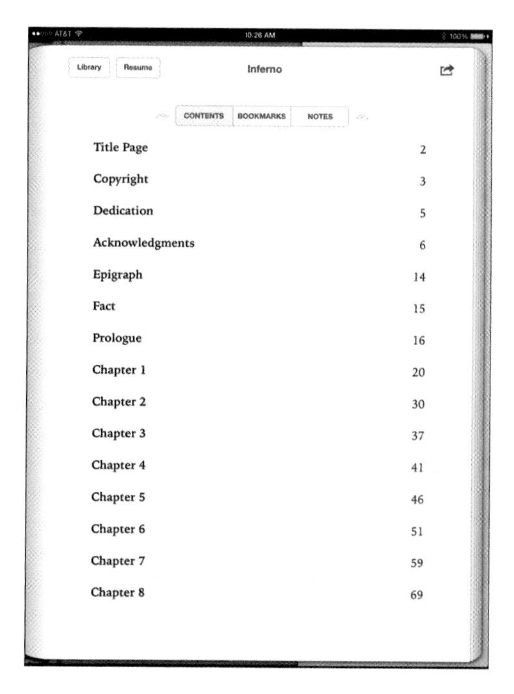

FIGURE 15.11

The Table of Contents screen for every eBook is interactive. Tap on the chapter number or chapter title to jump to the appropriate page.

As you're looking at a table of contents, tap on any chapter number or chapter title to immediately jump to that location in the book. Or, near the top center of the Table of Contents screen, tap on the Bookmarks option to see a list of manual bookmarks you have previously set as you were reading that eBook.

TIP Whenever you tap on the Library button while reading an eBook or press the Home button to return to the device's Home screen, your current location in the book is automatically bookmarked and saved.

At any time, however, you have the option to manually add a virtual bookmark to as many pages in the eBook as you want. Then, by tapping on the Table of Contents icon and then on the Bookmarks tab, you can see a complete listing of manually placed virtual bookmarks in that eBook and return to any of those pages quickly.

To exit the Table of Contents screen and return to reading your eBook, tap on the Resume button in the upper-left corner of the screen.

Three additional command icons appear to the right of the eBook title. Tap on the "aA" icon to reveal a pop-up window (refer to Figure 15.10). It offers a screen brightness slider and a small and large "A" button that are used to instantly decrease or increase the font size in the book you're reading. Tap on the Fonts button to change the text font, or tap on the Themes button to change the theme that's used to display the text and background color in the eBook you're reading.

Your theme choices include White, Sepia, and Night. Each displays the text and background in a different color combination. Choose the theme that is best suited for the lighting available and that is visually pleasing to you.

TIP When you tap on the Theme button, you can switch between White, Sepia, or the Night theme by tapping on the circular icon for your selection. However, near the bottom of the window, you can also switch between normal Book viewing mode, Full Screen mode (iPad only), or the Scroll mode.

The Book viewing mode shows each page of the book you're reading, as well as icons on the top of the page, and page number information on the bottom. Full Screen mode gets rid of some of this onscreen clutter, so you can just focus your eyes on the eBook's page.

The Scroll mode enables you to scroll up or down continuously within an eBook, as opposed to turning pages.

Tap on the Search icon (which is shaped like a magnifying glass) to display a Search field. Use this feature to locate any keyword or search phrase that appears in the eBook you're currently reading.

TIP Tap on the virtual bookmark icon to manually add a bookmark to the page you're on. You can then view a listing of your saved bookmarks by tapping on the Table of Contents icon and selecting the Bookmarks option.

As you're reading, to turn the page, swipe your finger from right to left (horizontally) across the screen to move one page forward, or swipe your finger from left to right to back up one page at a time.

> **TIP** To turn the page, you can also tap on the right side of the screen to advance or the left side of the screen to go back on the page. However, if you have the Both Margins Advance option activated (which can be done from within Settings), tapping either margin advances to the next page.

Displayed near the bottom center of the screen is the page number in the eBook you're currently reading, as well as the total number of pages in the eBook. The number of pages remaining in the current chapter is displayed to the right of the page number.

> **TIP** As you're reading an eBook, hold your finger on a single word. A group of six command tabs appears above that word labeled Copy, Define, Highlight, Note, Search, and Share.
>
> Use your finger to move the blue dots that appear to the left and right of the word to expand the selected text to a phrase, sentence, paragraph, or entire page, for example.
>
> Tap on the Copy tab to copy the selected text into iOS 7's virtual clipboard. You can then paste that text into another app or into a Note within iBooks.
>
> Tap on the Define tab to look up the definition of a selected word. Tap on the Highlight tab to highlight the selected text. It's possible to choose the color of your highlights or underline the selected text by tapping on the yellow circle icon displayed above the word. Tap on the white circle (with a red line through it) to remove highlights, or tap on the Note icon to create a new note. The Share icon also appears above the selected text after you tap on the Highlight option, as do the Copy, Define, and Search options, if you tap on the right-pointing arrow.
>
> If you tap on the Note tab, a virtual sticky note appears on your device's screen, along with the virtual keyboard. Using the keyboard, type notes to yourself about what you're reading. When you're finished typing, tap anywhere on the screen outside the sticky note box. A sticky note icon appears in the margin of the eBook. You can later tap on this icon to read your notes or annotations.
>
> When you tap on the Highlight option, you're given the option to choose a highlight color. The last highlight color you selected determines the color of the sticky note that appears when you tap on the Note option. This enables you to easily color-code your highlights and/or notes.

Tap on the Search tab to enter any word or phrase and find it in the eBook. A search window appears below the Search field. References to each occurrence of your keyword or search phrase are displayed by chapter and page number. Tap on a reference to jump to that point in the book.

When you tap on the Share option, a Share menu appears, giving you the option to email, text/instant message, tweet, or send the selected text to your Facebook friends. From the Share menu, you can also copy text to the virtual clipboard and then paste it elsewhere.

READ PDF FILES WITH iBOOKS

The iBooks app can also be used to read PDF files you download or transfer to your iPhone or iPad. When you receive an email with a PDF file as an attachment, tap on the PDF thumbnail in that email so the file downloads to your iPhone or iPad. Next, tap and hold your finger on that same PDF thumbnail for a few seconds, until a menu window appears. The options in this window are Quick Look, Open in iBooks, and, if applicable, Open In [Compatible App].

The Open in iBooks command automatically launches the iBooks app and enables you to read the PDF document as if you're reading an eBook you downloaded from iBookstore. It's also possible to use the Open in iBooks command to read eBooks published in the ePub format that were acquired from another online bookseller.

NOTE If applicable, the Open In command enables you to open a PDF file using another third-party app. When you tap on this menu option, a list of compatible apps for viewing, printing, sharing, and/or annotating PDF files that are currently installed on your iPhone or iPad is displayed. These apps might include PDF Reader, GoodReader, or PDFpen, for example.

When a PDF file opens in iBooks, you see command icons displayed along the top of the screen, as well as small thumbnails of the PDF document's pages displayed along the bottom of the screen.

Tap on the Library button that's displayed near the upper-left corner of the screen to return to iBook's main Library screen. When you do this, however, the Bookshelf displays all the PDF files stored on your device—not eBooks downloaded from iBookstore.

To once again access your eBooks, tap on the PDFs button on the iPhone or the Collections command icon on the iPad, and then select the Books option.

TIP As you're viewing a PDF file in iBooks, next to the Library icon is the Table of Contents icon. Tap on it to display larger thumbnails of each page in your PDF document, and then tap on any of the thumbnails to jump to that page. Or tap on the Resume icon to return to the main view of your PDF file.

To the immediate right of the Table of Contents icon (near the upper-left corner of the iBooks screen as you're reading a PDF file) is a Share icon that enables you to email or print the PDF document you're currently viewing. Near the upper-right corner of this screen are three additional command icons. The sun-shaped icon enables you to adjust the brightness of the screen. The magnifying glass–shaped icon enables you to search a PDF file for specific text in the document, and the Bookmark icon enables you to bookmark specific pages in the PDF file for later reference.

TIP As you're viewing a PDF file using iBooks, you can zoom in on or out of the page using a reverse pinch or pinch finger motion on the touchscreen display, or by double-tapping on the area you want to zoom in or out on.

Also, as you're reading a PDF file, you can hold the device in either a vertical or a horizontal position. If you tap anywhere on the screen (except on a command icon or page thumbnail), the icons and thumbnails on the top and bottom of the screen disappear, giving you more onscreen real estate to view your PDF document. Tap near the top or bottom of the screen to make these icons and thumbnails reappear at any time.

CREATE YOUR OWN EBOOKS USING APPLE'S iBOOKS AUTHOR SOFTWARE

If you want to create your own content to be viewed using the iBooks app on the iPhone or iPad (or iPad mini), create a PDF document, and then load it into iBooks. However, if you want to create interactive and visually compelling eBooks for the iPad (or iPad mini), use Apple's free iBooks Author software for the Mac. (It's available from the Mac App Store.) To learn more about what this software can do, visit www.apple.com/ibooks-author.

NOTE It's possible to create and view eBooks using the ePub file format with other eBook creation software, but these books can't offer the interactive elements that are possible when using iBooks Author to create and publish eBooks.

ALTERNATIVE METHODS FOR READING YOUR EBOOKS

Although Apple has worked out distribution deals with many major publishers and authors, the iBookstore does not offer an eBook edition of every book in publication.

TIP In some cases, eBook titles are available from Amazon.com or Barnes & Noble (BN.com) but not from iBookstore. Or if Amazon.com, BN.com, and iBookstore offer the same eBook title, the price for that eBook might be lower from one of these other online-based booksellers. So, if you're a price-conscious reader, it pays to shop around for the lowest eBook prices. Just because you're using an iPhone or iPad does not mean you must shop for eBooks exclusively from iBookstore.

Perhaps you owned a Kindle or Nook eBook reader before purchasing your iPhone or iPad and have already acquired a personal library of eBooks formatted for that device. If you want to access your current Kindle or Nook eBook library from your iPhone or iPad, download the free Kindle or Nook apps from the App Store. These apps prompt you for your Amazon or Barnes & Noble account information to sync your purchased content to the app. To purchase new Kindle- or Nook-formatted eBook titles, you must visit Amazon.com or BN.com using Safari or your primary computer. After you make your purchase, your eBooks can be automatically synced to the Kindle or Nook app on your device.

ACQUIRE DIGITAL EDITIONS OF NEWSPAPERS AND MAGAZINES WITH THE NEWSSTAND APP

Many local, regional, and national newspapers, as well as popular consumer and industry-oriented magazines, are now available in digital form and accessible from your iPhone or iPad via the Newsstand app. This app comes preinstalled with iOS 7.

WORKING WITH THE NEWSSTAND APP

Not to be confused with the iBooks app, which is used for eBooks, the Newsstand app is used to manage and access all of your digital newspaper and magazine single issues and subscriptions in one place. However, the iBooks and Newsstand apps have a similar user interface, so after you learn how to use one, you'll have no trouble using the other.

NOTE Many of the world's most popular newspapers, including *The New York Times*, *The Wall Street Journal*, *Barron's*, and *USA Today*, are now published in digital form, as are popular magazines, such as *Entertainment Weekly*, *TIME*, *Newsweek*, *Good Housekeeping*, *Mac/Life*, *National Geographic*, *US Weekly*, *Family Fun*, *The New Yorker*, *Wired*, *Sports Illustrated*, *GQ*, and *PEOPLE*.

After you launch Newsstand (shown in Figure 15.12), tap the Store button and browse through the ever-growing selection of digital newspapers and magazines that are available. With the tap of an icon, you can subscribe to any publication, or in most instances, purchase a single current or back issue.

FIGURE 15.12

The main Newsstand screen displays thumbnails for all newspaper and magazine issues currently stored on your iPhone or iPad.

The Newsstand is broken up by category. When you find a publication you're interested in, tap on its listing. This reveals a detailed description screen, which is very much like what you'd see in the App Store when shopping for apps. The description screen has Details, Reviews, and Related tabs that enable you to learn more about a publication.

NOTE The online digital newsstand operated by Apple, which is compatible with the Newsstand app, is actually part of the App Store. Access it by tapping on the Store button in the Newsstand app, or launch the App Store app, tap on the Featured button (near the bottom of the screen), and then, on the iPhone, tap the Categories button followed by the Newsstand option. On the iPad, tap on the Newsstand tab that's displayed near the top of the screen.

All purchases you make are automatically billed to the credit or debit card you have on file with your Apple ID account, or you can pay using iTunes gift cards.

After you purchase a digital newspaper or magazine subscription (or a single issue of a publication), it appears on your Newsstand shelf in the Newsstand app. Tap the publication's cover thumbnail to access the available issue(s).

If you've subscribed to a digital publication, Newsstand automatically downloads the most current issue as soon as it's published (assuming your phone or tablet has a Wi-Fi Internet connection available), so when you wake your iPhone or iPad from Sleep mode each morning, the latest edition of your favorite newspaper can be waiting for you.

NOTE Each digital publication has its own proprietary app associated with it. These publication-specific apps are free and automatically installed on your iOS mobile device when you select a publication in Newsstand. All of these publication-specific apps are then accessible in Newsstand, plus they have their own unique functionality and allow for publication-specific interactive content.

TIP To use a cellular data network to automatically download digital publications, you must turn on this feature in the Settings app. Launch Settings, select the iTunes & App Stores menu option, and then turn on the virtual switch associated with the Use Cellular Data option.

Keep in mind that downloading digital publications using a cellular data network quickly uses up your monthly data allocation, and could ultimately result in additional charges if you're not on an unlimited data plan.

Also from within Settings, tap on the Newsstand option to turn on the virtual switches associated with each specific newspaper or magazine subscription that's listed. After you do this once, when using a Wi-Fi connection, your iPhone or iPad automatically downloads all new publication content when it becomes available, without you having to worry about using up your monthly wireless data allocation.

A Home screen icon badge and/or the Notification Center notifies you immediately whenever a new issue of a digital publication is automatically downloaded to your iOS device and is ready for reading. When you access Newsstand, you also see a thumbnail of that publication's cover on the main Newsstand shelf screen.

READING DIGITAL PUBLICATIONS

Every publisher utilizes the iPhone or iPad's display in a different way to transform a traditionally printed newspaper or magazine into an engaging and interactive reading experience. Thus, each publication has its own user interface.

Figure 15.13 shows what a sample issue of *Geek* magazine looks like when being read in its digital form on the iPad.

FIGURE 15.13

Digital newspapers and magazines, and their proprietary apps, are accessible from the Newsstand app.

In most cases, a digital edition of a publication faithfully reproduces the printed edition and features the same content. However, sometimes the digital edition of a publication also offers bonus content, such as active hyperlinks to websites, video clips, animated slide shows, or interactive elements not offered by the printed edition.

Reading a digital publication is very much like reading an eBook. Use a finger swipe motion to turn the pages or to scroll up or down on a page. Tap the Table of Contents icon to view an interactive table of contents for each issue of the publication. When viewing some publications, you can also use a reverse pinch, pinch, or double-tap finger motion to zoom in or out on specific content. Depending on the publisher, you might be able to access past issues of a publication at any given time in addition to the current issue. An additional per-issue fee may apply.

MANAGING YOUR NEWSPAPER AND MAGAZINE SUBSCRIPTIONS

If you opt to subscribe to a digital publication, you often need to select a duration for your subscription, such as one year. However, almost all digital subscriptions acquired through the Newsstand app are auto-renewing. Thus, when the subscription ends, unless you manually cancel it, Newsstand automatically renews your subscription and bills your credit or debit card accordingly.

To manage your recurring subscriptions, launch the Newsstand app and tap the Store button. From the Newsstand store, tap the Featured command button that's located near the bottom of the screen. Scroll downward and tap the Apple ID [Your Username] button. When prompted, enter your Apple ID password.

Next, from the Account Settings window that appears, tap the Manage button that's displayed under the Subscriptions heading. Displayed on the Subscriptions screen is a listing of all publications to which you've subscribed. Tap any publication's listing to see the expiration date of your subscription, to cancel a subscription, or to renew your subscription.

NEWSSTAND QUICK TIPS

- The publication-specific app related to the digital edition of a newspaper or magazine is free; however, in most cases, you must pay for individual issues or for a subscription to a publication. From Newsstand, to determine the per-issue or subscription cost, tap on a publication listing, tap on the Details tab, and then scroll toward the button of the screen. Tap on the option called In-App Purchases.
- To entice you to become a paid subscriber, some publishers offer free issues of their digital newspaper or magazine that you can download and read before actually paying for a subscription. Some publications, however, give away the digital edition of their publication for free to paid subscribers of the print edition.

- When actually reading a publication using a proprietary app (via Newsstand), you'll often see several command buttons displayed near the bottom of the page, including Store and Library buttons. Tap on Store to acquire additional single issues or a subscription to that publication, or tap on Library to reopen issues you've already purchased.
- Although you can download a digital publication and then read it offline, an Internet connection might be required to access interactive content that's exclusive to that digital publication. Look for interactive speaker or movie icons in a publication, and tap on them to experience this extra content.

Appendix A

SET UP YOUR NEW iPHONE OR iPAD

If you purchased a brand-new iPhone or iPad (after September 2013), iOS 7 comes preinstalled; otherwise, you'll need to upgrade your iOS mobile device from iOS 6 to iOS 7 to take full advantage of the latest features and functionality that your iPhone or iPad is capable of and that you've been reading about in this book.

TIP To upgrade to iOS 7, make sure your iOS mobile device is connected to the Internet via a Wi-Fi connection. Also, make sure the battery is fully charged or that your iPhone or iPad is connected to an external power source. Next, use iCloud Backup or iTunes Sync to back up your device.

When you're ready to upgrade the iOS, launch Settings, tap on the General option, and then tap on the Software Update option. Follow the onscreen prompts to download and install iOS 7. The process takes about 15 minutes.

To set up your brand-new iPhone or iPad that's running iOS 7, follow these steps:

1. Unpack the iPhone or iPad and charge its battery.
2. Turn on your iPhone or iPad by holding down the Power button until the Apple logo appears.
3. When the device is turned on, the Hello screen is displayed (shown in Figure A.1). Swipe your finger from left to right across the Slide To Set Up slider.

FIGURE A.1

From the Hello screen, slide your finger across the Slide To Set Up slider to get started using your iPhone or iPad.

NOTE To display the most information possible, all the screen shots featured in this appendix were taken using an iPad running iOS 7.

NOTE If you purchased your iPhone from Apple or a cellular service provider, your smartphone's phone number will already be programmed into the device. However, if you're reactivating an iPhone using a new account with a (different) cellular service provider, you will need to have that service provider activate your iPhone and/or the SIM card installed in the iPhone.

4. Select your language by tapping on a menu option. English is listed first.
5. From the Select Your Country or Region screen, tap on the appropriate option (shown in Figure A.2).

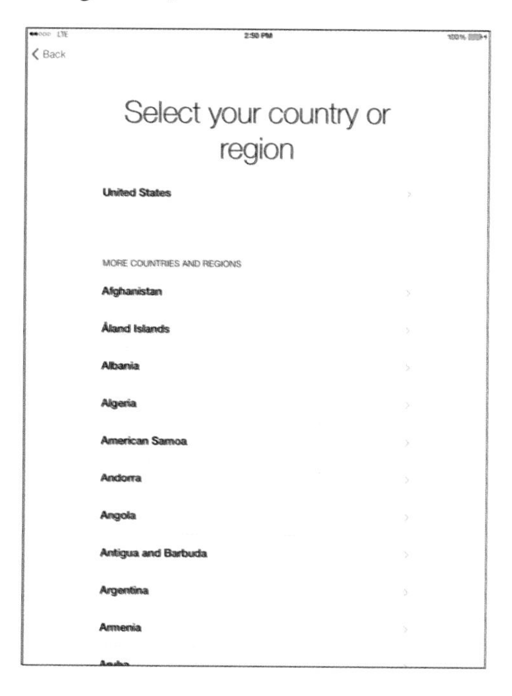

FIGURE A.2

Select your home country or region, where you'll primarily be using your iPhone or iPad.

6. When the Choose a Wi-Fi Network screen appears (shown in Figure A.3), tap on an available Wi-Fi network (hotspot). If applicable, you can tap on the Use Cellular Connection option to enable your mobile device to access a 3G/4G LTE cellular data network and complete the setup process.
7. Your iOS mobile device will now be activated. When the Location Services screen appears, tap on Enable Location Services to turn on this feature and enable your iPhone or iPad to pinpoint your location.

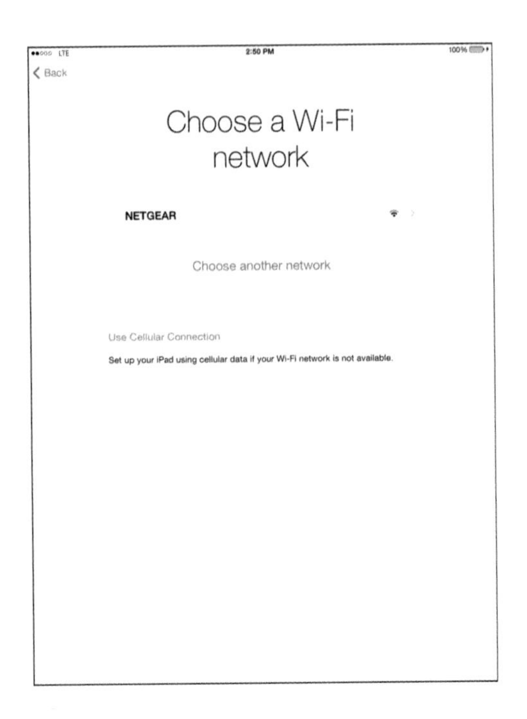

FIGURE A.3

Choose an available Wi-Fi network so your mobile device can connect to the Internet. If applicable, you also can tap on the Use Cellular Connection option.

8. The Set Up Your iPad (or iPhone) screen appears next (shown in Figure A.4). Here, you have three options: Set Up as New iPad (or iPhone), Restore from iCloud Backup, or Restore from iTunes Backup.

> **NOTE** When you select the Restore from iCloud Backup or Restore from iTunes Backup option, the setup process will automatically restore your personal settings, apps, files, and documents, for example, to the new iPhone or iPad using content from your backup files. If you're setting up a new iPhone or iPad and have no previously created backup files to restore, select the Set Up as New iPad [iPhone] option.

9. From the Apple ID screen, you can either sign in with your Apple ID or create a free Apple ID. If you already have another Apple device, use the same Apple ID username and password, so that all of your Macs and iOS mobile devices can sync information via iCloud, as well as share iTunes Store, App Store, iBookstore, and Newsstand purchases. As soon as you enter your Apple

ID information, any related content will be transferred from iCloud to your new mobile device. See Chapter 4, "Sync, Share, and Print Files Using iCloud, AirDrop, AirPlay, and AirPrint," for more information about iCloud's features.

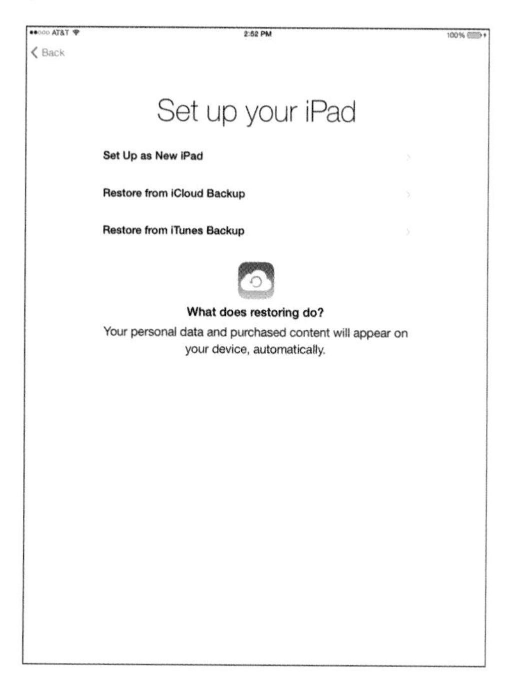

FIGURE A.4

If you are upgrading from an old iPhone to a new iPhone, or an older iPad to a new iPad, and want to restore your data from an existing iCloud backup or iTunes backup, select one of these options. Otherwise, choose the Set Up as New iPad (or iPhone) option.

10. Accept the Terms and Conditions by tapping on the Agree option that's displayed near the bottom-right corner of the screen. When the Terms and Conditions pop-up window appears, tap on the Agree button.
11. You now have the option of setting up and activating the Passcode option. To do this, create and enter a four-digit passcode, and then when prompted, enter the passcode again. To skip this step, tap on the Don't Add Passcode option. If you skip this step now, you can activate or deactivate this feature in the Settings app later.
12. To turn on and activate the Siri feature on your iOS mobile device, from the Set Up Siri screen, tap on the Use Siri option. Then, from the Diagnostics screen, tap on either the Automatically Send or Don't Send option, based on your personal preference.

13. The Welcome to iPad (or iPhone) screen appears next. Tap on the Get Started option to begin using your iOS mobile device. The Home screen will appear (shown in Figure A.5). You can now begin using your newly set up and activated iPhone or iPad.

> **TIP** If you're setting up an iPhone 5S, the activation and setup process will include additional steps for turning on and setting up the Touch ID fingerprint scanner that's built in to the Home button.

FIGURE A.5

From the Home screen, you can begin using any of the apps that come preinstalled with iOS 7.

From the Home screen, you can launch any of the apps that come preinstalled with iOS 7. Swipe from right to left across the Home screen to access additional screens of apps.

Displayed near the top-left corner of the screen is the cellular data network and/or Wi-Fi signal strength indicator. As long as one or both of these options are displayed, your iOS mobile device can freely access the Internet. Using the App Store app, it's now possible to find, purchase, download, and install new apps. Or using the iTunes Store app, you can acquire content, such as music, TV shows, movies, ringtones, music videos, or audiobooks, that you can enjoy using your iPhone or iPad.

TIP When your mobile device is set up and functional, be sure to use Settings to customize the functionality of your iPhone or iPad. How to do this is covered in Chapter 1, "Tips and Tricks for Customizing Settings."

Appendix B

TAKE ADVANTAGE OF THE PASSBOOK APP AND DISCOVER OTHER AWESOME THINGS YOUR iOS DEVICE CAN DO

One of the apps Apple offers as part of iOS 7 is called Passbook. It's an iPhone-only app that's designed to manage electronic airline boarding passes; movie, show, and sporting event tickets; store rewards cards and digital retail coupons—all from a single app.

For the Passbook app to function, it must be used with one or more third-party apps. Plus, it's necessary to have your iPhone's Location Service functionality turned on for use with this app.

Although it's been more than one year since it was first introduced, only a handful of companies are supporting Passbook functionality. Each company, however, is using it in a slightly different way to interact with iPhone users who are their customers.

For example, American Airlines, Delta, United Airlines, British Airways, Air Canada, Lufthansa, and Alaska Airlines have added Passbook integration into their iPhone apps. Thus, once you load your electronic boarding pass into your phone, it will appear on your phone's display when you arrive at the airport and need to check in. Currently, this option is only available at certain airports, however.

Likewise, when you purchase tickets online using the Fandango, Live Nation, or Ticketmaster apps, the electronic ticket displays automatically on your iPhone's screen when you arrive at a participating venue and can be scanned by the box office or ticket taker.

Companies such as Starbucks enable you to build up rewards and pay for your food and beverage purchases using a digital edition of a Starbucks pre-paid card, which is stored in the official Starbucks app. Meanwhile, Walgreen's and Target are among the first companies to integrate Passbook functionality into their apps so you can access online coupons, refill prescriptions, or track earned rewards for purchases.

When you launch the Passbook app for the first time, make sure your iPhone has Internet access, and then tap on the App Store button displayed near the bottom of the screen. This launches the iTunes app and enables you to view and download free apps from companies with proprietary apps that offer Passbook integration.

NOTE Apple Stores offer Passbook integration through the official Apple Store app. Among other things, this feature enables you to quickly pay for in-store purchases using the credit or debit card information that's linked with the app (and your Apple ID).

In the months and years to come, companies will innovate new ways to interact with their customers by taking advantage of Passbook functionality, combined with the iPhone's Location Services feature. However, this functionality and technology is still in its infancy.

THERE'S SO MUCH MORE YOUR iPHONE OR iPAD CAN DO

Much of this book has focused on ways to use your iPhone or iPad with the apps that come preinstalled with iOS 7, as well as a wide range of third-party apps that can dramatically enhance the functionality of your iOS mobile device. Keep in mind, however, that a vast selection of optional accessories are currently available for your iPhone or iPad that can be used with apps to also greatly expand what's possible. Plus, through wireless connectivity via Bluetooth, AirPlay, or a home network, you can link your iPhone or iPad with other devices.

With Apple's iOS In Your Car initiative and iOS 7's Siri Eyes Free feature, it's now possible to connect your iPhone to a growing selection of 2013 or 2014 model year vehicles from several manufacturers, including GM. You can then use your vehicle's in-dash infotainment system to access content from your iPhone and make or receive calls.

Here are just a few examples of what else is currently possible:

- Thanks to the Philips Hue lighting system (www.meethue.com), it's possible to replace the standard light bulbs throughout your home with special LED bulbs, and then control them wirelessly from your iPhone. The Philips Hue bulbs can be programmed to various intensities and/or change color. In addition to Hue's LED bulbs, Philips has introduced standalone LED light fixtures and LED light strips that work with the system. Prices start at $199 for three Hue LED bulbs and the control hub.
- Using a wireless home network or the Internet, you can control the temperature in your home using the Nest thermostat ($249, www.nest.com). This intelligent and programmable thermostat learns your day-to-day living habits and automatically finds ways to save you money on your utility bills, while keeping your home at a comfortable temperature while you're there.
- Whether you're concerned about home security or want to keep tabs on your kids and pets while you're away from the house, wireless baby monitor and security cameras are available that can be controlled from the iPhone or iPad via the Internet. The SmartBaby monitor from Withings ($299, www.withings.com/en/babymonitor) and the iBaby Monitor from iBaby Labs ($199.95, ibabylabs.com/ibabymonitor) are two products available for this purpose.
- For kids, teens, and those who are young at heart, a handful of companies offer remote control vehicles that can be controlled wirelessly via an iPhone or iPad. You'll find these toys at Brookstone stores (www.brookstone.com) and high-end toy stores.
- To get work done while on the go, you can find a wide range of battery-powered accessories for the iPhone or iPad, including a portable scanner, portable projector, external keyboards, external battery packs, and wireless (Bluetooth) speakers.
- If you're a musician, several companies offer optional microphones, specialized apps, and proprietary adapters for connecting instruments and professional-quality microphones directly to the phone or tablet, enabling you to create a professional-quality recording studio almost anywhere. iRig

from IK Multimedia ($39.99, www.ikmultimedia.com) is one product that can be used to connect an instrument directly to your iOS mobile device. Beyond using the optional GarageBand app to record music, many other apps are available for serious musicians that are designed for composing, recording, editing/mixing, and performing music.

- Nike offers a selection of running shoes and a monitoring device, called the Nike+ FuelBand SE (http://nikeplus.nike.com/plus/products/fuelband), which is worn on your wrist. When used with your iPhone or iPad, these tools can help you stay fit and/or lose weight. Thanks to Nike+ technology, the running shoes and FuelBand device link wirelessly to your iOS mobile device, enabling you to track your progress and achieve your fitness or weight loss goals faster.

And that's just the beginning. Companies in many different industries have begun inventing unique iPhone or iPad accessories that transform the way we handle everyday tasks and that can provide your iOS mobile device with dramatically enhanced functionality.

How Apple and other companies are utilizing iOS technology with proprietary accessories is only in its infancy. As English poet and playwright Robert Browning once said (back in the 1800s), "The best is yet to come!"

A SMART WATCH IS THE PERFECT COMPANION TO YOUR TABLET AND SMARTPHONE

Just as the iPhone has become the world's most popular smartphone, and Apple's iPad is the world's best-selling tablet, the next "must-have" device is quickly becoming a smart watch.

The Pebble Smart Watch ($150.00, www.getpebble.com), shown in Figure B.1, is available right now; however, Apple also is hard at work developing the iWatch for release most likely in 2014.

A smart watch is a digital watch, worn on your wrist, that can display the time and date, just like any watch. However, it also can communicate wirelessly with your smartphone or tablet and display details about incoming emails and text/instant messages, as well as inform you of alerts, alarms, or notifications generated by various apps running on your iOS mobile device.

FIGURE B.1

The Pebble Smart Watch communicates wirelessly with the iPhone or iPad.

Many of the smart watches already on the market can also run their own apps, enabling them to collect data and transmit that information wirelessly to an iOS mobile device. Thus, the screen of your wristwatch has become another viable way to interact wirelessly with your iPad.

Index

A

B

C

F

J-K

L

M

N

R

S

T

Z